EP Math
Algebra 1
Workbook

All-in-One
Homeschool

This workbook, made by permission of Easy Peasy All-in-One Homeschool, is based on the math component of Easy Peasy's curriculum. For EP's online curriculum, visit allinonehomeschool.com.

ISBN: 9798399284279

How to Use This Workbook

This is an offline workbook for Easy Peasy All-in-One Homeschool's Algebra 1 course. You can use this book by itself or along with EP's online course whenever extra practice would be helpful or a computer isn't available. This book can also be used as a stand-alone course.

This book provides 180 daily lessons with exercises that can replace all online activities, both lessons and exercises. The lessons are designed with the following objectives in mind:

- **To introduce an appropriate amount of new material each day**

  Each lesson is built upon the previous lessons and introduces new topics in a way that flows logically and makes sense. You'll learn new skills and strategies each day without getting overwhelmed.

- **To teach by examples and by practice**

  The lessons break down abstract concepts into practical skills that need to be developed. Each lesson teaches a new set of skills with detailed examples, followed by practice problems. Always work through the examples first. Be sure to understand them before proceeding to the practice problems.

- **To provide offline alternatives to online activities**

  Each lesson can replace the day's online activities. It provides offline activities comparable in both quantity and quality to those offered online, so that you can switch between online and offline without missing anything.

This book also includes grading sheets and a final exam to help you assess your understanding of the material and to provide a grading structure for the course.

It is recommended that you solve the problems in a separate notebook. Start each lesson on a fresh page. Write the lesson number on the top of the page and label each problem with its number. This will help you when you are checking the answers and when you review your work later.

Where to Find the Answer Key

Please note that the answer key is **not** included in this workbook. The answers (including worked-out solutions for most problems) are available on the Easy Peasy All-in-One Homeschool website, also for purchase in book form.

Contents

Completion Chart

ALGEBRA BASICS

LESSON 1	Order of Operations	☐
LESSON 2	Algebraic Expressions	☐

SOLVING LINEAR EQUATIONS

LESSON 3	Solving Basic Linear Equations	☐
LESSON 4	Solving Multi-Step Linear Equations	☐
LESSON 5	Solving Linear Equations with Fractions & Decimals	☐
LESSON 6	Solving Absolute Value Equations	☐
LESSON 7	Solving Linear Equations of All Types	☐
LESSON 8	Number of Solutions to Linear Equations	☐
LESSON 9	Applications of Linear Equations	☐
LESSON 10	Applications of Linear Equations (Distance)	☐
LESSON 11	Applications of Linear Equations (Mixtures)	☐
LESSON 12	Solving for a Variable	☐
LESSON 13	Catch Up and Review!	☐

GRAPHING LINES

LESSON 14	Graphing Lines by Plotting Points	☐
LESSON 15	Slope and Slope Formula	☐
LESSON 16	Graphing Lines in Slope-Intercept Form	☐
LESSON 17	Graphing Lines in Standard Form	☐
LESSON 18	Graphing Lines Using Intercepts	☐
LESSON 19	Horizontal, Vertical, Parallel, and Perpendicular Lines	☐
LESSON 20	Graphing Absolute Value Equations	☐
LESSON 21	Catch Up and Review!	☐

FINDING EQUATIONS OF LINES

SYSTEMS OF LINEAR EQUATIONS

LINEAR INEQUALITIES

QUARTERLY REVIEW

PSAT PRACTICE

Test Taking Tips & Self-Review

Review: All Topics in Algebra 1

Review: Solving All Types of Equations

Final Exam Week

LESSON 1 Order of Operations

☐ **BE SURE TO READ BEFORE STARTING** ···

✓ For those who need a course grade, grading sheets are available in Appendix A. Record your score after completing each lesson. See the grading sheets for details.

✓ It is a good practice to solve the problems in a separate notebook. Start each lesson on a fresh page. Write the lesson number on the top of the page and label each problem with its number. This will help you when you are checking the answers and when you review your work later.

✓ This workbook tries to provide ample practice problems. You will find problems marked "**EXTRA**" and "**CHALLENGE.**" They are optional and are not required assignments. Use extra problems for more practice, especially if you are struggling, or save them for later review.

☐ **BASIC DEFINITIONS** ···

An **expression** is a mathematical statement that does not contain an equal sign. **Evaluating an expression** means finding its value.

An **exponent** is a way to represent how many times a number is multiplied by itself. The expression b^n means the number b is multiplied n times. The repeated number b is called the **base**, and the number n is called the **exponent** or **power**. For example, 2^3 is the same as saying $2 \times 2 \times 2$. In words, 2^3 is read as "two to the third power" or "two cubed."

☐ **EVALUATING EXPONENTS** ···

To evaluate b^n, simply multiply b by itself n times.

Note that $(-5)^2$ and -5^2 evaluate to different values. The expression $(-5)^2$ represents $(-5) \times (-5)$ which evaluates to 25. The expression -5^2 represents $-(5 \times 5)$ which evaluates to -25.

➜ **EXAMPLE** Evaluate 2^3 and $(-5)^2$.

$2^3 = 2 \times 2 \times 2 = 8$

$(-5)^2 = (-5) \times (-5) = 25$

➜ **TRY IT** Evaluate.

1. 3^4

2. $(-10)^3$

☐ **USING THE ORDER OF OPERATIONS** ···

When evaluating expressions, remember to follow the **order of operations**. To get correct answers, you must perform operations in the proper order: Parentheses, Exponents, Multiplication and Division in order from left to right, then Addition and Subtraction in order from left to right. These rules are often referred to as **PEMDAS** (or **P**lease **E**xcuse **M**y **D**ear **A**unt **S**ally).

➜ **EXAMPLE** Evaluate $9 + 3 \times 3 - 5$.

$9 + 3 \times 3 - 5$ Multiplication

$= 9 + 9 - 5$ Addition, then Subtraction (left to right)

$= 18 - 5$

$= 13$

➜ **TRY IT** Evaluate.

3. $5 - 8 \times 4 + 2$

4. $3 \times 8 \div 6 - 2 + 7$

→ **EXAMPLE** Evaluate $10 \div 2 \times (4 - 6)$.

$10 \div 2 \times (4 - 6)$ Parentheses

$= 10 \div 2 \times (-2)$ Division, then
Multiplication
(left to right)

$= 5 \times (-2)$

$= -10$

→ **TRY IT** Evaluate.

5. $15 - 8 \times (3 + 2)$

6. $3 \times (6 \div 6) - 2 + 7$

→ **EXAMPLE** Evaluate $4 - 8 \div (5 - 3)^2 \times 5$.

$4 - 8 \div (5 - 3)^2 \times 5$ Parentheses

$= 4 - 8 \div 2^2 \times 5$ Exponents

$= 4 - 8 \div 4 \times 5$ Division

$= 4 - 2 \times 5$ Multiplication

$= 4 - 10$ Subtraction

$= -6$

→ **TRY IT** Evaluate.

7. $1^4 - 6 \times (3 \div 3)^6$

8. $5 + 2^5 \div 8 \times (2 - 4)^2 - 3$

□ **EXERCISE YOUR SKILLS** ···

Evaluate.

9. 1^8

10. $(-2)^5$

11. -3^3

12. $(-9)^2$

Evaluate using the order of operations.

13. $7 - 3 + 2$

14. $12 \div 3 \times 2$

15. $-34 + 3 \times 5$

16. $4 \times (5 + 6)$

17. $3^2 + 6 \times (-7)$

18. $(6 + 2)^2 \div (-4)^2$

19. $9 + 5 \times (8 \div 8)^5$

20. $(7 - 3) \div 2^2 \times (-2)^4$

21. $30 - 8^2 \div 2^5 - 5^2$

22. $4 + 3^3 \div 9 \times (6 - 7)^2$

CHALLENGE Evaluate using the order of operations.

23. $9 + (3 \times 2^3 - 8 \div 2) - 4^2$

24. $36 \div (6^2 - 7 \times 5)^4 + 7$

25. $\dfrac{(-4) \times (5 + 2) + 3}{3^2 - 2^4 \div 4}$

26. $\dfrac{5 - 4^2 \div 8 \times (3 - 5)^3}{(3^2 - 7) \times 2 + (-3)^1}$

LESSON 2 Algebraic Expressions

☐ BASIC DEFINITIONS

An **algebraic expression** is an expression that contains one or more variables. A **variable** is a letter that represents a quantity that can change. Any letter can be a variable. The most common variables are x, y, and z. For example, x^2, $3y + z$, and $x + y + z$ are all algebraic expressions.

An algebraic expressions is made up of **terms** separated by plus and minus signs. A term has two parts: the number part, also called the **coefficient**, and the variable part. A term with no variable part is called a **constant**. For example, the expression $x^2 - 4xy + 5$ has 3 terms: x^2, $-4xy$, and 5. x^2 and $-4xy$ are variable terms and 5 is a constant. In the term x^2, the coefficient is 1 and the variable part is x^2. In the term $-4xy$, the coefficient is -4 and the variable part is xy.

Like terms are terms that have the same variable part. For example, x^2 and $3x^2$ are like terms while x^2 and $5x$ are not. All constants are like terms.

☐ EVALUATING ALGEBRAIC EXPRESSIONS

The value of an algebraic expression changes as the values of the variables change. To evaluate an algebraic expression, replace the variables with the given values and evaluate using the order of operations. Review Lesson 1 if needed.

➔ **EXAMPLE** Evaluate when $x = -1$.

$x^2 + 2x + 1$

$= (-1)^2 + 2(-1) + 1$ Replace x with -1.

$= 1 - 2 + 1$ Evaluate.

$= 0$

➔ **TRY IT** Evaluate when $x = 3$.

1. $x^2 - 6x + 9$

2. $x^3 + x^2 - 9x - 5$

☐ SIMPLIFYING ALGEBRAIC EXPRESSIONS

When algebraic expressions become complex with multiple terms and parentheses, we often simplify them by using the distributive property and combining like terms. To combine like terms, simply combine their coefficients but keep the variable part the same.

➔ **EXAMPLE** Combine like terms.

$5x + x^2 - 4 + 3x^2 + 2$

$= 4x^2 + 5x - 2$

$x^2 + 3x^2 = 4x^2$

$-4 + 2 = -2$

➔ **TRY IT** Combine like terms.

3. $2x + 5x^2 + 3 - 4x^2 - x + 1$

➔ **EXAMPLE** Simplify.

$2(x - 1) + 4x + 5y - 3$

$= 2x - 2 + 4x + 5y - 3$ Distributive property

$= 6x + 5y - 5$ Combine like terms.

➔ **TRY IT** Simplify.

4. $9x - 6 + 2(x + 4) - 4x$

5. $2(x - 2y) + 5(y - 2x)$

☐ WRITING ALGEBRAIC EXPRESSIONS ··

When writing algebraic expressions for word problems, pay attention to the words (phrases) that indicate mathematical operations.

➜ **EXAMPLE** Write an expression.

An electrician charges a $45 flat fee plus $36 per hour. How much does the electrician charge for an h-hour job?

The word "plus" indicates addition, and the word "per" indicates multiplication.

Total charge = flat fee + hourly rate × hours on a job, so the answer is $45 + 36h$.

➜ **TRY IT** Write an expression.

6. Gasoline costs $2.90 per gallon. What's the cost of g gallons?

7. Larry has a 168-page reading assignment. He read 22 pages per day for d days. How many pages does he have left to read?

☐ EXERCISE YOUR SKILLS ··

Evaluate when $x = -3$, $y = 4$, and $z = 8$. Reduce fractions but leave them improper.

8. $2y + 3$

9. $xz + 8$

10. $\dfrac{-3y}{z}$

11. $\dfrac{-x}{y^2 - 1}$

Simplify by using the distributive property and combining like terms.

12. $2x + 4 + 4x - 6 - x$

13. $4x + 6 + 3(x - 5)$

14. $2(5x + 1) - 7 - 7x$

15. $6(x + 2) - 3(2x - 1)$

16. $5x - 4y - 3 + 4(y - x)$

17. $2(4x^2 - 7x) + 7x - 3x^2$

Write an expression that answers each question.

18. Lisa bought p pears at $10. What's the price of one pear?

19. Hannah drove for h hours at an average speed of 68 miles per hour. How far did she drive?

20. Carter bought b comic books at $2.70 each. He paid with a $20 bill. How much change did he get back?

☐ GO BACK AND REVIEW WHEN NECESSARY ··

Keep in mind that each lesson in this course is built upon the previous lessons. If you have trouble following any lesson, go back and review the concepts and examples from previous lessons. Make sure you understand each lesson before moving on to a new one.

LESSON 3 Solving Basic Linear Equations

☐ BASIC DEFINITIONS

An **equation** is a statement that two expressions are equal. A **solution to an equation** is the value(s) of the variable(s) that makes the equation true. **Solving an equation** means finding all the solutions to the equation. For example, $2x - 4 = 8$ is an equation with the solution $x = 6$.

An **inverse operation** is an operation that undoes another operation. Addition and subtraction are inverse operations, as are multiplication and division. For example, the inverse of adding 5 is subtracting 5. The inverse of multiplying 7 is dividing 7.

☐ SOLVING ONE-STEP LINEAR EQUATIONS

To solve an equation, you perform the same inverse operations on both sides of the equation until you get the variable alone on one side of the equal sign. Equations that take one step to isolate the variable are called **one-step equations**. To solve a one-step equation, you only need to perform one inverse operation on both sides of the equation.

➔ **EXAMPLE** Solve (find the value of x that makes each equation true).

a.
$$x + 3 = 5$$
$$-3 \quad -3$$
$$x = 2$$
Check:
$$2 + 3 = 5$$

b.
$$x - 3 = 5$$
$$+3 \quad +3$$
$$x = 8$$
Check:
$$8 - 3 = 5$$

c.
$$3x = 6$$
$$\div 3 \quad \div 3$$
$$x = 2$$
Check:
$$3 \cdot 2 = 6$$

d.
$$\frac{1}{3}x = -1$$
$$\times 3 \quad \times 3$$
$$x = -3$$
Check:
$$\frac{1}{3} \cdot -3 = -1$$

➔ **TRY IT** Solve.

1. $x + 8 = 9$

2. $x - 7 = 6$

3. $-4x = 12$

4. $\frac{1}{2}x = 5$

☐ SOLVING TWO-STEP LINEAR EQUATIONS

Equations that take two steps to isolate the variable are called **two-steps equations**. Two-step equations look more complicated than one-step equations, but the principle for solving them is the same: you perform the same inverse operations on both sides of the equation until you get the variable alone on one side of the equation.

➔ **EXAMPLE** Solve $2x + 3 = 9$.

$$2x + 3 = 9$$
$$-3 \quad -3 \qquad \text{Subtract 3 from both sides.}$$
$$2x = 6$$
$$\div 2 \quad \div 2 \qquad \text{Divide both sides by 2.}$$
$$x = 3 \qquad \text{Find the solution.}$$
Check:
$$2 \cdot 3 + 3 = 9 \qquad \text{Check the solution.}$$

➔ **TRY IT** Solve.

5. $4x + 3 = 11$

6. $3x - 8 = 13$

7. $-2x - 7 = 5$

Describe the step(s) to solve each equation. Do not solve.

8. $x - 2 = 5$

9. $-9x = 27$

10. $3x + 7 = 8$

11. $\dfrac{x}{5} - 4 = -6$

Solve. Check your solutions.

12. $x + 9 = 15$

13. $7x = 63$

14. $4x + 7 = 11$

15. $-14 = 6x - 2$

16. $6 - 5x = 21$

17. $4x + 34 = 10$

18. $\dfrac{1}{5}x = -6$

19. $\dfrac{1}{6}x = \dfrac{2}{3}$

20. $\dfrac{1}{3}x + 7 = 0$

21. $15 - \dfrac{1}{2}x = 11$

EXTRA Solve. Check your solutions.

22. $5x = -45$

23. $x - 8 = 16$

24. $30 + 6x = -24$

25. $8x - 14 = 74$

26. $7x - 16 = -65$

27. $-2x + 19 = 47$

28. $\dfrac{1}{9}x - 5 = 2$

29. $\dfrac{1}{5}x - 8 = -3$

☐ **IF YOU ARE CURIOUS** ···

We use algebra every day without even realizing it. If you are curious about some real-life applications, flip through this workbook and check out lessons with titles starting with "Applications of." The examples provided in those lessons are just the tip of the iceberg!

LESSON 4 Solving Multi-Step Linear Equations

☐ **REFRESH YOUR SKILLS** ··

Simplify by using the distributive property and combining like terms. Review Lesson 2 if needed.

1. $5x - 6 + 2x + 9 - x$

2. $9 + 5(3x - 2) - 7x$

☐ **SOLVING LINEAR EQUATIONS WITH VARIABLES ON BOTH SIDES** ·····················

When solving equations with variables on both sides, first use inverse operations to collect all variables on one side and all constants on the other. Then solve as usual.

➔ **EXAMPLE** Solve $2x + 3 = 9 - 4x$.

$$2x + 3 = 9 - 4x$$

$+ 4x \qquad + 4x$ Add $4x$ to both sides.

$$6x + 3 = 9$$

$- 3 \qquad - 3$ Subtract 3 from both sides.

$$6x = 6$$

$\div 6 \qquad \div 6$ Divide both sides by 6.

$$x = 1$$ Find the solution.

Check:

$$2 \cdot 1 + 3 = 9 - 4 \cdot 1$$ Check the solution.

➔ **TRY IT** Solve.

3. $4x - 8 = 2x$

4. $-2x = 6 + x$

5. $7x - 9 = -9x + 7$

☐ **SOLVING MULTI-STEP LINEAR EQUATIONS** ···

The first step in solving any linear equation is to simplify each side of the equation by removing parentheses and combining like terms. Then you can solve the equation as usual.

➔ **EXAMPLE** Solve $1 + 2x - 5 = 2(1 - x)$.

$$1 + 2x - 5 = 2(1 - x)$$

$2 - 2x$

$$2x - 4 = 2 - 2x$$ Simplify each side.

$+ 2x \qquad + 2x$ Add $2x$ to both sides.

$$4x - 4 = 2$$

$+ 4 \qquad + 4$ Add 4 to both sides.

$$4x = 6$$

$\div 4 \qquad \div 4$ Divide both sides by 4.

$$x = \frac{3}{2}$$ We usually leave a fraction improper.

Check:

$$1 + 2 \cdot \frac{3}{2} - 5 = 2(1 - \frac{3}{2})$$ Check the solution.

➔ **TRY IT** Solve.

6. $5 + 3(2x - 3) = 2$

7. $6x + 5 = 5(x - 3)$

8. $7(x - 4) + 2 = 6 - x$

9. $3x + x = 4(x + 3) + 4x$

□ **EXERCISE YOUR SKILLS** ···

Solve. Reduce fractions but leave them improper. Check your solutions.

10. $4x + 8 = 2x$

11. $-4x = 40 + x$

12. $8x - 3x + 5 = 0$

13. $5x + 2x - 9 = 6$

14. $20 - 3x = 5x - 2$

15. $3x - 9 = -5x + 7$

16. $3 + 7(2x - 8) = 17$

17. $2(4 + x) - 4(x - 3) = 7$

18. $4(x - 3) = 3x + 5$

19. $5x = 2(1 - 4x) + 6x$

20. $2 + x - 8 = 2x + 3(2 - x)$

21. $2(3x + 4) + 11 = 9(x + 2)$

EXTRA Solve. Reduce fractions but leave them improper. Check your solutions.

22. $x + 8 - 4x = -16$

23. $9x - 12 = -x + 8$

24. $4x - 8 - x = -29$

25. $4x + 5 = 10x - 13$

26. $9(3 + x) + 5 = 11$

27. $3(6 - 3x) = -36$

28. $7x + 4 = 2(x - 4) - 3$

29. $3(2x + 3) = -2x - 15$

30. $4x + x - 5 = 2(4x + 1)$

31. $5x + 4(2 - 3x) = 2x + 6$

CHALLENGE Solve. Reduce fractions but leave them improper. Check your solutions.

32. $\frac{1}{3}x + 5 = \frac{2}{3}x - 2$

33. $\frac{1}{2}(x - 2) + \frac{3}{4} = \frac{1}{4}$

34. $\frac{3}{4} + 4x = \frac{1}{2}(4x + 1)$

35. $\frac{5}{2}x - \frac{1}{5} = \frac{1}{2}(x + 2) + \frac{1}{5}$

LESSON 5 Solving Linear Equations with Fractions & Decimals

☐ **BASIC DEFINITIONS** ···

Equivalent equations are equations that have identical solutions. Performing the same operation on both sides of an equation results in an equivalent equation. For example, if you multiply both sides of the equation $x + 3 = 4$ by 2, you get an equivalent equation $2x + 6 = 8$. Notice that the solution will be the same no matter which equation you solve.

☐ **SOLVING LINEAR EQUATIONS WITH DECIMALS** ···

When solving an equation with decimals, multiply both sides by a power of 10 (10, 100, 1000, and so on) to clear the decimals. The resulting equation will be equivalent to the original equation, but with no decimals.

➜ **EXAMPLE** Solve $0.3x - 0.6 = 1.5$.

$$0.3x - 0.6 = 1.5$$

$10(0.3x - 0.6) \quad 10(1.5)$ Multiply both sides by 10.

$$3x - 6 = 15$$

$+6 \quad +6$ Add 6 to both sides.

$$3x = 21$$

$\div 3 \quad \div 3$ Divide both sides by 30.

$$x = 7$$ Find the solution.

Check:

$$0.3 \cdot 7 - 0.6 = 1.5$$ Check the solution.

➜ **TRY IT** Solve.

1. $0.3x + 0.5 = 0.8$

2. $0.2x - 0.01 = 0.04$

3. $1.4 - 0.06x = 1.1$

☐ **SOLVING LINEAR EQUATIONS WITH FRACTIONS** ···

When solving an equation with fractions, clear the fractions by multiplying both sides by the least common multiple (LCM) of the denominators of all the fractions in the equation. The resulting equation will be equivalent to the original equation, but with no fractions.

➜ **EXAMPLE** Solve $\frac{1}{3}x = \frac{1}{4}x - \frac{2}{3}$.

$$\frac{1}{3}x = \frac{1}{4}x - \frac{2}{3}$$ The LCM of 3 and 4 is 12.

$12 \cdot \frac{1}{3}x = 12\left(\frac{1}{4}x - \frac{2}{3}\right)$ Multiply both sides by 12.

$$4x = 3x - 8$$

$-3x \quad -3x$ Subtract $3x$ from both sides.

$$x = -8$$ Find the solution.

Check:

$$\frac{1}{3}(-8) = \frac{1}{4}(-8) - \frac{2}{3}$$ Check the solution.

➜ **TRY IT** Solve.

4. $\frac{3}{4}x - \frac{1}{4} = \frac{1}{2}$

5. $\frac{5}{6} + \frac{1}{4}x = \frac{5}{4}x$

6. $\frac{1}{5}x + \frac{7}{10} = \frac{1}{10}x + \frac{3}{5}$

Solve. Reduce fractions but leave them improper. Check your solutions.

7. $2x + 7.3 = 5.9$

8. $3.4 - 1.4x = -7.8$

9. $6x - 0.61 = 0.7(2 - x)$

10. $0.03x + 0.15 = -0.02x - 0.5$

11. $0.8x - 0.5(x + 3) = 0.2x$

12. $1.2(x - 1) = 1.5(x + 3) - 0.3$

13. $\dfrac{1}{5}x + \dfrac{3}{5} = 2$

14. $\dfrac{3}{8}x + \dfrac{1}{4} = -\dfrac{1}{2}$

15. $\dfrac{3}{5}x + \dfrac{2}{3} = \dfrac{4}{5}$

16. $\dfrac{3}{4}x + \dfrac{5}{6} = \dfrac{5}{4}$

17. $\dfrac{3}{4} - \dfrac{2}{5}x = -\dfrac{1}{5}$

18. $\dfrac{7}{10}x + \dfrac{2}{5} = \dfrac{1}{2}$

19. $\dfrac{2}{3}x + \dfrac{1}{4}x - x = 1$

20. $x = \dfrac{1}{2}(6x + 1) - \dfrac{3}{4}$

EXTRA Solve. Reduce fractions but leave them improper. Check your solutions.

21. $3x - 6.05 = 8.95$

22. $-0.8x + 0.95 = 0.35$

23. $2.1x - 4.7 = -5.7 + 1.6x$

24. $5.5 - 2x = 0.1x + 4.24$

25. $\dfrac{2}{3}x + \dfrac{5}{6} = 2$

26. $\dfrac{1}{10}x + \dfrac{1}{5} = \dfrac{3}{5}$

27. $\dfrac{2}{3} + \dfrac{7}{9}x = -\dfrac{1}{9}$

28. $\dfrac{4}{5}x - \dfrac{3}{4} = -\dfrac{11}{20}$

29. $\dfrac{3}{5}x - \dfrac{1}{2} = \dfrac{3}{5} - \dfrac{1}{2}x$

30. $\dfrac{1}{4}(3x - 1) - \dfrac{2}{3}x = \dfrac{1}{3}$

LESSON 6 Solving Absolute Value Equations

□ BASIC DEFINITIONS ·······

The **absolute value** of a number is its distance from zero on a number line. The absolute value of a number n is written as $|n|$. For example, on a number line, both 8 and -8 are at a distance of 8 from zero. So $|-8| = 8$ as well as $|8| = 8$. Remember, absolute value is never negative.

□ SOLVING ABSOLUTE VALUE EQUATIONS ·······

An **absolute value equation** is an equation that contains an absolute value expression. Consider an absolute value equation such as $|2x| = 8$. There are two numbers whose absolute value is 8: 8 itself and -8. This means the expression inside the absolute value bars is either 8 or -8. So we can rewrite the equation as two equations and solve each equation separately.

➔ **EXAMPLE** Solve $|2x| = 8$.

$$|2x| = 8$$

Positive   Negative

$2x = 8$ $2x = -8$

$x = 4$ $x = -4$

The solution is $x = 4$ or $x = -4$.

➔ **TRY IT** Solve.

1. $|5x| = 5$

2. $|x + 5| = 9$

Here is a general strategy. To solve an absolute value equation, first isolate the absolute value expression on one side of the equation. Then rewrite the equation as two equations and solve each equation separately.

➔ **EXAMPLE** Solve $2|4x - 2| + 3 = 23$.

$$2|4x - 2| + 3 = 23$$

Subtract 3 from both sides, then divide both sides by 2.

$$|4x - 2| = 10$$

Positive   Negative

$4x - 2 = 10$ $4x - 2 = -10$

$4x = 12$ $4x = -8$

$x = 3$ $x = -2$

The solution is $x = 3$ or $x = -2$.

Check:

$$2|4 \cdot \mathbf{3} - 2| + 3 = 2|10| + 3 = 23$$

$$2|4 \cdot \mathbf{-2} - 2| + 3 = 2|-10| + 3 = 23$$

➔ **TRY IT** Solve.

3. $|x - 3| + 2 = 8$

4. $|4 - 5x| + 1 = 5$

5. $5|x + 2| - 4 = 6$

6. $3|3x + 4| - 8 = 7$

Solve. Reduce fractions but leave them improper. Check your solutions.

7. $|4x| = 20$

8. $|-x| = 11$

9. $|x + 4| = 6$

10. $|8 - x| + 3 = 5$

11. $|6x| - 8 = -3$

12. $6 + 2|4x| = 10$

13. $|9 - 3x| = 12$

14. $|2x + 4| = 6$

15. $9 + |7x - 6| = 10$

16. $|1 - 5x| + 4 = 5$

17. $4|x + 4| + 2 = 6$

18. $9 - |5x - 3| = 2$

19. $\dfrac{|x - 7|}{3} = 8$

20. $\dfrac{3}{7}|5x + 1| = 6$

EXTRA Solve. Reduce fractions but leave them improper. Check your solutions.

21. $|9x| = 27$

22. $|-5x| = 3$

23. $|x - 4| = 9$

24. $6 - |x + 5| = 0$

25. $9 + |-4x| = 17$

26. $3|6x| - 6 = 12$

27. $|-2x + 5| = 9$

28. $|8x + 3| = 3$

29. $3|x + 6| = 9$

30. $9|2x - 5| = 63$

31. $5 - 3|x + 2| = -7$

32. $4|5 + 2x| + 7 = 11$

33. $\dfrac{|x + 9|}{5} = 7$

34. $\dfrac{|x|}{2} + 4 = 7$

LESSON 7 Solving Linear Equations of All Types

Redo the examples you have studied earlier.

1. Explain how to solve $x + 3 = 5$. Show your steps. Review Lesson 3 if needed.

2. Explain how to solve $2x + 3 = 9$. Show your steps. Review Lesson 3 if needed.

3. Explain how to solve $1 + 2x - 5 = 2(1 - x) - x$. Show your steps. Review Lesson 4 if needed.

4. Describe how to clear $0.3x - 0.6 = 1.5$ of decimals to make the equation easier to work with. Then solve the equation. Show your steps. Review Lesson 5 if needed.

5. Describe how to clear $\frac{1}{3}x = \frac{1}{4}x - \frac{2}{3}$ of fractions to make the equation easier to work with. Then solve the equation. Show your steps. Review Lesson 5 if needed.

6. Explain how to rewrite $2|4x - 2| + 3 = 23$ as two separate equations. Then solve each equation. Show your steps. Review Lesson 6 if needed.

☐ **EXERCISE YOUR SKILLS** ···

Solve. Reduce fractions but leave them improper. Check your solutions.

7. $x + 5 = -7$

8. $21x = 9$

9. $\dfrac{x}{5} = 8$

10. $\dfrac{x}{4} = -\dfrac{1}{6}$

11. $14 + 2x = -10$

12. $5x - 5 = 75$

13. $\dfrac{x}{8} - 14 = -12$

14 $7 = \dfrac{x}{5} + 12$

15. $2x = 3x - 5x + 8$

16. $8 - 2(3x + 5) = 16$

17. $4 - 2x = 1 - 5x + 6$

18. $7(x - 1) + 2 = 17 - x$

19. $0.3x + 0.25 = 1.45$

20. $7.7 - 3.2x = 23.7$

21. $\dfrac{3}{5}x - \dfrac{1}{4} = \dfrac{1}{2}$

22. $\dfrac{5}{6} - \dfrac{3}{4}x = \dfrac{4}{3}$

23. $|4x| = 12$

24. $|4x + 2| + 4 = 6$

EXTRA Solve. Reduce fractions but leave them improper. Check your solutions.

25. $3x + 15 = 3$

26. $-7x - 24 = 25$

27. $2 + x - 9 = 2x + 3(2 - x)$

28. $2(3x + 4) = 9(x + 2) - 43$

29. $3.2 - 0.6x = 3.74$

30. $0.008x + 0.027 = 0.075$

31. $\dfrac{2}{3}x - \dfrac{5}{7} = \dfrac{9}{7}$

32. $\dfrac{2}{3}x + \dfrac{5}{2} = \dfrac{1}{2}$

33. $2 - \dfrac{3}{4}x = -\dfrac{5}{8}$

34. $\dfrac{1}{3}(x - 2) + \dfrac{4}{9} = \dfrac{1}{9}(x + 6)$

35. $|x + 9| = 8$

36. $7 - 3|x| = 1$

37. $|3x - 12| = 6$

38. $12 - 5|2x - 6| = 2$

LESSON 8 Number of Solutions to Linear Equations

☐ **REFRESH YOUR SKILLS** ···

Solve. Review Lessons 3 through 6 if needed.

1. $8x + 17 = -79$

2. $5(3x + 1) + 28 = 4x$

3. $\dfrac{1}{6}x - \dfrac{2}{3} = \dfrac{1}{2} - x$

4. $3|2x + 1| + 2 = 5$

☐ **CLASSIFYING SOLUTIONS TO LINEAR EQUATIONS** ··

You may assume that all equations have solutions. However, equations can have no solution or infinitely many solutions. Look at the examples below.

➔ **EXAMPLE** Determine the number of solutions.

a.

$3x + 2 = 3x + 5$

$-3x \qquad -3x$

$0x + 2 = 5$

$-2 \quad -2$

$0x = 3$

The equation has **no solution** because there is no x value that will produce 3 when multiplied by 0.

b.

$3x + 2 = 3x + 2$

$-3x \qquad -3x$

$0x + 2 = 2$

$-2 \quad -2$

$0x = 0$

The equation has **infinitely many solutions** because any value of x will work. Multiply any value by 0, and you always get 0.

c.

$2|x + 5| + 3 = 1$

$-3 \quad -3$

$2|x + 5| = -2$

$\div 2 \quad \div 2$

$|x + 5| = -1$

The equation has **no solution** because an absolute value can never be negative.

➔ **TRY IT** Determine the number of solutions. Do not solve.

5. $4 - x = 9 - x$

6. $x - 4 = 2x + 5x$

7. $8 - 2x = x - 3x + 8$

8. $|2x + 5| + 3 = 1$

☐ **EXERCISE YOUR SKILLS** ···

Determine the number of solutions. Do not solve.

9. $2 - 5x = x - 6x + 2$

10. $3(x - 1) + 4 = 6x$

11. $2|x - 3| = 16$

12. $5|3x + 2| + 9 = 4$

Solve. Reduce fractions but leave them improper. Check your solutions.

13. $4x - 13 = 19$

14. $3(5 - 2x) = 15 - 6x$

15. $x + 17 - 6 = 51$

16. $4 + 2(5x - 7) = 60$

17. $8 - 9(2x - 1) = 27$

18. $3(5 - 2x) + 6x = -9$

19. $-|3x| + 9 = 3$

20. $5|x| + 6 = -14$

21. $\dfrac{x}{3} - 5 = \dfrac{2}{3}$

22. $\dfrac{2}{5}x + 3 = \dfrac{1}{5}(2x + 15)$

EXTRA Solve. Reduce fractions but leave them improper. Check your solutions.

23. $7(x - 6) = -7$

24. $3x + 5(3x - 2) = -10$

25. $6x + 9 - 2x = 4x + 9$

26. $4 + 3x = 3x + 5(1 - 2x)$

27. $6(2x + 5) - 10 = 4(5 + 3x)$

28. $1 + 5x = x + 4(2 + x)$

28. $4 - 3|5 - x| = 13$

30. $2|x + 3| - 6 = 6$

31. $\dfrac{3}{5}x - \dfrac{1}{3} = \dfrac{4}{15}$

32. $x + \dfrac{3}{4} = 2x + \dfrac{1}{4}$

33. $\dfrac{2}{3}x + \dfrac{1}{2} = \dfrac{3}{4}x + \dfrac{5}{6}$

34. $\dfrac{1}{2}(x - 3) + \dfrac{1}{3}x = \dfrac{5}{6}x$

CHALLENGE Solve. Reduce fractions but leave them improper. Check your solutions.

35. $\dfrac{|3x - 5|}{5} + 4 = 6$

36. $\dfrac{2}{5}|x + 4| - 2 = 0$

37. $\dfrac{6}{7}|2 - 7x| + \dfrac{2}{7} = 2$

38. $\dfrac{3}{10}|5x - 7| + \dfrac{4}{5} = \dfrac{1}{5}$

LESSON 9 Applications of Linear Equations

☐ **SOLVING LINEAR EQUATION WORD PROBLEMS** ···

There are many types of word problems that require algebra: number problems, geometry problems, money problems, percentage problems, distance problems, mixture problems, and so on. You may find some more difficult than others, but they all can be solved using the same strategy. To solve a word problem using algebra, 1) define a variable, 2) set up an equation to model the given situation, 3) solve the equation as usual, and then 4) answer what's being asked.

➔ **EXAMPLE** Consecutive integers

The sum of three consecutive even integers is 12. Find the integers.

1. Let x = the first even integer
2. $x + 2$ = the second even integer
   $x + 4$ = the third even integer
   The sum is 12, so $x + (x + 2) + (x + 4) = 12$.
3. Solve for x, and you get $x = 2$.
4. The numbers are 2, 4, and 6.

➔ **TRY IT** Solve.

1. The sum of two consecutive even integers is 26. Find the two integers.

2. The sum of two consecutive odd integers is 32. Find the two integers.

3. The sum of three consecutive integers is 27. Find the integers.

➔ **EXAMPLE** Percent

The price of an apple rose by 15% to $1.38/lb. What was the original price?

1. Let x = the original price
2. $0.15x$ = the price increase
   The new price = the original price + the price increase, so $1.38 = x + 0.15x$.
3. Solve for x, and you get $x = 1.2$.
4. The original price was $1.20/lb.

➔ **TRY IT** Solve.

4. Cammy bought a jacket at $43.50. The price was 25% off the regular price. What was the regular price?

5. Jim bought a pair of pants at $16.80. The price was 40% off the regular price. What was the regular price?

➔ **EXAMPLE** Age

Dale is 6 years older than Kate. Three years ago, Dale was twice as old as Kate. How old are they now?

1. Let x = Kate's age now
2. $x + 6$ = Dale's age now
   $x - 3$ = Kate's age 3 years ago
   $(x + 6) - 3$ = Dale's age 3 years ago
   Dale's age 3 years ago = twice Kate's age 3 years ago, so $(x + 6) - 3 = 2(x - 3)$.
3. Solve for x, and you get $x = 9$.
4. Kate is 9 years old. Dale is 15 years old.

➔ **TRY IT** Solve.

6. Jamie is 5 years older than Nicole. Two years ago, Jamie was twice as old as Nicole. How old are they now?

7. Mia's father is 42 years old. Six years ago, he was six times as old as Mia. How old is Mia?

8. Ellen is 10 years younger than Max. In two years, Max will be twice as old as Ellen. How old are they now?

→ **EXAMPLE** Geometry

The length of a rectangle is twice its width. The perimeter is 18 feet. Find the dimensions of the rectangle.

1. Let x = the width of the rectangle
2. $2x$ = the length of the rectangle
   Perimeter = 2(length + width),
   so $2(x + 2x) = 18$.
3. Solve for x, and you get $x = 3$.
4. The rectangle is 3 feet by 6 feet.

→ **EXAMPLE** Coins

Olivia has $0.90 in dimes and nickels. She has three more nickels than dimes. How many coins of each type does she have?

1. Let x = the number of dimes
2. $x + 3$ = the number of nickels
   Total value = x dimes at $0.10 each +
   ($x + 3$) nickels at $0.05 each,
   so $0.10x + 0.05(x + 3) = 0.90$.
3. Solve for x, and you get $x = 5$.
4. Olivia has 5 dimes and 8 nickels.

→ **TRY IT** Solve.

9. The length of a rectangle is three times its width. The perimeter is 40 feet. Find the dimensions of the rectangle.

10. The length of a rectangle is 5 cm less than three times its width. The perimeter is 22 cm. Find the dimensions of the rectangle.

→ **TRY IT** Solve.

11. Emma has $0.95 in dimes and nickels. She has five more dimes than nickels. How many coins of each type does she have?

12. Joey has $1.60 in quarters and nickels. He has two more nickels than quarters. How many coins of each type does he have?

□ **EXERCISE YOUR SKILLS** ···

For each problem, 1) define a variable, 2) set up an equation, 3) solve the equation, and 4) answer what's being asked. Show your work in your notebook.

13. One integer is 5 less than twice another. Their sum is 25. Find the two integers.

14. The sum of three consecutive odd integers is 27. Find the integers.

15. A company's stock price dropped by 10% to $108 per share. What was the previous price per share?

16. Currently, Joey is three times as old as Anna. In five years, Joey will be twice as old as Anna. How old is Joey? How old is Anna?

17. Two sides of a triangle are equal in length and twice the length of the shortest side. The perimeter is 45 inches. Find the dimensions of the triangle.

18. Max has one-, five-, and ten-dollar bills totaling $82. He has twice as many fives as ones and three times as many tens as ones. How many bills of each type does he have?

LESSON 10 Applications of Linear Equations (Distance)

☐ USING THE DISTANCE-RATE-TIME FORMULA

Distance problems ask you to find how far (*distance*), how fast (*rate* or *speed*), or how long (*time*) an object or objects have traveled. When you see a problem involving these concepts, think of the distance-rate-time formula shown on the right.

$$distance = rate \times time$$
$$D = rt$$

The idea behind the formula is simple, and you already know it: if you drive at 60 miles per hour (*r*) for 3 hours (*t*), you will travel $60 \times 3 = 180$ miles (*D*).

→ **EXAMPLE** Distance-rate-time formula

How long will it take to travel 150 miles at 75 miles per hour (mph)?

1. Let t = travel time in hours
2. $D = rt$, so $150 = 75t$.
3. Solve for t, and $t = 2$.
4. It will take 2 hours.

→ **TRY IT** Solve.

1. How long will it take an airplane to travel 1,600 miles at an average speed of 320 mph?

2. A train traveled 720 miles in 4 hours. What was its average speed?

☐ SOLVING DISTANCE WORD PROBLEMS

More complex distance problems will take some practice to get used to. Often the hardest part is setting up an equation. It helps to first organize the given information using a picture or a table. Here are four classic types of distance problems. Study each example carefully.

→ **EXAMPLE** Meeting in between

Two trains leave stations 300 miles apart at the same time and travel toward each other. One train travels at 70 mph while the other travels at 80 mph. How long will it take for the two trains to meet?

70*t* miles   80*t* miles

300 miles

OR

	r	t	$D = rt$
Train 1	70	t	70t
Train 2	80	t	80t

1. Let t = time it will take for the two trains to meet
2. Total distance traveled by the two trains in t hours = distance of train 1 + distance of train 2, so $70t + 80t = 300$.
3. Solve for t, and $t = 2$.
4. It will take 2 hours.

→ **TRY IT** Solve.

3. Two trains leave stations 800 miles apart at the same time and travel toward each other. One train travels at 110 mph while the other travels at 90 mph. How long will it take for the two trains to meet?

4. Brian and Jamie began jogging from the same spot at the same time in opposite directions on a 6-mile circular trail. Brian runs at 5 mph and Jamie at 7 mph. How long will it take them to meet?

→ **EXAMPLE** Traveling in opposite directions

Two cars leave a location at the same time and travel in opposite directions. One car travels 5 mph faster than the other. After 2 hours, they are 210 miles apart. Find the speed of each car.

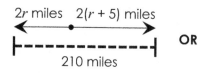

OR

	r	t	$D = rt$
Car 1	r	2	$2r$
Car 2	$r + 5$	2	$2(r + 5)$

1. Let r = speed of car 1
2. $r + 5$ = speed of car 2
   Total distance traveled by the two cars in 2 hours
   = distance of car 1 + distance of car 2,
   so $2r + 2(r + 5) = 210$.
3. Solve for r, and $r = 50$.
4. Car 1 travels at 50 mph. Car 2 travels at 55 mph.

→ **TRY IT** Solve.

5. Two trains leave a station at the same time and travel in opposite directions. One train travels 10 mph faster than the other. After 4 hours, they are 720 miles apart. Find the speed of each train.

6. Two airplanes depart from an airport at the same time and travel in opposite directions. One plane flies 150 mph faster than the other. After 3 hours, they are 2,250 miles apart. Find the speed of each airplane.

→ **EXAMPLE** Round-trip travel

Sam drove to work averaging 55 mph. On the way home, he averaged 45 mph. His total driving time was 2 hours. How far does Sam live from work?

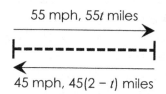

OR

	r	t	$D = rt$
To work	55	t	$55t$
To home	45	$2 - t$	$45(2 - t)$

1. Let t = time taken from home to work
2. $2 - t$ = time taken from work to home
   Distance from home to work = distance from work to home, so $55t = 45(2 - t)$.
3. Solve for t, and $t = 0.9$.
4. Sam lives $55 \times 0.9 = 49.5$ miles from work.

→ **TRY IT** Solve.

7. Mike hiked around a circular mountain trail twice in a total of 5 hours. He walked the circle at 6 mph the first time and at 4 mph the second time. How long is the trail?

8. Thomas rode his bike to a museum at an average speed of 15 mph. Then he rode back home at an average speed of 20 mph. His total riding time was 1.75 hours, or 1 hour and 45 minutes. How far does Thomas live from the museum?

Continued on the next page.

→ EXAMPLE Overtaking

Kyle starts jogging a trail at 4 mph. An hour later, Eli starts jogging the trail from the same point in the same direction at 6 mph. How long will it take Eli to overtake (catch up with) Kyle?

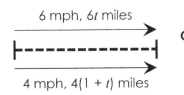

6 mph, 6*t* miles

4 mph, 4(1 + *t*) miles

OR

	r	*t*	*D = rt*
Eli	6	*t*	6*t*
Kyle	4	1 + *t*	4(1 + *t*)

1. Let *t* = time it takes Eli to overtake Kyle
2. 1 + *t* = time Kyle will jog until Eli overtakes him
   Eli's distance in *t* hours = Kyle's distance in (1 + *t*) hours, so 6*t* = 4(1 + *t*).
3. Solve for *t*, and *t* = 2.
4. It will take 2 hours for Eli to overtake Kyle.

→ TRY IT Solve.

9. The first bus leaves a station traveling at an average speed of 60 mph. An hour later, the second bus leaves the station traveling at an average speed of 70 mph in the same direction. How long will it take the second bus to overtake the first?

10. Josh starts walking a trail at an average speed of 3 mph. Thirty minutes later, Carol starts walking the trail from the same point in the same direction at an average speed of 5 mph. How long will it take Carol to catch up with Josh?

☐ EXERCISE YOUR SKILLS ··

For each problem, 1) define a variable, 2) set up an equation, 3) solve the equation, and 4) answer what's being asked. Show your work in your notebook.

11. Mark drove to visit his friend who lives 180 miles away. His average speed was 72 mph. How long did it take him to get to his friend's house?

12. Two trains leave stations 880 miles apart at the same time and travel toward each other. One train travels at 85 mph while the other travels at 75 mph. How long will it take for the two trains to meet?

13. Two airplanes depart from an airport at the same time and travel in opposite directions. One plane flies 60 mph faster than the other. After 5 hours, they are 4,300 miles apart. Find the speed of each airplane.

14. Sandra drove to work at an average speed of 60 mph. Later in the evening, she drove back home at an average speed of 45 mph. Her total driving time was 1.4 hours. How far does Sandra live from work?

15. The first train leaves a station traveling at an average speed of 100 mph. Two hours later, the second train leaves the station traveling at an average speed of 150 mph in the same direction. How long will it take the second train to overtake the first?

LESSON 11 Applications of Linear Equations (Mixtures)

☐ **USING THE CONCENTRATION FORMULA** ··

Mixture problems involve combining different quantities at different rates. One type of mixture problem is mixing liquids of different concentrations. To solve these liquid mixture problems, we use the formula:

> *concentration (%) × amount of solution = amount of substance in the solution*

It is basically the percent formula: *percent × whole = part*. Let's first understand how the formula works. Read carefully and check off each box if you understand it.

☐ Concentration is the percentage of a substance (*part*) in a solution (*whole*).

☐ Dissolve 2 g of salt in 18 g of water, and you get a 2/(18 + 2) = 10% saline solution.

☐ In other words, 20 g of a 10% saline solution contains 10% of 20 = 0.1 x 20 = 2 g of salt.

☐ Similarly, 30 g of a 20% saline solution contains 20% of 30 = 0.2 × 30 = 6 g of salt.

☐ Mix the two solutions, and you get 50 g of a saline solution with 8 g of salt in it.

☐ Hence, the concentration of the mixture is 8/50 = 16%.

Now let's try some problems.

→ **EXAMPLE** Concentration formula

You dissolve 5 g of salt in 15 g of water. What is the concentration of the solution?

1. Let c = concentration of the solution
2. Substance = salt = 5 g
   Solution = salt + water = 5 + 15 = 20 g
   Concentration = substance/solution (or percent = part/whole),
   so c = 5/20 = 0.25 = 25%.
3. You get a 25% saline solution.

→ **EXAMPLE** Concentration formula

How much water must be mixed with 5 g of salt to make a 20% saline solution?

1. Let w = amount of water to mix
2. Substance = salt = 5 g
   Solution = salt + water = 5 + w g
   Concentration = 20% = 0.2
   Concentration × solution = substance (or percent × whole = part), so 0.2(5 + w) = 5.
3. Solve for w, and w = 20.
4. You need to mix 20 g of water.

→ **TRY IT** Solve.

1. You dissolve 8 g of salt in 17 g of water. What is the concentration of the solution?

2. How much salt is in 45 ounces of a 40% saline solution?

→ **TRY IT** Solve.

3. How much water must be mixed with 15 g of salt to obtain a 30% saline solution?

4. How much water must be mixed with 2 milliliters of acid to produce a 4% acid solution?

→ EXAMPLE Concentration formula

You mix 10 g of a 10% saline solution with 20 g of a 25% saline solution. What is the concentration of the mixture?

1. Let c = concentration of the mixture
2. Salt in 10% solution = 0.1 × 10 = 1 g
   Salt in 25% solution = 0.25 × 20 = 5 g
   Salt in the mixture = 1 + 5 = 6 g
   Amount of the mixture = 10 + 20 = 30 g
   Concentration = substance/solution,
   so c = 6/30 = 0.2 = 20%.
3. The mixture is a 20% saline solution.

→ TRY IT Solve.

5. You mix 9 g of a 10% saline solution with 6 g of a 15% saline solution. What is the concentration of the mixture?

6. You mix 12 g of a 15% saline solution with 18 g of a 25% saline solution. What is the concentration of the mixture?

7. You mix 15 liters of water with 30 liters of a 12% alcohol solution. What is the concentration of the mixture?

☐ **SOLVING LIQUID MIXTURE WORD PROBLEMS** ···

Here is a typical liquid mixture problem. Just like distance problems, it helps to first organize the given information using a picture or a table and then set up an equation.

→ EXAMPLE Liquid mixture

How many liters of a 50% saline solution must be added to 2 liters of a 20% saline solution to produce a 40% saline solution?

	%	Solution	Substance
50% solution	0.5	x	$0.5x$
20% solution	0.2	2	0.4
Mixture (40%)	0.4	$x + 2$	$0.4(x + 2)$

1. Let x = liters of 50% solution
2. $x + 2$ = liters of 40% solution
   Salt in x liters of 50% solution + salt in 2 liters of 20% solution = salt in $(x + 2)$ liters of 40% solution, so $0.5x + 0.4 = 0.4(x + 2)$.
3. Solve for x, and $x = 4$
4. We need 4 liters of 50% solution.

→ TRY IT Solve.

8. How much of a 25% acid solution must be added to 15 ounces of a 10% acid solution to produce a 20% acid solution?

9. How much water must be added to 12 liters of a 30% saline solution to produce an 18% saline solution?

☐ **SOLVING DRY MIXTURE WORD PROBLEMS** ···

Another type of mixture problem is mixing non-liquid items with different unit prices. To solve these dry mixture problems, we use the familiar formula shown on the right.

$$unit\ price \times quantity = cost$$

The formula is simple: when you buy 5 pears at $2 each, you pay $2 × 5 = $10 in all.

Continued on the next page.

➜ EXAMPLE Dry mixture

Walnuts sell for $6 per pound. Cashews sell for $3 per pound. How many pounds of walnuts must be mixed with 8 pounds of cashews to make a mixture of nuts that costs $5 per pound?

	Unit price	Quantity	Total cost
Walnuts	6	x	$6x$
Cashews	3	8	24
Mixture	5	$x + 8$	$5(x + 8)$

1. Let x = pounds of walnuts
2. $x + 8$ = pounds of the mixture
   Cost of x pounds of walnuts at $6/lb + cost of 8 pounds of cashews at $3/lb = cost of $(x + 8)$ pounds of the mixture at $5/lb, so $6x + 3 \times 8 = 5(x + 8)$.
3. Solve for x, and $x = 16$.
4. We need 16 pounds of walnuts.

➜ TRY IT Solve.

10. Six pounds of candy costing $4.50 per pound is mixed with 4 pounds of candy costing $6.50 per pound. What is the price of the mixture per pound?

11. Coffee A costs $9 per pound. Coffee B costs $12 per pound. How many pounds of coffee A must be mixed with 3 pounds of coffee B to make a coffee blend that costs $10 per pound?

☐ EXERCISE YOUR SKILLS ···

For each problem, 1) define a variable, 2) set up an equation, 3) solve the equation, and 4) answer what's being asked. Show your work in your notebook.

12. How much salt is in 50 grams of a 40% saline solution?

13. How much water must be mixed with 15 ounces of salt to produce a 30% saline solution?

14. How much alcohol must be added to 60 liters of water to produce a 25% alcohol solution?

15. Five cups of a 10% hydrogen chloride solution is mixed with 15 cups of a 30% hydrogen chloride solution. What is the concentration of the mixture?

16. How much of a 60% alcohol solution must be added to 30 liters of a 20% alcohol solution to produce a 50% alcohol solution?

17. Six pounds of candy costing $5 per pound is mixed with 9 pounds of candy costing $4 per pound. What is the price of the mixture per pound?

18. Peanuts sell for $3 per pound. Almonds sell $8 per pound. How many pounds of peanuts must be mixed with 5 pounds of almonds to make a mixture of nuts that costs $5 per pound?

LESSON 12 Solving for a Variable

☐ **REFRESH YOUR SKILLS** ⋯⋯⋯⋯⋯⋯⋯⋯⋯⋯⋯⋯⋯⋯⋯⋯⋯⋯⋯⋯⋯⋯⋯⋯⋯⋯⋯⋯⋯⋯⋯⋯⋯⋯⋯⋯⋯

Describe the step(s) to solve each equation. Do not solve. Review Lesson 3 if needed.

1. $x - 4 = 9$

2. $-3x = 9$

3. $2x + 5 = 7$

4. $\dfrac{x}{4} - 3 = -5$

☐ **SOLVING FOR A VARIABLE** ⋯⋯⋯⋯⋯⋯⋯⋯⋯⋯⋯⋯⋯⋯⋯⋯⋯⋯⋯⋯⋯⋯⋯⋯⋯⋯⋯⋯⋯⋯⋯⋯⋯⋯⋯⋯⋯

Equations with several variables (letters) are called **literal equations**. Solving a literal equation for a variable means to isolate the variable on one side of the equation. We do this by performing the same inverse operations on both sides of the equation.

➔ **EXAMPLE** Solve for y.

$$6 - 5x = 2y - x$$

Switch the sides to put y on the left.

$$2y - x = 6 - 5x$$

$+x \qquad +x$ Add x to both sides.

$$2y = 6 - 4x$$

$\div 2 \quad \div 2$ Divide both sides by 2.

$$y = 3 - 2x$$

➔ **TRY IT** Solve for y.

5. $y - 7 = -x$

6. $x - 4y = 9x$

7. $4x + 5 = -6x + 5y$

☐ **REWRITING FORMULAS** ⋯⋯⋯⋯⋯⋯⋯⋯⋯⋯⋯⋯⋯⋯⋯⋯⋯⋯⋯⋯⋯⋯⋯⋯⋯⋯⋯⋯⋯⋯⋯⋯⋯⋯⋯⋯⋯⋯⋯

Formulas are examples of literal equations. In real-world situations, it is often useful to rewrite formulas by solving them for one of their variables.

➔ **EXAMPLE** The formula $V = lwh$ gives the volume V of a rectangular prism with length l, width w, and height h. Solve it for h.

Simply divide both sides by lw, as shown on the right. Now you can use the new formula to find the height of any rectangular prism with known length, height, and volume.

$$V = lwh$$

$\div lw \qquad \div lw$

$$\frac{V}{lw} = h$$

➔ **TRY IT** Rewrite each formula as indicated. Then use it to answer the question.

8. The formula $D = rt$ gives the distance D traveled at a speed of r over time t. Solve it for t. How long will it take to travel 165 miles at 55 mph?

9. The formula $P = 2l + 2w$ gives the perimeter P of a rectangle with width w and length l. Solve it for l. What is the length of a rectangle whose perimeter is 60 cm and whose width is 12 cm?

Solve for y.

10. $15x = -3y$

11. $6x - y = -7$

12. $y - 2 + 4x = 3$

13. $9x + 5 = 3y - 7$

Rewrite each formula as indicated. Then use it to answer the question.

14. The formula $A = lw$ gives the area A of a rectangle with width w and length l. Solve it for w. What is the width of a rectangle whose area is 90 cm² and whose length is 15 cm?

15. The formula $C = 2\pi r$ gives the circumference C of a circle of radius r. Solve it for r. What is the radius of a circle whose circumference is 31.4 inches? Use 3.14 for π.

16. The formula $A = \frac{1}{2}bh$ gives the area A of a triangle with base b and height h. Solve it for h. What is the height of a triangle whose area is 24 in² and whose base is 6 in?

17. The formula $V = \pi r^2 h$ gives the volume V of a cylinder with base radius r and height h. Solve it for h. What is the height of a cylinder whose volume is 785 in³ and whose base radius is 5 in? Use 3.14 for π.

18. The formula $SA = 2\pi rh + 2\pi r^2$ gives the surface area SA of a cylinder with base radius r and height h. Solve it for h. What is the height of a cylinder whose surface area is 942 cm² and whose base radius is 10 cm? Use 3.14 for π.

19. The formula $F = \frac{9}{5}C + 32$ gives the Fahrenheit temperature F for a given Celsius temperature C. Solve it for C. What is the temperature in Celsius when it is 50 °F?

20. The formula $I = Prt$ gives the amount of simple interest I earned by investing principal P for rate r over time t. Solve it for t. How long would it take $1,200 to earn simple interest of $360 at an annual interest rate of 6%?

CHALLENGE Solve for y.

21. $\dfrac{4x - 2y}{5} = -1$

22. $\dfrac{1}{2}x + \dfrac{2}{3}y = \dfrac{1}{2}y$

23. $\dfrac{1}{5}y - 1 + x = 2x + \dfrac{4}{5}$

24. $\dfrac{4}{9}x + \dfrac{1}{3}y = \dfrac{1}{3}x + \dfrac{2}{9}y$

LESSON 13 Catch Up and Review!

"Catch Up and Review!" lessons have no required assignments. Catch up if you are behind. Review lessons that caused you trouble. Redo problems you got wrong. If you do not need to catch up, you could use the review problems below to make sure you're on track.

LESSON 1 Evaluate.

1. $8 + 24 \div 4 \times 2$

2. $10 + 2^5 \div 2^4 \div (-2)^1$

3. $(9 + 2^2) \times (6 \div -6)^5$

4. $(3^2 - 8) \times 5 + (-3)^3 \div 9$

LESSON 2 Simplify.

5. $2x + 5 + 3x - 9 - 4x$

6. $4(8 - 7x) + 6(x + 2)$

LESSON 3 Solve.

7. $x + 9 = 2$

8. $3x = -12$

9. $2x - 7 = 3$

10. $6x + 4 = 7$

LESSON 4 Solve.

11. $21 - 2x = -5x$

12. $5x - 12 + x = 15 - 3x$

13. $3(x + 1) + 1 = 4x + 5$

14. $6x - x = 3(x + 5) + 7x$

LESSON 5 Solve.

15. $0.3x + 0.55 = 1.75$

16. $0.2x - 0.42 = 0.14x - 0.9$

17. $\frac{1}{3}x + 1 = \frac{3}{4}$

18. $\frac{2}{5}x + 2 = \frac{1}{5} - \frac{1}{2}x$

LESSON 6 Solve.

19. $|4x| = 2$

20. $3|x| - 6 = 0$

21. $2|x - 5| + 1 = 5$

22. $5|2x - 7| - 3 = 2$

LESSON 8 Determine the number of solutions.

23. $7 - 5x = x - 6x + 4$

24. $2x + 5 = x + 5 + x$

LESSONS 9–11 Solve.

25. The sum of three consecutive integers is 18. Find the integers.

26. A train traveled to another city at 80 mph and then returned at 70 mph. The whole round trip took 7.5 hours. How far away is the other city?

27. How many liters of a 70% saline solution must be added to 40 liters of a 40% saline solution to produce a 50% saline solution?

LESSON 12 Solve.

28. The formula $V = \frac{1}{3}\pi r^2 h$ gives the volume of a cone with base radius r and vertical height h. Solve it for h. Then find h when $V = 157$ cm^3 and $r = 5$ cm. Use 3.14 for π.

☐ **MIXED REVIEW: PRE-ALGEBRA** ··

Brush up on the topics covered in Pre-Algebra.

29. Round 0.275 to the nearest tenth.

30. Express 54 as a product of prime factors.

31. Find the greatest common factor of 16 and 24.

32. Find the least common multiple of 16 and 24.

33. In which quadrant is the point with coordinates (3, −2) located?

LESSON 14 Graphing Lines by Plotting Points

☐ **REFRESH YOUR SKILLS** ···

Determine whether the given value is a solution. Review Lesson 3 if needed.

1. $x + 8 = 9; x = 1$

2. $4x + 7 = 5; x = 3$

☐ **CHECKING SOLUTIONS TO LINEAR EQUATIONS** ·································

Equations in two variables often have infinitely many solutions. A **solution to an equation in two variables** is any ordered pair (x, y) that make the equation true. To check whether an ordered pair is a solution to an equation, simply plug it into the equation and see if the equation holds true.

➔ **EXAMPLE** Is $(1, 2)$ a solution to $2x + 3y = 5$?

$2(1) + 3(2) = 5$ Substitute 1 for x and 2 for y.

$8 = 5$ False. $(1, 2)$ is not a solution.

➔ **TRY IT** Is the point a solution?

3. $x + 2y = 4; (2, 1)$

➔ **EXAMPLE** Given $2x + 3y = 5$, find y when $x = 1$.

$2(1) + 3y = 5$ Substitute 1 for x.

$y = 1$ Solve for y.

➔ **TRY IT** Find y given x.

4. $x + 2y = 4; x = -2$

☐ **GRAPHING LINES BY PLOTTING POINTS** ·································

Graphing an equation in two variables means plotting all its solutions on the coordinate plane. Graphs of equations can have many different shapes. Equations whose graphs are straight lines are called **linear equations**.

To graph a linear equation, 1) choose any set of x-values, 2) substitute them into the equation to find the corresponding y-values, and then 3) plot the ordered pairs and connect them with a line.

➔ **EXAMPLE** Graph $y = x + 1$.

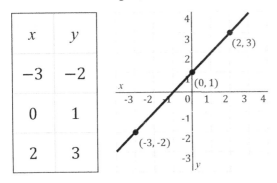

x	y
-3	-2
0	1
2	3

➔ **TRY IT 5.** Graph $y = -x + 1$.

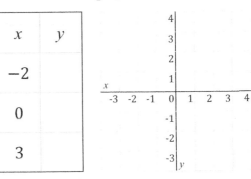

x	y
-2	
0	
3	

☐ **EXERCISE YOUR SKILLS** ·································

Determine whether the given point is a solution.

6. $y = -3x; (2, -6)$

7. $x + 4y = -8; (4, -3)$

Find the *y*-value for the given *x*-value.

8. $y = -x + 5; x = 3$

9. $x - 2y = 7; x = 3$

Find the *x*-value for the given *y*-value.

10. $y = x - 2; y = 4$

11. $5x - 3y = 9; y = -3$

Find at least three ordered-pair solutions, then graph.

12. $y = x$

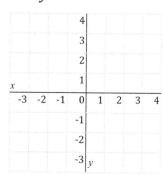

13. $y = -x$

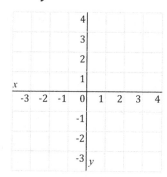

14. $y = x + 2$

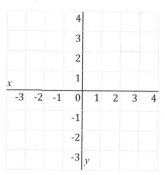

15. $y = -2x$

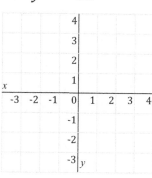

16. $y = 2x - 1$

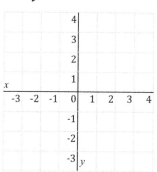

17. $y = -3x + 2$

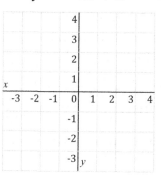

18. $x - y = 2$

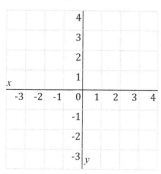

19. $x + 2y = 0$

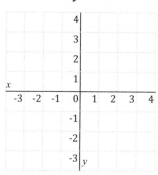

20. $2x - 3y = 6$

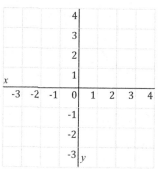

LESSON 15 Slope and Slope Formula

☐ **IDENTIFYING TYPES OF SLOPES** ··

The **slope** of a line is the steepness of the line. Slope can be positive, negative, zero, or undefined. **Positive slope** means that the line goes up from left to right. **Negative slope** means that the line goes down from left to right. **Zero slope** means that the line is horizontal. **Undefined slope** means that the line is vertical.

➔ **TRY IT** Identify each slope as positive, negative, zero, or undefined.

1.

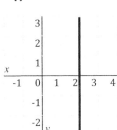

2.

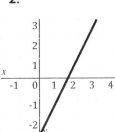

3.

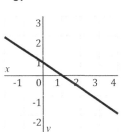

4.

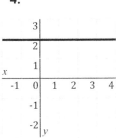

☐ **FINDING SLOPE FROM GRAPHS** ···

Slope is defined as **rise over run** (*rise/run*) where *rise* is the change in *y* (up or down) and *run* is the change in *x* (left or right). Up and right are positive, and down and left are negative.

To find the slope of a line from its graph, 1) pick any two points on the line, 2) determine the rise and run between the two points, and 3) divide the rise by the run to calculate the slope.

➔ **EXAMPLE** Find the slope.

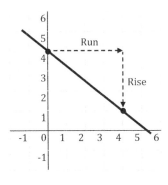

1. Pick two points (0, 4) and (4, 1).
2. The line has a run of 4 (right) and a rise of −3 (down).
3. The slope is −3/4.

➔ **TRY IT 5.** Find the slope.

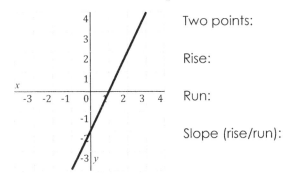

Two points:

Rise:

Run:

Slope (rise/run):

☐ **FINDING SLOPE FROM POINTS** ···

The formula for the slope of a line passing through two points (x_1, y_1) and (x_2, y_2) can be obtained using the definition of slope.

$$slope = \frac{rise}{run} = \frac{change\ in\ y}{change\ in\ x} = \frac{y_2 - y_1}{x_2 - x_1}$$

➔ **EXAMPLE** Find the slope of the line passing through (0, 4) and (3, 1).

$$slope = \frac{y_2 - y_1}{x_2 - x_1} = \frac{1 - 4}{3 - 0} = \frac{-3}{3} = -1$$

➔ **TRY IT 6.** Find the slope of the line passing through (2, 4) and (−3, 1).

Find the slope of each line.

7.

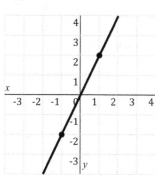

8.

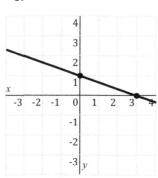

9.

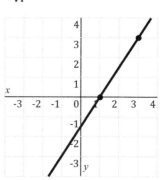

10.

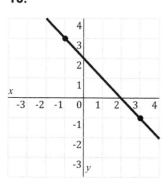

11.

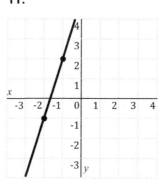

12.

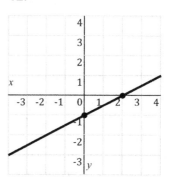

13.

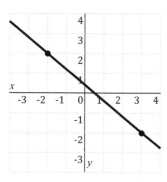

14.

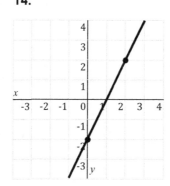

15.

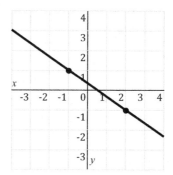

Find the slope given two points.

16. $(0, 5)$ and $(3, 8)$

17. $(4, 2)$ and $(-1, 3)$

18. $(-1, 7)$ and $(2, -5)$

19. $(3, 6)$ and $(2, 4)$

20. $(1, 4)$ and $(-2, 4)$

21. $(4, -3)$ and $(6, 7)$

LESSON 16 Graphing Lines in Slope-Intercept Form

☐ REFRESH YOUR SKILLS

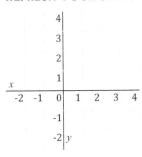

1. Graph $y = 2x + 1$ by plotting at least three points. Review Lesson 14 if needed.

2. What is the slope of your line?

3. Where does your line cross the y-axis?

☐ IDENTIFYING SLOPES AND Y-INTERCEPTS

When solved for y, all linear equations have the form $y = mx + b$. This is called **slope-intercept form** because it tells us the slope m and the y-intercept b of the line. The **y-intercept** is the point where the line intersects the y-axis. For example, by simply looking at the equation $y = 2x + 1$, we can say that its graph is a line with a slope of 2 and a y-intercept of 1.

> Slope-intercept form
>
> $$y = mx + b$$
>
> m = slope, b = y-intercept

➔ **EXAMPLE** Find the slope and y-intercept.

a. $y = 2x + 1$

$m = 2, b = 1$

b. $y = -1$

$m = 0, b = -1$

➔ **TRY IT** Find the slope and y-intercept.

4. $y = 5x - 4$

5. $y = 6$

☐ GRAPHING LINES IN SLOPE-INTERCEPT FORM

When an equation is in slope-intercept form, you can graph it using the slope and y-intercept.

➔ **EXAMPLE** Graph $y = 2x + 1$.

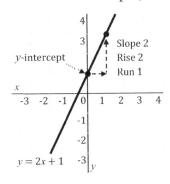

1. Identify the slope and y-intercept from the equation. The slope is 2, and the y-intercept is 1.
2. Use the y-intercept to plot the first point. The y-intercept is 1, so we first plot (0, 1).
3. From the first point, use the slope to find the second point and plot it. The slope is 2, so we move to the right 1 unit and up 2 units from (0, 1) to reach (1, 3) and plot it.
4. Draw a line through the two points.

➔ **TRY IT 6.** Graph $y = 2x - 1$.

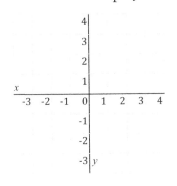

Slope:

y-intercept:

1st point:

2nd point:

➔ **TRY IT 7.** Graph $y = -x + 2$.

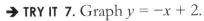
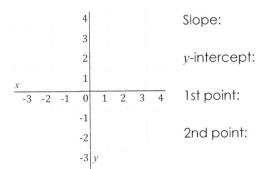

Slope:

y-intercept:

1st point:

2nd point:

Find the slope and *y*-intercept, then graph.

8. $y = x + 2$

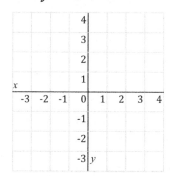

9. $y = -x + 3$

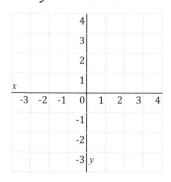

10. $y = 2x - 3$

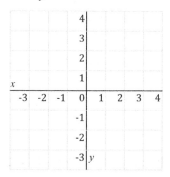

11. $y = -x - 1$

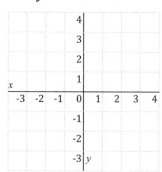

12. $y = -2x + 2$

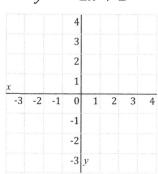

13. $y = 4x$

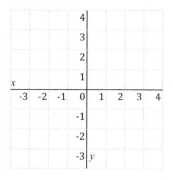

14. $y = x - 3$

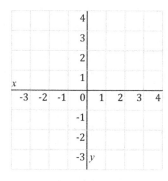

15. $y = -\frac{1}{2}x + 1$

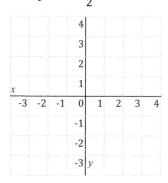

16. $y = \frac{1}{4}x - 1$

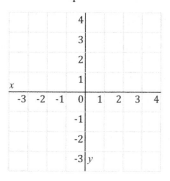

17. $y = \frac{3}{4}x - 1$

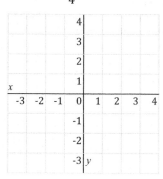

18. $y = -\frac{2}{3}x - 2$

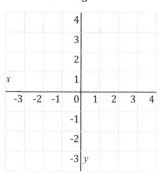

19. $y = \frac{1}{2}x + 3$

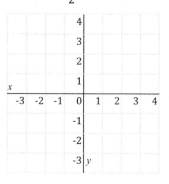

LESSON 17 Graphing Lines in Standard Form

☐ **REFRESH YOUR SKILLS** ···

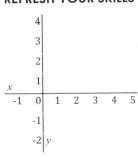

1. Graph $y = -\frac{2}{3}x + 2$ by using the slope and y-intercept. Review Lesson 16 if needed.

2. Where does your line cross the x-axis?

3. Which quadrants does your line pass through?

Solve for y. Review Lesson 12 if needed.

4. $3x - y = 2$

5. $x + 2y = 4$

☐ **CONVERTING STANDARD FORM TO SLOPE-INTERCEPT FORM** ·······················

The **standard form** of linear equations is $Ax + By = C$ where A, B and C are real numbers and A and B are not both zero. To convert standard form to slope-intercept form, simply solve for y.

Standard form
$Ax + By = C$

➜ **EXAMPLE** Put $2x + 3y = 6$ in slope-intercept form.

$2x + 3y = 6$

$\quad -2x \quad -2x$ Subtract $2x$ from both sides.

$3y = -2x + 6$

$\quad \div 3 \quad \div 3$ Divide both sides by 3.

$y = -\frac{2}{3}x + 2$ Solpe-intercept form

➜ **TRY IT** Put in slope-intercept form.

6. $x + 2y = 2$

7. $4x + 3y = 6$

☐ **GRAPHING LINES IN STANDARD FORM** ···

When an equation is given in standard form, first solve the equation for y to put it into slope-intercept form. Then use the slope and y-intercept to graph the equation.

➜ **EXAMPLE** Graph $2x + 3y = 6$.

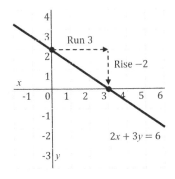

1. Find the slope and y-intercept:
   $$m = -\frac{2}{3}, \quad b = 2$$

2. Plot the 1st point (y-intercept) (0, 2).

3. Find and plot the 2nd point (3, 0).

4. Draw a line through the two points.

➜ **TRY IT 8.** Graph $x + 2y = 2$.

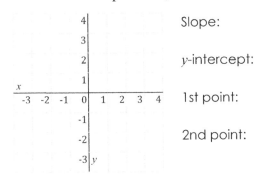

Slope:

y-intercept:

1st point:

2nd point:

Put in slope-intercept form.

9. $x + y = 4$

10. $5x + y = -4$

11. $x + 4y = 8$

12. $2x - 5y = 10$

Find the slope and y-intercept, then graph.

13. $x + y = 2$

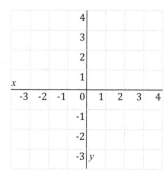

14. $4x - y = 4$

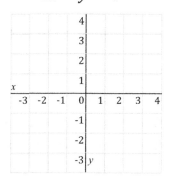

15. $x - 2y = 0$

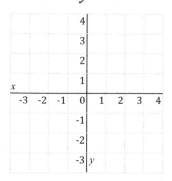

16. $3x - y = -3$

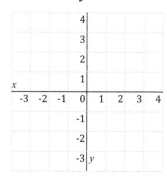

17. $x + 4y = 8$

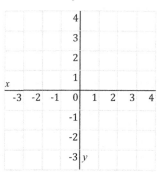

18. $2x + 3y = 3$

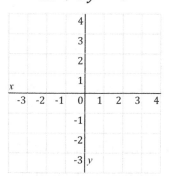

19. $5x - 3y = 6$

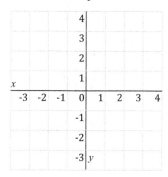

20. $2x + y = -1$

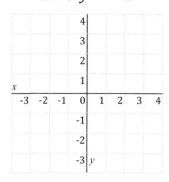

21. $x + 3y = -6$

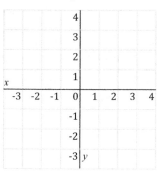

LESSON 18 Graphing Lines Using Intercepts

☐ **REFRESH YOUR SKILLS** ···

```
5
4
3
2
1
x
-1  0  1  2  3  4  5
  -1  y
```

1. Find the slope and y-intercept of the graph of $4x + 3y = 12$. Review Lesson 17 if needed.

2. Graph $4x + 3y = 12$ by using the slope and y-intercept.

3. Where does your line cross the x-axis?

☐ **GRAPHING LINES USING INTERCEPTS** ·····································

Regardless of what form an equation is given in, you can always graph it by plotting two points and drawing a line through them. Commonly the x- and y-intercepts are used because they are easy to find. The **x-intercept** is the point where $y = 0$. The **y-intercept** is the point where $x = 0$.

x-intercept
$(x, 0)$

y-intercept
$(0, y)$

To find the x-intercept, set $y = 0$ and solve for x. To find the y-intercept, set $x = 0$ and solve for y.

➔ **EXAMPLE** Find the intercepts of $4x + 3y = 12$.

$$4x + 3y = 12$$

> $4x = 12$ Set $y = 0$, then solve for x.
> $x = 3$

> $3y = 12$ Set $x = 0$, then solve for y.
> $y = 4$

The x-intercept is 3, and the y-intercept is 4.

➔ **TRY IT** Find the intercepts.

4. $x - y = -4$

5. $2x + 3y = 6$

➔ **EXAMPLE** Graph $4x + 3y = 12$.

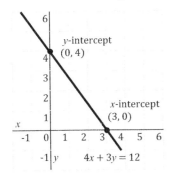

1. Find the intercepts:
    x-intercept = 3
    y-intercept = 4
2. Plot the two points (3, 0) and (0, 4).
3. Draw a line through the two points.

➔ **TRY IT 6.** Graph $2x + 3y = 6$.

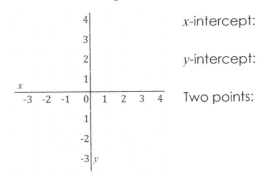

x-intercept:

y-intercept:

Two points:

☐ **EXERCISE YOUR SKILLS** ···

Find the intercepts.

7. $x - 4y = 8$

8. $5x + 3y = -15$

Find the intercepts, then graph.

9. $x - y = -2$

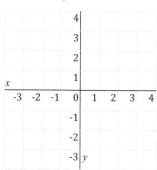

10. $x - 2y = 2$

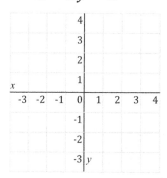

11. $3x + y = 3$

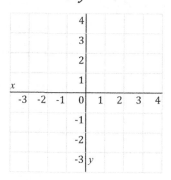

12. $2x - 3y = -6$

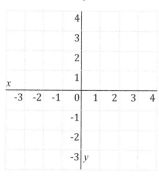

13. $x + y = -3$

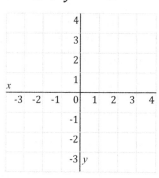

14. $-4x + y = 4$

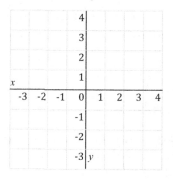

15. $-x + y = 1$

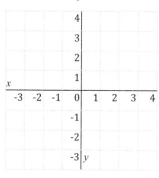

16. $4x - 3y = 12$

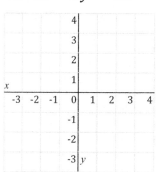

17. $-x + 3y = 3$

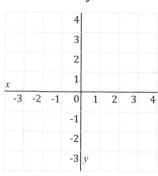

EXTRA Find the intercepts, then graph.

18. $2x + y = 2$

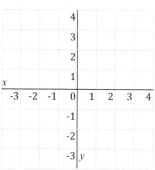

19. $x + 4y = -4$

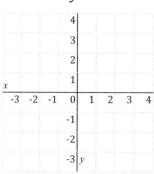

20. $3x + 2y = 6$

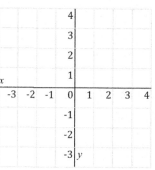

LESSON 19 Horizontal, Vertical, Parallel, and Perpendicular Lines

☐ **REFRESH YOUR SKILLS** ···

Find the slope given two points. Review Lesson 15 if needed.

1. $(0, 5)$ and $(4, 5)$

2. $(3, 1)$ and $(3, 7)$

Put in slope-intercept form, then identify the slope. Review Lessons 16 and 17 if needed.

3. $x + y = -2$

4. $x + 2y = 0$

5. $5x - 3y = 6$

6. $3x + 4y = -4$

☐ **GRAPHING HORIZONTAL AND VERTICAL LINES** ···

The slope of a horizontal line is zero because the change in y (or *rise*) is always zero. The equation of a horizontal line is in the form $y = k$ where k is a constant. The form $y = k$ means y is always k no matter what x is.

The slope of a vertical line is undefined because the change in x (or *run*) is always zero and division by zero is undefined. The equation of a vertical line is in the form $x = k$ where k is a constant. The form $x = k$ means x is always k no matter what y is.

Horizontal line
$y = k$
Vertical line
$x = k$

➔ **EXAMPLE** Graph $y = 2$ and $x = -2$.

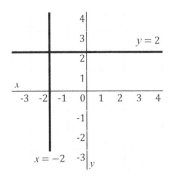

The graph of $y = 2$ is a horizontal line crossing the y-axis at $(0, 2)$.

The graph of $x = -2$ is a vertical line crossing the x-axis at $(0, -2)$.

➔ **TRY IT** Graph.

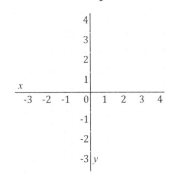

7. $x = 1$

8. $y = 0$

☐ **IDENTIFYING PARALLEL AND PERPENDICULAR LINES** ···

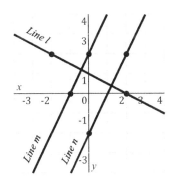

Two lines are parallel if and only if their slopes are equal. Lines m and n on the left are parallel because they both have a slope of 2.

Two lines are perpendicular if and only if the product of their slopes is -1. In other words, perpendicular lines have slopes that are negative reciprocals of one another. Lines l and m are perpendicular because line l has a slope of $-1/2$ and line m has a slope of 2. Notice that lines l and n are also perpendicular because line n has the same slope as line m.

To determine whether lines are parallel or perpendicular given their equations, put each equation in slope-intercept form and compare their slopes.

→ **EXAMPLE** Parallel or perpendicular?

$3x - y = 1$ and $x + 3y = 0$

$y = 3x - 1 \qquad y = -\frac{1}{3}x$ Solve each for y.

$3\left(-\frac{1}{3}\right) = -1$ Check the slopes.

The lines are perpendicular.

→ **TRY IT** Parallel or perpendicular?

9. $x - y = 0$ and $x + y = 5$

10. $y = 2x + 1$ and $2x - y = 3$

□ **EXERCISE YOUR SKILLS** ··

Graph.

11. $x = 2$

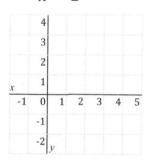

12. $y = 3$

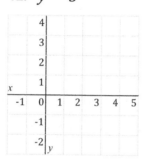

13. $x = 0$

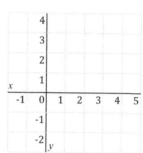

14. $y = -1$

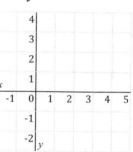

Use the graphs to solve.

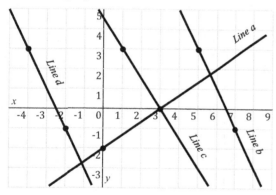

15. Determine which lines are parallel. Explain your answer.

16. Determine which lines are perpendicular. Explain your answer.

Determine if the lines are parallel, perpendicular, or neither.

17. $y = -x + 5$ and $x + y = 3$

18. $y = -3x + 1$ and $x - 3y = 9$

19. $2x - 3y = 9$ and $3x + 2y = 8$

20. $2x + 5y = 10$ and $5x + 2y = -10$

EXTRA Find the slopes of lines parallel and perpendicular to each of the following.

21. $5x - y = 1$

22. $4x - 3y = 3$

LESSON 20 Graphing Absolute Value Equations

□ **REFRESH YOUR SKILLS** ···

1. Graph $y = |x| + 1$ and $y = -|x - 2|$ by plotting as many points as you can. Review Lesson 14 if needed.

2. What is the corner point of your graph of $y = |x| + 1$?

3. What is the corner point of your graph of $y = -|x - 2|$?

□ **FINDING VERTICES OF ABSOLUTE VALUE EQUATIONS** ··························

Graphs of absolute value equations in two variables are symmetrical and V-shaped. The highest or lowest point on an absolute value graph is called the **vertex**, which occurs when the absolute value expression is zero.

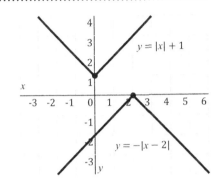

See the graphs on the right. The graph of $y = |x| + 1$ has a vertex at (0, 1) because $|x|$ is zero when $x = 0$. The graph of $y = -|x - 2|$ has a vertex at (2, 0) because $|x - 2|$ is zero when $x = 2$.

To find the vertex of the graph of an absolute value equation, first find the x-value that makes the absolute value expression zero. Then find the corresponding y-value.

➔ **EXAMPLE** Find the vertex of $y = -|x + 1| + 2$.

The vertex is (−1, 2) because

- $x = -1$ makes $|x + 1|$ zero.
- $y = 2$ when $x = -1$.

➔ **TRY IT** Find the vertex.

4. $y = |x - 3| - 1$

□ **GRAPHING ABSOLUTE VALUE EQUATIONS** ··

We can always graph absolute value equations by plotting lots of points. However, we know the graphs of these equations are always symmetrical and V-shaped, so we can graph them faster! Simply find and plot three points: the vertex, a point to the left of the vertex, and a point to the right of the vertex. Then draw rays from the vertex through the two points.

➔ **EXAMPLE** Graph $y = -|x + 1| + 2$.

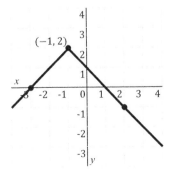

1. Find and plot the vertex (−1, 2).
2. Find and plot a point on each side of the vertex. We plot (−3, 0) and (2, −1).
3. Draw two rays.

➔ **TRY IT 5.** Graph $y = |x - 3| - 1$.

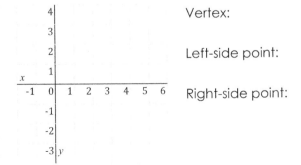

Vertex:

Left-side point:

Right-side point:

Find the vertex.

6. $y = -|x|$　　　　　　　　　　　**7.** $y = |x| + 3$

8. $y = |x + 2|$　　　　　　　　　　**9.** $y = -|x + 1|$

10. $y = |x - 1| + 3$　　　　　　　　**11.** $y = -|x - 3| - 2$

Find the vertex, then graph.

12. $y = |x|$

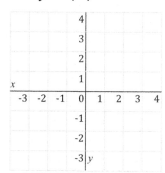

13. $y = |x| - 2$

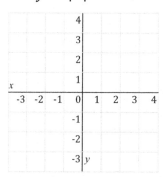

14. $y = -|x| + 1$

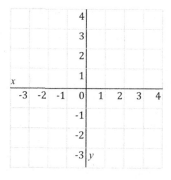

15. $y = |x + 1|$

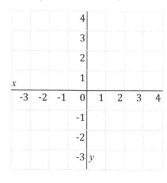

16. $y = |x - 1|$

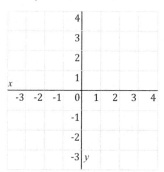

17. $y = -|x - 1|$

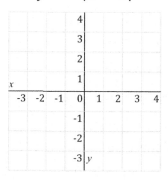

18. $y = |x - 2| + 1$

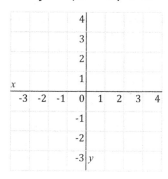

19. $y = -|x + 1| + 3$

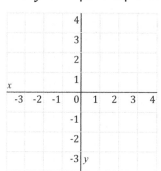

20. $y = |x + 3| - 1$

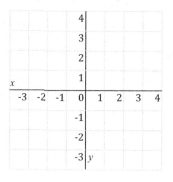

LESSON 21 Catch Up and Review!

Catch up if you are behind. Use the review problems below to make sure you're on track.

LESSON 14 Find three ordered-pair solutions, then graph.

1. $y = x - 2$

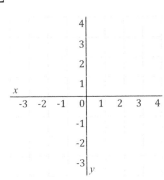

x	y
-1	
0	
3	

2. $x + 2y = 4$

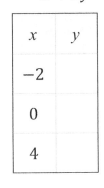

x	y
-2	
0	
4	

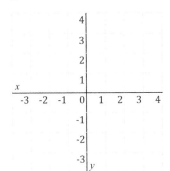

LESSON 15 Find the slope given two points.

3. $(8, 7)$ and $(3, 6)$

4. $(4, 2)$ and $(-2, 8)$

LESSONS 16–17 Find the slope and y-intercept, then graph.

5. $y = x - 1$

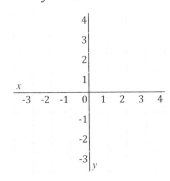

6. $y = 2x + 3$

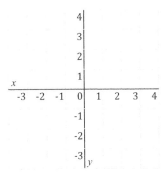

7. $y = -\frac{1}{2}x + 1$

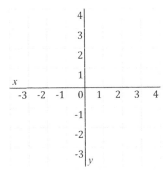

8. $x + 3y = 6$

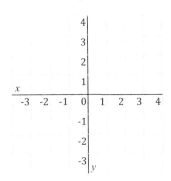

LESSONS 18 Find the intercepts, then graph.

9. $y = 2x + 2$

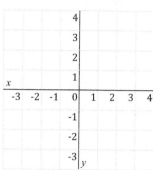

10. $4x + 3y = 12$

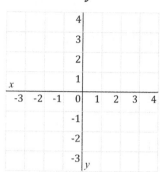

LESSON 20 Find the vertex, then graph.

11. $y = -|x - 2|$

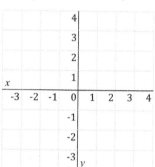

12. $y = |x + 1| - 3$

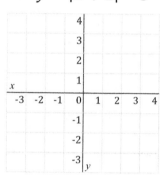

LESSON 19 Determine if the lines are parallel, perpendicular, or neither.

13. $y = 3$ and $x = -2$

14. $y = 3x + 4$ and $6x - 2y = 1$

15. $y = 4x + 1$ and $x - 4y = 6$

16. $2x - y = 9$ and $x + 2y = 6$

☐ **MIXED REVIEW: PRE-ALGEBRA** ···

Brush up on the topics covered in Pre-Algebra.

17. $|2 - 7| =$

18. $4.6 - 0.08 =$

19. $0.8 \times 0.12 =$

20. $0.9 \div 0.5 =$

21. $\dfrac{1}{2} - \dfrac{2}{3} =$

22. $\dfrac{1}{2} \div \dfrac{3}{4} =$

LESSON 22 Finding Equations of Lines in Slope-Intercept Form

☐ **REFRESH YOUR SKILLS** ··

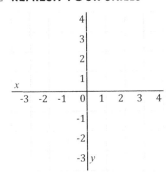

1. Find the slope and y-intercept of $y = 2x + 1$. Review Lesson 16 if needed.

2. Explain the steps to graph $y = 2x + 1$ using the slope and y-intercept, and then graph it. Review Lesson 16 if needed.

Find the slope given two points. Review Lesson 15 if needed.

3. $(2, 5)$ and $(-2, 3)$ **4.** $(0, 2)$ and $(4, -2)$

☐ **FINDING EQUATIONS OF LINES IN SLOPE-INTERCEPT FORM** ································

To find an equation in slope-intercept form ($y = mx + b$) given its graph, 1) pick any two points on the line, 2) find the slope (m) between the two points using the slope formula, 3) find the y-intercept (b) where the line crosses the y-axis, and 4) write an equation using the slope and y-intercept.

➔ **EXAMPLE** Find an equation of the line.

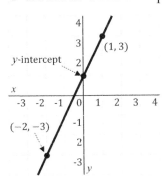

1. Pick two points: $(-2, -3)$ and $(1, 3)$
2. Find the slope: $m = \frac{3-(-3)}{1-(-2)} = 2$
3. The y-intercept b is 1.
4. Write an equation with $m = 2$ and $b = 1$: $y = 2x + 1$

➔ **TRY IT 5.** Find an equation of the line.

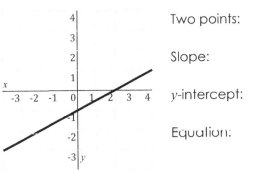

Two points:

Slope:

y-intercept:

Equation:

☐ **EXERCISE YOUR SKILLS** ··

Find an equation of each line in slope-intercept form.

6.

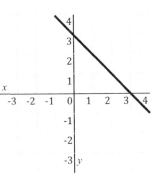

7.

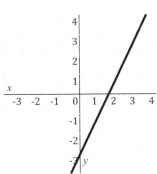

8.

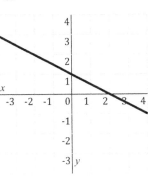

9.

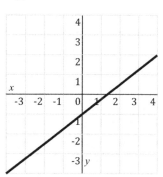

10.

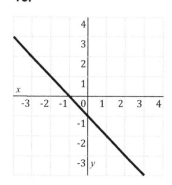

11.

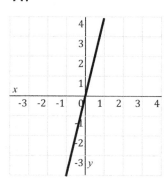

12.

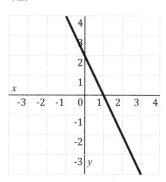

13.

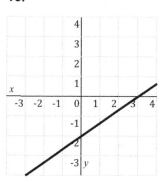

14.

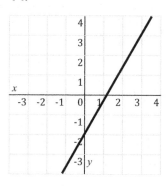

15.

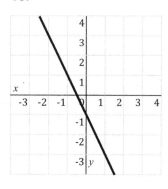

16.

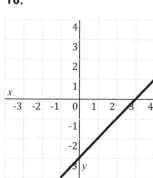

17.

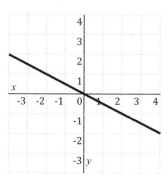

EXTRA Find an equation of each line in slope-intercept form.

18.

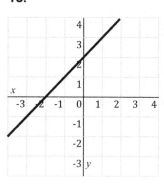

19.

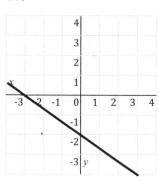

20.

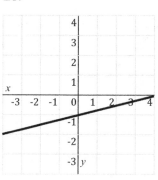

LESSON 23 Finding Equations of Lines in Slope-Intercept Form

☐ **REFRESH YOUR SKILLS** ···

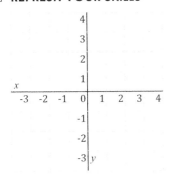

1. Graph a line that passes through $(-2, -3)$ and $(1, 3)$: plot the two points and draw a line through them. Then use your graph to find its equation in slope-intercept form. Review Lesson 22 if needed.

2. What is the slope of a line parallel to your line? What is the slope of a line perpendicular to your line? Review Lesson 19 if needed.

☐ **FINDING EQUATIONS OF LINES IN SLOPE-INTERCEPT FORM** ··································

You can find an equation of a line passing through two points algebraically (without graphing).

To find an equation of a line in slope-intercept form ($y = mx + b$) given two points (x_1, y_1) and (x_2, y_2) on the line, 1) find the slope (m) between the two points using the slope formula, 2) find the y-intercept (b) using the slope and one of the points, and 3) write an equation using the slope and y-intercept.

➔ **EXAMPLE** Find an equation of the line passing through $(-2, -3)$ and $(1, 3)$.

$m = \frac{3-(-3)}{1-(-2)} = 2$

1. Plug the two points into the slope formula to find m.

$y = mx + b$
$3 = 2 \cdot 1 + b$
$b = 1$

2. Substitute the slope and one of the points into $y = mx + b$, then solve for b.

$y = mx + b$
$y = 2x + 1$

3. Write an equation with $m = 2$ and $b = 1$.

➔ **TRY IT** Find an equation of each line given two points.

3. $(3, 7)$ and $(-2, -3)$

4. $(4, -1)$ and $(7, -4)$

How do you find an equation of a line in slope-intercept form ($y = mx + b$) given its slope (m) and a point (x_1, y_1) on the line? You already have the slope, so just find the y-intercept (b) using the point. Substitute m, x_1, and y_1 into $y = mx + b$ and solve for b. Then you have the slope and y-intercept needed to write an equation.

➔ **EXAMPLE** Find an equation of the line that has a slope of -2 and passes through $(1, 1)$.

$y = mx + b$
$1 = -2 \cdot 1 + b$
$b = 3$

1. Substitute the slope and the point into $y = mx + b$, then solve for b.

$y = mx + b$
$y = -2x + 3$

2. Write an equation with $m = -2$ and $b = 3$.

➔ **TRY IT** Find an equation of each line given the slope and a point.

5. $m = 1; (6, -2)$

6. $m = -5; (1, -3)$

FINDING EQUATIONS OF PARALLEL AND PERPENDICULAR LINES ·······················

When finding an equation of a parallel or perpendicular line, remember that parallel lines have the same slope and perpendicular lines have opposite reciprocal slopes.

➔ **EXAMPLE** Find an equation of the line that is parallel to $2x + y = 0$ and passes through $(1, 1)$.

The given line has a slope of -2, so a parallel line also has a slope of -2. As shown in the previous exmaple, the line with slope -2 passing through $(1, 1)$ is $y = -2x + 3$.

➔ **EXAMPLE** Find an equation of the line that is perpendicular to $x - 2y = 0$ and passes through $(1, 1)$.

The given line has a slope of $1/2$, so a perpendicular line has a slope of -2. As shown in the previous exmaple, the line with slope -2 passing through $(1, 1)$ is $y = -2x + 3$.

➔ **TRY IT** Find an equation of each line described.

7. parallel to $x + 4y = 4$; through $(8, 0)$

8. perpendicular to $3x - 2y = 0$; through $(3, 3)$

☐ EXERCISE YOUR SKILLS ···

Find an equation of each line given the slope and a point.

9. $m = 5; (1, 8)$

10. $m = \frac{1}{2}; (8, -5)$

Find an equation of each line given two points.

11. $(1, 5)$ and $(2, 8)$

12. $(5, -2)$ and $(9, -2)$

13. $(-2, -9)$ and $(1, 3)$

14. $(-6, -4)$ and $(8, 17)$

Find an equation of each line described.

15. parallel to $y = 3x - 5$; through $(-1, 4)$

16. perpendicular to $y = x + 2$; through $(2, 8)$

17. parallel to $x - 5y = 1$; through $(5, -1)$

18. perpendicular to $3x + y = 0$; through $(9, 0)$

EXTRA Find an equation of each line.

19. $m = 0; (-1, 4)$

20. $m = -2; (-3, 9)$

21. $(1, -1)$ and $(3, 7)$

22. $(0, 2)$ and $(-1, -3)$

23. $(2, 2)$ and $(-4, 5)$

24. $(7, -4)$ and $(3, -4)$

LESSON 24 Finding Equations of Lines in Point-Slope Form

☐ **REFRESH YOUR SKILLS** ···

Find an equation of each line in slope-intercept form. Review Lesson 23 if needed.

1. slope $= -1$; through $(-4, 7)$

2. slope $= 4$; through $(3, 9)$

3. through $(0, 1)$ and $(-6, -3)$

4. through $(-2, 1)$ and $(2, 9)$

☐ **FINDING EQUATIONS OF LINES IN POINT-SLOPE FORM** ··

Consider the following equations. Which have a slope of 2? Which pass through $(1, 3)$? Which have a slope of 2 *and* pass through $(1, 3)$? Can you tell just by looking at the equations?

$$y - 3 = 2(x - 1) \qquad y - 1 = 2(x - 3) \qquad y - 3 = -2(x - 1)$$

The **point-slope form** of a linear equation is $y - y_1 = m(x - x_1)$ where m is the slope of the line and (x_1, y_1) is a point on the line. It is just another way of expressing a linear equation. Point-slope form is useful when finding an equation of a line given its slope and a point on the line.

Point-slope form
$y - y_1 = m(x - x_1)$

➔ **EXAMPLE** Find an equation of the line that has a slope of 2 and passes through $(1, 3)$.

$y - y_1 = m(x - x_1)$ 1. Write point-slope form.
$y - 3 = 2(x - 1)$

$y - 3 = 2x - 2$ 2. Solve for y to get slope-
$y = 2x + 1$ intercept form.

➔ **TRY IT** Find an equation of each line given the slope and a point.

5. $m = -2$; $(-2, 7)$

6. $m = \frac{3}{4}$; $(4, 2)$

Point-slope form can also be used to find an equation of a line given two points on the line. Simply find first the slope between the two points using the slope formula. Then write the point-slope form using the slope and either point, as shown above.

➔ **EXAMPLE** Find an equation of the line passing through $(-2, -3)$ and $(1, 3)$.

$m = \frac{3 - (-3)}{1 - (-2)} = 2$ 1. Plug the two points into the slope formula to find m.

$y - y_1 = m(x - x_1)$ 2. Write point-slope form
$y - 3 = 2(x - 1)$ using $(1, 3)$.

$y - 3 = 2x - 2$ 3. Solve for y to get slope-
$y = 2x + 1$ intercept form.

➔ **TRY IT** Find an equation of each line given two points.

7. $(1, 3)$ and $(6, 8)$

8. $(2, 4)$ and $(4, 10)$

Find an equation of each line in point-slope form. Use the point marked on each line.

9.

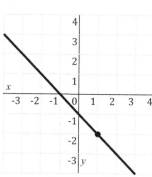

10.

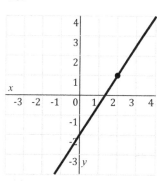

11.

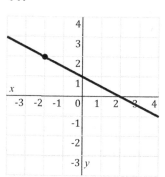

Find an equation of each line in point-slope form and in slope-intercept form. Use the first point for point-slope form when given two points.

12. A line has a slope of 2 and passes through (1, 5).

13. A line has a slope of 2/5 and passes through (10, −1).

14. A line passes through (2, 9) and (−1, 3).

15. A line passes through (9, −1) and (−3, −5).

16. A line is parallel to $x + y = 9$ and passes through (6, 2).

17. A line is perpendicular to $x + 6y = 5$ and passes through (−1, 1).

EXTRA Find an equation of each line in point-slope form and in slope-intercept form.

18. A line has a slope of 4 and passes through (3, −2).

19. A line has a slope of 1/4 and passes through (−2, 1).

20. A line passes through (−1, 5) and (2, −4).

21. A line passes through (−2, −2) and (4, 7).

LESSON 25 Finding Equations of Lines in All Forms

☐ **REFRESH YOUR SKILLS** ···

Find an equation of each line in point-slope form. Use the first point for point-slope form when given two points. Review Lesson 24 if needed.

1. slope $= 4$; through $(3, 1)$

2. slope $= -1$; through $(2, -5)$

3. through $(-5, 4)$ and $(1, 7)$

4. through $(3, 6)$ and $(-1, -2)$

☐ **FINDING EQUATIONS OF LINES IN STANDARD FORM** ····································

So far, you've learned three forms of linear equations. These three forms are equivalent to each other, meaning that they are just different ways of writing the same equation. Let's review.

Point-slope form	Slope-intercept form	Standard form
$y - y_1 = m(x - x_1)$	$y = mx + b$	$Ax + By = C$
where m = slope and (x_1, y_1) = a point on the line	where m = slope and b = y-intercept	where A, B, and C are constants

Once an equation is in slope-intercept form, it is easy to convert it to standard form. The constants A, B, and C in standard form can be any real numbers, but we usually write standard form using only integers and the smallest possible positive integer coefficient for x.

➔ **EXAMPLE** Put $y = \frac{2}{3}x + 4$ in standard form.

$y = \frac{2}{3}x + 4$

Multiply both sides by 3.

$3y = 2x + 12$

Subtract $2x$ from both sides.

$-2x + 3y = 12$

Multiply both sides by -1.

$2x - 3y = -12$

➔ **TRY IT** Put in standard form.

5. $y = -2x + 4$

6. $y = \frac{1}{2}x + 3$

☐ **EXERCISE YOUR SKILLS** ···

Put in slope-intercept form.

7. $x + 6y = 6$

8. $y - 4 = \frac{2}{3}(x - 6)$

Put in standard form. Use only integers and the smallest possible positive integer coefficient for x.

9. $y = -4x + 3$

10. $y = \frac{3}{5}x + 2$

Find an equation of each line in point-slope form, in slope-intercept form, and in standard form. For point-slope form, use the first point when given two points. For standard form, use only integers and the smallest possible positive integer coefficient for x.

11. A line has a slope of 4 and passes through $(-1, 2)$.

12. A line has a slope of -3 and passes through $(4, -3)$.

13. A line passes through $(-3, -1)$ and $(5, 3)$.

14. A line passes through $(3, 8)$ and $(-6, 2)$.

15. A line is parallel to $x + y = 5$ and passes through $(2, 0)$.

16. A line is perpendicular to $x + 4y = 8$ and passes through $(2, 5)$.

EXTRA Put each equation in standard form.

17. $y + 3 = -5(x - 1)$

18. $y + 8 = \dfrac{1}{2}(x + 6)$

EXTRA Find an equation of each line in slope-intercept form and in standard form.

19. A line has a slope of $-1/3$ and passes through $(6, -2)$.

20. A line has a slope of $3/4$ and passes through $(-8, 1)$.

21. A line passes through $(0, 6)$ and $(1, -2)$.

22. A line passes through $(5, 7)$ and $(1, -5)$.

23. A line is parallel to $4x - 7y = 0$ and passes through $(-1, -1)$.

24. A line is perpendicular to $5x + 3y = 10$ and passes through $(4, 2)$.

LESSON 26 Applications of Slope-Intercept Form

□ **REFRESH YOUR SKILLS** ···

Find the y value for the given x-value. Review Lesson 14 if needed.

1. $y = x - 5; x = 2$

2. $y = -3x + 5; x = -1$

Find the x-value for the given y-value. Review Lesson 14 if needed.

3. $y = x - 4; y = 3$

4. $y = 3x - 5; y = 4$

Find the slope and y-intercept of each line. Review Lesson 16 if needed.

5. $y = 2x + 1$

6. $y = 5x - 4$

□ **SOLVING WORD PROBLEMS USING SLOPE-INTERCEPT FORM** ···································

In real-world situations, the slope represents a constant rate of change, and the y-intercept represents an initial value or starting point. When solving a word problem involving these concepts, first identify the slope (m) and y-intercept (b) to write an equation in slope-intercept form ($y = mx + b$). Then use the equation to find what's being asked.

➜ **EXAMPLE** Solve using slope-intercept form.

A plumber charges a $50 flat fee plus $35 per hour. a) Write an equation for the cost, y, after x hours of service. b) How much will it cost for a job that takes 5 hours? c) If the plumber earned $120 on a job, how long did the job take?

🔎 Here's a tip! The word "per" indicates a rate.

a. Slope m = rate of change = $35/hour
    y-intercept b = initial value = $50
    So the equation is $y = 35x + 50$.

b. Given $x = 5$, $y = 35 \times 5 + 50 = 225$
    So a 5-hour job will cost $225.

c. Given $y = 120$, $120 = 35x + 50$
    Solve for x, and $x = 2$.
    So the job took 2 hours.

➜ **TRY IT** Solve.

7. An electrician charges a $40 flat fee plus $38 per hour.

    a. Write an equation representing the total cost, y, after x hours of service.
    b. How much will it cost for a job that takes 3 hours?
    c. If the electrician earned $116 on a job, how long did the job take?

8. A bike rental shop charges a flat fee of $15 plus $9 per hour for renting a bike.

    a. Write an equation representing the total cost, y, of renting a bike for x hours.
    b. How much will it cost to rent a bike for 3 hours?
    c. If you have $78, how many hours can you rent a bike?

Solve.

9. A taxi company charges an initial fee of $8 plus $1.50 per mile.

   a. Write an equation representing the total cost, y, of riding a taxi for x miles.
   b. How much will a taxi ride cost for 20 miles?
   c. If a taxi ride cost $29, how many miles did the taxi travel?

10. A water tank with 360 gallons of water is being emptied at a rate of 9 gallons per minute.

   a. Write an equation representing the amount of water, y, in the tank after x minutes.
   b. How much water will be in the tank after 15 minutes?
   c. How long will it take to empty the tank?

11. An online bookstore sells magazines for $2.50 each. The shipping cost is $7 for the whole order.

   a. Write an equation representing the total cost, y, of ordering x magazines.
   b. How much will it cost to order 12 magazines?
   c. If you have $62, how many magazines can you order?

12. A mountain climber starts descending from 750 feet above sea level at an average speed of 30 feet per hour.

   a. Write an equation representing the climber's elevation, y, after x hours.
   b. What is the elevation of the climber after 6 hours of descending?
   c. How long will it take the climber to reach sea level?

13. An airplane 32,000 feet above the ground begins descending at an average speed of 1,200 feet per minute.

   a. Write an equation representing the altitude, y, of the plane after x minutes.
   b. What is the altitude of the plane after 10 minutes of descending?
   c. How long will it take the plane to reach an altitude of 26,000 feet?

14. Tom has $2,800 in his bank account. Every month, Tom's company deposits his salary of $6,700, and his rent of $1,200 is withdrawn automatically.

   a. Write an equation representing the balance, y, of his account in x months.
   b. What will be the balance in 3 months?
   c. How long will it take his balance to go over $50,000?

LESSON 27 Applications of Standard Form

□ **REFRESH YOUR SKILLS** ....

Find the y-value for the given x-value. Review Lesson 14 if needed.

1. $x + 5y = 5; x = -5$

2. $3x - 2y = 6; x = -2$

Find the x-value for the given y-value. Review Lesson 14 if needed.

3. $x - 2y = 3; y = 2$

4. $2x - 5y = 4; y = 2$

Put each equation in standard form. Review Lesson 25 if needed.

5. $y = -2x + 4$

6. $y + 2 = 4(x + 1)$

□ **SOLVING WORD PROBLEMS USING STANDARD FORM** ·································

When a word problem involves a relationship between two quantities whose sum is a constant, you can write an equation in standard form ($Ax + By = C$) to model the relationship. Then you can use the equation to find what's being asked.

➜ **EXAMPLE** Solve using standard form.

A 100-point test has x questions worth 2 points each and y questions worth 4 points each. a) Write an equation relating x and y. b) If there are 20 4-point questions, how many 2-point questions are on the test? c) If there are 20 2-point questions, how many 4-point questions are on the test?

🔎 Here's a tip! Look for the total that is given. That is our constant C in the equation.

a. Points from 2-point questions = $2x$
    Points from 4-point questions = $4y$
    Total points from all questions = 100
    So the equation is $2x + 4y = 100$.

b. Given $y = 20$, $2x + 80 = 100$
    Solve for x, and $x = 10$
    So there are 10 2-point questions.

c. Given $x = 20$, $40 + 4y = 100$
    Solve for y, and $y = 15$
    So there are 15 4-point questions.

➜ **TRY IT** Solve.

7. A 100-point test has x multiple-choice questions worth 3 points each and y short-answer questions worth 5 points each.

   a. Write an equation relating x and y.
   b. If there are 20 3-point questions, how many 5-point questions are on the test?

8. Sarah has $56 to buy x pounds of beef and y pounds of pork for her barbecue party. Beef costs $6.80 per pound, and pork costs $4.40 per pound.

   a. Write an equation relating x and y.
   b. How many pounds of beef can Sarah buy if she buys 5 pounds of pork?

Solve.

9. Olivia has x dimes and y nickels totaling $1.80.

   a. Write an equation relating x and y.
   b. If she has 15 dimes, how many nickels does she have?

10. Laura has x five-dollar bills and y ten-dollar bills amounting to $80.

   a. Write an equation relating x and y.
   b. If she has 8 five-dollar bills, how many ten-dollar bills does she have?

11. A 100-point test has x multiple-choice questions worth 2 points each and y short-answer questions worth 5 points each.

   a. Write an equation relating x and y.
   b. If there are 6 5-point questions, how many 2-point questions are on the test?

12. Anna and her friends went to see a movie and spent $45 to buy 5 bags of popcorn and 4 sodas. Popcorn costs x per bag, and sodas cost y each.

   a. Write an equation relating x and y.
   b. If each bag of popcorn costs $6.20, how much does each soda cost?

13. To raise money for a trip to summer camp, Dale sold 20 muffins at $$x$ each and 46 cookies at $$y$ each at a bake sale. He made $113 in total.

   a. Write an equation relating x and y.
   b. If the price of cookies was $1.50 each, what was the price of a muffin?

14. At a festival, a group of people bought 7 adult tickets at $$x$ each and 5 child tickets at $$y$ each. They paid $81 in total.

   a. Write an equation relating x and y.
   b. If adult tickets cost $8 each, how much did each child ticket cost?

15. Max has $55 to buy x bags of flour and y bags of sugar for a church bake sale. A bag of flour costs $4, and a bag of sugar costs $6.50.

   a. Write an equation relating x and y.
   b. How many bags of sugar can Max buy if he buys 4 bags of flour?

16. A restaurant has x tables that seat 4 people and y tables that seat 8 people. The restaurant can seat a total of 96 people.

   a. Write an equation relating x and y.
   b. If 6 tables seat 8 people, how many tables seat 4 people?

LESSON 28 Catch Up and Review!

Catch up if you are behind. Use the review problems below to make sure you're on track.

LESSON 22 Find an equation of each line in slope-intercept form.

1.

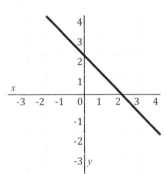

2.

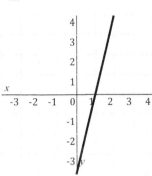

LESSON 23 Find an equation of each line in slope-intercept form.

3. slope $= 2$; through $(0, 4)$

4. slope $= 5$; through $(2, 9)$

5. through $(4, 9)$ and $(-1, -6)$

6. through $(3, 2)$ and $(4, 0)$

LESSON 24 Find an equation of each line in point-slope form. Use the first point for point-slope form when given two points.

7. slope $= -1$; through $(3, 0)$

8. slope $= 2$; through $(5, 4)$

9. through $(-2, -7)$ and $(1, 5)$

10. through $(3, -8)$ and $(2, -3)$

LESSON 25 Find an equation of each line in standard form. Use only integers and the smallest possible positive integer coefficient for x.

11. slope $= 5$; through $(2, 4)$

12. slope $= \dfrac{4}{5}$; through $(-5, 3)$

13. through $(5, 3)$ and $(-5, 1)$

14. through $(-4, 8)$ and $(6, 3)$

LESSON 26 Solve.

15. A taxi charges a flat fee of $5 and $1.60 per mile.

   a. Write an equation representing the total cost, y, of riding the taxi for x miles.

   b. How much will a taxi ride cost for 15 miles?

   c. If a taxi ride cost $45, how many miles did the taxi travel?

16. An internet service provider charges $32 per month plus an initial set-up fee of $58.

   a. Write an equation representing the total cost, y, after x months of service.

   b. How much will it cost after 5 months of service?

   c. If a customer spent a total of $442, how long was the service provided?

LESSON 27 Solve.

17. Mia has x quarters and y dimes amounting to $2.30.

   a. Write an equation relating x and y.

   b. If she has 6 quarters, how many dimes does she have?

18. At a grocery, Rodney bought 3 bags of onions and 2 bags of potatoes. He spent $20 in total. Onions cost x per bag, and potatoes cost y per bag.

   a. Write an equation relating x and y.

   b. If each bag of potatoes costs $5.50, how much does each bag of onions cost?

☐ **MIXED REVIEW: PRE-ALGEBRA** ···
Brush up on the topics covered in Pre-Algebra.

19. What is 20% of 80?

20. Convert 40% to a fraction. Simplify your answer.

21. You cut 17 feet from a 50-foot wire. What is the percent decrease in length?

22. One kilometer is 1000 meters. One meter is 100 centimeters. How many centimeters are there in one kilometer?

23. One meter is approximately 3 feet. How many centimeters are there in 1.2 feet?

LESSON 29 Solving Linear Systems by Graphing

··

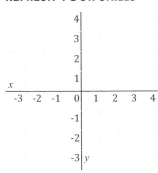

1. Graph $y = x$ 2. Review Lesson 16 if needed.

2. Graph $3x + 2y = 6$. Review Lessons 17 and 18 if needed.

3. Graph $x = 2$. Review Lesson 19 if needed.

☐ CHECKING SOLUTIONS TO LINEAR SYSTEMS ··

A **system of linear equations**, or a **linear system**, is a set of two or more linear equations. A **solution to a system of linear equations** is an ordered pair that is a solution to *every* equation in the system. The example on the right is a system of three linear equations.

$$x = 2$$
$$y = x - 2$$
$$3x + 2y = 6$$

To check whether an ordered pair is a solution to a system of linear equations, plug the ordered pair into each equation in the system and see if it makes all the equations true.

➜ **EXAMPLE** Is (2, 1) a solution to the system above?

$$2 = 2$$
$$1 \neq 2 - 2$$
$$3(2) + 2(1) \neq 6$$

(2, 1) is not a solution because it does not satisfy the second and third equations.

➜ **TRY IT** Is the point a solution?

4. $(-2, 3)$; $\begin{cases} y = 2x + 7 \\ x + 3y = 7 \end{cases}$

☐ SOLVING LINEAR SYSTEMS BY GRAPHING ··

One way of solving, or finding a solution to, a system of linear equations is by graphing. Remember, every point on a line is a solution to its corresponding equation. This means, when you graph each equation of the system on the same coordinate plane, a point where all the lines intersect is a solution to *every* equation in the system.

➜ **EXAMPLE** Solve $\begin{cases} y = x - 2 \\ 3x + 2y = 6 \end{cases}$

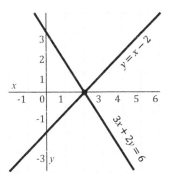

1. Graph $y = x - 2$.
2. Graph $3x + 2y = 6$.
3. Find the intersection point. The lines intersect at (2, 0).
4. Check if (2, 0) satisfies both the equations. If so, (2, 0) is the solution to the system.

➜ **TRY IT 5.** Solve $\begin{cases} y = x + 1 \\ x + 4y = 4 \end{cases}$

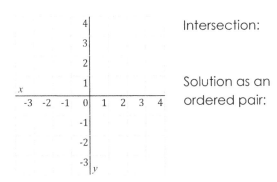

Intersection:

Solution as an ordered pair:

Determine whether the given point is a solution.

6. $(1, -1)$; $\begin{cases} x + 3y = -2 \\ 4x - y = 5 \end{cases}$ 7. $(2, 1)$; $\begin{cases} x + y = 3 \\ 2x - y = -3 \end{cases}$

Solve by graphing. Write your answers as an ordered pair. Check your solutions.

8. $x = 1$

    $x - y = 2$

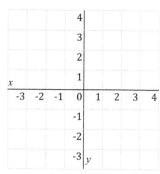

9. $x + 2y = 4$

    $4x - y = -2$

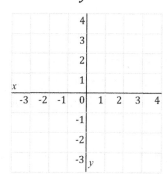

10. $x - y = -2$

    $2x + y = -4$

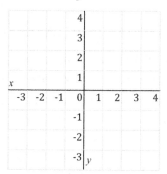

11. $-x + 3y = 3$

    $4x - 3y = 6$

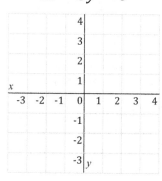

12. $y = 1$

    $3x + y = -2$

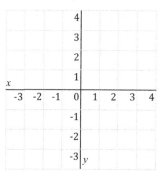

13. $x - 4y = 4$

    $5x - 3y = 3$

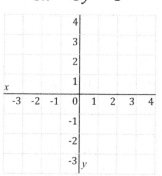

14. $2x + 3y = 3$

    $2x - 3y = 9$

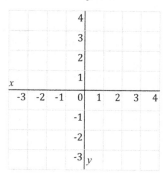

15. $x + 2y = -3$

    $-5x + y = 4$

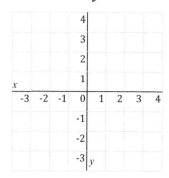

16. $2x + y = 2$

    $2x + 3y = -6$

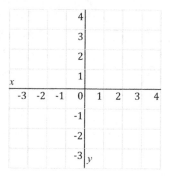

LESSON 30 Solving Linear Systems by Substitution

□ **REFRESH YOUR SKILLS** ···

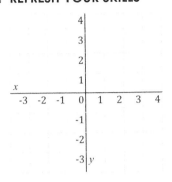

1. Graph $x \quad y = 3$. Review Lesson 17 if needed.

2. Graph $2x + y = 3$. Review Lesson 17 if needed.

3. Find the solution to the system of $x - y = 3$ and $2x + y = 3$ using your graphs. Review Lesson 29 if needed.

□ **SOLVING LINEAR SYSTEMS BY SUBSTITUTION** ···

Another way of solving a system of linear equations is by substitution. Let's see how our example system above can be solved using the substitution method.

Notice that you'll get the same result if you solve for x in the first step.

➔ **EXAMPLE** Solve the system of $x - y = 3$ and $2x + y = 3$ by substitution.

① $\quad x - y = 3$
$\quad\quad y = \boxed{x - 3}$

② $\quad 2x + \mathbf{y} = 3$
$\quad 2x + (x - 3) = 3$
$\quad\quad 3x - 3 = 3$
$\quad\quad\quad x = \boxed{2}$

③ $\quad y = \mathbf{x} - 3$
$\quad y = 2 - 3$
$\quad y = -1$

Solution: $(2, -1)$

1. Solve one equation for x or y (whichever is easier).

2. Substitute the expression for the isolated variable into the other equation, then solve to find the value of one variable.

3. Substitute the found value into either equation to find the value of the other variable. Write the solution as an ordered pair.

➔ **EXAMPLE** Solve by substitution.

① $\quad x - y = 3$
$\quad\quad x = \boxed{y + 3}$

② $\quad 2\mathbf{x} + y = 3$
$\quad 2(y + 3) + y = 3$
$\quad\quad 3y + 6 = 3$
$\quad\quad\quad y = \boxed{-1}$

③ $\quad x = \mathbf{y} + 3$
$\quad x = -1 + 3$
$\quad x = 2$

Solution: $(2, -1)$

➔ **TRY IT** Solve by substitution.

4. $x + y = 3$
$\quad 2x + y = 6$

5. $2x + 3y = 1$
$\quad 3x - y = 7$

6. $x - y = 4$
$\quad x + 3y = -8$

7. $4x + y = -3$
$\quad -2x + y = 9$

Solve by substitution. Write your answers as an ordered pair. Check your solutions.

8. $y = -2$
   $3x + 5y = -7$

9. $y = x + 3$
   $3x + y = 11$

10. $x + y = 5$
    $x + 3y = 1$

11. $x + 3y = 0$
    $2x - y = 7$

12. $x - 2y = -2$
    $x + 3y = 8$

13. $2x + y = -7$
    $-2x + y = 9$

14. $3x + y = 4$
    $5x + 2y = 8$

15. $x - 4y = -7$
    $2x - 5y = -5$

16. $x - 2y = 0$
    $3x - 4y = 2$

17. $x = 4$
    $6x + 5y = 4$

18. $7x + 8y = 1$
    $5x + y = -4$

19. $2x - y = -10$
    $4x + 5y = 8$

EXTRA Solve by substitution. Write your answers as an ordered pair. Check your solutions.

20. $x + 3y = 4$
    $4x + 5y = -12$

21. $2x + y = 3$
    $2x - 3y = 31$

22. $x + 2y = 0$
    $5x - 2y = 24$

23. $4x - 9y = 24$
    $4x - y = -8$

24. $x + 4y = 14$
    $7x - 5y = 32$

25. $3x - y = -9$
    $-5x + 2y = 19$

26. $3x - 4y = -20$
    $-9x + y = 5$

27. $x - 2y = 5$
    $9x - 4y = -11$

LESSON 31 Solving Linear Systems by Elimination

☐ **REFRESH YOUR SKILLS** ···

Solve by substitution. Review Lesson 30 if needed.

1. $y = x - 3$
$2x + 3y = -4$

2. $x + y = -1$
$4x + 5y = 3$

☐ **SOLVING LINEAR SYSTEMS BY ELIMINATION** ···

You can also solve a system of linear equations by elimination. The idea is to eliminate one variable by adding or subtracting equations. Watch what happens if you add $x - y = 1$ and $x + y = 3$. The variable y gets eliminated, and you get an equation in just one variable, x.

$$\begin{array}{r} x + y = 3 \\ +\quad x - y = 1 \\ \hline 2x + 0 = 4 \end{array}$$

Let's see how the first system above can be solved using the elimination method. Notice that, to eliminate y, we multiply the first equation by 3 before adding.

Notice that you'll get the same result if you eliminate x instead of y.

➔ **EXAMPLE** Solve the system of $y = x - 3$ and $2x + 3y = -4$ by elimination.

➀ $\quad x - y = 3$
$\quad 2x + 3y = -4$

➁ $\quad 3x - 3y = 9$
$+\ 2x + 3y = -4$

➂ $\quad 5x + \ 0 = 5$

➃ $\quad\quad 5x = 5$
$\quad\quad\quad x = 1$

➄ $\quad x - y = 3$
$\quad 1 - y = 3$
$\quad\quad\quad y = -2$

Solution: $(1, -2)$

1. Write both equations in standard form.

2. Multiply one or both of the equations by a constant so that adding or subtracting the equations will eliminate one of the variables.

3. Add or subtract the equations to eliminate one of the variables.

4. Solve the resulting equation for the remaining variable.

5. Substitute the found value into either equation to find the value of the eliminated variable. Write the solution as an ordered pair.

➔ **EXAMPLE** Solve by elimination.

➀ $\quad x - y = 3$
$\quad 2x + 3y = -4$

➁ $\quad 2x - 2y = 6$
$-\ (2x + 3y = -4)$

➂ $\quad 0 - 5y = 10$

➃ $\quad\quad -5y = 10$
$\quad\quad\quad y = -2$

➄ $\quad x - y = 3$
$\quad x - (-2) = 3$
$\quad\quad\quad x = 1$

Solution: $(1, -2)$

➔ **TRY IT** Solve by elimination.

3. $x + y = 5$
$5x - y = 7$

4. $x - y = -4$
$3x - 2y = -7$

Here is an example where both equations are multiplied by a constant in order to eliminate x.

➔ **EXAMPLE** Eliminate x.

$$3x + 2y = 4 \quad \times 2 \quad\longrightarrow\quad 6x + 4y = 8$$
$$2x + 3y = 1 \quad \times 3 \qquad\qquad\; - (6x + 9y = 3)$$
$$\overline{\qquad\qquad\qquad\; - 5y = 5}$$

➔ **TRY IT** Solve by elimination.

5. $4x - 3y = -2$
    $3x + 2y = 7$

□ **EXERCISE YOUR SKILLS** ···

Solve by elimination. Write your answers as an ordered pair. Check your solutions.

6. $7x + y = 0$
    $2x - y = -9$

7. $2x + y = 7$
    $3x - y = -2$

8. $x - 4y = 11$
    $-x + 3y = -9$

9. $x - y = 7$
    $x + 2y = -2$

10. $x - y = -1$
    $2x + 3y = 8$

11. $5x + y = -4$
    $3x - 2y = 8$

12. $x + y = 3$
    $3x + 5y = 9$

13. $x + 3y = -1$
    $2x + 9y = -8$

14. $3x + 4y = 6$
    $7x + 3y = -5$

15. $6x - 5y = -7$
    $5x - 4y = -5$

EXTRA Solve by elimination. Write your answers as an ordered pair. Check your solutions.

16. $2x + y = 3$
    $-2x + y = -5$

17. $3x + 2y = 4$
    $9x - 5y = -10$

18. $3x + 2y = 6$
    $3x + y = 9$

19. $3x + 2y = 7$
    $5x + 4y = 15$

20. $3x + 2y = 7$
    $2x + 5y = 1$

21. $2x + 9y = 3$
    $3x - 2y = 20$

LESSON 32 Solving Linear Systems Using Any Method

☐ **REFRESH YOUR SKILLS** ···

Redo the examples you have studied earlier.

1. Explain how to solve the system of $y = x - 2$ and $3x + 2y = 6$ by graphing. Why does the intersection of the two lines represent the solution to the system? Review Lesson 29 if needed.

2. Explain how to solve the system of $x - y = 3$ and $2x + y = 3$ by substitution. Which variable will you substitute for and how? Review Lesson 30 if needed.

3. Explain how to solve the system of $y = x - 3$ and $2x + 3y = -4$ by elimination. Which variable will you eliminate and how? Review Lesson 31 if needed.

☐ **EXERCISE YOUR SKILLS** ···

Determine whether the given point is a solution.

4. $(1, 1)$; $\begin{cases} x + 3y = 4 \\ 8x - 3y = 5 \end{cases}$

5. $(3, -2)$; $\begin{cases} 3x + 2y = 5 \\ 8x - 5y = 14 \end{cases}$

Solve by graphing. Write your answers as an ordered pair. Check your solutions.

6. $x - 2y = 4$

    $2x + y = -2$

7. $x = 2$

    $5x - 2y = 6$

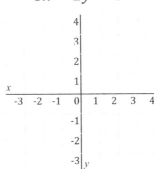

Solve by substitution. Check your solutions.

8. $y = -2x + 7$

    $3x - 5y = 4$

9. $5x - y = 3$

    $3x + y = 13$

Solve by elimination. Check your solutions.

10. $x + 3y = 16$

  $-x + 4y = 12$

11. $4x + 3y = -1$

  $5x + 2y = 11$

Solve. Use any method you prefer. Check your solutions.

12. $x + 2y = 10$

  $2x - 3y = -8$

13. $2x + y = 7$

  $4x + 3y = 11$

14. $y = x - 4$

  $5x + 2y = 6$

15. $2x - 7y = -4$

  $4x + 3y = -8$

16. $2x + 5y = 10$

  $4x - 3y = -6$

17. $5x - 10y = 0$

  $3x + 5y = 33$

18. $3x - 5y = -5$

  $4x - 7y = -8$

19. $x - y = 8$

  $3x + 8y = -9$

EXTRA Solve. Use any method you prefer. Check your solutions.

20. $x + 2y = -1$

  $4x + 9y = -9$

21. $5x - y = 18$

  $2x + y = 10$

22. $x + 2y = -8$

  $x + 3y = -13$

23. $2x + 7y = -4$

  $4x + 5y = 10$

24. $y = 6x - 11$

  $7x + 3y = -8$

25. $4x + 9y = -4$

  $5x + 12y = -2$

26. $5x - 3y = -4$

  $2x + 7y = 23$

27. $3x + 5y = 30$

  $2x - 5y = -30$

LESSON 33 Number of Solutions to Linear Systems

☐ **REFRESH YOUR SKILLS** ···

Solve each system of linear equations by graphing. Write your answers as an ordered pair, if possible. Review Lesson 29 if needed.

1. $y = x - 2$

    $2x + y = 4$

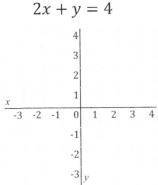

2. $2x - y = 1$

    $y = 2x + 3$

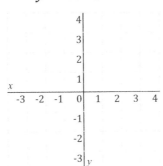

3. $y = -x + 2$

    $x + y = 2$

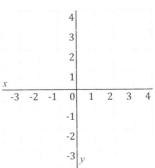

☐ **CLASSIFYING SOLUTIONS TO LINEAR SYSTEMS** ····································

A system of linear equations can have one solution, no solution, or infinitely many solutions. A system has one solution when the lines intersect at a point (different slopes). A system has no solution when the lines are parallel (the same slope but different y-intercepts). A system has infinitely many solutions when the lines are identical (the same slope and the same y-intercept).

Let's look again at the systems above. If we write all the equations in slope-intercept form, we can tell without graphing how many solutions there will be.

➜ **EXAMPLE** Determine the number of solutions.

a. $y = x - 2$

   $y = -2x + 4$

   Different slopes,
   so **exactly one solution**

b. $y = 2x - 1$

   $y = 2x + 3$

   The same slope but
   different y-intercepts,
   so **no solution**

c. $y = -x + 2$

   $y = -x + 2$

   The same slope and
   the same y-intercept,
   so **infinitely many solutions**

➜ **TRY IT** Determine the number of solutions. Do not solve.

4. $x - 2y = 2$

   $y = \frac{1}{2}x - 5$

5. $3x - y = -2$

   $y = -\frac{1}{3}x + 2$

6. $4x + 3y = 6$

   $y = -\frac{4}{3}x + 2$

7. $2x + 5y = 5$

   $y = -\frac{2}{5}x - 1$

Solve. Use any method you prefer. Write your answers as an ordered pair. Check your solutions.

8. $y = x + 2$
$3x - y = 2$

9. $x - 2y = 9$
$-2x + 4y = 5$

10. $4x + 3y = 11$
$3x - y = 5$

11. $2x - y = 7$
$2x - 5y = 19$

12. $x = 2y - 3$
$x - 2y = 5$

13. $4x - 3y = 0$
$8x - 6y = 0$

14. $3x - y = -2$
$-5x + 4y = 15$

15. $3x + 2y = -6$
$-x + 4y = 16$

16. $x = y + 9$
$3x - 2y = 22$

17. $3x + 2y = 1$
$4x - 5y = 9$

18. $-x + 4y = 9$
$2x + 3y = 4$

19. $x + 3y = 9$
$-x + 2y = 1$

EXTRA Solve. Use any method you prefer. Check your solutions.

20. $x - 3y = 5$
$-2x + 6y = 1$

21. $y = -4$
$3x - 2y = 11$

22. $2x + 7y = -6$
$4x - 3y = -12$

23. $y = 2x + 3$
$-5x + 3y = 11$

24. $4x - 5y = -5$
$-8x + 10y = 3$

25. $-3x + y = 2$
$9x - 3y = 7$

26. $4x + 3y = 6$
$6x - 5y = -10$

27. $9x - 8y = -67$
$3x + 4y = 11$

LESSON 34 Applications of Linear Systems

☐ **REFRESH YOUR SKILLS** ⋯⋯⋯⋯⋯⋯⋯⋯⋯⋯⋯⋯⋯⋯⋯⋯⋯⋯⋯⋯⋯⋯⋯⋯⋯⋯⋯⋯⋯⋯⋯⋯⋯⋯

Redo the examples you have studied earlier. For each problem, 1) define a variable, 2) set up an equation, 3) solve the equation, and 4) answer what's being asked. Show your work in your notebook. Review Lesson 9 if needed.

1. The sum of three consecutive even integers is 12. Find the integers.

2. The price of an apple rose by 15% to $1.38/lb. What was the original price?

3. Dale is 6 years older than Kate. Three years ago, Dale was twice as old as Kate. How old are they now?

4. The length of a rectangle is twice its width. The perimeter is 18 feet. Find the dimensions of the rectangle.

5. Olivia has $0.90 in dimes and nickels. She has three more nickels than dimes. How many coins of each type does she have?

☐ **SOLVING LINEAR SYSTEM WORD PROBLEMS** ⋯⋯⋯⋯⋯⋯⋯⋯⋯⋯⋯⋯⋯⋯⋯⋯⋯⋯⋯⋯⋯⋯⋯⋯⋯⋯

Sometimes, when a situation is complex, you may need more than one variable and more than one equation to model the situation. However, the basic strategy remains the same. To solve a word problem using algebra, 1) define a variable or variables, 2) set up an equation or a system of equations to model the given situation, 3) solve the equation or the system as usual, and then 4) answer what's being asked.

➔ **EXAMPLE** Solve using a system of linear equations.

Pears cost $2 each. Melons cost $3 each. Elijah bought a total of 8 pears and melons, and spent $19. How many pears and how many melons did Elijah buy?

1. Let x = the number of pears
   Let y = the number of melons
2. A total of 8 pears and melons, so $x + y = 8$.
   $19 at $2/pear and $3/melon, so $2x + 3y = 19$.
3. Solve the system, and you get $x = 5$, $y = 3$.
4. Elijah bought 5 pears and 3 melons.

➔ **TRY IT** Solve.

6. Movie tickets cost $9 for adults and $7 for children. A group bought 10 tickets and paid $78 in total. How many adults and how many children were in the group?

7. A 100-point test has a total of 20 questions. The multiple-choice questions are worth 4 points each, and the short-answer questions are worth 8 points each. How many questions of each type are on the test?

For each problem, 1) define variables, 2) set up a system of equations, 3) solve the system, and 4) answer what's being asked. Show your work in your notebook.

8. Consider two integers. The sum of three times the larger integer and the smaller is 3. The difference of the larger and three times the smaller is 11. Find the integers.

9. Max has 17 coins consisting of dimes and nickels. The value of the coins is $1.30. How many dimes and how many nickels does Max have?

10. Mr. Kim has a total of 27 bills in five- and ten-dollar bills. The total value of the money is $205. How many five-dollar bills and how many ten-dollar bills does Mr. Kim have?

11. Mark is five years younger than Dale. Five years ago, Dale was twice as old as Mark. How old are they now?

12. Emma bought five apples and four pears and paid $9.20. Kyle bought three apples and two pears and paid $5. How much does an apple cost, and how much does a pear cost?

13. A 100-point test has a total of 35 questions. The multiple-choice questions are worth 2 points each, and the short-answer questions are worth 5 points each. How many questions of each type are on the test?

14. A cafeteria has 12 tables that can seat a total of 58 people. Some tables seat 4 people, and the others seat 6 people. How many tables seat 6 people? How many tables seat 4 people?

EXTRA Solve.

15. Leah and Vicky bought a couch together for their dorm room. It cost $550 in total, and Leah paid $70 more than Vicky. How much did each pay?

16. The sum of the digits of a two-digit number is 5. When the digits are reversed, the number is decreased by 9. What is the number?

17. Lynn has a collection of nickels and quarters amounting to $2.65. There are five more nickels than quarters. How many nickels and how many quarters does Lynn have?

18. Joey is three times as old as Anna. In five years, Joey will be twice as old as Anna. How old are they now?

19. Josh used 24 flowers to make a bouquet of roses and lilies. Roses cost $2.20 each and lilies cost $1.80 each. He spent $48 in total. How many roses and how many lilies did Josh use?

LESSON 35 Applications of Linear Systems (Distance)

☐ **REFRESH YOUR SKILLS** ··

Redo the examples you have studied earlier. For each problem, 1) define a variable, 2) set up an equation, 3) solve the equation, and 4) answer what's being asked. Show your work in your notebook. Review Lesson 10 if needed.

1. How long will it take to travel 150 miles at 75 miles per hour (mph)?

2. Two trains leave stations 300 miles apart at the same time and travel toward each other. One train travels at 70 mph while the other travels at 80 mph. How long will it take for the two trains to meet?

3. Two cars leave a location at the same time and travel in opposite directions. One car travels 5 mph faster than the other. After 2 hours, they are 210 miles apart. Find the speed of each car.

4. Sam drove to work averaging 55 mph. On the way home, he averaged 45 mph. His total driving time was 2 hours. How far does Sam live from work?

5. Kyle starts jogging a trail at 4 mph. An hour later, Eli starts jogging the trail from the same point in the same direction at 6 mph. How long will it take Eli to overtake (or catch up with) Kyle?

☐ **SOLVING DISTANCE WORD PROBLEMS** ··

We solved distance problems using one variable and one equation in Lesson 10. Here are two examples requiring two variables and two equations.

➔ **EXAMPLE** Two-part trip

Mia traveled 270 km by car and by train. The car averaged 60 km/hr. The train averaged 90 km/hr. The whole trip took 4 hours. How much time did she spend in the car and in the train?

	r	t	$D = rt$
By car	60	x	$60x$
By train	90	y	$90y$

1. Let x = time spent in the car
   Let y = time spent in the train
2. Total travel time = 4 hours, so $x + y = 4$.
   Distance traveled in the car + distance traveled in the train = 270, so $60x + 90y = 270$.
3. Solve the system, and $x = 3$, $y = 1$.
4. Mia spent 3 hours in the car and 1 hour in the train.

➔ **TRY IT** Solve.

6. Logan took two buses to travel 235 miles. The first bus averaged 70 mph, and the second bus averaged 65 mph. The whole trip took 3.5 hours. How much time did Logan spend on each bus?

➜ **EXAMPLE** Flying with and against the wind

A plane flying with the wind traveled 1,200 miles in 4 hours. The return trip took 5 hours flying against the wind. Find the speed of the wind and the speed at which the plane would travel in still air.

1. Let x = speed of the plane in still air
   Let y = speed of the wind
2. Distance with the wind = 1,200 and distance against the wind = 1,200, so $4(x + y) = 1,200$ and $5(x - y) = 1,200$.
3. Solve the system, and $x = 270$, $y = 30$.
4. The speed of the airplane in still air would be 270 mph, and the speed of the wind was 30 mph.

	r	t	$D = rt$
With wind	$x + y$	4	$4(x + y)$
Against wind	$x - y$	5	$5(x - y)$

➜ **TRY IT** Solve.

7. Flying with the wind, an airplane can fly 1,440 miles in 4 hours. Flying against the wind, the plane can fly the same distance in 6 hours. Find the speed of the plane in still air and the speed of the wind.

☐ **EXERCISE YOUR SKILLS** ···

For each problem, 1) define variables, 2) set up a system of equations, 3) solve the system, and 4) answer what's being asked. Show your work in your notebook.

8. Owen traveled 554 miles by car and by train. The car averaged 67 mph. The train averaged 120 mph. The whole trip took 5.5 hours. How much time did he spend in the train and in the car?

9. Jessie took two buses to travel 273 miles. The first bus averaged 72 mph, and the second bus averaged 66 mph. The whole trip took 4 hours. How many miles did she travel by each bus?

10. An airplane flying with the wind traveled 2,240 miles in 7 hours. The return trip took 8 hours flying against the wind. Find the speed of the plane in still air and the speed of the wind.

11. A boat traveled 56 km downstream in 2 hours. The return trip, going upstream, took twice as long. Find the speed of the boat in still water and the speed of the current.

12. Two trains leave a station at the same time and travel in opposite directions. One train travels 25 mph faster than the other train. After 2 hours, they are 530 miles apart. Find the speed of each train.

13. Two buses traveled the same distance from one city to another. One bus traveled 20 km/h faster than the other and took 2 hours and 30 minutes. The other bus took 30 minutes longer. Find the distance between the two cities.

LESSON 36 Applications of Linear Systems (Mixtures)

☐ **REFRESH YOUR SKILLS** ···

Redo the examples you have studied earlier. For each problem, 1) define a variable, 2) set up an equation, 3) solve the equation, and 4) answer what's being asked. Show your work in your notebook. Review Lesson 11 if needed.

1. You dissolve 5 g of salt in 15 g of water. What is the concentration of the solution?

2. How much water must be mixed with 5 g of salt to make a 20% saline solution?

3. You mix 10 g of a 10% saline solution with 20 g of a 25% saline solution. What is the concentration of the mixture?

4. How many liters of a 50% alcohol solution must be added to 2 liters of a 20% alcohol solution to produce a 40% alcohol solution?

5. Walnuts sell for $6 per pound. Cashews sell for $3 per pound. How many pounds of walnuts must be mixed with 8 pounds of cashews to make a mixture of nuts that costs $5 per pound?

☐ **SOLVING MIXTURE WORD PROBLEMS** ···

We solved mixture problems using one variable and one equation in Lesson 11. Here are two examples requiring two variables and two equations.

➔ **EXAMPLE** Liquid mixture

A 50% saline solution is mixed with a 20% saline solution to produce 6 liters of a 40% saline solution. How much of each is used?

	%	Solution	Substance
50% solution	0.5	x	$0.5x$
20% solution	0.2	y	$0.2y$
Mixture	0.4	6	2.4

1. Let x = amount of 50% solution used
   Let y = amount of 20% solution used
2. Amount of the mixture = 6, so $x + y = 6$.
   Salt in 50% solution + salt in 20% solution = salt in the mixture, so $0.5x + 0.2y = 2.4$.
3. Solve the system, and $x = 4$, $y = 2$.
4. Four liters of the 50% saline solution and 2 liters of the 20% saline solution are used.

➔ **TRY IT** Solve.

6. A 10% alcohol solution is to be mixed with a 55% alcohol solution to produce 30 liters of a 37% alcohol solution. How much of each should be used?

7. A chemist wants to make 22 ounces of a 27% acid solution by mixing a 42% acid solution and a 20% acid solution. How much of each should be used?

→ **EXAMPLE** Dry mixture

Walnuts worth $6/lb are mixed with cashews worth $3/lb to make a 24-pound mixture that is worth $5/lb. How much of each is used?

	Unit price	Quantity	Total cost
Walnuts	6	x	$6x$
Cashews	3	y	$3y$
Mixture	5	24	120

1. Let x = amount of walnuts
   Let y = amount of cashews
2. Amount of the mixture = 24, so $x + y = 24$.
   Cost of walnuts + cost of cashews = cost of the mixture, so $6x + 3y = 120$.
3. Solve the system, and $x = 16$, $y = 8$.
4. 16 pounds of walnuts and 8 pounds of cashews are used.

→ **TRY IT** Solve.

8. Chocolate sells for $5 per pound. Nuts sell for $3 per pound. A grocer wants to make 8 pounds of a mixture to sell for $4.50 per pound. How much of each should be used?

9. Coffee A costs $12 per pound. Coffee B costs $8 per pound. How much of each should be mixed to produce 20 pounds of a coffee blend that costs $9.60 per pound?

☐ **EXERCISE YOUR SKILLS** ···

For each problem, 1) define variables, 2) set up a system of equations, 3) solve the system, and 4) answer what's being asked. Show your work in your notebook.

10. A 30% saline solution is to be mixed with a 50% saline solution to produce 20 gallons of a 44% saline solution. How much of each should be used?

11. A nurse wants to make 24 ounces of a 60% alcohol solution by mixing a 50% alcohol solution and a 65% alcohol solution. How much of each should be used?

12. One juice drink is 10% orange juice. Another is 15% pineapple juice. How much of each should be mixed to make 15 cups of 13% fruit juice?

13. Solution A is 45% acid. Solution B is 80% acid. How much of each should be used to produce 14 milliliters of a solution that is 65% acid?

14. Pretzels sell for $2.50 a pound. Cereal sells for $2.00 a pound. A store wants to make 10 pounds of a mixture to sell for $2.20 per pound. How much of each should be used?

15. White rice sells for $1.10 per pound. Wild rice sells for $2.40 per pound. A 5-pound bag of white and wild rice sells for $1.88 per pound. How much of each is in the bag?

16. A cook mixed ground beef and ground pork to make 25 pounds of a ground meat mixture. Ground beef cost $6.90 per pound, ground pork cost $4.90 per pound, and the cook spent $142.50 in total. How much of each meat did the cook use?

LESSON 37 Catch Up and Review!

Catch up if you are behind. Use the review problems below to make sure you're on track.

LESSON 29 Determine whether the given point is a solution.

1. $(3,0)$; $\begin{cases} x = 3 \\ y = x - 3 \end{cases}$

2. $(2,1)$; $\begin{cases} x + y = 3 \\ 2x - y = -3 \end{cases}$

LESSON 29 Solve by graphing.

3. $x + y = 0$

   $x + 2y = 2$

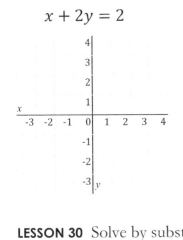

4. $y = 3$

   $5x - 3y = 6$

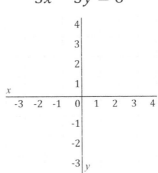

LESSON 30 Solve by substitution.

5. $x = 2y - 5$

   $3x - 4y = -1$

6. $y = 1$

   $2x + 7y = 21$

7. $-2x + y = 1$

   $2x - 3y = -11$

8. $x - 2y = -7$

   $-5x + 2y = -5$

LESSON 31 Solve by elimination.

9. $x + 3y = 4$

   $8x - 3y = 5$

10. $5x + 7y = 6$

    $5x + 2y = 16$

11. $-2x + 5y = 3$

    $3x + y = 21$

12. $2x - 3y = -2$

    $-3x + 5y = 6$

LESSONS 32–33 Solve. Use any method you prefer. Check your solutions.

13. $2x - y = 10$
    $x + 4y = 5$

14. $4x - y = 3$
    $-4x + y = -3$

15. $-3x + 2y = 4$
    $6x - 4y = 9$

16. $9x + y = 6$
    $2x - 5y = 17$

17. $x + 5y = -26$
    $2x + 3y = -10$

18. $3x - 4y = -22$
    $2x + 7y = 24$

LESSONS 34–36 Solve.

19. Three muffins and four cookies cost $12.30. Five muffins and a dozen cookies cost $28.50. How much does a muffin cost, and how much does a cookie cost?

20. A boat traveled 80 miles upstream in 4 hours. The return trip downstream took only 2 hours. Find the speed of the boat in still water and the speed of the current.

21. A 15% saline solution is mixed with a 60% saline solution to produce 10 liters of a 51% saline solution. How much of each is used?

☐ **MIXED REVIEW: PRE-ALGEBRA** ···

Brush up on the topics covered in Pre-Algebra.

22. True or false? The square root of 9 is 3 because 3 x 3 = 9.

23. Evaluate $3^2 + \sqrt{64}$.

24. Evaluate $(-10)^3 + \sqrt[3]{27}$.

25. Simplify $\sqrt{28}$.

26. The Pythagorean Theorem states that if a triangle is a right triangle, then the sum of the squares of its legs equals the square of its hypotenuse. A right triangle has leg lengths 6 and 8. What is the length of the hypotenuse?

LESSON 38 Linear Inequalities in One Variable

☐ **REFRESH YOUR SKILLS** ···

Use < or > to compare each pair of expressions. Review Pre-Algebra if needed.

1. 2 _____ 5

2. -1×2 _____ -1×5

Solve. Review Lessons 3, 4, and 5 if needed.

3. $4 - 5x = -6$

4. $3x + x = 4(x + 3) + 4x$

5. $\dfrac{1}{4}x - \dfrac{1}{2} = \dfrac{3}{4}$

6. $\dfrac{3}{10}x + \dfrac{1}{5} = \dfrac{4}{5}x + \dfrac{7}{10}$

☐ **BASIC DEFINITIONS** ···

An **inequality** is a statement that contains an inequality symbol. A **solution to an inequality** is the value(s) of the variable(s) that makes the inequality true. Inequalities often have multiple solutions, or a **solution set**. For example, $2x - 4 < 8$ is an inequality with the solution set $x < 6$. The solution set $x < 6$ means that every value less than 6 is a solution to this inequality.

☐ **GRAPHING LINEAR INEQUALITIES IN ONE VARIABLE** ································

Inequalities in one variable can be graphed on a number line. When graphing an inequality on a number line, we use an open circle for < or > and a closed circle for ≤ or ≥.

➡ **EXAMPLE** Graph $x < 1$.

➡ **TRY IT** Graph.

7. $x > -2$

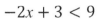

8. $x \le 0$

☐ **SOLVING LINEAR INEQUALITIES IN ONE VARIABLE** ································

Solving linear inequalities is just like solving linear equations, except for one thing: when multiplying or dividing by a negative number, you must flip the inequality sign.

➡ **EXAMPLE** Solve $-2x + 3 < 9$.

$-2x + 3 < 9$

$\underline{-3 \quad -3}$ Subtract 3 from both sides.

$-2x < 6$

$\div -2 \quad \div -2$ Divide both sides by −2, then flip the inequality sign.

$x > -3$

➡ **TRY IT** Solve.

9. $x + 5 < 8$

10. $8 - 3x \le -4$

Graph.

11. $x < -1$

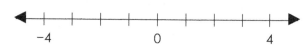

12. $x \geq 6$

Solve, then graph the solution set.

13. $3 - 2x \leq -1$

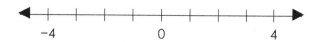

14. $5(x + 6) - 13 < 17$

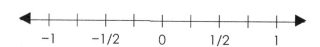

Solve. Reduce fractions but leave them improper.

15. $x + 45 > 21$

16. $5x > -40$

17. $-39 \geq 16x + 25$

18. $45 > 18 - 3x$

19. $6x - 4(2x + 3) \geq -8$

20. $3(x - 2) \leq 19 - 2x$

21. $6 - \dfrac{x}{3} > 7$

22. $5x - \dfrac{3}{4} < \dfrac{1}{4}$

23. $-2 + \dfrac{4}{5}x \geq \dfrac{3}{5}$

24. $\dfrac{1}{3}x - x + \dfrac{1}{6} \leq -\dfrac{1}{6}$

CHALLENGE For each problem, write an inequality and solve it. Then interpret your solution.

25. The width of a rectangle is 9 cm. Its perimeter is at most 54 cm. What are the possible lengths of the rectangle?

26. Matt earns a 25% commission on his sales. Last month he made more than $2,000 in commissions. What were his total sales for last month?

27. There are three exams in the algebra course. Ron scored 87 and 88 on the first two exams. What does Ron need to score on the third exam to get an average of at least 90?

LESSON 39 Compound Inequalities

☐ **REFRESH YOUR SKILLS** ···

Solve. Review Lesson 38 if needed.

1. $9x - 2 \leq -56$

2. $7(5 - 3x) > -28$

☐ **GRAPHING COMPOUND INEQUALITIES** ···

A **compound inequality** is two simple inequalities joined by the word *and* or *or*. A compound inequality with *and* is true only if both inequalities are true. Its graph is the **intersection** of the graphs of the two inequalities. A compound inequality with *or* is true if either inequality is true. Its graph is the **union** of the graphs of the two inequalities.

Note that a compound inequality with *and* can be combined and written without using *and*. For example, the inequality $x > -2$ *and* $x \leq 3$ shown below is equivalent to $-2 < x \leq 3$.

➜ **EXAMPLE** Graph.

a. $2 \leq x < 6$

b. $x > -2$ and $x \leq 3$

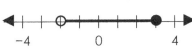

c. $x \leq -2$ or $x > 4$

➜ **TRY IT** Graph.

3. $1 < x < 5$

4. $x \geq -3$ and $x \leq 2$

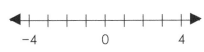

5. $x < -4$ or $x \geq 0$

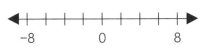

☐ **SOLVING COMPOUND INEQUALITIES** ···

To solve a compound inequality, first solve each inequality separately. Then graph the two solution sets on the same number line and determine their intersection (*and*) or union (*or*).

➜ **EXAMPLE** AND inequality

$2x + 7 \geq 1$ and $3x - 4 < -1$

$2x + 7 \geq 1$	$3x - 4 < -1$
$x \geq -3$	$x < 1$

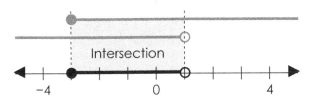

The solution set is $-3 \leq x < 1$.

➜ **EXAMPLE** OR inequality

$4x + 1 < -3$ or $-2x + 7 \geq 3$

$4x + 1 < -3$	$-2x + 7 \geq 3$
$x < -1$	$x \leq 2$

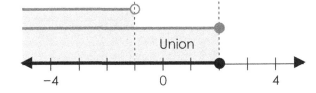

The solution set is $x \leq 2$.

➔ **TRY IT** Solve, then graph the solution set.

6. $-8 < 3x + 1 \le 7$

7. $5x - 3 > 7$ or $-2x + 7 < -3$

☐ **EXERCISE YOUR SKILLS** ···

Graph.

8. $1 < x \le 6$

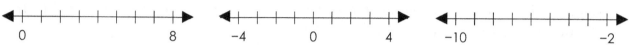

9. $x \le -2$ or $x > 1$

10. $x < -8$ or $x > -4$

Solve, then graph the solution set.

11. $-13 \le 4x + 15 < -1$

12. $5x + 2 < 27$ or $3x - 5 > 16$

Solve. Reduce fractions but leave them improper.

13. $23 < x + 9 \le 45$

14. $-5x > 75$ or $x + 19 > 13$

15. $-7 \le 3 - 5x < 6$

16. $2x + 7 \le -3$ or $4x + 1 \le -11$

17. $-1 < \dfrac{1}{3}x + 1 < \dfrac{3}{4}$

18. $\dfrac{x}{4} - 1 < -1$ or $\dfrac{1}{4} - x \ge \dfrac{5}{4}$

EXTRA Solve. Reduce fractions but leave them improper.

19. $-15 < 8x - 7 \le 17$

20. $x + 9 > 16$ and $3x + 4 < 19$

21. $-11 \le 3(x - 5) + 1 < 10$

22. $x + 6(x + 1) < 6$ or $3(1 - 2x) < 9$

23. $-2 < \dfrac{x}{4} + 5 \le 6$

24. $\dfrac{x - 7}{3} \le -2$ and $\dfrac{1}{5} - x > \dfrac{6}{5}$

LESSON 40 Absolute Value Inequalities

☐ **REFRESH YOUR SKILLS** ···

Solve. Review Lesson 6 if needed.

1. $|x - 7| = 3$

2. $2|4x - 2| + 1 = 13$

☐ **GRAPHING ABSOLUTE VALUE INEQUALITIES** ······························

An **absolute value inequality** is an inequality that contains an absolute value expression. We solve absolute value inequalities using equivalent compound inequalities. For example, consider two inequalities $|x| < 2$ and $|x| > 2$. The inequality $|x| < 2$ means the distance from 0 to x is less than 2, so it is equivalent to $-2 < x < 2$. The inequality $|x| > 2$ means the distance from 0 to x is greater than 2, so it is equivalent to $x < -2 \text{ or } x > 2$.

➜ **EXAMPLE** Graph $|x| < 2$.

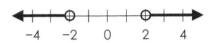

➜ **EXAMPLE** Graph $|x| > 2$.

➜ **TRY IT** Graph.

3. $|x| \leq 3$

4. $|x| \geq 1$

5. $|x| > 4$

☐ **SOLVING ABSOLUTE VALUE INEQUALITIES** ·····························

To solve an absolute value inequality, first isolate the absolute value expression on one side of the inequality. Then rewrite the inequality as an equivalent compound inequality and solve the compound inequality. Remember that

✓ $|x| < n$ is equivalent to $-n < x < n$.

✓ $|x| \leq n$ is equivalent to $-n \leq x \leq n$.

✓ $|x| > n$ is equivalent to $x < -n \text{ or } x > n$.

✓ $|x| \geq n$ is equivalent to $x \leq -n \text{ or } x \geq n$.

➜ **EXAMPLE** AND inequality

$|4x - 2| + 3 \leq 9$

⟶ Subtract 3 from both sides.

$|4x - 2| \leq 6$

⟶ Rewrite as an "AND" compound inequality.

$-6 \leq 4x - 2 \leq 6$

⟶ Add 2 to all sides.
Divide all sides by 4.

$-1 \leq x \leq 2$

➜ **EXAMPLE** OR inequality

$5|2x| - 6 > 14$

⟶ Add 6 to both sides.
Divide both sides by 5.

$|2x| > 4$

⟶ Rewrite as an "OR" compound inequality.

$2x < -4 \text{ or } 2x > 4$

⟶ Divide both sides by 2.

$x < -2 \text{ or } x > 2$

➜ TRY IT Solve, then graph the solution set.

6. $3|x + 2| + 5 \leq 8$

7. $3|2x - 5| + 2 > 11$

☐ **EXERCISE YOUR SKILLS** ···

Graph.

8. $|x| < 3$

9. $|x| \geq 4$

10. $|x| < \frac{1}{2}$

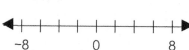

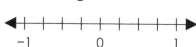

Solve, then graph the solution set.

11. $|4x - 3| < 2$

12. $|5 - 2x| + 4 \geq 6$

Solve. Reduce fractions but leave them improper.

13. $|5x| < 20$

14. $|x + 4| \geq 7$

15. $|8 - x| + 3 > 7$

16. $|9 - 3x| < 12$

17. $3 + |4x| \geq 5$

18. $3 - |7x - 6| \geq 7$

19. $\dfrac{|x - 6|}{5} < 2$

20. $\dfrac{|x|}{3} + 4 > 2$

EXTRA Solve. Reduce fractions but leave them improper.

21. $5 - |x + 4| < 9$

22. $|-2x + 8| > 20$

23. $|1 - 5x| + 4 \geq 5$

24. $\dfrac{2}{5}|2 - x| - 9 \geq -7$

LESSON 41 Linear Inequalities in Two Variables

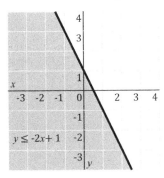

1. Find the slope and y-intercept of $y = 2x + 1$, then graph it. Review Lesson 16 if needed.

2. Find the slope and y-intercept of $2x + 3y = 6$, then graph it. Review Lesson 17 if needed.

3. Is $(1, 2)$ a solution to $2x + 3y = 6$? Explain how you know. Review Lesson 14 if needed.

☐ **CHECKING SOLUTIONS TO LINEAR INEQUALITIES** ·······································

Inequalities in two variables often have infinitely many solutions. A **solution to an inequality in two variables** is any ordered pair (x, y) that make the inequality true. To check whether an ordered pair is a solution to an inequality, simply plug it into the inequality and see if the inequality holds true.

➔ **EXAMPLE** Is $(1, 2)$ a solution to $2x + 3y < 5$?

$2(1) + 3(2) < 5$ Substitute 1 for x and 2 for y.

$8 < 5$ False. $(1, 2)$ is not a solution.

➔ **TRY IT** Is the point a solution?

4. $x + 2y \leq 4; (2, -3)$

☐ **GRAPHING LINEAR INEQUALITIES** ···

The graph of a linear inequality in two variables is a half-plane bounded by a boundary line. On the right is the graph of $y > 2x$. The shaded half-plane represents all the solutions to $y > 2x$. That is, every point in the shaded region makes $y > 2x$ true. The boundary line is $y = 2x$. It is dashed because the inequality does not include an equal sign, meaning the points on the line do not belong to the solution set. Otherwise, the line will be solid.

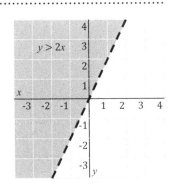

➔ **EXAMPLE** Graph $2x + y \leq 1$.

1. Solve the inequality for y. We get $y \leq -2x + 1$.
2. Graph the related equation. Use a solid line for $\geq$ or $\leq$, and a dashed line for $<$ or $>$. We graph $y = -2x + 1$ as a solid line.
3. Shade the appropriate side. Shade above the boundary line for $>$ or $\geq$, or below the line for $<$ or $\leq$. We shade below $y = -2x + 1$.
4. To verify the graph, pick a point from the shaded region and test if it is a solution to the inequality. $(0, 0)$ is a solution, so our shading is correct.

➡ **TRY IT 5.** Graph $x < y + 1$.

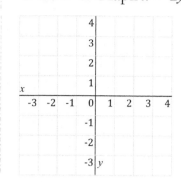

Solve for y:

Related equation:

Solid or dashed?

Test point:

➡ **TRY IT 6.** Graph $x + 2y \leq 4$.

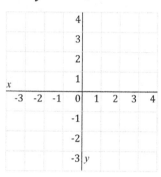

Solve for y:

Related equation:

Solid or dashed?

Test point:

☐ **EXERCISE YOUR SKILLS** ··

Graph the solution set.

7. $y > x + 1$

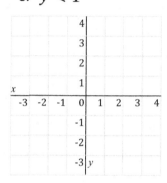

8. $y < 1$

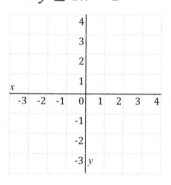

9. $y \leq 3x - 1$

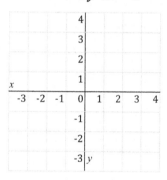

10. $2x + 3y \leq -3$

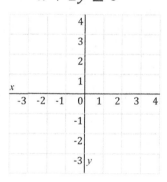

11. $x + 2y \geq 0$

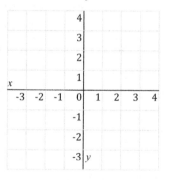

12. $5x + 4y < -8$

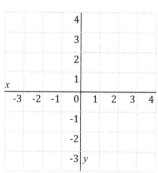

13. $x \geq 2$

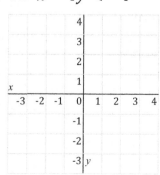

14. $x - 4y < -4$

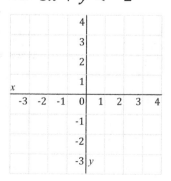

15. $3x + y < -2$

LESSON 42 Systems of Linear Inequalities

☐ **REFRESH YOUR SKILLS** ···

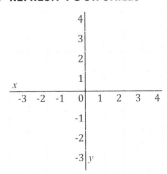

1. Graph $y > 2x$. Review Lesson 41 if needed.

2. Graph $2x + y \leq 1$. Review Lesson 41 if needed.

☐ **CHECKING SOLUTIONS TO SYSTEMS OF LINEAR INEQUALITIES** ······························

A **system of linear inequalities** is a set of two or more linear inequalities. A **solution to a system of linear inequalities** is an ordered pair that satisfies *all* the inequalities in the system. The example on the right is a system of three linear inequalities.

$$y > 2x$$
$$y \leq 1$$
$$x + y < 3$$

To check if an ordered pair is a solution to a system of linear inequalities, plug the ordered pair into each inequality in the system and very that it makes all the inequalities true.

➡ **EXAMPLE** Is (0, 1) a solution to the system above?

$$1 > 2 \cdot 0$$
$$1 \leq 1$$
$$0 + 1 < 3$$

(0, 1) is a solution because it satisfies all three inequalities in the system.

➡ **TRY IT** Is the point a solution?

3. $(1, 2);$ $\begin{cases} y < x + 5 \\ 2x - 3y > 3 \end{cases}$

☐ **GRAPHING SYSTEMS OF LINEAR INEQUALITIES** ·······································

The graph of a system of linear inequalities is the intersection of the graphs of each inequality in the system. To graph a system of linear inequalities, first graph each inequality in the same coordinate plane. Then find the intersection of the shaded regions.

➡ **EXAMPLE** Graph $\begin{cases} y > 2x \\ y - 1 \leq 0 \end{cases}$

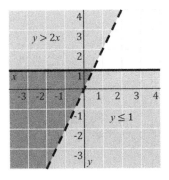

1. Graph $y > 2x$.
2. Graph $y - 1 \leq 0$.
3. Find the intersection of the shaded regions. The double-shaded region represents all the solutions to the system.
4. Pick a point and test. $(-1, 0)$ is a solution, so our shading is correct.

➡ **TRY IT 4.** Graph $\begin{cases} y < 1 \\ 3x + y > 1 \end{cases}$

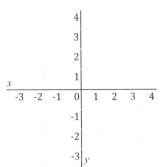

Determine whether the given point is a solution.

5. $(-1,0); \begin{cases} y < x - 2 \\ 2x - 7y > -6 \end{cases}$

6. $(6,-1); \begin{cases} x + 3y \le 3 \\ x + 4y > 4 \end{cases}$

Graph the solution set.

7. $x - y \le 1$

 $2x + 3y < -3$

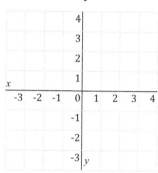

8. $x - 4y \ge 4$

 $5x - 3y \le 3$

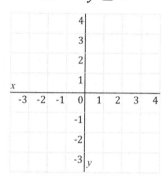

9. $x > 2$

 $5x + 2y > 8$

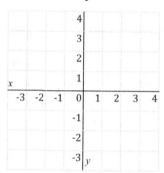

10. $4x - y > -4$

 $4x - y < 4$

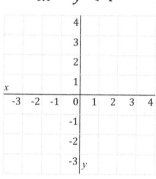

11. $2x + y > 1$

 $2x + 3y \le 3$

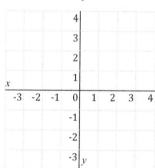

12. $y < -2$

 $4x - 3y > 6$

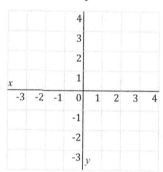

13. $x - y \le -2$

 $2x + y > -4$

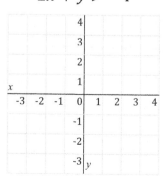

14. $4x + y \ge 1$

 $x - 3y < -3$

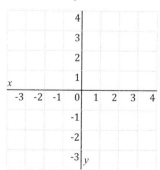

15. $x - 4y > -2$

 $3x + 2y < 8$

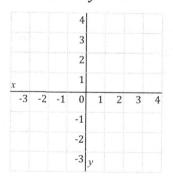

LESSON 43 Catch Up and Review!

Catch up if you are behind. Use the review problems below to make sure you're on track.

LESSON 38 Solve.

1. $5x + 8 \leq 9$

2. $-4x + 7 < 19$

3. $4(x + 1) - 5x \geq -11$

4. $3(x + 6) - 5x < 10 - 3x$

5. $\dfrac{x}{5} + 6 \leq 9$

6. $-\dfrac{3}{4}x + \dfrac{1}{8} < 2 + \dfrac{1}{2}x$

LESSON 39 Solve.

7. $3x \geq -6$ and $-2x < 10$

8. $-4 \leq 5 - 3x < 8$

9. $4 - 5x < 9$ or $3x - 5 \geq 10$

10. $7x - 5 < 9$ or $5(x + 1) - 7 > 13$

11. $-2 < \dfrac{x}{3} + 2 \leq 6$

12. $\dfrac{x}{6} - 3 \leq \dfrac{1}{3}$ or $\dfrac{1}{2} - x \geq \dfrac{3}{4}$

LESSON 40 Solve.

13. $|x + 2| < 5$

14. $|4x| + 1 \leq 9$

15. $4 + |1 - 2x| > 7$

16. $2|x - 6| + 5 \geq 9$

LESSONS 38–40 Graph.

17. $2 \leq x < 7$

18. $|x| < 6$

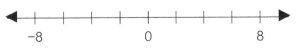

LESSON 41 Graph the solution set.

19. $y > -2x$

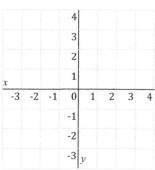

20. $x - 4y \geq 4$

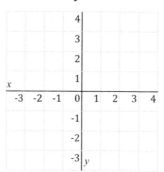

LESSON 42 Graph the solution set.

21. $y < -1$

  $x + y < 1$

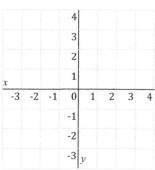

22. $y - x \geq 3$

  $2x + y > -3$

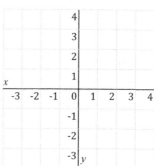

☐ **MIXED REVIEW: PRE-ALGEBRA** ···

Brush up on the topics covered in Pre-Algebra.

23. Any number with a negative exponent is equal to the reciprocal of that number with the same positive exponent. Evaluate and write without exponents: 5^{-2}.

24. Simplify and write with positive exponents only: $x^6 x^{-4}/x^3$.

25. Simplify and write with positive exponents only: $(x^5 x^{-2})^3$.

26. Scientific notation is a way of writing very large or very small numbers in decimal form. In scientific notation, a number is written in the form $a \times 10^n$ where $1 \leq a < 10$ and n is an integer. Write 0.00000125 in scientific notation.

27. Simplify and write in scientific notation: $(4 \times 10^3) \cdot (5 \times 10^7)$.

LESSON 44 Review: 1st Quarter

Let's review the topics covered in the first quarter.

LESSON 1 Evaluate.

1. $(16 - 3 \times 2)^3$

2. $6^2 \div 2^2 + 4 \times (3 - 2^3)$

LESSONS 3–5 Solve.

3. $3x + 5 = 11$

4. $3x - 4 = 2(4x + 7) - 6x$

5. $0.4x + 0.13 = 0.49$

6. $\dfrac{1}{10}x - \dfrac{3}{5} = \dfrac{1}{5}x + \dfrac{1}{2}$

LESSON 6 Solve.

7. $|x + 1| = 9$

8. $3|2x - 4| - 5 = 7$

LESSONS 30–31 Solve.

9. $x - y = 5$
   $3x + 2y = 5$

10. $2x + y = 3$
    $2x - 9y = -7$

LESSONS 38–39 Solve.

11. $2 \geq 3x - 7$

12. $-6x + 4 < 3x - 5$

13. $0 < 2x + 4 \leq 10$

14. $4x + 9 \geq x$ or $x + 6 < 3x + 2$

LESSON 40 Solve.

15. $|x + 3| \leq 4$

16. $2|4 - 3x| + 3 > 7$

LESSONS 9–11 Solve.

17. The sum of three consecutive integers is 30. Find the integers.

18. Nicole bought a shirt at $20.50. The price was 18% off the regular price. What was the regular price?

19. It takes 6 minutes to ride a bike to a park at an average speed of 12 mph. How long will it take to walk to the park at an average speed of 4 mph?

20. Two trains leave stations 810 miles apart at the same time and travel toward each other. One train travels at 120 mph, while the other travels at 150 mph. How long will it take for the two trains to meet?

21. How much pure water must be added to 10 liters of a 60% iodine solution to produce a 40% iodine solution?

22. Walnuts sell for $6 per pound. Almonds sell $7.50 per pound. How many pounds of walnuts must be mixed with 4 pounds of almonds to make a mixture of nuts that costs $7 per pound?

LESSONS 34–36 Solve.

23. Mike is 9 years older than Jason. In four years, Mike will be twice as old as Jason. How old is Mike?

24. An airplane flying with the wind traveled 2,100 miles in 6 hours. The return trip took 7 hours flying against the wind. What was the speed of the wind?

25. A 30% saline solution is mixed with a 50% saline solution to produce 12 gallons of a 45% saline solution. How much of the 50% solution is used?

26. Coffee A costs $8.50 per pound. Coffee B costs $6 per pound. How much of each should be mixed to produce 10 pounds of a coffee blend that costs $7 per pound?

LESSON 45 Review: 1st Quarter

Let's review the topics covered in the first quarter.

LESSON 15 Find the slope given two points.

1. $(4, 7)$ and $(1, -2)$

2. $(-3, 5)$ and $(7, 5)$

LESSONS 16–19 Graph.

3. $y = -x + 2$

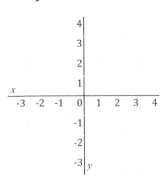

4. $y = \frac{1}{3}x - 1$

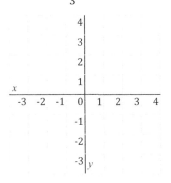

5. $4x + y = 0$

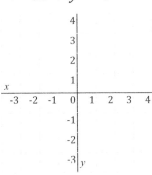

6. $2x - 3y = 6$

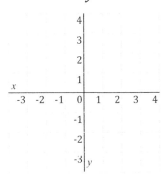

LESSON 20 Graph.

7. $y = -|x|$

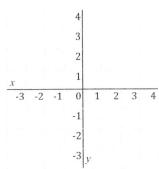

8. $y = |x + 1| - 2$

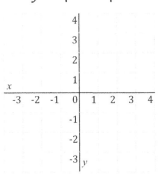

LESSONS 22–25 Find an equation of each line in slope-intercept form and in standard form. Use only integers and the smallest possible positive integer coefficient for x.

9. slope = 3; through $(2, -2)$

10. slope = $-\frac{1}{2}$; through $(4, -5)$

11. through $(4, 1)$ and $(-5, 10)$

12. through $(1, 7)$ and $(-2, -8)$

13. parallel to $y + 2x = 2$; through $(2, 3)$

14. perpendicular to $2x + 3y = 6$; through $(4, 4)$

LESSONS 38–40 Graph.

15. $1 \leq x < 5$

16. $|x| \geq 4$

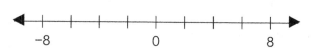

LESSON 41 Graph the solution set.

17. $y > 2x$

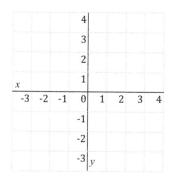

18. $x - 3y < -3$

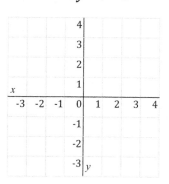

LESSON 42 Graph the solution set.

19. $y \leq 1$
   $2x + y < 3$

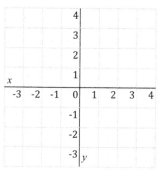

20. $x - 2y < 2$
   $4x + y \geq -1$

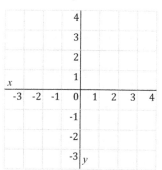

LESSON 46 PSAT Practice

This is a timed practice test. Get a timer, a bubble answer sheet (provided in Appendix B), and blank sheets of paper for your calculations. When you are ready, set the timer for **25 minutes** and begin. Do not use a calculator. Mark all your answers on the answer sheet. Only answers marked on the answer sheet can be scored. After the test, make sure you review what you missed.

1. Which of the following is equivalent to the expression $4 - 3(x - 2) + 2x$?

   A) $-x - 2$ B) $-x + 10$

   C) $5x - 2$ D) $5x + 10$

2. $2x - 5 = 4 - x$

   If x is the solution to the equation above, what is the value of $x + 3$?

   A) -3 B) 0 C) 3 D) 6

3. $2x + y = 2$ and $x + 3y = -9$

   Which ordered pair (x, y) satisfies the system of equations above?

   A) $(-2, 6)$ B) $(0, -3)$

   C) $(1, 0)$ D) $(3, -4)$

4. Which of the following is equivalent to the inequality $14 - 2x > 3(x - 2)$?

   A) $x > -4$ B) $x > 4$

   C) $x < 4$ D) $x > 8$

5. $7 + 3x = 3(x + c) - 5$

   Which value of c makes the equation above have infinitely many solutions?

   A) 0 B) 1 C) 2 D) 4

6. $|3 - 2x| = 7$

   If a and b are the solutions to the equation above, what is the value of $a + b$?

   A) 3 B) 5 C) 7 D) 9

7. $x - y = 5$ and $x + 2y = -1$

   If (p, q) is a solution to the system above, what is the value of p ?

   A) -1 B) -2 C) 3 D) 6

8. $F = \dfrac{9}{5}C + 32$

   The formula above gives the Fahrenheit temperature F for a given Celsius temperature C. Which formula gives the Celsius temperature C for a given Fahrenheit temperature F ?

   A) $C = \dfrac{5}{9}F - 32$ B) $C = \dfrac{5}{9}(F - 32)$

   C) $C = \dfrac{9}{5}F - 32$ D) $C = \dfrac{9}{5}(F - 32)$

9. A recipe calls for 2 quarts of milk, but Josh has only 2 cups of milk. How much more milk does he need in cups? (1 quart = 2 pints and 1 pint = 2 cups)

   A) 2 B) 4 C) 6 D) 8

Continue to the next page.

10. A hiking club has 45 members. The ratio of males to females is 2:3. How many males are in the club?

A) 9   B) 18   C) 27   D) 30

11. The line with the equation $x - y = 3$ does NOT pass through which of the four quadrants?

A) I   B) II   C) III   D) IV

12. $y = 50 + 30x$

The equation above models the total cost, y, that an electrician charges for x hours of service. The total cost consists of a one-time fee plus an hourly charge. If the equation is graphed in the xy-plane, what is indicated by the y-intercept of the graph?

A) A one-time fee of $30

B) A one-time fee of $50

C) An hourly charge of $30

D) An hourly charge of $50

13. An airplane 8 kilometers above the ground begins descending at an average speed of 350 meters per minute. Which expression represents the altitude of the plane, in kilometers, after t minutes?

A) $8 - 0.35t$ B) $8 - 350t$

C) $8000 - 0.35t$ D) $8000 - 350t$

14. Mark is 18 years old now. Two years ago, Mark was twice as old as Kate. How many years older than Kate is Mark?

A) 6   B) 8   C) 10   D) 12

15. Natalie bought a hat using a $2 coupon off the regular price. With sales tax of 5% added, she paid $8.40 in total. Which equation can be used to determine the regular price, x, of the hat?

A) $1.05x + 2 = 8.4$

B) $1.05x - 2 = 8.4$

C) $1.05(x + 2) = 8.4$

D) $1.05(x - 2) = 8.4$

16. A group of x adults and y children went to see a movie. Movie tickets cost $8 for adults and $6 for children. The group bought 10 tickets and paid $72 in total. Which system of equations represents the relationship between x and y ?

A) $x + y = 10$ and $8x + 6y = 72$

B) $x + y = 10$ and $8x + 6y = 10 \cdot 72$

C) $x + y = 72$ and $8x + 6y = 10$

D) $x + y = 72$ and $8x + 6y = 10 \cdot 72$

17. $x - y > 1$ and $2x + y \leq 2$

The system of inequalities above is graphed below. Which region represents the solution to the system?

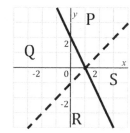

A) Region P

B) Region Q

C) Region R

D) Region S

STOP

This is the end of the test. If you finish before time is up, check your work.

LESSON 47 PSAT Practice

This is a timed practice test. Get a timer, a bubble answer sheet, and blank sheets of paper for your calculations. When you are ready, set the timer for **25 minutes** and begin. Do not use a calculator. Mark all your answers on the answer sheet. Only answers marked on the answer sheet can be scored. After the test, make sure you review what you missed.

1. If $x = -5$ and $y = 2$, what is the value of the expression $x^2 + 2xy + y^2$?

   A) -31 B) -9 C) 9   D) 49

2. If 40% of x is 16 and $\frac{2}{3}$ of y is 12, what is the value of $x - 2y$?

   A) 4   B) 22   C) 24   D) 28

3. $\frac{1}{2}x + \frac{1}{4} = \frac{1}{3}$

   What is the solution to the equation above?

   A) -6 B) $\frac{1}{6}$ C) $\frac{5}{6}$ D) 6

4. Which of the following is the value(s) of x that satisfies the equation $|x - 7| + 3 = 2$?

   A) 6   B) 6 and 8

   C) None   D) All real numbers

5. $y = -2x + 8$ and $3x - y = 7$

   If each equation in the system of equations above is graphed in the xy-plane, which ordered pair (x, y) represents the point where the lines intersect?

   A) $(0, 8)$ B) $(1, 6)$

   C) $(3, 2)$ D) $(4, 5)$

6. The formula $D = rt$ gives the distance D traveled at a speed of r over time t. Which formula can be used to determine the time it takes to travel a certain distance at a certain speed?

   A) $t = \dfrac{D}{r}$ B) $t = Dr$

   C) $t = Drt$ D) $t = \dfrac{r}{D}$

7. $2x + 6y = 3$ and $4x + 12y = k$

   Which value of k makes the system above have infinitely many solutions?

   A) 3   B) 6   C) 9   D) 12

8. A line has a slope of -3 and passes through the points $(-1, 4)$ and $(3, k)$. What is the value of k ?

   A) -8 B) -2 C) $\dfrac{8}{3}$ D) $\dfrac{11}{3}$

9. Which equation represents the line below?

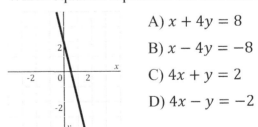

   A) $x + 4y = 8$

   B) $x - 4y = -8$

   C) $4x + y = 2$

   D) $4x - y = -2$

Continue to the next page.

10. A rental car company charges \$20 per day plus \$0.10 per mile traveled. Isaac rented a car for three days and was charged \$105 plus tax. How many miles did he drive?

    A) 300   B) 450   C) 850   D) 1,050

11. A typical page contains around 200 words when double-spaced. Jessica can type 40 words per minute. What is her rate in pages per hour?

    A) 5 pages/hour   B) 8.3 pages/hour

    C) 12 pages/hour   D) 30 pages/hour

12. A bus leaves a station at 1 PM traveling at an average speed of 60 miles per hour. An hour later, a second bus leaves the station traveling at an average speed of 70 miles per hour in the same direction. At what time will the second bus overtake the first?

    A) 6 PM   B) 7 PM

    C) 8 PM   D) 9 PM

13. $h = 5 + 1.5x$

    Sam planted a new tree in his garden. The equation above gives the height h, in feet, of the tree in x years. What does the number 5 represent in the equation?

    A) The height of the tree in 1.5 years

    B) The height the tree grows each year

    C) The height of the tree when it was planted

    D) The number of years the tree had grown when it was planted

14. Two pumps are used to fill a water tank that already contains 50 gallons of water. One pump fills at a rate of 3 gallons per minute and the other pump at a rate of 5 gallons per minute. Which expression represents the amount of water in the tank after t minutes?

    A) $(50 + 3 + 8)t$ B) $(50 + 5) + 3t$

    C) $(50 + 3) + 5t$ D) $50 + (3 + 5)t$

15. Olivia is filling up 60-milliliter bottles with 0.2 liters of water. What is the maximum number of bottles she can fill up?

    A) 3   B) 4   C) 33   D) 34

16. Which inequality represents the graph shown below?

    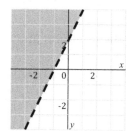

    A) $x - 2y < -4$

    B) $x - 2y > -4$

    C) $2x - y < -2$

    D) $2x - y > -2$

17. A restaurant has 15 tables that can seat a total of 70 people. Some tables seat 4 people, and the others seat 6 people. How many tables seat 4 people?

    A) 6   B) 8   C) 10   D) 12

STOP

This is the end of the test. If you finish before time is up, check your work.

LESSON 48 Relations and Functions

☐ **IDENTIFYING FUNCTIONS FROM RELATIONS** ···

A **relation** is a set of inputs and outputs. A relation can be represented by a set of ordered pairs, a table, a mapping, or a graph. On the right is the relation {(1, 4), (2, 5), (2, 6)} expressed as a table and a mapping.

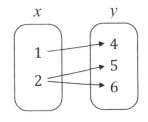

A **function** is a special type of relation where every input has exactly one output. All functions are relations, but not all relations are functions. To determine whether a relation is a function or not, check the inputs and outputs. If any input has more than one output, the relation is not a function.

➜ **EXAMPLE** Is the relation above a function?

The relation above is not a function because input 2 has two different outputs: 5 and 6.

➜ **TRY IT** Identify as a function or not a function. Explain your answer.

1. {(1, 1), (2, 3), (3, 5), (4, −7)}   2. {(2, 7), (3, 1), (3, 8), (5, 4)}

☐ **USING THE VERTICAL LINE TEST** ···

The **vertical line test** is a visual way to determine whether a graph represents a function. If you can draw any vertical line that intersects a graph more than once, then the graph does not represent a function because a function has only one output value for each input value.

➜ **EXAMPLE** Identify as a function or not a function.

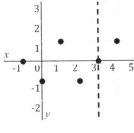
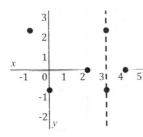
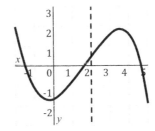
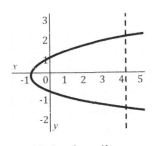

Function   Not a function   Function   Not a function

➜ **TRY IT** Identify as a function or not a function. Explain your answer.

3.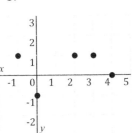

4.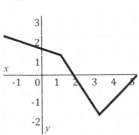

5.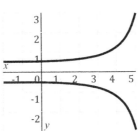

6.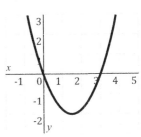

Identify as a function or not a function. Explain your answer.

7. $\{(5, 8), (6, 0), (7, 9), (3, 2)\}$

8. $\{(0, 1), (2, 1), (4, 1), (6, 1)\}$

9. $\{(4, 3), (1, 3), (4, 2), (5, 8)\}$

10. $\{(4, 8), (5, 4), (6, 4), (7, 6)\}$

11.

x	-2	-1	0	1	2
y	4	2	0	2	4

12.

x	1	3	1	5	0
y	5	3	2	7	5

13.

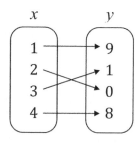

14.

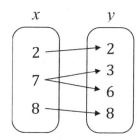

15.

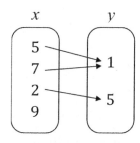

16.

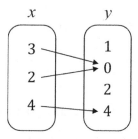

17.

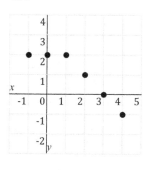

18.

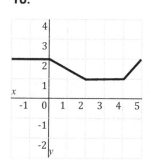

19.

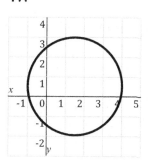

20.

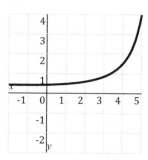

Graph, then identify as a function or not a function.

21. $x = 3$

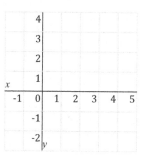

22. $x + 2y = 4$

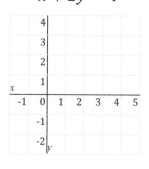

23. $y = |x - 2|$

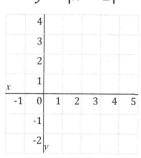

24. $y = -|x| + 3$

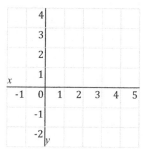

LESSON 49 Domain and Range

☐ **REFRESH YOUR SKILLS** ···

Identify as a function or not a function. Explain your answer. Review Lesson 48 if needed.

1. $\{(-4, 4), (2, 2), (4, 4), (-2, 2)\}$ **2.** $\{(1, 9), (9, 1), (2, -7), (9, -7)\}$

☐ **FINDING DOMAIN AND RANGE OF FUNCTIONS** ···

In a relation, the set of all input values is called the **domain**, and the set of all output values is called the **range**. Domains can be discrete or continuous. A **discrete domain** is a set of input values that are distinct and separate. A **continuous domain** is a set of input values without gaps. It contains an infinite number of values. In our example below, the first graph has a discrete domain, while the second graph has a continuous domain.

➜ **EXAMPLE** Find the domain and range, then identify as a function or not a function.

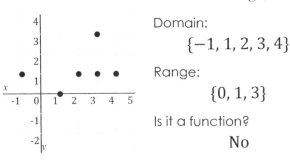

Domain:
$\{-1, 1, 2, 3, 4\}$

Range:
$\{0, 1, 3\}$

Is it a function?
No

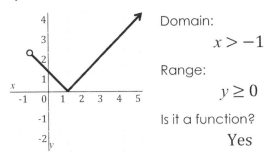

Domain:
$x > -1$

Range:
$y \geq 0$

Is it a function?
Yes

➜ **TRY IT** Find the domain and range, then identify as a function or not a function.

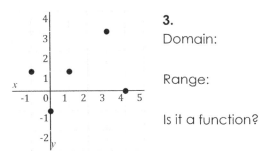

3.
Domain:

Range:

Is it a function?

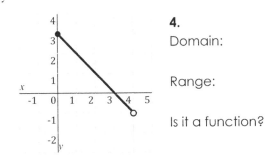

4.
Domain:

Range:

Is it a function?

☐ **IDENTIFYING DEPENDENT AND INDEPENDENT VARIABLES** ···

In a function, the variable representing the input values is called the **independent variable**, and the variable representing the output values is called the **dependent variable**. This is because the value of the output depends on the value of the input.

➜ **EXAMPLE** You buy cupcakes at $2 each. The function $C = 2n$ represents the amount of money, C, you spend for n cupcakes. a) Identify the dependent and independent variables. b) Find the range for the domain $\{0, 1, 2\}$.

  a. The amount of money you spend depends on the number of cupcakes you buy. So, C is the dependent variable, and n is the independent variable.
  b. Given the values of n, the corresponding values of C are $\{0, 2, 4\}$. So, the range is $\{0, 2, 4\}$.

→ **TRY IT** Solve.

5. You walk 4 miles per hour. The function $D = 4t$ represents the number of miles, D, you walk for t hours. a) Identify the dependent and independent variables. b) Find the range for the domain {1, 2, 3}.

☐ **EXERCISE YOUR SKILLS** ···

Find the domain and range, then identify as a function or not a function.

6.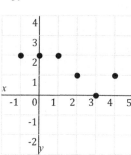

7.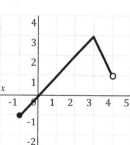

8.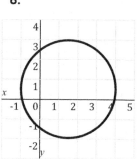

9.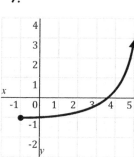

For each function, a) identify the dependent and independent variables and b) find the range for the domain {1, 2, 3}.

10. A recipe calls for 2 eggs to make 12 cookies. The function $C = 6e$ represents the number of cookies, C, you can bake using e eggs.

11. A bike rental shop charges a flat fee plus an additional charge per hour for renting a bike. The function $C = 9h + 15$ represents the total cost, C, of renting a bike for h hours.

12. A water tank is being emptied at a constant rate. The function $w = 200 - 10m$ represents the amount of water, w, in the tank after m minutes.

13. A taxi company charges a flat fee plus an additional charge per mile. The function $C = 1.5m + 8$ represents the total cost, C, of riding a taxi for m miles.

Find the range given the domain. (*Hint*: Sketch the graph first!)

14. $y = x + 5; -2 < x < 3$

15. $y = -2x + 1; -4 < x \leq 0$

16. $x + 5y = -5; 0 \leq x < 5$

17. $2x - 3y = 6; -3 \leq x \leq 6$

18. $y = |x|; -5 < x \leq 5$

19. $y = |x - 3|; 0 < x < 9$

LESSON 50 Function Notation

☐ **REFRESH YOUR SKILLS** ···

Solve for y. Review Lesson 12 if needed.

1. $x + y = 7$

2. $x + 4y = -8$

☐ **WRITING EQUATIONS IN FUNCTION FORM** ·······························

An equation is **in function form** when it is solved for y. For example, $2x + y = 5$ is not in function form, while its equivalent equation $y = -2x + 5$ is in function form.

➜ **TRY IT** Write in function form by solving for y.

3. $x - y = 2$

4. $2x^2 + y = 7$

☐ **EVALUATE FUNCTIONS IN FUNCTION NOTATION** ·····················

Instead of using y, you can use **function notation** to give a different name to each function. Often letters, such as f, g, and h, are used to name functions. The function notation $f(x)$ means the output of function f when the input is x, and is read "f of x."

Two ways of writing functions

As an equation	In function notation
$y = x + 1$	$f(x) = x + 1$
$y = x^2 - x$	$g(x) = x^2 - x$

To evaluate a function in function notation, replace the variable with the given value.

➜ **EXAMPLE** Evaluate, given f and g above.

a. $f(2) = 2 + 1 = 3$ Replace x with 2.

b. $g(1) = 1^2 - 1 = 0$ Replace x with 1.

➜ **TRY IT** Evaluate, given f and g above.

5. $f(-5)$

6. $g(4)$

☐ **EVALUATE FUNCTIONS FROM GRAPHS** ································

To evaluate a function from its graph, find the y-value for the given x-value.

➜ **EXAMPLE** Evaluate $f(4)$.

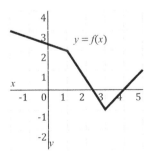

Find y when $x = 4$. The graph passes $(4, 0)$, so $f(4) = 0$.

➜ **TRY IT** Evaluate.

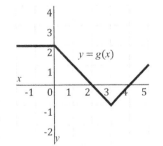

7. $g(0)$

8. $g(3)$

Write in function form by solving for y.

9. $x + y = -9$

10. $x - 3y = 6$

11. $x^2 - 4y = 0$

12. $2xy - 3 = 1$

Evaluate when $x = -2, 0,$ and 4. Write your answers in function notation.

13. $f(x) = x + 2$

14. $g(x) = 1 - 4x$

15. $h(x) = |x - 3|$

16. $k(x) = x^2 + 7$

Find the value(s) of x given the functions above.

17. $f(x) = 7$

18. $g(x) = 13$

19. $h(x) = 3$

20. $k(x) = 56$

Find the value(s) of n given the graphs of p and q.

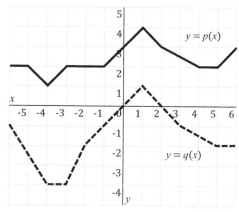

21. $p(-3) = n$

22. $q(3) = n$

23. $p(n) = 1$

24. $q(n) = 0$

25. $p(0) + q(1) = n$

26. $p(1) \cdot q(-2) = n$

CHALLENGE Evaluate, given the functions above. (*Hint*: To evaluate nested functions, start with the innermost parentheses and work your way out.)

27. $k(\sqrt{3})$

28. $f(1) + g(4) \div h(-2)$

29. $h(g(2))$

30. $h(-1) + k(h(-1))$

LESSON 51 Linear Functions

☐ **REFRESH YOUR SKILLS** ⸱⸱

Find the slope given two points. Review Lesson 15 if needed.

1. $(2, 5)$ and $(-2, 3)$

2. $(0, 2)$ and $(4, -2)$

Find an equation of each line in slope-intercept form. Review Lessons 22 and 23 if needed.

3.
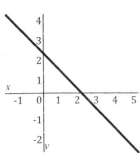

4.
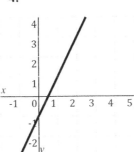

5.
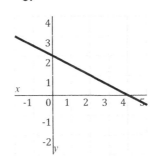

6.
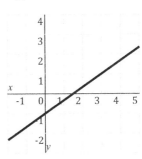

7. slope $= 2$; through $(1, 5)$

8. through $(1, -2)$ and $(2, -9)$

☐ **IDENTIFYING LINEAR FUNCTIONS FROM GRAPHS** ⸱⸱

A **linear function** is a function whose graph is a straight line. A **function rule** is an equation that describes the relationship between inputs (independent variable) and outputs (dependent variable).

➜ **TRY IT** Identify as linear or nonlinear. If linear, write a rule.

9.
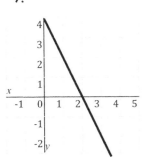

10.
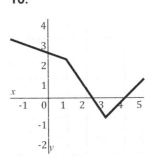

11.
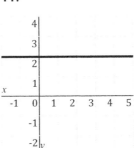

12.
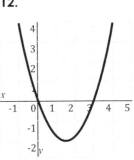

☐ **IDENTIFYING LINEAR FUNCTIONS FROM EQUATIONS** ⸱⸱⸱

An equation represents a linear function if it can be written in slope-intercept form.

➜ **TRY IT** Write in function form by solving for y, then identify as linear or nonlinear.

13. $6x - y = 2y$

14. $x^2 - y = 2x$

15. $xy + x = 3$

16. $x - 5y = -10$

A table represents a linear function if the rate of change, or slope, is constant. In other words, a table is linear if the y-values change by the same amount over equal intervals of x-values.

→ **EXAMPLE** Linear or not?   → **TRY IT** Identify as linear or nonlinear. If linear, write a rule.

Check the slope!

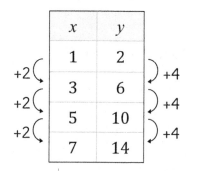

17.

x	y
−2	6
−1	3
0	0
1	3

18.

x	y
0	5
3	2
6	−1
9	−4

19.

x	y
−1	1
0	0
1	1
3	9

↳ The table is linear because the y-values increase by 4 every time the x-values increase by 2. An equation of the line that passes through (1, 2) and (3, 6) is $y = 2x$.

□ **EXERCISE YOUR SKILLS** ··

Identify as linear or nonlinear. If linear, write a rule.

20.

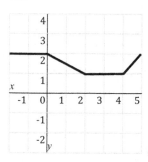

21.

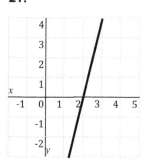

22.

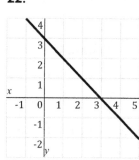

23.

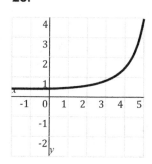

Write in function form by solving for y, then identify as linear or nonlinear.

24. $xy + 2 = 7$ **25.** $x - y = -6$ **26.** $9x - 3y = 6$ **27.** $x^2 + x - y = 0$

Identify as linear or nonlinear. If linear, write a rule.

28.

x	y
2	2
3	5
4	8
5	11

29.

x	y
0	9
3	8
6	6
9	3

30.

x	y
0	5
1	5
2	5
3	5

31.

x	y
−4	7
−2	5
0	3
2	1

LESSON 52 Linear, Exponential, and Quadratic Functions

☐ **IDENTIFYING TYPES OF FUNCTIONS FROM EQUATIONS AND GRAPHS** ·······················

There are many different types of functions that are used to model real-world data. Below are three important types of functions and their general forms and graphs. The graph of a linear function is a line. The graph of an exponential function is a L-shaped curve called an exponential curve. The graph of a quadratic function is a U-shaped curve called a parabola. Notice that the directions of these graphs can be different depending on their coefficients.

Linear function	Exponential function	Quadratic function
$y = mx + b$	$y = ab^x$	$y = ax^2 + bx + c$

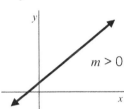 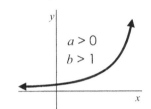 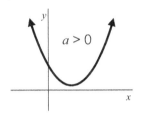

➜ **TRY IT** Classify as linear, exponential, quadratic, or none of these.

1. $y = x^2 + 3$ 2. $y = 2x + 5$ 3. $y = 5^x$ 4. $y = 2x^3$

5. 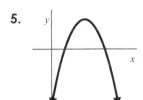   6.    7. 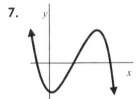   8.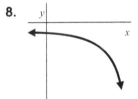

☐ **IDENTIFYING TYPES OF FUNCTIONS FROM TABLES** ·····································

To determine which type of function best describes the data in a table, look for a pattern in the y values. The differences of consecutive y-values are called **first differences**. The differences of consecutive first differences are called **second differences**. Linear functions have a constant first difference. Quadratic functions have a constant second difference. Exponential functions have a constant ratio between consecutive y-values.

➜ **EXAMPLE** Classify as linear, exponential, quadratic, or none of these.

	x	y	
+3	−1	12	−4
+3	2	8	−4
+3	5	4	−4
	8	0	

Linear function

	x	y	
+1	0	1	×5
+1	1	5	×5
+1	2	25	×5
	3	125	

Exponential function

	x	y		
+2	1	2	+8	
+2	3	10	+16	+8
+2	5	26	+24	+8
	7	50		

Quadratic function

➜ **TRY IT** Classify as linear, exponential, quadratic, or none of these.

9.

x	−4	−2	0	2	4
y	13	1	−3	1	13

10.

x	−1	0	1	2	3
y	0.25	1	4	16	64

☐ **EXERCISE YOUR SKILLS** ··

Classify as linear, exponential, quadratic, or none of these.

11. $y = 2^x + 1$ **12.** $y = x^2 - 2$ **13.** $y = -x + 4$ **14.** $y = -2x^2$

Match each function above with its graph.

15. 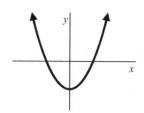   **16.** 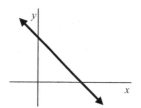   **17.** 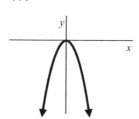   **18.**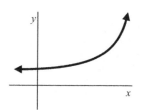

Classify as linear, exponential, quadratic, or none of these.

19.

x	−2	−1	0	1	2
y	1	2	4	8	16

20.

x	−2	−1	0	1	2
y	−8	−1	0	1	8

21.

x	2	4	6	8	10
y	11	15	19	23	27

22.

x	1	3	5	7	9
y	4	16	36	64	100

23.

x	1	2	4	5	10
y	20	10	5	4	2

24.

x	0	1	2	3	4
y	5	2	−1	−4	−7

LESSON 53 Average Rate of Change

☐ **REFRESH YOUR SKILLS** ···

Find the slope given two points. Review Lesson 15 if needed.

1. $(1, 7)$ and $(3, -5)$

2. $(4, -2)$ and $(8, 1)$

Use the graphs of g and h below to find each value. Review Lesson 50 if needed.

3. $g(4)$ **4.** $g(-2)$ **5.** $h(-1)$ **6.** $h(4)$

☐ **FINDING AVERAGE RATES OF CHANGE FROM TABLES** ·······························

The **average rate of change** measures how much a function is changed, on average, over a given interval. For linear functions, it is constant. For non-linear functions, it varies over different intervals. The formula for the average rate of change of function f over the interval $x_1 \leq x \leq x_2$ is the same as the slope formula, as shown below.

$$averate\ rate\ of\ change = \frac{changes\ in\ y}{changes\ in\ x} = \frac{y_2 - y_1}{x_2 - x_1} = \frac{f(x_2) - f(x_1)}{x_2 - x_1}$$

➜ **EXAMPLE** Find the average rate of change of f over the interval $-2 \leq x \leq 0$.

x	-2	-1	0	1	2
$f(x)$	0	1	4	9	16

Use the formula:

$$\frac{f(0) - f(-2)}{0 - (-2)} = \frac{4 - 0}{2} = 2$$

➜ **TRY IT** Find the average rate of change of f on the left over each given interval.

7. $0 \leq x \leq 1$ **8.** $-1 \leq x \leq 1$

9. $-1 \leq x \leq 2$ **10.** $-2 \leq x \leq 2$

☐ **FINDING AVERAGE RATES OF CHANGE FROM GRAPHS** ·······························

➜ **EXAMPLE** Find the average rate of change of g over the interval $1 \leq x \leq 5$.

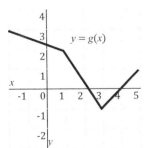

Use the formula:

$$\frac{g(5) - g(1)}{5 - 1}$$

$$= \frac{1 - 2}{4} = -\frac{1}{4}$$

➜ **TRY IT** Find the average rate of change of h over each given interval.

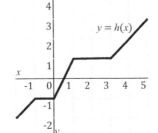

11. $1 \leq x \leq 5$

12. $0 \leq x \leq 2$

➔ **EXAMPLE** Find the average speed.

A ball is dropped from a height of 400 feet. Its height h, in feet, after t seconds is given by $h(t) = 400 - 16t^2$. What is the average rate of change (average speed) from $t = 1$ to $t = 2$?

Use the formula:

$$\frac{h(2) - h(1)}{2 - 1} = \frac{336 - 384}{1}$$

$$= -48 \, feet \, per \, second$$

➔ **TRY IT** Solve.

13. A ball is dropped from a height of 256 feet. Its height h, in feet, after t seconds is given by $h(t) = 256 - 16t^2$. What is the average rate of change from $t = 1$ to $t = 3$?

□ **EXERCISE YOUR SKILLS** ···

Use the table to find the average rate of change of f over each given interval.

x	−5	−3	−1	1	3
$f(x)$	25	9	1	1	9

14. $-3 \leq x \leq 3$

15. $-5 \leq x \leq 1$

Use the graphs to find the average rate of change of p and q over each given interval.

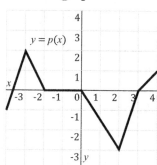

16. $2 \leq x \leq 3$

17. $-4 \leq x \leq 4$

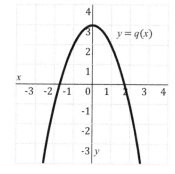

18. $-2 \leq x \leq 2$

19. $0 \leq x \leq 1$

Find the average rate of change of each function over the given interval.

20. $f(x) = (x - 3)^2; \; -4 \leq x \leq 4$

21. $f(x) = 2x^3; \; -1 \leq x \leq 3$

22. $f(x) = \dfrac{x + 5}{x - 3}; \; -1 \leq x \leq 2$

23. $f(x) = \dfrac{x^3 + 8}{x + 2}; \; 0 \leq x \leq 4$

Solve.

24. A ball is thrown up from a window 8 feet above ground level. Its height h, in feet, after t seconds is given by $h(t) = -16t^2 + 64t + 8$. What is the average rate of change from $t = 0$ to $t = 4$?

LESSON 54 Inverse of Linear Functions

☐ **FINDING INVERSES OF RELATIONS** ··

An **inverse relation** is a relation that switches the inputs and outputs of another relation. To find the inverse of a relation, switch the x- and y-values. Notice that, in our example below, the original relation is a function, but its inverse relation is *not* a function.

➜ **EXAMPLE** Find the inverse.

$(1, 5), (2, 6), (3, 6)$

Simply switch the x- and y-values.

$(5, 1), (6, 2), (6, 3)$

➜ **TRY IT** Find the inverse.

1. $(1, -5), (2, 3), (5, -2), (7, 0)$

2. $(-2, 4), (0, 0), (2, 4), (4, 8)$

☐ **EVALUATING INVERSES OF FUNCTIONS FROM GRAPHS** ··

The inverse of function f is written f^{-1} and read "f inverse." Note that the superscript $^{-1}$ in f^{-1} is not an exponent.

$$If\ f(x) = y, then\ f^{-1}(y) = x$$

To evaluate the inverse of a function from its graph, find the x-value that yields the given y-value.

➜ **EXAMPLE** Evaluate $f^{-1}(2)$.

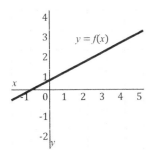

Find x when $y = 2$. The graph passes $(3, 2)$, so $f(3) = 2$ and $f^{-1}(2) = 3$.

➜ **TRY IT** Evaluate.

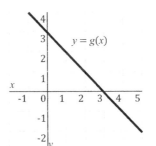

3. $g^{-1}(2)$

4. $g^{-1}(-1)$

☐ **FINDING INVERSES OF LINEAR FUNCTIONS** ···

To find the inverse of a function given its equation, simply switch x and y and solve for y.

➜ **EXAMPLE** Find the inverse of $f(x) = 2x + 4$.

$f(x) = 2x + 4$

$y = 2x + 4$ Set y equal to $f(x)$.

$x = 2y + 4$ Switch x and y.

$y = \dfrac{1}{2}x - 2$ Solve for y.

$f^{-1}(x) = \dfrac{1}{2}x - 2$ Write in function notation.

➜ **TRY IT** Find the inverse.

5. $f(x) = -x + 3$

6. $g(x) = 2x - 6$

7. $h(x) = -\dfrac{1}{3}x + 1$

Find the inverse.

8. $(-5, 1), (0, 0), (5, -1), (10, -2)$

9. $(-1, 0.5), (1, 2), (3, 8), (5, 32)$

Evaluate.

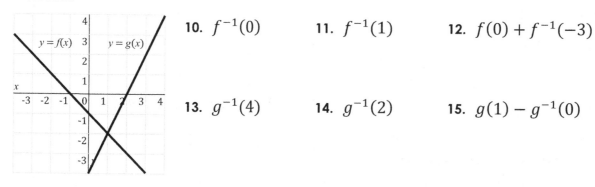

10. $f^{-1}(0)$

11. $f^{-1}(1)$

12. $f(0) + f^{-1}(-3)$

13. $g^{-1}(4)$

14. $g^{-1}(2)$

15. $g(1) - g^{-1}(0)$

Find the inverse algebraically, then graph both the original function and its inverse.

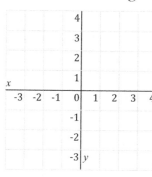

16. $f(x) = x - 2$

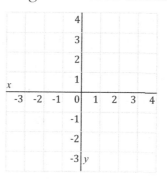

17. $g(x) = \dfrac{1}{4}x$

Find the inverse algebraically. Write your answers in function notation.

18. $p(x) = x + 7$

19. $q(x) = 3x - 2$

20. $r(x) = \dfrac{5 - 2x}{6}$

21. $s(x) = \dfrac{1}{4}x + \dfrac{1}{2}$

CHALLENGE Evaluate. Use the functions above. (*Hint*: To evaluate nested functions, start with the innermost parentheses and work your way out.)

22. $p^{-1}(9) + q^{-1}(1)$

23. $p(3) + r^{-1}(r(1))$

24. $r^{-1}\left(-\dfrac{1}{2}\right) \times q^{-1}(4)$

25. $p^{-1}(s^{-1}(3)) - r^{-1}\left(\dfrac{1}{2}\right)$

LESSON 55 Catch Up and Review!

Catch up if you are behind. Use the review problems below to make sure you're on track.

LESSON 48 Identify as a function or not a function.

1.
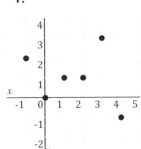

2.
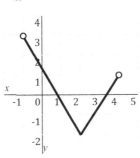

3.
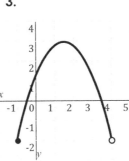

4.
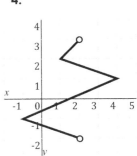

LESSON 49 Find the domain and range of each relation above.

5.

6.

7.

8.

LESSON 50 Evaluate when $x = -1, 0$, and 5. Write your answers in function notation.

9. $f(x) = 4x + 3$

10. $g(x) = x^2 - 9$

LESSONS 51–52 Classify as linear, exponential, quadratic, or none of these. If linear, write a rule.

11.

x	-3	0	3	6	9
y	2	0	-2	-4	-6

12.

x	0	1	2	3	4
y	1	0	1	4	9

13.

x	0	1	2	3	4
y	1	2	4	8	16

14.

x	-2	-1	0	1	2
y	4	3	2	1	0

15.

x	0	1	2	3	4
y	0	1	8	27	64

16.

x	-2	-1	0	1	2
y	0	3	4	3	0

LESSON 53 Find the average rate of change.

17. $f(x) = x^2 + x;\ 3 \leq x \leq 8$

18. $g(x) = 3 \cdot 2^x\ 0 \leq x \leq 3$

19. $h(x) = \dfrac{x^2 - 9}{x + 3};\ -2 \leq x \leq 4$

20. $k(x) = 5 + \dfrac{x}{x - 1};\ 3 \leq x \leq 6$

LESSON 54 Find the inverse algebraically. Write your answers in function notation.

21. $f(x) = x + 5$

22. $g(x) = 2x - 1$

23. $h(x) = \dfrac{6 + 2x}{3}$

24. $k(x) = \dfrac{1}{5}x + \dfrac{1}{10}$

☐ **MIXED REVIEW: PRE-ALGEBRA** ··

Brush up on the topics covered in Pre-Algebra.

25. There are six basic types of quadrilaterals: parallelogram, rhombus, rectangle, square, trapezoid, and kite. Name all quadrilaterals that have four right angles.

26. Polygons are closed plane figures formed by three or more line segments. Is a circle a polygon or not? Explain.

27. The Pythagorean Theorem states that, if a triangle is a right triangle, the sum of the squares of its legs equals the square of its hypotenuse. Can side lengths of 5, 6, and 9 form a right triangle? Why or why not?

28. One common property of all triangles is that the sum of their interior angles is always 180°. Find the value of x.

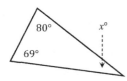

29. Classify the marked angle pair as corresponding, alternate interior, alternate exterior, or consecutive interior. Then find the value of x.

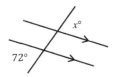

LESSON 56 Direct Variation

☐ **REFRESH YOUR SKILLS** ···

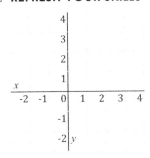

1. Find the slope and y-intercept of $y = 2x$, then graph it. Review Lesson 16 if needed.

2. Find the slope and y-intercept of $x + y = 1$, then graph it. Review Lesson 17 if needed.

☐ **IDENTIFYING DIRECT VARIATION FROM GRAPHS** ·································

Direct variation is a relationship between two variables x and y that can be written in the form $y = kx$, or $k = y/x$, where k is a nonzero constant. Direct variation $y = kx$ means that y is directly proportional to x, or y varies directly with (or as) x. The constant k is called the **constant of proportionality** or **constant of variation**.

> Direct variation
>
> $$y = kx \text{ or } k = \frac{y}{x}$$

The graph of $y = kx$ is a line with a slope of k that passes through the origin. So the graph of a direct variation always goes through the origin, and its slope is the constant of variation.

➔ **TRY IT 3.** See your graphs above. Which graph represents a direct variation?

☐ **IDENTIFYING DIRECT VARIATION FROM EQUATIONS** ····························

To determine whether an equation represents a direct variation, solve for y and see if it ends up in the form $y = kx$.

➔ **EXAMPLE** Direct variation?

a. $2y = 4x$

$y = 2x$

Yes ($k = 2$)

b. $x + y = 1$

$y = -x + 1$

No

➔ **TRY IT** Direct variation? If so, find k.

4. $x + y = 0$

5. $xy - 3 = 2$

☐ **FINDING DIRECT VARIATION EQUATIONS** ····································

To find a direct variation equation given a point, plug the given point into $y = kx$ and solve for k.

➔ **EXAMPLE** Solve using direct variation.

Suppose y varies directly with x, and $y = 6$ when $x = 3$. Find y when $x = 5$.

1. Plug $x = 3$ and $y = 6$ into $y = kx$ and solve for k, and you get $k = 2$.
2. The direct variation equation is $y = 2x$.
3. Use the equation to find the unknown. Plug $x = 5$ into $y = 2x$, and you get $y = 10$.

➔ **TRY IT** Solve.

6. Suppose y varies directly with x, and $y = 12$ when $x = 4$. Find y when $x = 6$.

7. Suppose y varies directly with x, and $y = 2$ when $x = 8$. Find x when $y = -1$.

☐ SOLVING DIRECT VARIATION WORD PROBLEMS ···

To solve a problem involving direct variation, 1) identify the independent variable x and dependent variable y, 2) plug the given values for x and y into $y = kx$ to solve for k, 3) write the direct variation equation with k, and 4) use the equation to find the unknown.

→ **EXAMPLE** Solve using direct variation.

The distance a car travels varies directly with (is directly proportional to) the amount of gas it uses. A car uses 7 gallons of gas to travel 210 miles. How much gas will it use to travel 180 miles?

1. x = amount of gas used
   y = distance traveled
2. $210 = 7k$, so $k = 30$.
3. The equation is $y = 30x$.
4. $180 = 30x$, so $x = 6$.
   It will use 6 gallons of gas.

🔎 The phrase "varies directly with" indicates direct variation.

→ **TRY IT** Write a direct variation equation, then solve.

8. The distance sound travels varies directly with the time it travels. Sound travels 1,700 meters in 5 seconds in air. How far will it travel in 12 seconds?

9. The height of an object varies directly with the length of its shadow. If a tree 12 feet tall casts a shadow 18 feet long, how long will be the shadow of a tree that is 16 feet tall?

☐ EXERCISE YOUR SKILLS ···

Identify as direct variation or not direct variation.

10. $2x + y = 0$ 11. $xy = 1$ 12. $4y = 2x$ 13. $2x + y = 3$

Write a direct variation equation, then solve.

14. Suppose y varies directly with x, and $y = 8$ when $x = 2$. Find y when $x = 3$.

15. Suppose y varies directly with x, and $y = 6$ when $x = 9$. Find x when $y = 4$.

16. The cost to paint a wall varies directly with the area of the wall. If it costs $50 to paint 400 square feet of wall space, how much will it cost to paint 500 square feet of wall space?

17. The number of calories in a can of soda varies directly with the amount of soda in the can. If a 12-ounce can of soda has 150 calories, how many calories will be in a 20-ounce bottle of soda?

18. The weight of an object on Earth is directly proportional to its weight on Mars. An object that weighs 50 pounds on Earth would weigh about 19 pounds on Mars. How much will an 80-pound object on Earth weigh on Mars?

LESSON 57 Inverse Variation

☐ **REFRESH YOUR SKILLS** ··

Solve. Review Lesson 56 if needed.

1. Suppose y varies directly with x, and $y = 15$ when $x = -5$. Find y when $x = 4$.

2. The distance a car travels varies directly with the amount of gas it uses. A car uses 4 gallons of gas to travel 100 miles. How much gas will it use to travel 150 miles?

☐ **IDENTIFYING INVERSE VARIATION FROM GRAPHS** ··

Inverse variation is a relationship between two variables x and y that can be written in the form $y = k/x$, or $k = xy$, where k is a nonzero constant. Inverse variation $y = k/x$ means y varies inversely with (or as) x. The constant k is also called the **constant of proportionality** or **constant of variation**.

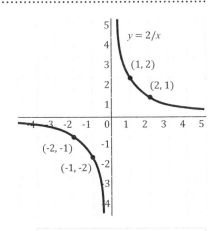

The graph of $y = k/x$ is a curve called a **hyperbola**. The curve never passes through the origin and never crosses the x- or y-axis. It just gets closer and closer to the axes. Shown on the right is the graph of $y = 2/x$.

☐ **IDENTIFYING INVERSE VARIATION FROM EQUATIONS** ··································

To determine whether an equation represents an inverse variation, solve for y and see if it ends up in the form $y = k/x$.

> Inverse variation
> $$y = \frac{k}{x} \text{ or } k = xy$$

➜ **EXAMPLE** Inverse variation?

   a. $2xy = 4$ **b.** $x + y = 1$

       $y = 2/x$ $y = -x + 1$

       Yes (k = 2)   No

➜ **TRY IT** Inverse variation? If so, find k.

  3. $2xy = -6$ **4.** $3y = 9x$

☐ **FINDING DIRECT VARIATION EQUATIONS** ··

To find an inverse variation equation given a point, plug the given point into $xy = k$ to find k.

➜ **EXAMPLE** Solve using inverse variation.

Suppose y varies inversely with x, and $y = 1$ when $x = 6$. Find y when $x = -3$.

1. Plug $x = 6$ and $y = 1$ into $xy = k$, and $k = 6$.
2. The inverse variation equation is $xy = 6$.
3. Use the equation to find the unknown. Plug $x = -3$ into $xy = 6$ and solve for y, and you get $y = -2$.

➜ **TRY IT** Solve.

5. Suppose y varies inversely with x, and $y = 2$ when $x = 6$. Find y when $x = 4$.

6. Suppose y varies inversely with x, and $y = 5$ when $x = -2$. Find x when $y = -10$.

☐ **SOLVING DIRECT VARIATION WORD PROBLEMS** ···

Solving an inverse variation problem is just like solving a direct variation problem except that you use $y = k/x$, or $xy = k$, instead of $y = kx$. Review Lesson 56 if needed.

➔ **TRY IT** Write an inverse variation equation, then solve.

7. The resale value of a car varies inversely with its age. If a 2-year-old car costs $18,000, what will be the value of the car when it is 5 years old?

8. The time it takes to finish a painting job varies inversely with the number of people working on the job. If it takes 3 hours for 4 people to finish a painting job, how long will it take for 6 people to finish the job?

☐ **EXERCISE YOUR SKILLS** ··

Identify as direct variation, inverse variation, or neither.

9. $xy = -2$ 10. $3y = -6$ 11. $5xy - 1 = 0$ 12. $x - 3y = 0$

Assume y varies directly with x. Write a direct variation equation relating x and y.

13. $y = -3$ when $x = 3$ 14. $y = 0.6$ when $x = 2$

Assume y varies inversely with x. Write an inverse variation equation relating x and y.

15. $y = 4$ when $x = 1$ 16. $y = 4$ when $x = -2$

Write a direct or inverse variation equation, then solve.

17. Suppose y varies directly with x, and $y = 15$ when $x = 3$. Find x when $y = 30$.

18. Suppose y varies inversely with x, and $y = 4$ when $x = -5$. Find y when $x = 2$.

19. The distance a car travels varies directly with the time it travels. If a car travels 72 kilometers in 3/4 hour, how far will it travel in 4 hours?

20. The time it takes to empty a water tank varies inversely with the rate of pumping. If a pump can empty a tank in 36 minutes at 12 gpm (gallons per minute), how long will it take to empty the same tank at 16 gpm?

21. The current in an electrical circuit varies inversely with the resistance. If the current is 9 amperes when the resistance is 4 ohms, what will be the current when the resistance is 12 ohms?

LESSON 58 Arithmetic Sequences

☐ **IDENTIFYING ARITHMETIC SEQUENCES** ···

An **arithmetic sequence** is an ordered list of numbers in which the difference between consecutive terms is constant. This difference is called a **common difference**, denoted d. In an arithmetic sequence, each term is found by adding its common difference to the previous term. See the example on the right.

Arithmetic sequence ($d = 2$)

$$1,\ 3,\ 5,\ 7,\ 9, \ldots$$

+2 +2 +2 +2

To determine if a sequence is arithmetic, subtract each term from the next term and see if there is a common difference.

➔ **EXAMPLE** Arithmetic or not?

1, 3, 6, 10, 15, 21, …

1. Subtract each term from the next term.
   $3 - 1 = 2, 6 - 3 = 3, 10 - 6 = 4, \ldots$
2. This sequence is not arithmetic because there is no common difference.

➔ **TRY IT** Arithmetic or not?

1. 1, 8, 15, 22, 29, …

2. 1, 2, 4, 8, 16, 32, …

☐ **FINDING RULES FOR ARITHMETIC SEQUENCES** ···

If the first term of an arithmetic sequence is a_1 and the common difference is d, then the nth term of the sequence is given by the rule:

$$a_n = a_1 + (n - 1)d$$

To find the rule for the nth term of an arithmetic sequence, first identify the first term and the common difference of the sequence. Then find the rule using the pattern on the right and simplify. (Don't just memorize the rule. Understand how it is derived.)

How the rule is derived:

$$a_2 = a_1 + d$$
$$a_3 = a_1 + d + d$$
$$a_4 = a_1 + d + d + d$$
…
$$a_n = a_1 + (n - 1)d$$

➔ **EXAMPLE** Find the rule for the nth term.

15, 10, 5, 0, −5, …

1. Identify a_1 and d: a_1 = 15 and d = −5
2. Find the rule: a_n = 15 + (n − 1) × (−5)
3. Simplify: a_n = = −5n + 20

➔ **TRY IT** Find the rule for the nth term.

3. 9, 7, 5, 3, 1, …

4. 6, 15, 24, 33, 42, …

Once you have the rule for the nth term of a sequence, you can find any term in the sequence.

➔ **EXAMPLE** Find the 28th term.

15, 10, 5, 0, −5, …

1. Find the rule: a_n = −5n + 20
2. Use the rule for n = 28:
   a_{28} = −5 × 28 + 20 = −120

➔ **TRY IT** Find the rule and the 10th term.

5. −5, 0, 5, 10, 15, …

6. 4, 10, 16, 22, 28, …

Identify as arithmetic or not arithmetic. If arithmetic, find the common difference.

7. $1, 4, 7, 10, 13, \ldots$

8. $5, 8, 13, 21, 34, \ldots$

9. $6, 13, 20, 27, 34, \ldots$

10 $7, 1, -5, -11, -17, \ldots$

Write the first five terms.

11. $a_1 = 2$ and $d = -5$

12. $a_1 = 5$ and $d = 9$

13. $a_1 = -1$ and $d = 4$

14. $a_1 = -9$ and $d = -3$

Find the rule for the nth term, then find the 10th term.

15. $-3, 2, 7, 12, 17, \ldots$

16. $8, 4, 0, -4, -8, \ldots$

17. $2, 9, 16, 23, 30, \ldots$

18. $-5, -1, 3, 7, 11, \ldots$

19. $3, -4, -11, -18, -25, \ldots$

20. $-2, 4, 10, 16, 22, \ldots$

EXTRA Find the rule for the nth term, then find the 10th term.

21. $7, 10, 13, 16, 19, \ldots$

22. $23, 18, 13, 8, 3, \ldots$

23. $35, 27, 19, 11, 3, \ldots$

24. $-23, -20, -17, -14, -11, \ldots$

CHALLENGE Find the value of x.

25. 35 is the xth term of the arithmetic sequence 3, 7, 11, 15, 19, …

26. 41 is the xth term of the arithmetic sequence 5, 8, 11, 14, 17, …

27. –50 is the xth term of the arithmetic sequence 20, 15, 10, 5, 0, …

28. 192 is the xth term of the arithmetic sequence –60, –48, –36, –24, –12, …

LESSON 59 Geometric Sequences

☐ IDENTIFYING GEOMETRIC SEQUENCES

A **geometric sequence** is an ordered list of numbers in which the ratio between consecutive terms is constant. This ratio is called a **common ratio**, denoted r. In a geometric sequence, each term is found by multiplying the previous term by its common ratio. See the example on the right.

Geometric sequence ($r = 2$)

3, 6, 12, 24, 48, ...

×2 ×2 ×2 ×2

To determine if a sequence is geometric, divide each term by the previous term and see if there is a common ratio.

➔ **EXAMPLE** Geometric or not?

1, 3, 9, 27, 81, ...

1. Divide each term by the previous term.
   $3 ÷ 1 = 3$, $9 ÷ 3 = 3$, $27 ÷ 9 = 3$, $81 ÷ 27 = 3$
2. This sequence is a geometric sequence with a common ratio of 3.

➔ **TRY IT** Geometric or not?

1. 2, 4, 6, 8, 10, ...

2. 2, 4, 8, 16, 32, ...

☐ FINDING RULES FOR GELOMETRIC SEQUENCES

If the first term of a geometric sequence is a_1 and the common ratio is r, then the nth term of the sequence is found by the rule:

$$a_n = a_1 \cdot r^{n-1}$$

To find the rule for the nth term of a geometric sequence, first identify the first term and the common ratio of the sequence. Then find the rule using the pattern on the right and simplify.

How the rule is derived:

$$a_2 = a_1 \cdot r$$
$$a_3 = a_1 \cdot r \cdot r$$
$$a_4 = a_1 \cdot r \cdot r \cdot r$$
...
$$a_n = a_1 \cdot r^{n-1}$$

➔ **EXAMPLE** Find the rule for the nth term.

3, 6, 12, 24, 48, ...

1. Identify $a_1 = 3$ and $r = 2$.
2. Find the rule: $a_n = 3(2)^{n-1}$

➔ **TRY IT** Find the rule for the nth term.

3. 2, 4, 8, 16, 32, ...

4. 4, 12, 36, 108, 324, ...

Once you have the rule for the nth term of a sequence, you can find any term in the sequence.

➔ **EXAMPLE** Find the 8th term.

3, −6, 12, −24, 48, ...

1. Identify $a_1 = 3$ and $r = -2$.
2. Find the rule: $a_n = 3(-2)^{n-1}$
3. Use the rule for $n = 8$:
   $a_8 = 3(-2)^{8-1} = -384$

➔ **TRY IT** Find the rule and the 7th term.

5. 4, −12, 36, −108, 324, ...

6. $9, 3, 1, \dfrac{1}{3}, \dfrac{1}{9}, ...$

Identify as geometric or not geometric. If geometric, find the common ratio.

7. $2, 8, 32, 128, 512, \ldots$

8. $81, 27, 9, 3, 1, \ldots$

9. $4, 9, 16, 25, 36, \ldots$

10 $-3, 6, -12, 24, -48, \ldots$

Write the first five terms.

11. $a_1 = 3$ and $r = 2$

12. $a_1 = 2$ and $r = 5$

13. $a_1 = 6$ and $r = -3$

14. $a_1 = -5$ and $r = -2$

Find the rule for the nth term, then find the 7th term.

15. $1, 5, 25, 125, 625, \ldots$

16. $5, -10, 20, -40, 80, \ldots$

17. $-4, -8, -16, -32, -64, \ldots$

18. $5, 20, 80, 320, 1280, \ldots$

19. $2, \dfrac{1}{2}, \dfrac{1}{8}, \dfrac{1}{32}, \dfrac{1}{128}, \ldots$

20. $5, \dfrac{1}{2}, \dfrac{1}{20}, \dfrac{1}{200}, \dfrac{1}{2000}, \ldots$

EXTRA Find the rule for the nth term, then find the 7th term.

21. $3, 12, 48, 192, 768, \ldots$

22. $5, -15, 45, -135, 405, \ldots$

23. $-4, 12, -36, 108, -324, \ldots$

24. $4, 20, 100, 500, 2500, \ldots$

CHALLENGE Find the value of x.

25. 768 is the xth term of the geometric sequence 3, 6, 12, 24, 48, ...

26. 1,024 is the xth term of the geometric sequence 1, –2, 4, –8, 16, ...

27. –4,374 is the xth term of the geometric sequence –2, –6, –18, –54, –162, ...

28. 1 is the xth term of the geometric sequence 512, 256, 128, 64, 32, ...

LESSON 60 Recursive Formulas for Sequences

☐ **REFRESH YOUR SKILLS** ··

Find the rule for the nth term. Review Lessons 58 and 59 if needed.

1. 15, 12, 9, 6, 3, ...

2. 3, 12, 48, 192, 768, ...

3. 6, 15, 24, 33, 42, ...

4. 5, −10, 20, −40, 80, ...

☐ **FINDING RECURSIVE FORMULAS FOR SEQUENCES** ···

Arithmetic and geometric sequences can be described using explicit formulas or recursive formulas. So far we have learned explicit formulas. An **explicit formula** is a formula that defines the nth term of a sequence as a function of n. A **recursive formula** is a formula that defines each term of a sequence using preceding term(s). Here are the formulas for the nth term.

Arithmetic sequence		Geometric sequence	
Explicit formula	Recursive formula	Explicit formula	Recursive formula
$a_n = a_1 + (n-1)d$	$a_n = a_{n-1} + d$	$a_n = a_1 \cdot r^{n-1}$	$a_n = r \cdot a_{n-1}$

Be sure to state the first term when you write a recursive formula. A recursive formula is a two-part formula: the first term and the rule for the nth term in terms of the preceding term(s). On the right is the recursive formula for a geometric sequence with a first term of 5 and a common ratio of 2.

Two-part formula:

$$a_1 = 5$$

$$a_n = 2a_{n-1}$$

To find the recursive formula for a sequence, 1) determine if the sequence is arithmetic or geometric, 2) find the first term and the common difference or ratio of the sequence, then 3) express the nth term in terms of the previous term. (Think about how to find the current term using the previous term.)

➔ **EXAMPLE** Arithmetic sequence

2, 5, 8, 11, 14, ...

1. The sequence is arithmetic.
2. Find a_1 and d: $a_1 = 2$ and $d = 3$
3. Find the two-part recursive formula:
   $a_1 - 2, a_n = a_{n-1} + 3$

➔ **TRY IT** Find the recursive formula.

5. 7, 9, 11, 13, 15, ...

6. 26, 20, 14, 8, 2, ...

➔ **EXAMPLE** Geometric sequence

4, 12, 36, 108, 324, ...

1. The sequence is geometric.
2. Find a_1 and r: $a_1 = 4$ and $r = 3$
3. Find the two-part recursive formula:
   $a_1 = 4, a_n = 3a_{n-1}$

➔ **TRY IT** Find the recursive formula.

7. 1, 2, 4, 8, 16, ...

8. 2, 10, 50, 250, 1250, ...

Find the first five terms and the explicit formula.

9. $a_1 = 5, a_n = a_{n-1} + 8$

10. $a_1 = 4, a_n = -2a_{n-1}$

11. $a_1 = 32, a_n = a_{n-1} - 7$

12. $a_1 = 5, a_n = 3a_{n-1}$

Find the first five terms and the recursive formula.

13. $a_n = 4n + 5$

14. $a_n = 3(2)^{n-1}$

15. $a_n = -5n + 21$

16. $a_n = 2(-3)^{n-1}$

Identify as arithmetic or geometric, then find the explicit formula and the recursive formula.

17. $2, -8, 32, -128, 512, \ldots$

18. $22, 13, 4, -5, -14, \ldots$

19. $35, 25, 15, 5, -5, \ldots$

20. $4, 20, 100, 500, 2500, \ldots$

EXTRA Find the explicit formula and the recursive formula.

21. $5, -15, 45, -135, 405, \ldots$

22. $13, 21, 29, 37, 45, \ldots$

23. $42, 47, 52, 57, 62, \ldots$

24. $1, \dfrac{1}{2}, \dfrac{1}{4}, \dfrac{1}{8}, \dfrac{1}{16}, \ldots$

CHALLENGE Find the explicit formula and the recursive formula for each arithmetic sequence with the two terms given. (*Hint*: Plug each term into the explicit formula. Then you get a system of two linear equations with two variables, a_1 and d.)

25. $a_8 = 19$ and $a_{12} = 27$

26. $a_3 = 1$ and $a_9 = 25$

27. $a_9 = -13$ and $a_{15} = -31$

28. $a_5 = 44$ and $a_{10} = 89$

29. $a_7 = 38$ and $a_{14} = 73$

30. $a_{13} = -40$ and $a_{18} = -70$

LESSON 61 Applications of Sequences

□ **REFRESH YOUR SKILLS** ···

Identify as arithmetic or geometric, then find the explicit formula and the recursive formula.
Review Lessons 58, 59, and 60 if needed.

1. 5, 10, 20, 40, 80, ...

2. 10, 15, 20, 25, 30, ...

□ **SOLVING SEQUENCE WORD PROBLEMS** ···

When solving a sequence word problem, 1) write out the first few terms to see if the sequence is arithmetic or geometric, 2) identify the first term and the common difference or ratio, 3) find the explicit formula for the sequence, and 4) answer what's being asked.

➜ **EXAMPLE** Arithmetic sequence

Emma put $3,000 in her savings account with a simple interest rate of 3% per year. What will be the balance of her account at the end of the 9th year?

    🔎 Notice that, at the end of the 1st year, the balance will be $3000 + 3% interest on $3000. So a_1= 3090, not 3000.

1. 3090, 3180, 3270, 3360, 3450, ...
   It is an arithmetic sequence.
2. a_1 = 3090 and d = 3000 · 3% = 90
3. a_n = 90n + 3000
4. When n = 9, a_9 = 3810.
   The balance will be $3,810.

➜ **TRY IT** Write the explicit formula, then solve.

3. Samantha put $5,000 in her savings account with a simple interest rate of 4% per year. What will be the balance of her account at the end of the 10th year?

4. A tree in Lisa's backyard grows 1.2 feet per year. It was 5 feet tall at the beginning of this year. What will be the height of the tree at the beginning of the 8th year?

➜ **EXAMPLE** Geometric sequence

A ball is dropped from a height of 256 feet. After the ball hits the floor, it rebounds to 50% of its previous height. How high will the ball rebound after its fifth bounce?

    🔎 Notice that, in our sequence, we define a_n as the height AFTER the nth bounce. So a_1 = 128, not 256.

1. 128, 64, 32, ...
   It is a geometric sequence.
2. a_1 = 128 and r = 0.5
3. a_n = 128$(0.5)^{n-1}$
4. When n = 5, a_5 = 8.
   It will bounce to 8 feet.

➜ **TRY IT** Write the explicit formula, then solve.

5. A ball is dropped from a height of 128 feet. After the ball hits the floor, it rebounds to 75% of its previous height. How high will the ball rebound after its seventh bounce?

6. As a car gets older, its resale value goes down by 10% each year. Kris bought a new car for $20,000. What will be the value of the car after 6 years?

Find the explicit formula for the sequence.

7. −12, −5, 2, 9, 16, ...

8. 2, 6, 18, 54, 162, ...

For each problem, 1) identify the sequence as arithmetic or geometric, 2) write the explicit formula for the sequence, and 3) answer what's being asked. Round your answers to the nearest hundredth.

9. Mia is studying algebra. She scored 72% on her first quiz. Then she scored 76% and 80% on her next two quizzes. If this pattern continues, what will be her score on her 7th quiz?

10. During a science experiment, Jessica found that bacteria double every hour. There were 10 bacteria at 1 pm. How many bacteria will be there at 8 pm on the same day?

11. Mark started a job that paid $62,000 a year. Each year after the first, he received a raise of $800. What was Mark's salary in his 8th year of employment?

12. As a car gets older, its resale value goes down by 20% each year. Kris bought a new car for $18,000. What will be the value of the car after 7 years?

13. The population of a town is 30,000 this year, and it is expected to increase by 10% per year. What will be the population of the town after 5 years?

14. Sandra has been practicing for a marathon. She ran 5 km daily during the first week, 7 km daily during the second week, and 9 km daily during the third week. If this pattern continues, how far will she run daily during the 10th week?

EXTRA Solve. Round your answers to the nearest hundredth.

15. A new website had a total of 500 hits this week. The traffic is estimated to increase by 100% per week. How many hits will the website have in the 5th week?

16. The starting salary for Alex's job is $52,000 a year. He is to receive a 5% raise each year. What will his salary be in the 7th year?

17. Joe has been practicing for a 43–km marathon. He ran 4 km daily during the first week, 7 km daily during the second week, and 10 km daily during the third week. If this pattern continues, in which week will he run the full distance of a marathon?

18. The sum of the interior angles of a triangle is 180, of a quadrilateral is 360, and of a pentagon is 540. If this pattern continues, what will be the sum of the interior angles of a decagon (10 sides)?

LESSON 62 Catch Up and Review!

Catch up if you are behind. Use the review problems below to make sure you're on track.

LESSON 56 Write a direct variation equation, then solve.

1. Suppose y varies directly with x, and $y = 8$ when $x = 2$. Find y when $x = 3$.

2. Suppose y varies directly with x, and $y = -4$ when $x = 9$. Find x when $y = -8$.

3. The distance a car travels varies directly with the time it travels. If a car travels 285 kilometers in 3 hours, how far will it travel in 5 hours?

4. The weight of an object on Earth varies directly with its weight on Pluto. An object that weighs 50 pounds on Earth would weigh only about 4 pounds on Pluto. How much will a 10-pound object on Pluto weigh on Earth?

LESSON 57 Write an inverse variation equation, then solve.

5. Suppose y varies inversely with x, and $y = 4$ when $x = 3$. Find y when $x = 4$.

6. Suppose y varies inversely with x, and $y = 3/4$ when $x = 2$. Find x when $y = 3$.

7. The monthly sales of a certain product varies inversely with its price. If 180 units are sold at $5.50, how many units will be sold at $6.00?

8. The length of a guitar string varies inversely with the frequency of its vibrations. If a 10-inch guitar string vibrates at 420 cycles per second (Hz), what will be the frequency of a 15-inch string?

LESSON 58 Find the explicit formula, then find the 10th term.

9. 8, 10, 12, 14, 16, ...

10. −1, 3, 7, 11, 15, ...

11. 3, 0, −3, −6, −9, ...

12. −5, −13, −21, −29, −37, ...

LESSON 59 Find the explicit formula, then find the 7th term.

13. 2, 6, 18, 54, 162, ...

14. 8, −16, 32, −64, 128, ...

15. 2, −10, 50, −250, 1250, ...

16. 128, 64, 32, 16, 8, ...

LESSON 60 Identify as arithmetic or geometric, then find the explicit and recursive formulas.

17. 8, 17, 26, 35, 44, ...

18. 4, 20, 100, 500, 2500, ...

LESSON 61 Solve. Round your answers to the nearest hundredth.

19. A new online store had 32 orders on the day it opened. Then it had 48 and 64 orders on the next two days. If this pattern continues, how many orders will the store have on its 20th day?

20. A ball is dropped from a height of 12 meters. After the ball hits the floor, it rebounds to 75% of its previous height. How high will the ball rebound after its tenth bounce?

☐ **MIXED REVIEW: PRE-ALGEBRA** ··

Brush up on the topics covered in Pre-Algebra.

21.

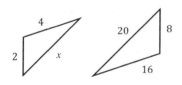

When two figures are similar, their corresponding sides are proportional, meaning that the ratios of the corresponding sides are equal.

The two triangles on the left are similar. Find the value of x.

22. On a sunny day, two trees cast shadows of 15 feet and 25 feet. The shorter tree is 12 feet tall. How tall is the taller tree?

23. A map has a scale of 0.5 in = 25 miles. What is the actual distance when the distance on the map is 1.8 inches?

24. A point with coordinates (−3, 1) is translated 4 units right and 2 units down and then reflected across the x-axis. What are the new coordinates?

LESSON 63 Radicals

☐ FINDING SQUARE ROOTS OF NUMBERS ···

A **square root** of a number a is a number x such that $x^2 = a$. For example, both 3 and -3 are square roots of 9 because $3^2 = 9$ and $(-3)^2 = 9$. Every positive number has two square roots, one positive and one negative. Zero has exactly one square root, and negative numbers do not have square roots. The **radical sign** $\sqrt{}$ indicates the non-negative square root.

➔ **EXAMPLE** Find the square root.

$\sqrt{0} = 0 \qquad$ because $0^2 = 0$

$\sqrt{9} = 3 \qquad$ because $3^2 = 9$

$\sqrt{0.25} = 0.5 \qquad$ because $0.5^2 = 0.25$

$\sqrt{-1} = ? \qquad$ Not a real number

➔ **TRY IT** Find the square root.

1. $\sqrt{4}$ 2. $\sqrt{64}$

3. $\sqrt{0.01}$ 4. $\sqrt{0.49}$

☐ FINDING CUBE ROOTS OF NUMBERS ···

A **cube root** of a number a is a number x such that $x^3 = a$. For example, 2 is the cube root of 8 because $2^3 = 8$. The cube root of a positive number is positive, and the cube root of a negative number is negative. The cube root symbol $\sqrt[3]{}$ is the radical sign with a little 3 that indicates the cube root.

➔ **EXAMPLE** Find the cube root.

$\sqrt[3]{0} = 0 \qquad$ because $0^3 = 0$

$\sqrt[3]{8} = 2 \qquad$ because $2^3 = 8$

$\sqrt[3]{-8} = -2 \qquad$ because $(-2)^3 = -8$

$\sqrt[3]{0.001} = 0.1 \qquad$ because $0.1^3 = 0.001$

➔ **TRY IT** Find the cube root.

5. $\sqrt[3]{1}$ 6. $\sqrt[3]{125}$

7. $\sqrt[3]{-27}$ 8. $\sqrt[3]{0.008}$

☐ FINDING NTH ROOTS OF NUMBERS ···

An **nth root** of a number a is a number x such that $x^n = a$. It is also called a **radical**. The nth root symbol is the radical sign with a little n that indicates the nth root. In the radical $\sqrt[n]{x}$, the integer n is called the **index** and the number x is called the **radicand**. When $n = 2$, the radical is a square root and the index 2 is usually omitted. When $n = 3$, the radical is a cube root.

➔ **EXAMPLE** Find the nth root.

$\sqrt[4]{81} = 3 \qquad$ because $3^4 = 81$

$\sqrt[5]{32} = 2 \qquad$ because $2^5 = 32$

$\sqrt[7]{-1} = -1 \qquad$ because $(-1)^7 = -1$

$\sqrt[5]{-243} = -3 \qquad$ because $(-3)^5 = -243$

➔ **TRY IT** Find the nth root.

9. $\sqrt[6]{1}$ 10. $\sqrt[4]{16}$

11. $\sqrt[4]{625}$ 12. $\sqrt[5]{-100,000}$

Find the square root.

13. $\sqrt{1}$ **14.** $\sqrt{9}$ **15.** $\sqrt{49}$ **16.** $\sqrt{144}$

17. $\sqrt{0.01}$ **18.** $\sqrt{0.36}$ **19.** $\sqrt{1.21}$ **20.** $\sqrt{1.96}$

Find the cube root.

21. $\sqrt[3]{0}$ **22.** $\sqrt[3]{8}$ **23.** $\sqrt[3]{27}$ **24.** $\sqrt[3]{1{,}000}$

25. $\sqrt[3]{-1}$ **26.** $\sqrt[3]{-64}$ **27.** $\sqrt[3]{-125}$ **28.** $\sqrt[3]{-0.027}$

Find the nth root.

29. $\sqrt[5]{0}$ **30.** $\sqrt[7]{-1}$ **31.** $\sqrt[5]{-32}$ **32.** $\sqrt[6]{64}$

33. $\sqrt[4]{81}$ **34.** $\sqrt[7]{-128}$ **35.** $\sqrt[4]{10{,}000}$ **36.** $\sqrt[4]{160{,}000}$

CHALLENGE Evaluate using the order of operations. (*Hint*: Radical expressions such as square roots are treated the same as exponents in the order of operations.)

37. $2^3 - \sqrt{16} \times (-4)$ **38.** $\sqrt{25} \times \sqrt[3]{27} - 3^2$

39. $\sqrt{4 + 7 \times 3} + \sqrt[3]{64}$ **40.** $\sqrt{144} \div \sqrt{36} - \sqrt{(2^2 \times 5^2)}$

41. $\left(3^3 - \sqrt{49}\right)^2 \div \sqrt[5]{10^5}$ **42.** $(\sqrt{81} - 6)^3 \div 3^3 \times 5^2 \times \sqrt[5]{1}$

CHALLENGE Find the mystery numbers.

43. I am a 2-digit perfect square (a square of a whole number). The sum of my digits is my square root. What number am I?

44. I am a 2-digit perfect square. My square root is a prime number. All of my digits are also prime numbers. What number am I?

45. I am a 2-digit number divisible by 3 and 5 but not by 10. The sum of my digits is a perfect square number. What number am I?

LESSON 64 Simplifying Radicals

□ **REFRESH YOUR SKILLS** ···

Evaluate. Review Lesson 63 if needed.

1. $\sqrt{25}$ **2.** $\sqrt{81}$ **3.** $\sqrt[3]{-27}$ **4.** $\sqrt[5]{32}$

□ **SIMPLIFYING SQUARE ROOTS** ···

Simplifying a radical is to make the radicand, the number under the radical sign, as small as possible. There are two rules that can be used when simplifying radicals. The **product rule for radicals** says that the product of two radicals is the radical of the product. The **quotient rule for radicals** says that the quotient of two radicals is the radical of the quotient.

Product rule: $\sqrt[n]{ab} = \sqrt[n]{a} \cdot \sqrt[n]{b}$

Quotient rule: $\sqrt[n]{\dfrac{a}{b}} = \dfrac{\sqrt[n]{a}}{\sqrt[n]{b}}$

A **perfect square** is a square of a whole number. 4 is a perfect square because it is the square of 2.

To simplify a square root, look for the largest perfect square factor of the radicand and pull its square root out of the radical. For example, in the radical $\sqrt{20}$ below, 4 is the largest perfect square factor of 20 and so we can pull its square root 2 out of the radical.

➜ **EXAMPLE** Simplify.

a. $\sqrt{20} = \sqrt{4 \cdot 5} = \sqrt{4} \cdot \sqrt{5} = 2\sqrt{5}$

b. $2\sqrt{18} = 2 \cdot \sqrt{9} \cdot \sqrt{2} = 6\sqrt{2}$

c. $\sqrt{\dfrac{8}{49}} = \dfrac{\sqrt{8}}{\sqrt{49}} = \dfrac{\sqrt{4} \cdot \sqrt{2}}{7} = \dfrac{2\sqrt{2}}{7}$

➜ **TRY IT** Simplify.

5. $\sqrt{32}$ **6.** $4\sqrt{28}$

7. $\sqrt{\dfrac{27}{25}}$ **8.** $\sqrt{\dfrac{45}{64}}$

□ **SIMPLIFYING CUBE ROOTS** ···

A **perfect cube** is a cube of a whole number. To simplify a cube root, look for the largest perfect cube factor of the radicand and pull its cube root out of the radical.

➜ **EXAMPLE** Simplify.

a. $3\sqrt[3]{16} = 3 \cdot \sqrt[3]{8} \cdot \sqrt[3]{2} = 6\sqrt[3]{2}$

b. $\sqrt[3]{-54} = \sqrt[3]{-27} \cdot \sqrt[3]{2} = -3\sqrt[3]{2}$

c. $\sqrt[3]{\dfrac{40}{27}} = \dfrac{\sqrt[3]{40}}{\sqrt[3]{27}} = \dfrac{\sqrt[3]{8} \cdot \sqrt[3]{5}}{\sqrt[3]{27}} = \dfrac{2\sqrt[3]{5}}{3}$

➜ **TRY IT** Simplify.

9. $\sqrt[3]{24}$ **10.** $5\sqrt[3]{-40}$

11. $\sqrt[3]{\dfrac{81}{64}}$ **12.** $\sqrt[3]{\dfrac{32}{125}}$

☐ SIMPLIFYING RADICALS USING PRIME FACTORIZATION ·······································

You can also use prime factorization to simplify radicals. **Prime factorization** is a way of writing a number using only factors that are prime. For example, the prime factorization of 12 is $2 \times 2 \times 3$.

To simplify a square root using prime factorization, factor the radicand into its prime factors and pull out any factors that occur in pairs. To simplify a cube root, pull out any factors that occur three times.

➜ **EXAMPLE** Simplify using prime factorization.

a. $\sqrt{48} = \sqrt{2^2 \cdot 2^2 \cdot 3} = \sqrt{2^2} \cdot \sqrt{2^2} \cdot \sqrt{3} = 2 \cdot 2 \cdot \sqrt{3} = 4\sqrt{3}$

b. $\sqrt[3]{432} = \sqrt[3]{2^3 \cdot 3^3 \cdot 2} = \sqrt[3]{2^3} \cdot \sqrt[3]{3^3} \cdot \sqrt[3]{2} = 2 \cdot 3 \cdot \sqrt[3]{2} = 6\sqrt[3]{2}$

➜ **TRY IT** Simplify.

13. $\sqrt{80}$ 14. $\sqrt{112}$ 15. $\sqrt[3]{135}$ 16. $\sqrt[3]{250}$

☐ EXERCISE YOUR SKILLS ·······································

Simplify.

17. $\sqrt{8}$ 18. $\sqrt{18}$ 19. $\sqrt{24}$ 20. $\sqrt{50}$

21. $7\sqrt{20}$ 22. $2\sqrt{28}$ 23. $\sqrt[3]{40}$ 24. $5\sqrt[3]{-16}$

25. $\sqrt{\dfrac{18}{25}}$ 26. $3\sqrt{\dfrac{50}{81}}$ 27. $\sqrt[3]{\dfrac{48}{125}}$ 28. $10\sqrt[3]{\dfrac{81}{1000}}$

EXTRA Simplify.

29. $\sqrt{12}$ 30. $\sqrt{27}$ 31. $\sqrt{45}$ 32. $\sqrt{63}$

33. $9\sqrt{48}$ 34. $2\sqrt{72}$ 35. $\sqrt[3]{-54}$ 36. $2\sqrt[3]{81}$

37. $\sqrt{\dfrac{45}{16}}$ 38. $4\sqrt{\dfrac{27}{64}}$ 39. $\sqrt[3]{\dfrac{135}{64}}$ 40. $6\sqrt[3]{\dfrac{32}{27}}$

LESSON 65 Simplifying Radicals with Variables

Simplify. Review Lesson 64 if needed.

1. $\sqrt{18}$ **2.** $2\sqrt{20}$ **3.** $\sqrt[3]{-16}$ **4.** $3\sqrt[3]{54}$

□ **SIMPLIFYING RADICALS WITH VARIABLES** ···

To simplify a radical with variables as the radicand, look for factors with powers that match the index and pull them out. Remember, the square root of any number squared is simply that number. Likewise, the cube root of any number cubed is simply that number.

$$\sqrt{a^2} = a, \text{ if } a \geq 0$$
$$\sqrt[3]{a^3} = a$$

➜ **EXAMPLE** Simplify. Assume that all variables are positive.

a. $\sqrt{a^5} = \sqrt{a^2 \cdot a^2 \cdot a} = \sqrt{a^2} \cdot \sqrt{a^2} \cdot \sqrt{a} = a \cdot a \cdot \sqrt{a} = a^2\sqrt{a}$

b. $\sqrt{8a^3b^2} = \sqrt{2^2 \cdot 2 \cdot a^2 \cdot a \cdot b^2} = \sqrt{2^2} \cdot \sqrt{a^2} \cdot \sqrt{b^2} \cdot \sqrt{2a} = 2ab\sqrt{2a}$

c. $\sqrt{\dfrac{27a^3}{b^6}} = \dfrac{\sqrt{27a^3}}{\sqrt{b^6}} = \dfrac{\sqrt{3^2 \cdot 3 \cdot a^2 \cdot a}}{\sqrt{b^2 \cdot b^2 \cdot b^2}} = \dfrac{\sqrt{3^2} \cdot \sqrt{a^2} \cdot \sqrt{3a}}{\sqrt{b^2} \cdot \sqrt{b^2} \cdot \sqrt{b^2}} = \dfrac{3 \cdot a \cdot \sqrt{3a}}{b \cdot b \cdot b} = \dfrac{3a\sqrt{3a}}{b^3}$

➜ **TRY IT** Simplify. Assume that all variables are positive.

5. $\sqrt{x^3}$ **6.** $\sqrt{24x^2y^6}$ **7.** $\sqrt{\dfrac{16x^5}{25y^8}}$

➜ **EXAMPLE** Simplify. Assume that all variables are positive.

a. $\sqrt[3]{a^7} = \sqrt[3]{a^3 \cdot a^3 \cdot a} = \sqrt[3]{a^3} \cdot \sqrt[3]{a^3} \cdot \sqrt[3]{a} = a \cdot a \cdot \sqrt[3]{a} = a^2\sqrt[3]{a}$

b. $\sqrt[3]{24a^3b^5} = \sqrt[3]{2^3 \cdot 3 \cdot a^3 \cdot b^3 \cdot b^2} = \sqrt[3]{2^3} \cdot \sqrt[3]{a^3} \cdot \sqrt[3]{b^3} \cdot \sqrt[3]{3b^2} = 2ab\sqrt[3]{3b^2}$

c. $\sqrt[3]{\dfrac{6a^8}{b^3c^6}} = \dfrac{\sqrt[3]{6a^8}}{\sqrt[3]{b^3c^6}} = \dfrac{\sqrt[3]{6 \cdot a^3 \cdot a^3 \cdot a^2}}{\sqrt[3]{b^3 \cdot c^3 \cdot c^3}} = \dfrac{\sqrt[3]{a^3} \cdot \sqrt[3]{a^3} \cdot \sqrt[3]{6 \cdot a^2}}{\sqrt[3]{b^3} \cdot \sqrt[3]{c^3} \cdot \sqrt[3]{c^3}} = \dfrac{a \cdot a \cdot \sqrt[3]{6a^2}}{b \cdot c \cdot c} = \dfrac{a^2\sqrt[3]{6a^2}}{bc^2}$

➜ **TRY IT** Simplify. Assume that all variables are positive.

8. $\sqrt[3]{x^4}$ **9.** $\sqrt[3]{27x^3y^6}$ **10.** $\sqrt[3]{\dfrac{16x^3y^2}{125z^3}}$

Simplify. Assume that all variables are positive.

11. $\sqrt{x^4}$

12. $\sqrt{16x^6}$

13. $\sqrt{mn^7}$

14. $\sqrt{25m^2n^2}$

15. $\sqrt{p^3q^3r}$

16. $\sqrt{75p^2qr}$

17. $\sqrt{\dfrac{x^3}{y^4}}$

18. $\sqrt{\dfrac{72x}{y^8}}$

19. $\sqrt[3]{x^6}$

20. $\sqrt[3]{125x^5}$

21. $\sqrt[3]{\dfrac{x^4}{y^6z^3}}$

22. $\sqrt[3]{\dfrac{-32x^2y^3}{27z^3}}$

EXTRA Simplify. Assume that all variables are positive.

23. $\sqrt{y^5}$

24. $\sqrt{12y^2}$

25. $\sqrt{a^4b^4}$

26. $\sqrt{8a^2b^3}$

27. $\sqrt{s^3t^6u^4}$

28. $\sqrt{98s^8t^2u^5}$

29. $\sqrt{\dfrac{x^6}{y^2z^2}}$

30. $\sqrt{\dfrac{75x^7z^3}{36y^2}}$

31. $\sqrt[3]{a^4b}$

32. $\sqrt[3]{27a^3b^2}$

33. $\sqrt[3]{\dfrac{x^7}{y^3}}$

34. $\sqrt[3]{\dfrac{-8x^4y^2}{z^6}}$

LESSON 66 Adding and Subtracting Radicals

Simplify by combining like terms. Review Lesson 2 if needed.

1. $x - 2 + 4x - 5$

2. $3x + 5y + 2 - x - y + 3$

Simplify. Review Lesson 64 if needed.

3. $\sqrt{27}$

4. $\sqrt{72}$

5. $4\sqrt{28}$

6. $3\sqrt{45}$

☐ **ADDING AND SUBTRACTING LIKE RADICALS** ·································

Radicals with the same index and radicand are called **like radicals**. Here are some examples.

$\sqrt{2}$ and $3\sqrt{2}$	$\sqrt{5}$ and $\sqrt[3]{5}$	$-2\sqrt{ab}$ and $5\sqrt{ab}$	$\sqrt{ab}$ and $\sqrt{2ab}$
Like radicals	Not like radicals	Like radicals	Not like radicals

You can add and subtract like radicals in the same way you add and subtract like terms. To add or subtract like radicals, add or subtract the coefficients and keep the radicals the same.

➜ **EXAMPLE** Simplify.

a. $2\sqrt{2} + 3\sqrt{2} = (2 + 3)\sqrt{2} = 5\sqrt{2}$

b. $4\sqrt{5} - 5\sqrt{5} = (4 - 5)\sqrt{5} = -\sqrt{5}$

➜ **TRY IT** Simplify.

7. $5\sqrt{3} + \sqrt{3}$

8. $2\sqrt{7} - 6\sqrt{7}$

☐ **ADDING AND SUBTRACTING RADICALS** ····································

When adding and subtracting radicals, you can combine only like radicals. To add or subtract radicals, simplify each radical separately and then add or subtract like radicals.

➜ **EXAMPLE** Simplify.

a. $\sqrt{8} + \sqrt{18} = \sqrt{4 \cdot 2} + \sqrt{9 \cdot 2} = 2\sqrt{2} + 3\sqrt{2} = (2 + 3)\sqrt{2} = 5\sqrt{2}$

b. $3\sqrt{12} - 4\sqrt{27} = 3\sqrt{4 \cdot 3} - 4\sqrt{9 \cdot 3} = 6\sqrt{3} - 12\sqrt{3} = (6 - 12)\sqrt{3} = -6\sqrt{3}$

c. $2\sqrt{7} + \sqrt{20} - \sqrt{45} = 2\sqrt{7} + 2\sqrt{5} - 3\sqrt{5} = 2\sqrt{7} + (2 - 3)\sqrt{3} = 2\sqrt{7} - \sqrt{5}$

➜ **TRY IT** Simplify.

9. $\sqrt{12} + \sqrt{3}$

10. $\sqrt{24} - \sqrt{6}$

11. $4\sqrt{8} - 3\sqrt{32}$

12. $\sqrt{20} - \sqrt{28} + 3\sqrt{63}$

Simplify.

13. $\sqrt{20} - \sqrt{5}$

14. $\sqrt{7} + \sqrt{28}$

15. $\sqrt{63} - \sqrt{28}$

16. $\sqrt{75} + \sqrt{27}$

17. $\sqrt{48} + 5\sqrt{12}$

18. $3\sqrt{90} - 4\sqrt{40}$

19. $2\sqrt{18} - 3\sqrt{98}$

20. $2\sqrt{96} - 2\sqrt{150}$

21. $5\sqrt{5} + 5\sqrt{20} - \sqrt{125}$

22. $3\sqrt{50} - 3\sqrt{24} - 2\sqrt{98}$

EXTRA Simplify.

23. $\sqrt{18} - \sqrt{2}$

24. $\sqrt{8} + \sqrt{72}$

25. $\sqrt{12} - \sqrt{48}$

26. $\sqrt{45} - \sqrt{80}$

27. $\sqrt{24} + \sqrt{54}$

28. $\sqrt{50} + \sqrt{98}$

29. $\sqrt{32} - \sqrt{18}$

30. $\sqrt{99} + \sqrt{44}$

31. $3\sqrt{45} + 5\sqrt{20}$

32. $4\sqrt{80} + 2\sqrt{180}$

33. $2\sqrt{18} + \sqrt{8} - 4\sqrt{27}$

34. $3\sqrt{27} + 2\sqrt{20} - 2\sqrt{45}$

CHALLENGE Simplify.

35. $16\sqrt{\dfrac{5}{64}} + \sqrt{20}$

36. $14\sqrt{\dfrac{16}{49}} - \sqrt{169}$

37. $6\sqrt{\dfrac{12}{9}} - 8\sqrt{\dfrac{27}{16}}$

38. $3\sqrt{\dfrac{8}{81}} + 4\sqrt{\dfrac{8}{36}}$

LESSON 67 Multiplying and Dividing Radicals

☐ **REFRESH YOUR SKILLS** ···

Simplify. Review Lessons 64 through 66 if needed.

1. $\sqrt{8x^3}$

2. $4\sqrt{2} - \sqrt{18}$

☐ **MULTIPLYING RADICALS** ···

When multiplying radicals with the same index, we use the product rule for radicals. Simply multiply the coefficients and multiply the radicands. Then simplify the result.

➔ **EXAMPLE** Multiply.

a. $\sqrt{2} \cdot \sqrt{6} = \sqrt{2 \cdot 6} = \sqrt{12} = \sqrt{2^2 \cdot 3} = 2\sqrt{3}$

b. $2\sqrt{6} \cdot 4\sqrt{3} = 2 \cdot 4 \cdot \sqrt{6 \cdot 3} = 8\sqrt{18} = 8\sqrt{3^2 \cdot 2} = 8 \cdot 3 \cdot \sqrt{2} = 24\sqrt{2}$

c. $\sqrt{6}(\sqrt{2} + 3\sqrt{6}) = \sqrt{6} \cdot \sqrt{2} + \sqrt{6} \cdot 3\sqrt{6} = \sqrt{12} + 3\sqrt{36} = 2\sqrt{3} + 18$

d. $\sqrt{3x^3} \cdot 5\sqrt{8x} = 5 \cdot \sqrt{24x^4} = 5 \cdot \sqrt{2^2 \cdot 6 \cdot x^2 \cdot x^2} = 5 \cdot 2 \cdot x \cdot x \cdot \sqrt{6} = 10x^2\sqrt{6}$

➔ **TRY IT** Multiply.

3. $\sqrt{5} \cdot \sqrt{10}$

4. $3\sqrt{2} \cdot 5\sqrt{3}$

5. $\sqrt{3}(5\sqrt{5} - \sqrt{6})$

6. $3\sqrt{6x} \cdot \sqrt{8x}$

☐ **DIVIDING RADICALS** ··

Division works the same way, using the quotient rule for radicals. Simply divide the coefficients and divide the radicands. Then simplify the result.

➔ **EXAMPLE** Divide.

a. $\dfrac{\sqrt{40}}{\sqrt{5}} = \sqrt{\dfrac{40}{5}} = \sqrt{8} = 2\sqrt{2}$

b. $\dfrac{3\sqrt{3}}{\sqrt{27}} = 3 \cdot \sqrt{\dfrac{3}{27}} = 3 \cdot \sqrt{\dfrac{1}{9}} = 3 \cdot \dfrac{1}{3} = 1$

c. $\dfrac{\sqrt{18x^3y^2}}{\sqrt{3xy}} = \sqrt{\dfrac{18x^3y^2}{3xy}} = \sqrt{6x^2y} = x\sqrt{6y}$

➔ **TRY IT** Divide.

7. $\dfrac{\sqrt{18}}{\sqrt{2}}$

8. $\dfrac{4\sqrt{5}}{\sqrt{20}}$

9. $\dfrac{\sqrt{48x^5y}}{\sqrt{6xy}}$

RATIONALIZING DENOMINATORS

Note that, when simplifying radicals, you do not leave a radical in the denominator of a fraction. You must rewrite the fraction as an equivalent fraction with a rational number in the denominator. This process is called **rationalizing the denominator**. To rationalize a denominator, multiply both numerator and denominator by a radical that will get rid of the radical in the denominator.

➜ **EXAMPLE** Simplify.

a. $\dfrac{3}{\sqrt{3}} = \dfrac{3}{\sqrt{3}} \cdot \dfrac{\sqrt{3}}{\sqrt{3}} = \dfrac{3\sqrt{3}}{3} = \sqrt{3}$

b. $\dfrac{\sqrt{2}}{\sqrt{7}} = \dfrac{\sqrt{2}}{\sqrt{7}} \cdot \dfrac{\sqrt{7}}{\sqrt{7}} = \dfrac{\sqrt{14}}{7}$

➜ **TRY IT** Simplify.

10. $\dfrac{1}{\sqrt{5}}$

11. $\dfrac{4}{\sqrt{2}}$

12. $\dfrac{\sqrt{7}}{\sqrt{3}}$

13. $\dfrac{3\sqrt{5}}{\sqrt{6}}$

EXERCISE YOUR SKILLS

Simplify. Assume that all variables are positive.

14. $\sqrt{3} \cdot \sqrt{5}$

15. $\sqrt{2} \cdot 3\sqrt{14}$

16. $\sqrt{5}(\sqrt{3} - \sqrt{10})$

17. $\sqrt{6x^2} \cdot \sqrt{2x^3}$

18. $\dfrac{4\sqrt{15}}{\sqrt{60}}$

19. $\dfrac{\sqrt{27x^3}}{\sqrt{3x}}$

Rationalize the denominator.

20. $\dfrac{2}{\sqrt{2}}$

21. $\dfrac{4}{\sqrt{6}}$

22. $\dfrac{5}{2\sqrt{5}}$

23. $\dfrac{3\sqrt{2}}{\sqrt{3}}$

EXTRA Simplify. Assume that all variables are positive.

24. $\sqrt{6} \cdot \sqrt{3}$

25. $2\sqrt{5} \cdot \sqrt{15}$

26. $\sqrt{2}(4 + 2\sqrt{6})$

27. $\sqrt{x^3} \cdot \sqrt{x^7}$

28. $\dfrac{\sqrt{90}}{\sqrt{5}}$

29. $\dfrac{\sqrt{75x^4y^6}}{\sqrt{3x^2y^3}}$

LESSON 68 Solving Radical Equations

□ **REFRESH YOUR SKILLS** ···

Solve. Review Lesson 3 if needed.

1. $2x + 3 = 9$

2. $3x - 5 = x + 7$

□ **SOLVING RADICAL EQUATIONS** ···

A **radical equation** is an equation that contains a radical expression with a variable in the radicand. To solve a radical equation involving a square root, 1) isolate the radical on one side, 2) eliminate the radical by squaring both sides, and then 3) solve for the variable.

➜ **EXAMPLE** Solve $2\sqrt{x + 1} + 3 = 9$.

$$2\sqrt{x + 1} + 3 = 9$$

$$\sqrt{x + 1} = 3 \qquad \text{Isolate the radical.}$$

$$\left(\sqrt{x + 1}\right)^2 = 3^2 \qquad \text{Square both sides.}$$

$$x + 1 = 9 \qquad \text{Solve for } x.$$

$$x = 8 \qquad \text{Solution}$$

➜ **TRY IT** Solve.

3. $\sqrt{x - 5} + 2 = 4$

4. $3\sqrt{2x + 4} - 5 = 7$

➜ **EXAMPLE** Solve $\sqrt{3x - 1} = \sqrt{x + 5}$.

$$\sqrt{3x - 1} = \sqrt{x + 5}$$

$$\left(\sqrt{3x - 1}\right)^2 = \left(\sqrt{x + 5}\right)^2 \qquad \text{Square both sides, then}$$

$$3x - 1 = x + 5 \qquad \text{solve for } x.$$

$$x = 3 \qquad \text{Solution}$$

➜ **TRY IT** Solve.

5. $\sqrt{x + 2} = \sqrt{6 - x}$

6. $\sqrt{4x - 9} = \sqrt{3x}$

Solving an equation involving a cube root is not much different. Instead of squaring both sides, you cube both sides to eliminate the radical.

➜ **EXAMPLE** Solve $2\sqrt[3]{2x + 7} = 6$.

$$2\sqrt[3]{2x + 7} = 6$$

$$\sqrt[3]{2x + 7} = 3 \qquad \text{Isolate the radical.}$$

$$\left(\sqrt[3]{2x + 7}\right)^3 = 3^3 \qquad \text{Cube both sides.}$$

$$2x + 7 = 27 \qquad \text{Solve for } x.$$

$$x = 10 \qquad \text{Solution}$$

➜ **TRY IT** Solve.

7. $\sqrt[3]{x} + 4 = 7$

8. $\sqrt[3]{x + 6} = \sqrt[3]{2x}$

☐ **CHECKING FOR EXTRANEOUS SOLUTIONS** ···

When solving a radical equation, you sometimes get a solution to the squared equation that is not a solution to the original equation. Such a solution is called an **extraneous solution**. So you must always check your solution in the original equation and discard the solution if it is an extraneous solution.

➜ **EXAMPLE** Solve $\sqrt{x} + 6 = 4$.

$$\sqrt{x} + 6 = 4$$

$$\sqrt{x} = -2 \qquad \text{Isolate the radical.}$$

$$\left(\sqrt{x}\right)^2 = (-2)^2 \qquad \text{Square both sides.}$$

$$x = 4 \qquad \text{Solve for } x.$$

$$\sqrt{4} + 6 \neq 4 \qquad \text{Check.}$$

The equation has no solution.

➜ **TRY IT** Solve.

9. $\sqrt{x} + 7 = 4$

10. $\sqrt{x - 5} + 3 = 2$

☐ **EXERCISE YOUR SKILLS** ···

Solve. Check for extraneous solutions.

11. $\sqrt{x + 9} = 6$

12. $\sqrt{3x + 7} = 5$

13. $\sqrt{x} + 2 = 7$

14. $5\sqrt{x} + 3 = 8$

15. $\sqrt{x - 4} + 8 = 2$

16. $3\sqrt{7x + 2} - 5 = 7$

17. $\sqrt{x} = \sqrt{2x - 5}$

18. $\sqrt{5x - 1} = \sqrt{3x + 7}$

19. $\sqrt[3]{x - 5} + 4 = 2$

20. $\sqrt[3]{x + 4} = \sqrt[3]{5x - 8}$

EXTRA Solve. Check for extraneous solutions.

21. $\sqrt{x} + 4 = 6$

22. $\sqrt{4x} = \sqrt{x + 6}$

23. $1 + \sqrt{4x + 1} = 6$

24. $2 - 3\sqrt{x} = 11$

25. $\sqrt[3]{x + 2} - 1 = 0$

26. $\sqrt[3]{9x} = \sqrt[3]{2x - 7}$

LESSON 69 Applications of Radicals and Radical Equations

☐ **REFRESH YOUR SKILLS** ··

Solve. Check for extraneous solutions. Review Lesson 68 if needed.

1. $2\sqrt{x} - 1 = 3$

2. $\sqrt{x-2} + 3 = 6$

☐ **USING THE PYTHAGOREAN THEOREM** ···

A **right triangle** is a triangle with one right angle (90 degrees). The side opposite the right angle is called the **hypotenuse**. The sides adjacent to the right angle are called **legs**.

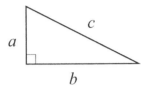

The **Pythagorean Theorem** states that, if a triangle is a right triangle, the sum of the squares of its legs equals the square of its hypotenuse. See the figure on the right.

$$a^2 + b^2 = c^2$$

You can use the Pythagorean Theorem to find the unknown side lengths of right triangles.

➜ **EXAMPLE** Find b when $a = 9$ and $c = 12$.

$9^2 + b^2 = 12^2$	Pythagorean Theorem
$b^2 = 63$	Isolate b.
$b = \sqrt{63}$	Take the squre root.
$b = 3\sqrt{7}$	Simplify.

➜ **TRY IT** Find the missing side.

3. Find c when $a = 3$ and $b = 3$.

4. Find a when $b = 5$ and $c = 13$.

When solving a word problem involving right triangles, draw a picture to illustrate the situation. Then use the Pythagorean Theorem to find the missing side.

➜ **EXAMPLE** Solve using the Pythagorean Theorem.

A 12-foot ladder is leaning against a wall. The top of the ladder is 9 feet above the ground. How far is the bottom of the ladder from the wall?

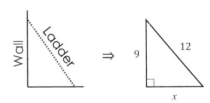

🔎 See the pictures on the right. Notice that this problem is essentially the same as the example above.

Find b when $a = 9$ and $c = 12$.

➜ **TRY IT** Solve. Leave your answers in simplest radical form, if applicable.

5. A 13-foot ladder is leaning against a wall. The bottom of the ladder is 5 feet from the wall. How high up on the wall will the top of the ladder reach?

6. Mike's house is 3 km east and 6 km north of Leah's house. What is the straight-line distance between the two houses?

☐ **SOLVING RADICAL EQUATION WORD PROBLEMS** ···

Many real-world formulas involve square roots. When solving a word problem given a formula, 1) plug the given value(s) into the formula and 2) solve for the unknown.

➔ **EXAMPLE** Solve.

The formula $v = \sqrt{64d}$ relates the speed v (in feet per second) and distance d (in feet) of a falling object. What is the distance an object has fallen when its speed reaches 32 feet per second?	1. Replace v with 32. $32 = \sqrt{64d}$ 2. Solve for d, and $d = 16$. It has fallen 16 feet.

➔ **TRY IT** Solve. Leave your answers in simplest radical form, if applicable.

7. The formula $v = \sqrt{64d}$ relates the speed v (in feet per second) and distance d (in feet) of a falling object. What is the distance an object has fallen when its speed reaches 24 feet per second?

8. The formula $d = \sqrt{(x_2 - x_1)^2 + (y_2 - y_1)^2}$ gives the distance, d, between two points (x_1, y_1) and (x_2, y_2). What is the distance between the two points $(1, 5)$ and $(2, 7)$?

☐ **EXERCISE YOUR SKILLS** ···

Find the missing side. Leave your answers in simplest radical form, if applicable.

9.
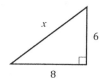

10.

11.
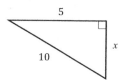

Solve. Leave your answers in simplest radical form, if applicable.

12. The area of a square is 49 cm². What is the length of the diagonal?

13. The hypotenuse of a right triangle is 15 cm, and one of its leg is 12 cm. What is the perimeter of the triangle?

14. The diagonal of a monitor is 16 inches. The width of the monitor is 12 inches. What is the height of the monitor?

15. A 10-foot ladder is leaning against a wall. The ladder reaches a height of 8 feet. How far is the bottom of the ladder from the wall?

16. The formula $P = 2\pi\sqrt{\dfrac{L}{32}}$ relates the length L (in feet) and period P (in seconds) of a pendulum. What is the length of a pendulum with a period of 2 seconds? Give your answer in terms of π.

LESSON 70 Catch Up and Review!

Catch up if you are behind. Use the review problems below to make sure you're on track.

LESSON 63 Evaluate.

1. $\sqrt{16}$

2. $\sqrt[3]{-8}$

3. $\sqrt[4]{81}$

4. $\sqrt[5]{32}$

LESSON 64 Simplify.

5. $\sqrt{8}$

6. $\sqrt[3]{24}$

7. $\sqrt{\dfrac{12}{25}}$

8. $\sqrt[3]{\dfrac{16}{27}}$

LESSON 65 Simplify. Assume that all variables are positive.

9. $\sqrt{x^5}$

10. $\sqrt[3]{x^4 y^3}$

11. $\sqrt{\dfrac{x^2}{y^6}}$

12. $\sqrt[3]{\dfrac{x^5}{y^9}}$

LESSON 66 Simplify.

13. $\sqrt{45} + 2\sqrt{5}$

14. $\sqrt{96} - 2\sqrt{24} + \sqrt{32}$

LESSON 67 Simplify. Rationalize all denominators. Assume that all variables are positive.

15. $\sqrt{2} \cdot \sqrt{8}$

16. $\sqrt{10x^3} \cdot \sqrt{5x}$

17. $\dfrac{10\sqrt{24}}{\sqrt{75}}$

18. $\dfrac{3\sqrt{2}}{\sqrt{3}}$

LESSON 68 Solve. Check for extraneous solutions.

19. $\sqrt{x-3} = 2$

20. $\sqrt{x} + 3 = 5$

21. $\sqrt{2x+5} - 4 = 1$

22. $3\sqrt{x+1} + 7 = 4$

23. $\sqrt[3]{x-3} + 2 = 5$

24. $\sqrt[3]{x+2} = \sqrt[3]{4x-1}$

LESSON 69 Find the missing side. Leave your answers in simplest radical form, if applicable.

25.

26.
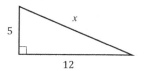

☐ **MIXED REVIEW: PRE-ALGEBRA** ···

Brush up on the topics covered in Pre-Algebra.

Reference

$A = lw$ $\qquad$ $A = bh$ $\qquad$ $A = \frac{1}{2}bh$ $\qquad$ $A = \frac{1}{2}h(b_1 + b_2)$

Find the area.

27.
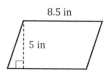

28.
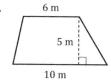

29.
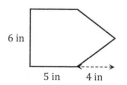

30.

LESSON 71 Zero and Negative Exponents

☐ **REFRESH YOUR SKILLS** ··

Evaluate. Review Lesson 1 if needed.

1. 1^7 **2.** 2^5 **3.** -3^4 **4.** $(-4)^3$

☐ **EVALUATING ZERO AND NEGATIVE EXPONENTS** ··

Any nonzero number with an exponent of 0 is always 1. For example, 2^0 is 1 and $2,157^0$ is also 1. Why? Look at the pattern on the right. Each time you divide by 10, the exponent decreases by 1. When you divide by 10 the last time, you cancel out all the 10s and have 1 left. The exponent now is 0. This pattern is true for any nonzero number. Get a piece of paper and try it yourself!

$10^3 = 1000$

                  Divide by 10

$10^2 = 100$

                  Divide by 10

$10^1 = 10$

                  Divide by 10

$10^0 = 1$

Any number with a negative exponent is equal to the reciprocal of that number with the same positive exponent. For example, 2^{-1} is equal to $1/2^1$ and 4^{-3} is equal to $1/4^3$. Look at the pattern on the right. What happens if we continue dividing by 10 and decreasing the exponent by 1? Do you see that 10^{-1} is equal to $1/10^1$, 10^{-2} to $1/10^2$, and 10^{-3} to $1/10^3$?

$10^0 = 1$

                  Divide by 10

$10^{-1} = {}^1/_{10}$

                  Divide by 10

$10^{-2} = {}^1/_{100}$

                  Divide by 10

$10^{-3} = {}^1/_{1000}$

As shown above, any number (except 0) with a zero exponent equals 1. A number with a negative exponent can be rewritten as its reciprocal with a positive exponent.

$$x^0 = 1$$

$$x^{-n} = \frac{1}{x^n}$$

➜ **EXAMPLE** Evaluate.

a. $3^0 = 1$ **b.** $(-3)^0 = 1$

c. $-3^1 = -3$ **d.** $(-3)^1 = -3$

➜ **TRY IT** Evaluate.

5. 9^0 **6.** $(-5)^0$

7. -2^1 **8.** $(-4)^1$

To evaluate a negative exponent, take the reciprocal of the base and change the exponent to positive.

➜ **EXAMPLE** Evaluate.

a. $5^{-2} = \dfrac{1}{5^2} = \dfrac{1}{25}$

b. $\dfrac{1}{(-4)^{-2}} = (-4)^2 = 16$

➜ **TRY IT** Evaluate.

9. 9^{-2} **10.** $(-4)^{-3}$

11. $\dfrac{1}{3^{-2}}$ **12.** $\dfrac{1}{(-2)^{-5}}$

☐ SIMPLIFYING EXPRESSIONS WITH ZERO AND NEGATIVE EXPONENTS ·············

To simplify an expression with zero and negative exponents, rewrite the expression using the definitions of zero and negative exponents and cancel all the common factors.

➜ **EXAMPLE** Evaluate.

$$4^3 \cdot 2^{-4} = \frac{4^3}{2^4} = \frac{4 \cdot 4 \cdot 4}{2 \cdot 2 \cdot 2 \cdot 2} = 4$$

➜ **TRY IT** Evaluate.

13. $4^{-2} \cdot 2^4$

14. $3^3 \cdot 9^{-2}$

☐ EXERCISE YOUR SKILLS ·················

Evaluate. Write your answers without exponents.

15. 8^0

16. -6^2

17. 2^{-5}

18. $(-3)^{-3}$

19. $\dfrac{1}{2^{-3}}$

20. $\dfrac{1}{3^{-4}}$

21. $\dfrac{1}{(-2)^{-1}}$

22. $\dfrac{1}{10^{-2}}$

23. $5^{-7} \cdot 5^9$

24. $4^3 \cdot 4^{-5}$

25. $2^{-2} \cdot 5^{-2}$

26. $(-9)^5 \cdot 27^{-4}$

EXTRA Evaluate. Write your answers without exponents.

27. $(-9)^0$

28. $(-11)^2$

29. 1^{-1}

30. -5^{-3}

31. $\dfrac{1}{3^{-3}}$

32. $\dfrac{1}{5^{-2}}$

33. $\dfrac{1}{(-7)^{-2}}$

34. $\dfrac{1}{(-10)^{-3}}$

35. $3^5 \cdot 3^{-5}$

36. $7^7 \cdot 7^{-5}$

37. $6^{-4} \cdot 3^6$

38. $(-18)^3 \cdot (-3)^{-5}$

CHALLENGE Find the value of x.

39. $2^3 \cdot 2^4 = 2^x$

40. $4^5 \cdot 4^{-3} = 4^x$

41. $3^2 \cdot 3^4 = 3^x \cdot 3^3$

42. $7^{-2} \cdot 7^4 = 7^2 \cdot 7^x$

43. $6^2 \cdot 6^{-5} = 6^x \cdot 6^{-2}$

44. $2^{-4} \cdot 2^{-3} = 2^x \cdot 2^{-5}$

LESSON 72 Product and Quotient Rules of Exponents

☐ **REFRESH YOUR SKILLS** ··

Evaluate. Write your answers without exponents. Review Lesson 71 if needed.

1. $(-4)^0$ **2.** 8^{-2} **3.** -3^4 **4.** 10^{-3}

☐ **USING THE PRODUCT RULE OF EXPONENTS** ···

When simplifying expressions with exponents, you can use the **rules of exponents**. These rules are derived from the definition of exponents, so you don't have to memorize them if you understand the principles. Make sure you understand the definition of exponent.

The **product rule of exponents** says that when multiplying exponential terms with the same base, you can add the exponents. Shown below is how the rule is derived.

$$5^2 \cdot 5^3 = (5 \cdot 5) \cdot (5 \cdot 5 \cdot 5) = 5^{2+3} = 5^5$$
$$a^4 \cdot a^2 = (a \cdot a \cdot a \cdot a) \cdot (a \cdot a) = a^{4+2} = a^6$$

Find the rule!

$$\boxed{x^m x^n = x^{m+n}}$$

➜ **EXAMPLE** Simplify.

a. $4x^5 \cdot 2x^3 = 4 \cdot 2 \cdot x^{5+3} = 8x^8$

b. $x^2 y^3 x^5 y^{-2} = x^{2+5} y^{3-2} = x^7 y$

➜ **TRY IT** Simplify.

5. $3x^4 \cdot 5x^2$ **6.** $x^6 y \cdot 3x^{-4} y^2$

☐ **USING THE QUOTIENT RULE OF EXPONENTS** ···

The **quotient rule of exponents** says that when dividing exponential terms with the same base, you can subtract the exponents.

$$\frac{5^8}{5^3} = \frac{5 \cdot 5 \cdot 5 \cdot 5 \cdot 5 \cdot 5 \cdot 5 \cdot 5}{5 \cdot 5 \cdot 5} = 5^{8-3} = 5^5$$

Find the rule!

$$\boxed{\frac{x^m}{x^n} = x^{m-n}}$$

➜ **EXAMPLE** Simplify.

a. $\dfrac{9x^5}{3x^4} = \dfrac{9}{3} \cdot x^{5-4} = 3x$

b. $\dfrac{4x^5 y^2}{x^3 y^2} = 4 \cdot x^{5-3} \cdot y^{2-2} = 4x^2$

➜ **TRY IT** Simplify.

7. $\dfrac{4x^4}{2x^2}$ **8.** $\dfrac{5x^4 y^5}{-5x^2 y^2}$

☐ **SIMPLIFYING USING ONLY POSITIVE EXPONENTS** ···

Generally, unless the instruction says otherwise, simplifying an exponential expression means to rewrite it so that each base is written one time with one positive exponent.

→ **EXAMPLE** Simplify.

a. $2x^3x^{-9} = 2x^{3-9} = 2x^{-6} = \dfrac{2}{x^6}$

b. $\dfrac{x^2x^{-4}}{x^3} = x^{2-4-3} = x^{-5} = \dfrac{1}{x^5}$

→ **TRY IT** Simplify.

9. $5x^{-4}x^2$

10. $\dfrac{x^2x^{-1}}{x^3x^2}$

□ **EXERCISE YOUR SKILLS** ··

Simplify. Write your answers in the form a^n, where n is an integer.

11. $a^3 \cdot a^2$

12. $a^4 \cdot a^{-7}$

13. $\dfrac{a^8}{a^4}$

14. $\dfrac{a^6}{a^8}$

Simplify. Write your answers with positive exponents.

15. $4x^8x^{-5}$

16. $2x^3 \cdot 7x^{-5}$

17. $x^8y^{-2}x^{-2}y^5$

18. $9x^2y^5 \cdot (-3x^{-4})$

19. $\dfrac{10x^5x^2}{-2x^4}$

20. $\dfrac{9x^{-4}x^5}{3x^3}$

21. $\dfrac{8x^5x^{-2}}{2x^4}$

22. $\dfrac{(-4x^3) \cdot 5x^2}{-2x^{-1}}$

23. $\dfrac{3x^3y^{-1}}{9x^3y^{-5}}$

24. $\dfrac{24x^4y^5}{-8x^3y^7}$

CHALLENGE Evaluate. Write your answers without exponents. Do not use a calculator.

25. $5^9 \cdot 5^{-7}$

26. $15^3 \cdot 15^7 \cdot 15^{-9}$

27. $\dfrac{(-16)^7}{(-16)^6}$

28. $\dfrac{8^7 \cdot 4^3}{8^5 \cdot 4^6}$

LESSON 73 Power Rules of Exponents

REFRESH YOUR SKILLS ···

Simplify. Write your answers with positive exponents. Review Lesson 72 if needed.

1. $3x^4 \cdot 2x^3$
2. $7x^5 x^{-2} x^{-5}$
3. $\dfrac{x^4 x^{-1}}{x^2}$
4. $\dfrac{8x^3 x^{-2}}{-4x^2 x^{-5}}$

☐ **USING THE POWER OF A POWER RULE OF EXPONENTS** ···

The **power of a power rule of exponents** says that when raising a power to a power, multiply the exponents. Shown below is how the rule is derived.

$(5^2)^3 = 5^2 \cdot 5^2 \cdot 5^2 = 5^{2+2+2} = 5^6 = 5^{2\times3}$

$(a^{-4})^2 = a^{-4} \cdot a^{-4} = a^{-4-4} = a^{-8} = a^{-4\times2}$

Find the rule!

$$(x^m)^n = x^{mn}$$

➔ **EXAMPLE** Simplify.

$(x^4)^{-3} = x^{4\times-3} = x^{-12} = \dfrac{1}{x^{12}}$

➔ **TRY IT** Simplify.

5. $(x^{-1})^5$
6. $(x^{-3})^{-2}$

☐ **USING THE POWER OF A PRODUCT RULE OF EXPONENTS** ···

The **power of a product rule of exponents** says that when raising a product to a power, distribute the exponent to each factor in the product.

$(ab)^3 = ab \cdot ab \cdot ab = (aaa) \cdot (bbb) = a^3 b^3$

$(2ab)^2 = (2ab) \cdot (2ab) = 2^2 a^2 b^2$

Find the rule!

$$(xy)^n = x^n y^n$$

➔ **EXAMPLE** Simplify.

$(-2xy)^3 = (-2)^3 x^3 y^3 = -8x^3 y^3$

➔ **TRY IT** Simplify.

7. $(-3x)^2$
8. $(5xy)^{-1}$

☐ **USING THE POWER OF A QUOTIENT RULE OF EXPONENTS** ···

The **power of a quotient rule of exponents** says that when raising a quotient to a power, distribute the exponent to the numerator and denominator.

$\left(\dfrac{a}{b}\right)^4 = \dfrac{a}{b} \cdot \dfrac{a}{b} \cdot \dfrac{a}{b} \cdot \dfrac{a}{b} = \dfrac{a \cdot a \cdot a \cdot a}{b \cdot b \cdot b \cdot b} = \dfrac{a^4}{b^4}$

Find the rule!

$$\left(\dfrac{x}{y}\right)^n = \dfrac{x^n}{y^n}$$

➔ **EXAMPLE** Simplify.

$\left(\dfrac{-2}{x}\right)^{-4} = \dfrac{(-2)^{-4}}{x^{-4}} = \dfrac{x^4}{(-2)^4} = \dfrac{x^4}{16}$

➔ **TRY IT** Simplify.

9. $\left(\dfrac{3}{x}\right)^3$
10. $\left(\dfrac{5}{x}\right)^{-2}$

☐ USING THE POWER RULES OF EXPONENTS ···

These rules of exponents can be combined to simplify more complicated expressions.

➜ **EXAMPLE** Simplify.

a. $(5x^{-3}y^4)^2 = 5^2x^{-3\times2}y^{4\times2} = \dfrac{25y^8}{x^6}$

b. $\left(\dfrac{x^{-1}}{3y^2}\right)^{-3} = \dfrac{x^3}{3^{-3}y^{-6}} = 27x^3y^6$

➜ **TRY IT** Simplify.

11. $(2x^2y^{-1})^4$

12. $\left(\dfrac{x}{y^2}\right)^{-2}$

☐ EXERCISE YOUR SKILLS ···

Simplify. Write your answers in the form ka^n, where k is a real number and n is an integer.

13. $(2a^2)^3$

14. $(-a^4)^{-5}$

15. $\left(\dfrac{a}{2}\right)^2$

16. $\left(\dfrac{3}{a}\right)^{-2}$

Simplify. Write your answers with positive exponents.

17. $(8x^5)^2$

18. $(3x^{-4})^3$

19. $(2x^3)^{-5}$

20. $(4x^{-5})^{-3}$

21. $(-3xy)^4$

22. $(7x^3y^{-5})^2$

23. $\left(\dfrac{x^2}{10}\right)^2$

24. $\left(\dfrac{-1}{x^{-5}}\right)^3$

25. $\left(\dfrac{1}{x^3y^{-4}}\right)^3$

26. $\left(\dfrac{y^3}{9x^4}\right)^{-2}$

CHALLENGE Evaluate. Write your answers without exponents. Do not use a calculator.

27. $(9^4)^3 \cdot 9^{-10}$

28. $(4 \cdot 8)^2 \cdot 4^{-3}$

29. $\dfrac{(7^2)^7}{7^{15}}$

30. $\dfrac{6^7 \cdot 12^3}{(6 \cdot 12)^5}$

LESSON 74 Simplifying Integer Exponents

The following table summarizes the exponent rules you've learned so far. Complete the table with your own examples that demonstrate the rules. Review Lessons 71, 72, and 73 if needed.

Rule	In Symbols		Example(s)
Zero exponent	$x^0 = 1$	1.	
Negative exponent	$x^{-n} = \dfrac{1}{x^n}$	2.	
Product of powers	$x^m x^n = x^{m+n}$	3.	
Quotient of powers	$\dfrac{x^m}{x^n} = x^{m-n}$	4.	
Power of a power	$(x^m)^n = x^{mn}$	5.	
Power of a product	$(xy)^n = x^n y^n$	6.	
Power of a quotient	$\left(\dfrac{x}{y}\right)^n = \dfrac{x^n}{y^n}$	7.	

☐ **SIMPLIFYING INTEGER EXPONENTS** ··

These rules of exponents can be combined to simplify more complicated expressions.

➜ **EXAMPLE** Simplify.

a. $(-x)^{-4} \cdot (x^2)^2 = (-1)^{-4} x^{-4} x^4 = \dfrac{x^0}{(-1)^4} = 1$

b. $\left(\dfrac{-8x^2}{4x^3}\right)^5 = (-2x^{-1})^5 = (-2)^5 x^{-5} = -\dfrac{32}{x^5}$

c. $(2x^3 y)^2 \cdot x^{-3} y^3 = 2^2 x^6 y^2 \cdot x^{-3} y^3 = 4x^3 y^5$

d. $\dfrac{(-2x^3 y^2)^2}{(-x^2 y^{-1})^3} = \dfrac{(-2)^2 x^6 y^4}{(-1)^3 x^6 y^{-3}} = \dfrac{4}{-1} \cdot x^0 y^7 = -4y^7$

e. $\left(\dfrac{5x^2 y^4}{x^3 y^2}\right)^{-2} = (5x^{-1} y^2)^{-2} = 5^{-2} x^2 y^{-4} = \dfrac{x^2}{25y^4}$

➜ **TRY IT** Simplify.

8. $(3x)^{-3} \cdot (x^4)^0$

9. $\left(\dfrac{9x^2}{3x^5}\right)^4$

10. $(x^2 y)^4 \cdot x^{-5} y^3$

11. $\dfrac{(x^3 y^3)^4}{(x^{-2} y^2)^2}$

12. $\left(\dfrac{3x^3 y^3}{x^2 y^6}\right)^{-3}$

Notice that there are multiple ways to simplify an expression. For example, in the last example on the previous page, you could find the reciprocal of the base first because the exponent is negative.

➜ **EXAMPLE** Simplify.

$$\left(\frac{5x^2y^4}{x^3y^2}\right)^{-2} = \left(\frac{x^3y^2}{5x^2y^4}\right)^2 = \left(\frac{x}{5y^2}\right)^2 = \frac{x^2}{25y^4}$$

➜ **TRY IT** Simplify.

13. $\left(\dfrac{4x^5y^2}{x^2y^4}\right)^{-2}$

□ **EXERCISE YOUR SKILLS** ···

Select all the expressions that are equivalent.

14. $a^5 \cdot a^{-2}$ a. $\dfrac{a^5}{a^2}$ b. $a^{5-(-2)}$ c. $\dfrac{a^2}{a^5}$ d. a^{5-2}

15. $(s^3 t^{-3})^2$ a. $s^{-6}t^6$ b. $\left(\dfrac{s^3}{t^3}\right)^2$ c. $s^6 t^{-6}$ d. $\left(\dfrac{t}{s}\right)^6$

16. $\dfrac{x^4 y^5}{(xy^2)^3}$ a. $\dfrac{x}{y}$ b. $x^{-1}y$ c. $\dfrac{x^4 y^5}{x^3 y^6}$ d. $x^{-1}y^{-1}$

Simplify. Write your answers with positive exponents.

17. $7x^{-1}x^{-3}x^{-2}$ 18. $5x^{-4} \cdot 7x^3$

19. $9x \cdot (9x^{-3})^{-3}$ 20. $x^5 \cdot (-2x^2)^3$

21. $xy^{-2} \cdot (2x^3 y)^2$ 22. $(7xy^4)^3 \cdot (7x^{-2}y^3)^{-2}$

23. $\dfrac{9x^5 x^{-2} x^4}{3x^4}$ 24. $\dfrac{(25x^3 y^2)^2}{(5x^2 y)^3}$

EXTRA Simplify. Write your answers with positive exponents.

25. $3x^{-2} x^4 x^{-2}$ 26. $4x^{-5} \cdot 2x^2$

27. $x^7 \cdot (2x)^{-5}$ 28. $x^{-5} \cdot (-4x^5)^2$

29. $x^5 y^{-3} \cdot (x^{-2}y)^4$ 30. $(xy^{-4})^3 \cdot (x^2 y^{-6})^{-2}$

LESSON 75 Scientific Notation

☐ **REFRESH YOUR SKILLS** ··

Evaluate. Write your answers without exponents. Review Lesson 71 if needed.

1. $(10)^0$ **2.** 10^{-2} **3.** 10^4 **4.** 10^{-3}

Simplify. Write your answers in the form 10^n, where n is an integer. Review Lesson 72 if needed.

5. $10^3 \cdot 10^5$ **6.** $10^2 \cdot 10^{-7}$ **7.** $\dfrac{10^2}{10^6}$ **8.** $\dfrac{10^{-3}}{10^{-2}}$

☐ **IDENTIFYING SCIENTIFIC NOTATION** ··

Scientists often write numbers in a special way called **scientific notation** to make the numbers easier to deal with. In scientific notation, a number is written in the form $a \times 10^n$, where $1 \le a < 10$ and n is an integer. Using this notation, you can shorten very large or very small numbers in a consistent form. For example, 320,000,000 can be written in scientific notation as 3.2×10^8.

> Scientific notation
>
> $a \times 10^n$
>
> $1 \le a < 10$, n = integer

➜ **EXAMPLE** In scientific notation?

   0.3×10^{-4} No, 0.3 is less than 1.

➜ **TRY IT** In scientific notation?

9. 5.02×10^6 **10.** 14×10^{-3}

☐ **WRITING NUMBERS IN SCIENTIFIC NOTATION** ··

To convert a number to scientific notation, move the decimal point until there is one nonzero digit to the left of the decimal point. The number of places the decimal point moves is the exponent of 10. The exponent is positive if you moved the decimal to the left and negative if you moved the decimal to the right. Look at the examples below. You'll find it's easier than it sounds.

➜ **EXAMPLE** Write 2,780,000 and 0.000325 in scientific notation.

a. $2\ 7\ 8\ 0\ 0\ 0\ 0 = 2.78 \times 10^6$

We have to move the decimal point
6 places to the left, so the exponent is 6.

b. $0\ .\ 0\ 0\ 0\ 3\ 2\ 5 = 3.25 \times 10^{-4}$

We have to move the decimal point
4 places to the right, so the exponent is −4.

➜ **TRY IT** Convert to standard form.

11. 2.3×10^4

12. 3.28×10^{-5}

➜ **TRY IT** Convert to scientific notation.

13. 1,590,000,000

14. 0.00000032

☐ MULTIPLYING AND DIVIDING SCIENTIFIC NOTATION ·······································

When numbers are expressed in scientific notation, it becomes easy to perform common arithmetic operations like multiplication and division. You just need to simplify expressions using the product rule and the quotient rule. See the examples below. Notice that, after simplifying, the result is converted to scientific notation.

➜ **EXAMPLE** Simplify. Write your answers in scientific notation.

a. $(5 \times 10^{-3})(4 \times 10^7) = (5 \times 4)(10^{-3} \times 10^7) = 20 \times 10^{-3+7} = 20 \times 10^4 = 2 \times 10^5$

b. $\dfrac{5 \times 10^4}{8 \times 10^{-3}} = \dfrac{5}{8} \times 10^{4-(-3)} = 0.625 \times 10^7 = 6.25 \times 10^6$

➜ **TRY IT** Simplify. Write your answers in scientific notation.

15. $(3 \times 10^2)(5 \times 10^3)$

16. $\dfrac{3 \times 10^6}{4 \times 10^2}$

☐ EXERCISE YOUR SKILLS ·······································

Convert to scientific notation or standard notation, as appropriate.

17. 1.5×10^3

18. 9.16×10^{-5}

19. $1{,}950{,}000{,}000$

20. 0.0000005

Simplify. Write your answers in scientific notation.

21. $(6 \times 10^2)(9 \times 10^7)$

22. $(1.1 \times 10^{-5})(3 \times 10^3)$

23. $(5 \times 10^6)(4 \times 10^{-3})$

24. $(2.3 \times 10^{-4})(5 \times 10^{-4})$

25. $\dfrac{8 \times 10^{-4}}{5 \times 10^{-7}}$

26. $\dfrac{4 \times 10^{-2}}{5 \times 10^3}$

EXTRA Simplify. Write your answers in scientific notation.

27. $(1.4 \times 10^{-8})(5 \times 10^3)$

28. $(3 \times 10^3)(8 \times 10^7)$

29. $\dfrac{2.5 \times 10^4}{5 \times 10^{-3}}$

30. $\dfrac{1.5 \times 10^4}{3 \times 10^9}$

LESSON 76 Rational Exponents

☐ **REFRESH YOUR SKILLS** ···

Evaluate. Review Lesson 63 if needed.

1. $\sqrt{49}$ 2. $\sqrt[3]{27}$ 3. $\sqrt[5]{32}$ 4. $\sqrt[4]{9^4}$

☐ **CONVERTING BETWEEN RADICALS AND RATIONAL EXPONENTS** ··

Radicals and exponents are closely related, and you can write an nth root as a **rational exponent** (fractional exponent). Here is one way to find the rule connecting the two.

$$\left(\sqrt{2}\right)^2 = 2 \text{ and } \left(2^{1/2}\right)^2 = 2^{(1/2)\cdot 2} = 2^1 = 2 \;\Rightarrow\; \sqrt{2} = 2^{1/2}$$
$$\left(\sqrt[3]{5}\right)^3 = 5 \text{ and } \left(5^{1/3}\right)^3 = 5^{(1/3)\cdot 3} = 5^1 = 5 \;\Rightarrow\; \sqrt[3]{5} = 5^{1/3}$$

Find the rule! $\sqrt[n]{a} = a^{\frac{1}{n}}$

Now, consider rational exponents whose numerator is an integer other than 1.

$$\left(\sqrt{2^3}\right)^2 = 2^3 \text{ and } \left(2^{3/2}\right)^2 = 2^{(3/2)\cdot 2} = 2^3 \;\Rightarrow\; \sqrt{2^3} = 2^{3/2}$$
$$\left(\sqrt[3]{5^4}\right)^3 = 5^4 \text{ and } \left(5^{4/3}\right)^3 = 5^{(4/3)\cdot 3} = 5^4 \;\Rightarrow\; \sqrt[3]{5^4} = 5^{4/3}$$

Find the rule! $\sqrt[n]{a^m} = a^{\frac{m}{n}}$

Note that it doesn't matter if you apply the power first or the root first.

$$\sqrt{2^3} = \sqrt{2}\cdot\sqrt{2}\cdot\sqrt{2} = \left(\sqrt{2}\right)^3 \qquad\qquad \Rightarrow \left(\sqrt{2}\right)^3 = 2^{3/2}$$
$$\sqrt[3]{5^4} = \sqrt[3]{5}\cdot\sqrt[3]{5}\cdot\sqrt[3]{5}\cdot\sqrt[3]{5} = \left(\sqrt[3]{5}\right)^4 \qquad \Rightarrow \left(\sqrt[3]{5}\right)^4 = 5^{4/3}$$

Find the rule! $\left(\sqrt[n]{a}\right)^m = a^{\frac{m}{n}}$

➜ **TRY IT** Convert to exponential form.   ➜ **TRY IT** Convert to radical form.

5. $\sqrt{3}$ 6. $\sqrt[5]{6^3}$ 7. $7^{1/2}$ 8. $4^{2/3}$

☐ **EVALUATING RATIONAL EXPONENTS** ···

Notice that you can evaluate rational exponents in more than one way.

➜ **EXAMPLE** Evaluate.

a. $4^{1/2} = (2^2)^{1/2} = 2^{2\cdot(1/2)} = 2^1 = 2$ OR $4^{1/2} = \sqrt{4} = \sqrt{2^2} = 2$

b. $27^{-2/3} = (3^3)^{-2/3} = 3^{-2} = \dfrac{1}{9}$ OR $27^{-2/3} = \dfrac{1}{27^{2/3}} = \dfrac{1}{\left(\sqrt[3]{27}\right)^2} = \dfrac{1}{3^2} = \dfrac{1}{9}$

c. $\left(\dfrac{1}{32}\right)^{3/5} = \dfrac{1^{3/5}}{32^{3/5}} = \dfrac{1}{(2^5)^{3/5}} = \dfrac{1}{2^3} = \dfrac{1}{8}$ OR $\left(\dfrac{1}{32}\right)^{3/5} = \dfrac{1^{3/5}}{32^{3/5}} = \dfrac{1}{\left(\sqrt[5]{32}\right)^3} = \dfrac{1}{2^3} = \dfrac{1}{8}$

→ **TRY IT** Evaluate. Use whichever method you find easier.

9. $25^{1/2}$

10. $64^{2/3}$

11. $36^{-1/2}$

12. $\left(\dfrac{1}{100}\right)^{3/2}$

□ **EXERCISE YOUR SKILLS** ···

Convert to exponential form.

13. $\sqrt{2}$

14. $\sqrt[6]{8^5}$

15. $\sqrt[9]{3^2}$

16. $\left(\sqrt[7]{6}\right)^2$

Convert to radical form.

17. $3^{1/2}$

18. $7^{3/2}$

19. $5^{4/3}$

20. $8^{1/5}$

Evaluate. Write your answers without exponents. Do not use a calculator.

21. $9^{1/2}$

22. $8^{1/3}$

23. $4^{5/2}$

24. $27^{2/3}$

25. $25^{-1/2}$

26. $64^{-1/3}$

27. $16^{-3/2}$

28. $125^{-2/3}$

29. $\left(\dfrac{1}{8}\right)^{5/3}$

30. $\left(\dfrac{1}{64}\right)^{1/6}$

31. $\left(\dfrac{1}{27}\right)^{4/3}$

32. $\left(\dfrac{1}{1000}\right)^{1/3}$

EXTRA Evaluate. Write your answers without exponents. Do not use a calculator.

33. $4^{1/2}$

34. $81^{1/4}$

35. $32^{3/5}$

36. $64^{2/3}$

37. $8^{-1/3}$

38. $36^{-1/2}$

39. $27^{-4/3}$

40. $10000^{-5/4}$

CHALLENGE Find the value of n.

41. $\sqrt[4]{8} = 2^n$

42. $\sqrt[3]{25} = 5^{2n}$

43. $\sqrt{32} = 2^{n+2}$

44. $\sqrt[5]{3^4} = 9^{n/5}$

45. $36^{2/3} = \sqrt[3]{6^n}$

46. $\sqrt[4]{4^3} = 64^n$

LESSON 77 Simplifying Rational Exponents

☐ **REFRESH YOUR SKILLS** ···

Make sure you understand the rules of exponents. Simplify each expression. Write your answers with positive exponents. Review Lessons 71 through 74 if needed.

1. $2x^5 \cdot 3x^{-3}$

2. $x^{-7} \cdot (2x^2)^3$

3. $\dfrac{x^7 x^{-2}}{3x^2}$

4. $\left(\dfrac{-x^3}{x^2 x^{-2}}\right)^4$

☐ **SIMPLIFYING RATIONAL EXPONENTS** ···

You can simplify expressions with rational exponents just as you simplify expressions with integer exponents. All the rules of exponents apply to rational exponents as well.

➜ **EXAMPLE** Simplify.

a. $2^{1/3} \cdot 2^{1/2} = 2^{1/3 + 1/2} = 2^{5/6}$

b. $\left(9^{1/3}\right)^{3/2} = 9^{1/3 \times 3/2} = 9^{1/2} = 3$

c. $\dfrac{x^{2/5}}{x^{1/3}} = x^{2/5 - 1/3} = x^{1/15}$

d. $\left(\dfrac{25x^{5/2}}{x^{1/2}}\right)^{3/2} = (5^2 x^2)^{3/2} = 5^3 x^3 = 125x^3$

➜ **TRY IT** Simplify.

5. $5^{1/3} \cdot 5^{1/4}$

6. $\left(4^{1/5}\right)^{5/2}$

7. $\dfrac{x^{3/5}}{x^{1/2}}$

8. $\left(\dfrac{27x^{5/6}}{x^{1/3}}\right)^{1/3}$

☐ **SIMPLIFY RADICAL EXPRESSIONS** ···

You can use rational exponents to simplify radical expressions. Convert radicals to exponential form, apply the rules for exponents, and then convert back to radical form.

➜ **EXAMPLE** Simplify.

a. $\sqrt{5} \cdot \sqrt[4]{5} = 5^{1/2} \cdot 5^{1/4} = 5^{3/4} = \sqrt[4]{5^3}$

b. $\dfrac{\sqrt[5]{8}}{\sqrt{2}} = \dfrac{\sqrt[5]{2^3}}{\sqrt{2}} = \dfrac{2^{3/5}}{2^{1/2}} = 2^{1/10} = \sqrt[10]{2}$

c. $\sqrt[3]{\sqrt[5]{27}} = \sqrt[3]{\sqrt[5]{3^3}} = \left(3^{3/5}\right)^{1/3} = 3^{1/5} = \sqrt[5]{3}$

➜ **TRY IT** Simplify.

9. $\sqrt{2} \cdot \sqrt[3]{4}$

10. $\dfrac{\sqrt[4]{1000}}{\sqrt{10}}$

11. $\sqrt[3]{\sqrt[5]{8}}$

→ **EXAMPLE** Simplify.

a. $\sqrt{x} \cdot \sqrt[3]{x^2} = x^{1/2} \cdot x^{2/3} = x^{7/6} = \sqrt[6]{x^7} = x\sqrt[6]{x}$

b. $\dfrac{\sqrt[4]{x^7}}{\sqrt[3]{x}} = \dfrac{x^{7/4}}{x^{1/3}} = x^{17/12} = \sqrt[12]{x^{17}} = x\sqrt[12]{x^5}$

c. $\sqrt{\sqrt[3]{x^4}} = \left(x^{4/3}\right)^{1/2} = x^{2/3} = \sqrt[3]{x^2}$

→ **TRY IT** Simplify.

12. $\sqrt[4]{x} \cdot \sqrt[3]{x}$

13. $\dfrac{\sqrt[8]{x^5}}{\sqrt{x}}$

14. $\sqrt[4]{\sqrt[3]{x^2}}$

□ **EXERCISE YOUR SKILLS** ···

Simplify. Write your answers in exponential form with positive exponents.

15. $3^{3/4} \cdot 3^{1/4}$

16. $x^{1/3} \cdot x^{2/5}$

17. $\left(8^{1/2}\right)^{1/3}$

18. $\left(4x^{4/5}\right)^{5/2}$

19. $\dfrac{125^{5/6}}{125^{1/2}}$

20. $\left(\dfrac{64x^{2/3}}{x^{1/6}}\right)^{1/2}$

Simplify. Write your answers in radical form.

21. $\sqrt{3} \cdot \sqrt[4]{9}$

22. $\sqrt[6]{x} \cdot \sqrt[6]{x^2}$

23. $\sqrt[3]{4} \cdot \sqrt[6]{32}$

24. $\sqrt[4]{x^3} \cdot \sqrt{x}$

25. $\sqrt[3]{\sqrt{64}}$

26. $\sqrt[5]{\sqrt[7]{x^5}}$

CHALLENGE Find the value of n.

27. $3^n \cdot 3^{1/3} = \sqrt[3]{27}$

28. $\left(4^{1/3}\right)^{1/2} = \sqrt[3]{n}$

29. $x^{1/4} \cdot x^n = \sqrt[4]{x^3}$

30. $\left(x^{2/5}\right)^n = \sqrt[10]{x}$

31. $\sqrt{\sqrt[3]{x}} = \dfrac{x^{2/3}}{x^n}$

32. $\sqrt[6]{\sqrt{x^6}} = \left(x^{1/6}\right)^n$

LESSON 78 Exponential Growth and Decay

☐ **REFRESH YOUR SKILLS**

Classify as linear, exponential, or quadratic. Review Lesson 52 if needed.

1. $y = ab^x$

2. $y = mx + b$

3. $y = ax^2 + bx + c$

4.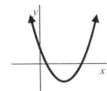

5.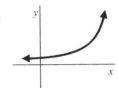

6.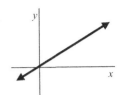

☐ **IDENTIFYING EXPONENTIAL GROWTH AND DECAY**

The general form of an exponential function is

$$y = ab^x, \text{ where } a = \text{initial value and } b = \text{growth factor}$$

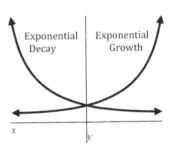

When $a > 0$ and $b > 1$, the function is called an **exponential growth function** because y increases exponentially as x increases. When $a > 0$ and $0 < b < 1$, the function is called an **exponential decay function** because y decreases exponentially as x increases. On the right are the basic shapes of exponential growth and decay graphs.

➜ **EXAMPLE** Exponential growth, decay, or neither?

a. $y = 3(2)^x$

Exponential growth
$a = 3, b = 2 \ (b > 1)$

b. $y = 5x^2$

Neither

c. $y = 5(0.3)^x$

Exponential decay
$a = 5, b = 0.3 \ (b < 1)$

d. $y = 0.1(4)^x$

Exponential growth
$a = 0.1, b = 4 \ (b > 1)$

➜ **TRY IT** Exponential growth, decay, or neither?

7. $y = 2(3)^x$

8. $y = 0.5^x$

9. $y = 1.5^x$

10. $y = 7x^3$

☐ **SOLVING EXPONENTIAL GROWTH AND DECAY WORD PROBLEMS**

Suppose you put \$1,000 in an account that earns 6% interest compounded annually. What is the function that models the balance y of the account after x years? Here's how you find it.

First, understand each year's balance:

Each year's new balance
= previous balance + interest
= previous balance + previous balance × 6%
= previous balance + previous balance × 0.06
= previous balance × (1 + 0.06)
= previous balance × 1.06

Then, find an exponential function:

Let B_n = balance after year n
B_0 = initial balance = 1,000
$B_1 = B_0 \times 1.06$
$B_2 = B_1 \times 1.06 = B_0 \times 1.06 \times 1.06 = B_0 \times 1.06^2$
$B_3 = B_2 \times 1.06 = \ldots = B_0 \times 1.06^3$
$B_n = B_{n-1} \times 1.06 = \ldots = B_0 \times 1.06^n$

The function to represent this situation is:

$$y = 1{,}000(1.06)^x$$

When solving real-world problems involving exponential growth or decay, it is important to 1) identify the initial value and growth factor and 2) determine an exponential function that models the situation. Then you can use the function to answer whatever is being asked.

→ EXAMPLE Exponential growth

You put $800 in an account that earns 4% interest compounded annually. What will be the balance after 5 years?

1. a = initial balance = 800
   b = 100% + 4% = 1.04 because
   new balance = previous + previous × 0.04
              = previous × 1.04
2. The function is $y = 800(1.04)^x$.
3. When $x = 5$, $y = 973.32...$
   The balance will be about $973.

→ EXAMPLE Exponential decay

The value of a car is $20,000. It loses 20% of its value every year. What will be the value after 6 years?

1. a = initial value = 20,000
   b = 100% − 20% = 0.8 because
   new value = previous − previous × 0.2
              = previous × 0.8
2. The function is $y = 20,000(0.8)^x$.
3. When $x = 6$, $y = 5,242.88...$
   The value will be about $5,243.

→ TRY IT Write a function that models each situation, then solve. Use a calculator.

11. The starting salary for Alex's job is $50,000 a year. He is to receive a 5% raise each year. What will his salary be after 7 years?

12. The population of a town is 50,000 this year, and it is expected to decline at a rate of 5% per year. What will be the population of the town after 7 years?

☐ **EXERCISE YOUR SKILLS** ···

Classify as exponential growth, exponential decay, or neither.

13. $y = x^{-2}$ 14. $y = 0.9^x$ 15. $y = 0.5(3)^x$ 16. $y = 7(0.1)^x$

For each problem, 1) classify the situation as exponential growth or exponential decay, 2) write a function that models the situation, and then 3) answer what's being asked. Use a calculator.

17. As a car gets older, its resale value goes down by 10% each year. Alex bought a new car for $15,000. What will be the value of the car after 10 years?

18. Melissa put $3,000 in her account that earns 4% interest compounded annually. What will be the balance of her account after 8 years?

19. During a science experiment, Jessica found that bacteria double every 30 minutes. There were 10 bacteria in the beginning. How many bacteria will be there after 5 hours?

20. The atmospheric pressure at sea level is 1,013 millibars. The pressure decreases by 14% for every kilometer you go up. What is the pressure at an altitude of 5 km?

LESSON 79 Catch Up and Review!

Catch up if you are behind. Use the review problems below to make sure you're on track.

LESSON 71 Evaluate.

1. 3^0

2. 2^{-3}

3. $10^4 \cdot 5^{-4}$

4. $3^{-7} \cdot 9^3$

LESSON 72 Simplify using positive exponents.

5. $2x^6 \cdot 4x^{-4}$

6. $2x^2y^{-2} \cdot (-3x^{-5}y^2)$

7. $\dfrac{12x^4x^{-5}}{3x^3}$

8. $\dfrac{5x^4y^{-1}}{15x^3y^{-2}}$

LESSON 73 Simplify using positive exponents.

9. $(4x^4)^2$

10. $(x^4y^{-3})^3$

11. $\left(\dfrac{-x^5}{2}\right)^3$

12. $\left(\dfrac{x^2}{3y^{-2}}\right)^3$

LESSON 74 Simplify using positive exponents.

13. $(4x)^{-2} \cdot (2x^4)^5$

14. $x^{-8}y^4 \cdot (2x^3y)^5$

15. $\dfrac{(-3x)^4}{3x^8}$

16. $\dfrac{(-2x^4y^{-2})^4}{(-2x^4y^{-3})^3}$

LESSON 75 Simplify and write in scientific notation.

17. $(4 \times 10^2)(8 \times 10^{-8})$

18. $\dfrac{2 \times 10^{-3}}{8 \times 10^{-6}}$

LESSON 76 Evaluate.

19. $49^{1/2}$ **20.** $27^{2/3}$ **21.** $\left(\dfrac{1}{32}\right)^{1/5}$ **22.** $\left(\dfrac{1}{10000}\right)^{3/4}$

LESSON 77 Simplify using positive exponents.

23. $5^{2/5} \cdot 5^{3/5}$ **24.** $\left(9^{1/3}\right)^{1/2}$

25. $\dfrac{81^{3/4}}{81^{1/2}}$ **26.** $\left(\dfrac{32x}{x^{1/6}}\right)^{2/5}$

LESSON 78 Write a function that models each situation, and then solve.

27. Samantha put $8,000 in her account that earns 5% interest compounded annually. What will be the balance of her account after 4 years?

28. The population of a town is 40,000 this year, and it is expected to decline at a rate of 3% per year. What will be the population of the town after 5 years?

☐ **MIXED REVIEW: PRE-ALGEBRA** ···

Brush up on the topics covered in Pre-Algebra. Use 3.14 for π.

Reference

$$C = 2\pi r;\; A = \pi r^2 \qquad V = \pi r^2 h \qquad V = \tfrac{1}{3}\pi r^2 h$$

29. Find the circumference of a circle with radius 6 cm.

30. Find the area of a circle with diameter 10 in.

31. Find the volume of a cylinder with base radius 10 in and height 5 in.

32. The volume of a cone is one-third the volume of a cylinder with the same radius and height. Find the volume of a cone with a radius of 4 m and a height of 3 m.

LESSON 80 Adding and Subtracting Polynomials

☐ **IDENTIFYING MONOMIALS** ··

A **monomial** is a term consisting of a number, a variable, or a product of numbers and variables with whole number exponents. The **degree of a monomial** is the sum of the exponents of its variables.

➜ **EXAMPLE** Monomials

$$2 \quad -5x \quad 3x^3 \quad 4xy^2z^3$$

These are all monomials whose degrees are 0, 1, 3, and 6 respectively.

➜ **EXAMPLE** Not monomials

$$\frac{1}{x} \quad x^{-2} \quad \sqrt{x} \quad 5^x$$

These are not monomials because their exponents are not whole numbers.

☐ **IDENTIFYING POLYNOMIALS** ··

A **polynomial** is a monomial or the sum or difference of monomials. A polynomial with two terms is called a **binomial**. A polynomial with three terms is called a **trinomial**. The **degree of a polynomial** is the greatest of the degrees of its terms.

A polynomial is in **standard form** when its terms are listed in decreasing degree. The term with the highest degree is called the **leading term** because it comes first in standard form. The coefficient of the leading term is called the **leading coefficient**.

➜ **EXAMPLE** A polynomial in standard form

$$4x^5 - 3x^3 + 6x$$

This is a trinomial with a degree of 5 and a leading coefficient of 4.

➜ **EXAMPLE** Not a polynomial

$$4x^5 - 3x^{-3} + 6x$$

This is not a polynomial because $3x^{-3}$ is not a monomial.

➜ **TRY IT** Identify as a polynomial or not a polynomial.

1. $2x^2 - x + 3$

2. $4x^{-2} + xy + 2$

3. $4x^3y - 5x^2y^3z$

➜ **TRY IT** Write in standard form. Identify the degree and leading coefficient.

4. $7 - 2x + 4x^2$

5. $4 - x^3 - x - 6x^2$

6. $5 + x + 3x^5 - 2x^4$

☐ **ADDING AND SUBTRACTING POLYNOMIALS** ···

To add or subtract polynomials, simply combine like terms.

➜ **EXAMPLE** Subtract.

$$(3x^3 - 5x^2 + x) - (3x^3 - x + 1)$$
$$= (3x^3 - 3x^3) - 5x^2 + (x - (-x)) - 1$$
$$= -5x^2 + 2x - 1$$

➜ **TRY IT** Add or subtract.

7. $(x^2 + 3x - 1) + (7x + 5)$

8. $(3x^2 + 6x + 1) - (4x^2 + x - 2)$

☐ ADDING AND SUBTRACTING POLYNOMIALS VERTICALLY ································

You can also add and subtract polynomials vertically. First align like terms vertically, then add or subtract. Leave a space for a missing term.

➜ **EXAMPLE** Subtract vertically.

$$3x^3 - 5x^2 + x$$
$$-\ \underline{(3x^3 - x + 1)} \quad \text{Align like terms.}$$
$$0x^3 - 5x^2 + 2x - 1 \quad \text{Subtract.}$$
$$= -5x^2 + 2x - 1 \quad \text{Answer}$$

➜ **TRY IT** Add or subtract.

9. $(3x^2 + 2x + 5) + (2x^2 - 6x - 3)$

10. $(2x^2 + x + 2) - (4x + 3)$

☐ EXERCISE YOUR SKILLS ································

Identify as a polynomial or not a polynomial.

11. $7 + 4x^4 y^3$

12. $2x + \sqrt{x} + 3$

13. $5x^{-4} + 5x$

Write in standard form. Identify the degree and leading coefficient.

14. $5x^2 + 4 - 2x$

15. $4x + 5 + x^3$

16. $x + 4x^3 - x^4 - 5x^2$

Add or subtract. Use any method you prefer. Write your answers in standard form.

17. $(3x + 1) + (x - 5)$

18. $(4x + 3) - (3x - 2)$

19. $(x^2 - 2x + 4) + (2x - 5)$

20. $(3x + 7) - (4 - 5x^2 + x)$

21. $(6 + 5x^2 + x) + (2 - 4x - x^2)$

22. $(x^3 + 5x + 2 - x^2) - (1 - 3x + 2x^3)$

EXTRA Add or subtract. Use any method you prefer. Write your answers in standard form.

23. $(2x + 7) + (1 - 3x)$

24. $(8 - x) - (6x + 5)$

25. $(-x + 9) + (6x - x^2 - 3)$

26. $(5x^2 - x + 3) - (4x - 2)$

27. $(x^2 + 2x + 1) + (x^2 + x + 5)$

28. $(x^2 + x + 9) - (4x^2 + x + 8)$

29. $(5 - 2x^2 - 4x) - (-2x + x^2 - 1)$

30. $(x^3 + 2x + x^2) + (x^2 + 7 - 4x)$

LESSON 81 Multiplying Monomials and Binomials

☐ **MULTIPLYING MONOMIALS** ⋯⋯⋯⋯⋯⋯⋯⋯⋯⋯⋯⋯⋯⋯⋯⋯⋯⋯⋯⋯⋯⋯

To multiply a monomial by a monomial, use the product rule for exponents.

➜ **EXAMPLE** Multiply $3x^3$ by $4x^2$.

$$(3x^3)(4x^2) = 3 \cdot 4 \cdot x^{3+2}$$
$$= 12x^5$$

➜ **TRY IT** Multiply.

1. $2x(8x^2)$

2. $(-4x^5)(5x^3)$

To multiply a monomial by a polynomial, apply the distributive property.

➜ **EXAMPLE** Multiply $2x^3$ by $4x^2 - x + 5$.

$$2x^3(4x^2 - x + 5)$$

$$= 2x^3(4x^2) + 2x^3(-x) + 2x^3(5)$$
$$= 8x^5 - 2x^4 + 10x^3$$

➜ **TRY IT** Multiply.

3. $3x(2x + 1)$

4. $-3x^2(x^3 - 2x + 1)$

☐ **MULTIPLYING BINOMIALS BY DISTRIBUTING** ⋯⋯⋯⋯⋯⋯⋯⋯⋯⋯⋯⋯⋯⋯

To multiply a binomial by a binomial, apply the distributive property twice.

➜ **EXAMPLE** Multiply $x + 3$ by $x - 4$.

$$(x + 3)(x - 4)$$
$$= x(x - 4) + 3(x - 4)$$
$$= x^2 - 4x + 3x - 12$$
$$= x^2 - x - 12$$

➜ **TRY IT** Multiply.

5. $(x + 1)(x + 2)$

6. $(2x + 5)(x - 3)$

☐ **MULTIPLYING BINOMIALS USING THE FOIL METHOD** ⋯⋯⋯⋯⋯⋯⋯⋯⋯

You can multiply two binomials using a shortcut method called **FOIL**. Multiply the **F**irst terms, the **O**uter terms, the **I**nner terms, and the **L**ast terms of each binomial. Then add them all up.

➜ **EXAMPLE** Multiply $x + 3$ by $x - 4$.

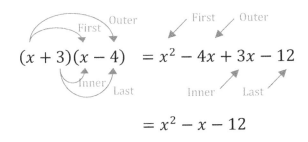

$$(x + 3)(x - 4) = x^2 - 4x + 3x - 12$$

$$= x^2 - x - 12$$

➜ **TRY IT** Multiply.

7. $(x + 2)(x + 3)$

8. $(x + 2)(x - 2)$

9. $(x - 4)(3x - 2)$

☐ MULTIPLYING BINOMIALS USING TABLES $\cdots\cdots\cdots\cdots\cdots\cdots\cdots\cdots\cdots\cdots\cdots\cdots\cdots\cdots\cdots\cdots$

You can also multiply two binomials using a table. Simply make a table of products, then add the products together. As shown below, you will get the same result as before.

➔ **EXAMPLE** Multiply $x - 4$ by $x + 3$.

×	x	-4
x	x^2	$-4x$
3	$3x$	-12

Make a table of products, then add up each product:

$x^2 - 4x + 3x - 12$
$= x^2 - x - 12$

➔ **TRY IT** Multiply.

10. $(x - 2)(x + 3)$

11. $(2x - 3)(x - 1)$

☐ EXERCISE YOUR SKILLS $\cdots\cdots\cdots\cdots\cdots\cdots\cdots\cdots\cdots\cdots\cdots\cdots\cdots\cdots\cdots\cdots\cdots\cdots\cdots\cdots$

Multiply. Use any method you prefer. Write your answers in standard form.

12. $x(2x^4)$

13. $(-2x^2)(6x^5)$

14. $5x(3x - 2)$

15. $x(x^2 + x + 5)$

16. $(x + 8)(x + 3)$

17. $(x + 7)(x - 4)$

18. $(2x + 5)(x + 1)$

19. $(x - 2)(4x - 1)$

20. $(3x + 2)(3x - 2)$

21. $(3x - 1)(2x + 3)$

EXTRA Multiply. Use any method you prefer. Write your answers in standard form.

22. $x(5x^3)$

23. $(3x^3)(-5x^2)$

24. $-2x(x^2 + 4x - 3)$

25. $4x^3(x^3 - 4x^2 + 2x - 8)$

26. $(x + 5)(x - 5)$

27. $(x - 2)(x - 3)$

28. $(x - 6)(3x - 1)$

29. $(3x + 1)(x - 3)$

30. $(2x + 1)(5x + 3)$

31. $(4x + 3)(4x - 3)$

LESSON 82 Multiplying Polynomials

☐ **REFRESH YOUR SKILLS** ··

Multiply. Review Lesson 81 if needed.

1. $(-2x^3)(-4x^2)$

2. $-x(x^2 - 5x + 1)$

3. $(x - 2)(x - 6)$

4. $(x + 3)(2x - 1)$

☐ **MULTIPLYING POLYNOMIALS** ···

To multiply a polynomial by a polynomial, apply the distributive property repeatedly. In other words, multiply each term of the first polynomial by each term of the second polynomial.

➜ **EXAMPLE** Multiply $x + 3$ by $2x^2 - x + 4$.

$(x + 3)(2x^2 - x + 4)$

$= 2x^3 - x^2 + 4x + 6x^2 - 3x + 12$

$= 2x^3 + 5x^2 + x + 12$

➜ **TRY IT** Multiply.

5. $(x + 2)(x^2 + x + 4)$

6. $(x^2 - 5x + 4)(x - 3)$

7. $(x^2 - x + 1)(x^2 - 2x + 1)$

☐ **FINDING AREA USING POLYNOMIALS** ···

Consider a rectangle with a length of $x + 3$ and a width of $2x^2 - x + 4$. The area of the rectangle can be expressed as a polynomial 1) by multiplying $x + 3$ by $2x^2 - x + 4$ using the distributive property as shown above, or 2) by adding up the area of each part of the rectangle as shown below. Either way, you will get the same result.

➜ **EXAMPLE** Find a polynomial representing the area of the entire rectangle.

First, find the area of each part.

$\times$	$2x^2$	$-x$	4
x	$2x^3$	$-x^2$	$4x$
3	$6x^2$	$-3x$	12

Then, add up all the areas.

$2x^3 - x^2 + 4x + 6x^2 - 3x + 12$

$= 2x^3 + 5x^2 + x + 12$

➜ **TRY IT** Find a polynomial representing the area of each rectangle given its dimensions.

8. $x + 4$ by $x - 3$

9. $x + 2$ by $x^2 + 3x - 2$

10. $x^2 - 3x + 1$ by $2x^2 + x + 1$

Multiply. Write your answers in standard form.

11. $(x + 3)(x + 1)$

12. $(x - 6)(x + 5)$

13. $(2x - 1)(x - 2)$

14. $(4x - 3)(5x + 3)$

15. $(x + 1)(x^2 - x + 1)$

16. $(4x + 3)(x^2 + 3x - 2)$

17. $(x^2 - 3x + 1)(x + 5)$

18. $(2x^2 - x - 5)(3x - 7)$

19. $(x^2 + x + 1)(x^2 + 4x + 5)$

20. $(x^2 - 5x + 1)(2x^2 - x + 3)$

Express the area as a polynomial in standard form.

21. [rectangle] $x - 1$
$x + 5$

22. [rectangle] $x + 1$
$x^2 + 2x + 1$

23. [rectangle] $x + 3$
$2x^2 - x + 3$

24. [rectangle] $5x^2$
$x^3 + 2x^2 - 3x + 1$

EXTRA Multiply. Write your answers in standard form.

25. $(x + 2)(x - 7)$

26. $(x - 2)(x - 2)$

27. $(4x - 1)(x + 4)$

28. $(3x + 7)(2x + 5)$

29. $(x - 4)(x^2 + 3x - 5)$

30. $(5x - 3)(2x^2 + 3x - 2)$

31. $(x^2 - 2x + 4)(x + 2)$

32. $(4x^2 - 2x + 1)(2x - 1)$

33. $(x^2 + x + 3)(x^2 - x + 4)$

34. $(3x^2 - x - 2)(3x^2 - 3x - 2)$

LESSON 83 Special Products of Binomials

□ **REFRESH YOUR SKILLS** ···

Multiply. Review Lesson 82 if needed.

1. $(a + b)(a + b)$ **2.** $(a - b)(a - b)$ **3.** $(a + b)(a - b)$

□ **MULTIPLYING BINOMIALS USING SPECIAL PRODUCTS** ···

The three binomial products you've just worked out have special patterns worth memorizing because they occur so frequently in algebra. The first two products are called **perfect square trinomials**, and the third product is called **difference of squares**. See the patterns and examples below. Familiarize yourself with these patterns enough to work out the problems mentally.

Squaring a binomial produces a perfect square trinomial:

$$(a + b)^2 = a^2 + 2ab + b^2 \quad \Rightarrow \quad (x + 1)^2 = x^2 + 2 \cdot x \cdot 1 + 1^2 = x^2 + 2x + 1$$

$$(a - b)^2 = a^2 - 2ab + b^2 \quad \Rightarrow \quad (x - 2)^2 = x^2 - 2 \cdot x \cdot 2 + 4^2 = x^2 - 4x + 4$$

Multiplying the sum and the difference of two terms produces a difference of squares:

$$(a + b)(a - b) = a^2 - b^2 \quad \Rightarrow \quad (x + 3)(x - 3) = x^2 - 3^2 = x^2 - 9$$

➜ **EXAMPLE** Square of a binomial

$(2x + 1)^2$

$= (2x)^2 + 2 \cdot 2x \cdot 1 + 1^2$

$= 4x^2 + 4x + 1$

➜ **TRY IT** Multiply.

4. $(x + 2)^2$ **5.** $(x + 3)^2$

6. $(4x + 1)^2$ **7.** $(3x + 2)^2$

➜ **EXAMPLE** Square of a binomial

$(3x - 2)^2$

$= (3x)^2 - 2 \cdot 3x \cdot 2 + 2^2$

$= 9x^2 - 12x + 4$

➜ **TRY IT** Multiply.

8. $(x - 1)^2$ **9.** $(x - 5)^2$

10. $(6x - 1)^2$ **11.** $(4x - 3)^2$

➜ **EXAMPLE** Sum and difference

$(5x + 4)(5x - 4)$

$= (5x)^2 - 4^2$

$= 25x^2 - 16$

➜ **TRY IT** Multiply.

12. $(x + 4)(x - 4)$ **13.** $(x + 8)(x - 8)$

14. $(2x + 1)(2x - 1)$ **15.** $(7x - 2)(7x + 2)$

☐ **USING SPECIAL PRODUCT PATTERNS** ···

You can use special product patterns to evaluate numerical expressions.

➜ **EXAMPLE** Use special product patterns to evaluate. Do not use a calculator.

a. 34^2

$= (30 + 4)^2$

$= 30^2 + 2 \cdot 30 \cdot 4 + 4^2$

$= 900 + 240 + 16$

$= 1156$

b. 49^2

$= (50 - 1)^2$

$= 50^2 - 2 \cdot 50 \cdot 1 + 1^2$

$= 2500 - 100 + 1$

$= 2401$

c. 23×17

$= (20 + 3)(20 - 3)$

$= 20^2 - 3^2$

$= 400 - 9$

$= 391$

➜ **TRY IT** Evaluate. Do not use a calculator.

16. 52^2

17. 67^2

18. 32×28

☐ **EXERCISE YOUR SKILLS** ···

Multiply. Write your answers in standard form.

19. $(x + 4)^2$

20. $(3x + 1)^2$

21. $(x - 3)^2$

22. $(5x - 4)^2$

23. $(x + 1)(x - 1)$

24. $(8x + 5)(8x - 5)$

Use special product patterns to evaluate. Do not use a calculator.

25. 21^2

26. 78^2

27. 81×79

28. 190×210

EXTRA Multiply. Write your answers in standard form.

29. $(x + 6)^2$

30. $(2x + 5)^2$

31. $(x - 7)^2$

32. $(3x - 2)^2$

33. $(x - 8)^2$

34. $(6x + 1)^2$

35. $(x + 9)(x - 9)$

36. $(4x + 1)(4x - 1)$

LESSON 84 Multiplying Binomials and Special Products

☐ **REFRESH YOUR SKILLS** ···

Be sure you know special product patterns. Multiply. Review Lesson 83 if needed.

1. $(a + b)^2$ 2. $(a - b)^2$ 3. $(a + b)(a - b)$

4. $(x + 1)^2$ 5. $(x - 2)^2$ 6. $(x + 3)(x - 3)$

7. $(2x + 1)^2$ 8. $(3x - 2)^2$ 9. $(5x + 4)(5x - 4)$

☐ **EXERCISE YOUR SKILLS** ···

Multiply. Write your answers in standard form.

10. $(x - 4)^2$ 11. $(x - 1)(x + 3)$

12. $(x + 6)(x - 2)$ 13. $(x + 9)^2$

14. $(x + 4)(x + 3)$ 15. $(x + 2)(x - 7)$

16. $(x + 3)^2$ 17. $(x + 9)(x + 1)$

18. $(x + 2)(x - 2)$ 19. $(x - 8)^2$

20. $(x - 4)(x - 1)$ 21. $(x + 9)(x - 9)$

22. $(3x + 1)^2$ 23. $(9x - 1)^2$

24. $(2x - 1)(x - 3)$ 25. $(2x + 5)(2x - 5)$

26. $(3x + 1)(x - 6)$ 27. $(x + 5)(4x + 1)$

28. $(4x - 7)(3x + 2)$ 29. $(5x - 4)^2$

EXTRA Multiply. Write your answers in standard form.

30. $(x + 2)^2$

31. $(x + 1)(x - 2)$

32. $(x + 4)(x - 4)$

33. $(x + 2)(x - 5)$

34. $(x - 7)^2$

35. $(x + 3)(x + 5)$

36. $(x - 9)(x + 3)$

37. $(x + 6)^2$

38. $(x + 1)(5x + 2)$

39. $(2x + 9)(2x - 9)$

40. $(4x + 7)^2$

41. $(4x + 3)(2x - 1)$

42. $(3x - 2)(3x - 4)$

43. $(6x - 1)(5x + 6)$

44. $(7x + 2)^2$

45. $(4x + 7)(4x - 7)$

CHALLENGE Find the values of m and n.

46. $(x + m)(x + n) = x^2 + 3x + 2$

47. $(x + m)(x + n) = x^2 + 4x + 3$

48. $(x + m)(x + n) = x^2 + x - 2$

49. $(x + m)(x + n) = x^2 + x - 6$

50. $(x + m)(x + n) = x^2 - 5x + 6$

51. $(x + m)(x + n) = x^2 - 7x + 10$

CHALLENGE Find two binomials whose product is each given polynomial.

52. $x^2 - 2x + 1$

53. $4x^2 + 4x + 1$

54. $x^2 - 64$

55. $16x^2 - 25$

LESSON 85 Dividing Polynomials

☐ **DIVIDING BY MONOMIALS** ···

To divide a monomial by a monomial, use the quotient rule for exponents.

➜ EXAMPLE Divide $25x^4$ by $5x^2$.

$$\frac{25x^4}{5x^2} = \frac{25}{5} \cdot x^{4-2} = 5x^2$$

➜ TRY IT Divide.

1. $\dfrac{x^5}{x^3}$

2. $\dfrac{16x^3}{4x^2}$

To divide a polynomial by a monomial, divide each term of the polynomial by the monomial.

➜ EXAMPLE Divide $6x^3 - 3x^2 + 9x$ by $3x$.

$$\frac{6x^3 - 3x^2 + 9x}{3x} = \frac{6x^3}{3x} - \frac{3x^2}{3x} + \frac{9x}{3x}$$

$$= \frac{6}{3}x^{3-1} - \frac{3}{3}x^{2-1} + \frac{9}{3}x^{1-1}$$

$$= 2x^2 - x + 3$$

➜ TRY IT Divide.

3. $\dfrac{x^3 - 5x^2 + x}{x}$

4. $\dfrac{2x^6 - 6x^5 + 4x^4 - 2x^3}{2x^3}$

☐ **DIVIDING POLYNOMIALS WITH NO REMAINDER** ··

To divide a polynomial by a polynomial, use long division just as you would with numbers. Be sure you understand long division with numbers <u>before</u> working with polynomials.

➜ EXAMPLE Divide $3x^2 - 4x - 4$ by $x - 2$.

Step 1. Set up the division problem.

$$x - 2 \,\big|\, 3x^2 - 4x - 4$$

Step 2. Divide, multiply, subtract, and bring down.

$$
\begin{array}{r}
3x \phantom{{}- 4x - 4} \\
x - 2 \,\big|\, \overline{3x^2 - 4x - 4} \\
\underline{3x^2 - 6x} \phantom{{}- 4} \\
2x - 4
\end{array}
$$

Divide: $3x^2 \div x = 3x$

Multiply: $(x - 2) \times 3x$

Subtract & bring down.

Step 3. Repeat.

$$
\begin{array}{r}
3x + 2 \\
x - 2 \,\big|\, \overline{3x^2 - 4x - 4} \\
\underline{3x^2 - 6x} \phantom{{}- 4} \\
2x - 4 \\
\underline{2x - 4} \\
0
\end{array}
$$

$2x \div x = 2$

$(x - 2) \times 2$

Subtract.

Step 4. Write the answer: $3x + 2$

Step 5. Check the answer:

$$(x - 2)(3x + 2) = 3x^2 - 4x - 4$$

➔ **TRY IT** Divide.

5. $x + 2 \overline{\smash{)}\,x^2 + 3x + 2}$

6. $2x + 1 \overline{\smash{)}\,2x^2 - 5x - 3}$

☐ **EXERCISE YOUR SKILLS** ··

Divide. Write your answers in standard form. Check your answers by multiplying.

7. $(6x^5) \div (3x)$

8. $(4x^6 - 16x^5 + 8x^4) \div (4x^3)$

9. $(x^2 + 5x + 6) \div (x + 3)$

10. $(x^2 - 2x + 1) \div (x - 1)$

11. $(x^2 - 8x + 16) \div (x - 4)$

12. $(x^2 - 8x + 12) \div (x - 6)$

13. $(3x^2 - 8x - 3) \div (x - 3)$

14. $(2x^2 + 5x + 2) \div (x + 2)$

15. $(4x^2 - 7x - 2) \div (4x + 1)$

16. $(10x^2 - 9x - 9) \div (5x + 3)$

EXTRA Divide. Write your answers in standard form. Check your answers by multiplying.

17. $(12x^6) \div (-2x^2)$

18. $(15x^2 - 10x) \div (5x)$

19. $(9x^4 + 4x^2) \div (x^2)$

20. $(2x^3 - 8x^2 + 6x) \div (-2x)$

21. $(x^2 + 7x + 10) \div (x + 2)$

22. $(x^2 + 3x - 28) \div (x - 4)$

23. $(5x^2 + 9x + 4) \div (x + 1)$

24. $(4x^2 + 19x - 5) \div (x + 5)$

25. $(8x^2 + 2x - 3) \div (2x - 1)$

26. $(6x^2 + 16x + 8) \div (3x + 2)$

CHALLENGE Divide. Write your answers in standard form. Check your answers by multiplying.

27. $(2x^3 - x^2 - x) \div (x^2 - x)$

28. $(x^4 + 6x^2 + 9) \div (x^2 + 3)$

29. $(x^3 + 4x^2 + 5x + 2) \div (x + 2)$

30. $(4x^3 - 7x^2 + 11x - 6) \div (x^2 - x + 2)$

LESSON 86 Dividing Polynomials

Divide. Review Lesson 85 if needed.

1. $(-10x^8) \div (5x^3)$

2. $(x^2 - 4x + 4) \div (x - 2)$

☐ **DIVIDING POLYNOMIALS WITH REMAINDERS** ··

Be sure you understand long division with numbers <u>before</u> working with polynomials.

When dividing polynomials, if there is a remainder, put the remainder as part of the answer. Simply write the remainder as a fraction with the divisor as the denominator.

➜ **EXAMPLE** Divide $6x^2 + 5x - 7$ by $2x + 3$.

$$
\begin{array}{r}
3x \ -2 \\
2x + 3 \overline{)\ 6x^2 + 5x - 7} \\
\underline{6x^2 + 9x} \quad (2x+3) \times 3x \\
-4x - 7 \\
\underline{-4x - 6} \quad (2x+3) \times (-2) \\
-1 \quad \text{Remainder}
\end{array}
$$

Write the answer:

$$3x - 2 - \dfrac{1}{2x + 3}$$ Write the remainder as a fraction.

Check the answer:

$$(2x + 3)(3x - 2) - 1 = 6x^2 + 5x - 7$$

➜ **TRY IT** Divide.

3. $(x^2 - x - 5) \div (x + 2)$

4. $(x^2 - 3x + 5) \div (x - 1)$

5. $(3x^2 + 4x + 2) \div (x + 2)$

6. $(6x^2 + 7x + 7) \div (3x - 1)$

☐ **DIVIDING POLYNOMIALS WITH MISSING TERMS** ···

When dividing polynomials, if the dividend has missing terms, insert the missing terms with a coefficient of 0. This will make it more convenient to perform long division.

➜ **EXAMPLE** Divide $x^2 - 9$ by $x - 3$.

$$
\begin{array}{r}
x \ +3 \\
x - 3 \overline{)\ x^2 + 0x - 9} \quad \text{Fill in the missing term.} \\
\underline{x^2 - 3x} \\
3x - 9 \\
\underline{3x - 9} \\
0
\end{array}
$$

➜ **TRY IT** Divide.

7. $(x^2 - 15) \div (x - 4)$

8. $(4x^2 + 8x) \div (2x + 1)$

Check if the answer is correct. Show how you check.

9. $(x^2 + 6x + 7) \div (x + 3)$

$= x + 3 - \dfrac{2}{x + 3}$

10. $(x^2 + 5x + 9) \div (x + 4)$

$= x + 1 - \dfrac{5}{x + 4}$

11. $(3x^2 - 8x + 3) \div (x - 3)$

$= 3x + 1 + \dfrac{6}{x - 3}$

12. $(20x^2 - 13x + 9) \div (5x - 2)$

$= 4x - 1 + \dfrac{2}{5x - 2}$

Divide. Write your answers in standard form. Check your answers.

13. $(8x^5) \div (4x)$

14. $(x^4 - 2x^2) \div x$

15. $(x^2 - 5x - 14) \div (x - 7)$

16. $(x^2 + 6x + 9) \div (x + 3)$

17. $(x^2 - x - 5) \div (x - 4)$

18. $(x^2 + 6x + 7) \div (x + 2)$

19. $(2x^2 - 5x + 3) \div (2x - 5)$

20. $(49x^2 + 1) \div (7x - 1)$

EXTRA Divide. Write your answers in standard form. Check your answers.

21. $(15x^4) \div (-5x^3)$

22. $(3x^6 - 9x^5 + 6x^3) \div (3x^3)$

23. $(x^2 + 9x + 18) \div (x + 6)$

24. $(x^2 + 4x - 32) \div (x - 4)$

25. $(x^2 - 25) \div (x + 5)$

26. $(x^2 + 9x + 14) \div (x + 2)$

27. $(9x^2 + 6x + 1) \div (3x + 1)$

28. $(4x^2 - 9) \div (2x + 3)$

29. $(x^2 + x - 10) \div (x + 3)$

30. $(x^2 + 4x) \div (x + 5)$

31. $(4x^2 + 4x + 9) \div (2x + 1)$

32. $(9x^2 + 15x - 1) \div (3x + 4)$

LESSON 87 Catch Up and Review!

Catch up if you are behind. Use the review problems below to make sure you're on track.

LESSON 80 Add or subtract.

1. $(x + 4) + (3x - 2)$

2. $(4x^2 + x + 7) + (2x^2 - x - 5)$

3. $(2x + 5) - (4x - 3)$

4. $(9x^2 - 6x + 4) - (2x^2 + x - 2)$

LESSON 81 Multiply.

5. $x(5x^3)$

6. $2x^2(3x^2 - x)$

7. $(x - 3)(x + 2)$

8. $(x - 4)(x + 7)$

9. $(2x + 1)(x - 5)$

10. $(2x + 3)(3x + 4)$

LESSON 82 Multiply.

11. $(x + 5)(x^2 + 3x - 2)$

12. $(x^2 + 2x + 4)(x - 2)$

13. $(2x + 1)(4x^2 - 2x + 1)$

14. $(x^2 + 2x + 1)(x^2 - 3x + 2)$

LESSONS 83–84 Multiply.

15. $(x + 3)^2$

16. $(x + 5)(x - 5)$

17. $(x + 5)(x + 2)$

18. $(2x - 1)^2$

19. $(4x + 3)(4x - 3)$

20. $(3x + 5)(2x - 7)$

LESSON 85 Divide.

21. $(x^2 - 3x + 2) \div (x - 2)$

22. $(x^2 - x - 12) \div (x + 3)$

23. $(2x^2 - 5x + 2) \div (2x - 1)$

24. $(20x^2 + x - 12) \div (5x + 4)$

LESSON 86 Divide.

25. $(x^2 + 8x + 11) \div (x + 3)$

26. $(2x^2 - 5x + 5) \div (2x - 1)$

27. $(x^2 - 20) \div (x - 5)$

28. $(9x^2 - 5) \div (3x + 2)$

☐ **MIXED REVIEW: PRE-ALGEBRA** ···

Brush up on the topics covered in Pre-Algebra.

Reference

$$A = lw$$

$$A = \frac{1}{2} bh$$

$$V = lwh$$

$$V = \frac{1}{3} lwh$$

29. Find the volume of a cube with side length of 8 in.

30. A cube has six square faces. Find the surface area of a cube with side length of 8 in.

31. Find the volume of a rectangular prism that is 6 in long, 5 in wide, and 10 in tall.

32. A rectangular prism has three pairs of identical faces: top and bottom, front and back, and left and right. Find the surface area of a rectangular prism that is 6 in long, 5 in wide, and 10 in tall.

33. Find the volume of a square pyramid whose height is 8 ft and base side length is 12 ft.

34. A square pyramid has one square base and four triangular sides. Find the surface area of a square pyramid whose height is 8 ft and whose sides are identical triangles with a base of 12 ft and a height of 10 ft.

LESSON 88 Review: 1st Quarter

Let's review the topics covered in the first quarter.

LESSONS 3–6 & 38–40 Solve.

1. $4x + 7 = 35$

2. $-2x + 4 > 8$

3. $3x + x = 4(x + 3) + 4x$

4. $x + 9 > 16$ and $3(x - 2) < 4x$

5. $|8 - x| + 3 = 5$

6. $|1 - 5x| + 4 \geq 5$

LESSONS 9–11 Solve.

7. The sum of Kyle's age and Alex's age is 35. Ten years ago, Kyle's age was double Alex's age. How old are they now?

8. It takes 6 minutes (or 0.1 hour) to drive to a community park at an average speed of 30 mph. How long will it take to walk to the park at an average speed of 4 mph?

9. How much water must be added to 12 grams of a 70% iodine solution to produce a 40% iodine solution?

10. Two trains leave a station at the same time and travel in opposite directions. One train travels at 85 mph while the other travels at 75 mph. How long does it take for the two trains to be 880 miles apart?

LESSONS 29–33 Solve.

11. $y = x - 5$
    $3x + y = 3$

12. $y = -2x + 1$
    $2x - 3y = -11$

13. $x + y = 5$
    $5x - y = 7$

14. $3x + 2y = 7$
    $2x + 3y = 3$

LESSONS 34–36 Solve

15. Logan drove to a park at an average speed of 30 mph and then to a library at an average speed of 40 mph. He spent 1 hour driving 35 miles in total. What is the distance between the park and the library?

16. An airplane can fly 700 miles with the wind in 2.5 hours. The same plane can fly 1,200 miles against the wind in 5 hours. Find the speed of the plane in still air and the speed of the wind.

17. Candy A that costs $5.60 per pound is mixed with candy B that costs $3.20 per pound. How much of each should be used to make 18 pounds of a mixture that costs $4 per pound?

LESSONS 16–20 & 41–42 Graph.

18. $y = 2x - 1$

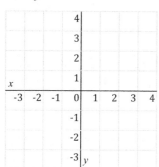

19. $2x + 3y = -6$

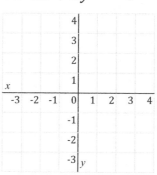

20. $y = |x - 1|$

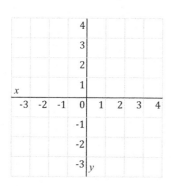

21. $\begin{cases} y \geq x - 1 \\ x - 3y > 3 \end{cases}$

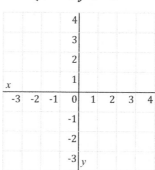

LESSONS 22–25 Find an equation of each line in slope-intercept form and in standard form. Use only integers and the smallest possible positive integer coefficient for x.

22. through $(4, 3)$ and $(-2, 0)$

23. perpendicular to $3x + y = 1$, through $(6, 4)$

LESSON 89 Review: 2nd Quarter

Let's review the topics covered in the second quarter.

LESSONS 48–49 Find the domain and range, then identify as a function or not a function.

1.
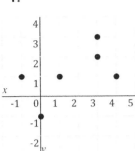

2.
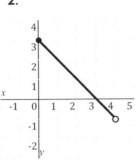

3.
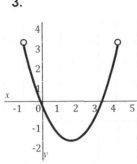

4.
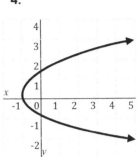

LESSON 50 Evaluate when $x = -1, 0$, and 5. Write your answers in function notation.

5. $f(x) = |x - 9|$

6. $g(x) = x^2 - 2x + 1$

LESSONS 51–52 Classify as linear, exponential, quadratic, or none of these. If linear, write a rule.

7.

x	0	1	2	3	4
y	3	6	12	24	48

8.

x	−1	0	1	2	3
y	−8	−5	−2	1	4

9.

x	−2	−1	0	1	2
y	−8	−1	0	1	8

10.

x	−2	0	2	4	6
y	9	1	1	9	25

LESSON 53 Find the average rate of change.

11. $f(x) = x^2 - 2x;\ 2 \le x \le 5$

12. $g(x) = 4 \cdot 3^x;\ 0 \le x \le 4$

13. $h(x) = \dfrac{x^2 - 16}{x + 4};\ -3 \le x \le 3$

14. $k(x) = 6 + \dfrac{x + 2}{x};\ 2 \le x \le 8$

LESSON 54 Find the inverse algebraically. Write your answers in function notation.

15. $f(x) = x + 3$

16. $g(x) = 2x - 6$

17. $h(x) = \dfrac{3 - 2x}{4}$

18. $k(x) = \dfrac{1}{6}x + \dfrac{1}{3}$

LESSONS 56–57 Write a direct or inverse variation equation, then solve.

19. Suppose y varies directly with x, and $y = 6$ when $x = 4$. Find y when $x = 6$.

20. Suppose y varies inversely with x, and $y = 8$ when $x = 3$. Find y when $x = -4$.

21. The amount of sales tax varies directly with the cost of the purchase. If the sales tax is $2.70 on a purchase of $45, what will be the sales tax on a purchase of $32?

22. The time it takes to travel a certain distance varies inversely with the speed traveled. If it takes 1 hour to drive to work at 40 mph, how long will it take to drive back home at 50 mph?

LESSONS 58–60 Identify as arithmetic or geometric, then find the explicit and recursive formulas.

23. 5, 10, 20, 40, 80, ...

24. 12, 14, 16, 18, 20, ...

25. −7, 2, 11, 20, 29, ...

26. 1, −5, 25, −125, 625, ...

LESSON 61 Solve. Round your answers to the nearest hundredth.

27. Amy put $2,000 in her savings account with a simple interest rate of 2% per year. What will be the balance of her account at the end of the 6th year?

28. A ball is dropped from a height of 5 meters. On each bounce, the ball rises to 80% of the height it reached on the previous bounce. Determine how high the ball rebounds on its fifth bounce.

LESSON 90 Review: 2nd Quarter

Let's review the topics covered in the second quarter.

LESSONS 63–65 Simplify. Assume that all variables are positive.

1. $\sqrt{25}$

2. $\sqrt[3]{27}$

3. $\sqrt{24}$

4. $\sqrt[3]{54}$

5. $\sqrt{x^3}$

6. $\sqrt[3]{x^3 y^4}$

LESSONS 66-67 Simplify. Rationalize all denominators. Assume that all variables are positive.

7. $\sqrt{50} + \sqrt{72}$

8. $\sqrt{10x^3} \cdot \sqrt{5x}$

9. $\dfrac{10}{\sqrt{5}} + \sqrt{80}$

10. $\dfrac{\sqrt{72x^2 y}}{2\sqrt{9xy}}$

LESSON 68 Solve. Check for extraneous solutions.

11. $\sqrt{x-7} + 4 = 6$

12. $5 - \sqrt{2x+5} = 8$

13. $\sqrt{6x-1} = \sqrt{4x+7}$

14. $9 + \sqrt[3]{x-15} = 6$

LESSON 69 Find the missing side. Leave your answers in simplest radical form, if applicable.

15.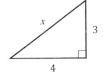

16.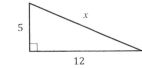

17. A 10-foot ladder is leaning against a wall. The ladder reaches a height of 8 feet. How far is the bottom of the ladder from the wall?

LESSON 71 Evaluate.

18. 9^0

19. $4^5 \cdot 2^{-9}$

LESSONS 72–74 Simplify using positive exponents.

20. $5x^{-4} \cdot 2x^3$

21. $x^{-2} \cdot (2x^3)^4$

22. $\dfrac{7x^{-4}x^2}{x^5x^3}$

23. $\dfrac{27x^2}{(3x^{-3})^2}$

LESSON 76 Evaluate.

24. $16^{1/2}$

25. $(-8)^{1/3}$

26. $81^{-1/4}$

27. $\left(\dfrac{1}{125}\right)^{2/3}$

LESSON 77 Simplify using positive exponents.

28. $x^{1/3} \cdot x^{1/4}$

29. $\left(8x^{3/4}\right)^{4/3}$

30. $\dfrac{6x^{3/4}}{3x^{1/2}}$

31. $\left(\dfrac{25x^{1/2}}{x^{1/6}}\right)^{1/2}$

LESSONS 80-86 Simplify. Write your answers in standard form.

32. $(x - 6)(x + 3)$

33. $(2x - 3)(x^2 + 4x - 1)$

34. $(x^2 - 5x - 14) \div (x + 2)$

35. $(x^2 - 8) \div (x + 2)$

LESSON 91 PSAT Practice

This is a timed practice test. Get a timer, a bubble answer sheet, and blank sheets of paper for your calculations. When you are ready, set the timer for **25 minutes** and begin. Do not use a calculator. Mark all your answers on the answer sheet. Only answers marked on the answer sheet can be scored. After the test, make sure you review what you missed.

1. $3x + 5 = 6(x + 1)$

   If x is a solution to the equation above, what is the value of $3x + 1$?

   A) 0   B) 2   C) 7   D) 5

2. $f(x) = |x| + 3$

   What is the range of the function above?

   A) $f(x) \geq 0$ B) $f(x) \geq 3$

   C) $f(x) \leq 3$ D) All real numbers

3. $(2x^2 + x + 3y) - (x^2 - x + 2y)$

   Which of the following is equivalent to the expression above?

   A) $x^2 + 5y$ B) $x^2 + 2x + y$

   C) $3x^2 + 5y$ D) $3x^2 + 2x + 5y$

4. If $x + 6$ is multiplied by $x - 3$, what is the resulting coefficient of x ?

   A) -9 B) -3 C) 3   D) 9

5. Which of the following is equivalent to the expression $\sqrt{12} - \sqrt{3}$?

   A) $\sqrt{3}$ B) $2\sqrt{6} - \sqrt{3}$

   C) $3\sqrt{3}$ B) $6\sqrt{2} - \sqrt{3}$

6. If $16^{-2} = \left(\frac{1}{2}\right)^n$, what is the value of n ?

   A) 4   B) 6   C) 8   D) 10

7. $\left(x^{\frac{1}{2}} y^{\frac{1}{4}}\right)(x^2 y^4) = x^a y^b$

   If the equation above is true for all positive values of x and y, what is the value of $a + 2b$?

   A) 2   B) 3   C) 9   D) 11

8. If y varies directly with x, and $y = 3$ when $x = 2$, which equation relates x and y ?

   A) $xy = 6$ B) $y = 6x$

   C) $y = \frac{3}{2}x$ D) $y = x + 1$

9. What is the value of x in the right triangle below?

   A) $2\sqrt{3}$

   B) $3\sqrt{2}$

   C) 5

   D) 9

Continue to the next page.

10. Kyle's car uses 4 gallons of gas to travel 96 miles. How many miles can Kyle drive on 3 gallons of gas?

    A) 24
    B) 72
    C) 125
    D) 168

11. Lillian bought 2 yards of fabric. She cut it into strips that are 8 inches wide. How many strips did she make? (1 yard = 3 feet and 1 foot = 12 inches)

    A) 3   B) 6   C) 9   D) 12

12. A group of 5 friends went out for dinner. The bill was $90 plus a 20% tip. If they split the bill evenly, which expression can be used to determine the amount of money, x, each person paid?

    A) $\dfrac{90 + 0.2}{5}$

    B) $\dfrac{90 + 1.2}{5}$

    C) $\dfrac{90}{5} + 90 \cdot 0.2$

    D) $\dfrac{90 + 90 \cdot 0.2}{5}$

13. Liam deposited $1,000 in his savings account. The table below shows the balance y, in dollars, of the account after x years. Which of the following best describes the data in the table?

x	0	1	2	3	4
y	1,000	1,030	1,060	1,090	1,120

    A) Linear, increasing by $30 per year

    B) Linear, increasing by $50 per year

    C) Exponential, increasing by 3% per year

    D) Exponential, increasing by 6% per year

14. A line has a slope of 3 and a y-intercept of -2. Which of the following is an equation of the line?

    A) $x - 3y = 6$
    B) $x + 3y = -6$
    C) $3x - y = 2$
    D) $3x + y = -2$

15. A moving truck rental costs $20 for the first day and $10 for each day after the first. Which function gives the total cost, C, of renting a truck for d days?

    A) $C(d) = 20 + 10d$

    B) $C(d) = 20 + 10(d - 1)$

    C) $C(d) = 30 + 10d$

    D) $C(d) = 30 + 10(d - 1)$

16. A gym membership costs $30 to join and $15 each month. Carol joined the gym and also rented a locker at $2 per month. Which expression represents Carol's total cost after x months?

    A) $30 + 2 + 15x$
    B) $30 + (15 + 2)x$
    C) $30 + 15 + 2x$
    D) $(30 + 15 + 2)x$

17. A 100-point test has a total of 16 questions. The multiple-choice questions are worth 6 points each, and the short-answer questions are worth 8 points each. What is the ratio of the number of multiple-choice questions to the number of short-answer questions?

    A) 2:1   B) 3:1   C) 3:2   D) 7:1

STOP

This is the end of the test. If you finish before time is up, check your work.

LESSON 92 PSAT Practice

This is a timed practice test. Get a timer, a bubble answer sheet, and blank sheets of paper for your calculations. When you are ready, set the timer for **25 minutes** and begin. Do not use a calculator. Mark all your answers on the answer sheet. Only answers marked on the answer sheet can be scored. After the test, make sure you review what you missed.

1. $|3 + 4x| = 5$

   If a and b are the solutions to the equation above, what is the value of ab ?

   A) -2 B) -1 C) 1   D) 2

2. $f(x) = 4x - 5$

   Given the function above, what is the value of x when $f(x) = 3$?

   A) -12 B) 2   C) 3   D) 7

3. $\sqrt[3]{-64x^{12}y^6}$

   Which of the following is equivalent to the expression above?

   A) $8x^6y^3$ B) $-8x^4y^2$

   C) $4x^6y^3$ D) $-4x^4y^2$

4. $\sqrt{5x - 1} = \sqrt{3x + 7}$

   If x is a solution to the equation above, what is the value of x^2 ?

   A) 4   B) 9   C) 16   D) 25

5. If $x^2 - 3x + k$ is divisible by $x - 4$, what is the value of k ?

   A) -4 B) -3 C) 2   D) 4

6. $(2x + 1)(x - 3)$

   Which of the following is equivalent to the expression above?

   A) $-6x^2 + x$ B) $2x^2 - 3$

   C) $2x^2 - 5x - 3$ D) $2x^2 - 7x + 3$

7. $\dfrac{6^4 \cdot 3^2}{2^4}$

   Which of the following is equal to the value above?

   A) 3^3 B) 3^6 C) 3^8 D) $\dfrac{3^6}{2^3}$

8. $(x^2y^3)^{\frac{1}{6}} = x^a y^b$

   If the equation above is true for all positive values of x and y, what is the value of ab ?

   A) $\dfrac{1}{6}$ B) $\dfrac{5}{6}$ C) 1   D) 6

9. $x^3 = \sqrt[n]{x^m}$

   If the equation above is true for all positive values of x, what is the ratio of m^2 to n^2 ?

   A) 1:3   B) 3:1   C) 1:9   D) 9:1

Continue to the next page.

10. A book club has 20 members. The ratio of boys to girls is 3:2. How many more girls should join the club to make the ratio 1:1 ?

A) 2   B) 4   C) 6   D) 8

11. Luke made exactly 40% of the free throws he shot. Which of the following could be the number of free throws he shot?

A) 21   B) 23   C) 25   D) 27

12. $y = 100 - 0.5x$

The equation above models the remaining balance, y, on a prepaid phone card after making a total of x minutes of calls. If the equation is graphed in the xy-plane, what does the slope of the graph represent?

A) The initial balance of $100

B) The remaining balance of $100

C) The rate per call of $0.50

D) The rate per minute of $0.50

13. Line l has the equation $2x + y = 1$. Line m has the equation $x - 2y = 1$. Which of the following is true about the two lines?

A) They are parallel.

B) They are perpendicular.

C) They are the same.

D) They intersect, but not at a right angle.

14. A bacteria culture starts with 100 bacteria and doubles in size every hour. Which function gives the number of bacteria, N, after t hours?

A) $N(t) = 100t^2$

B) $N(t) = (100t)^2$

C) $N(t) = 100(2)^t$

D) $N(t) = (100 \cdot 2)^t$

15. The area of a triangle is one-half base times height. A triangle has a base of 8 cm and a height of x cm. What are all the values of x for which the area of the triangle is at least 16 cm² and at most 48 cm² ?

A) $2 < x < 6$ B) $2 \leq x \leq 6$

C) $4 < x < 12$ D) $4 \leq x \leq 12$

16. The resale value of a car varies inversely with its age. If a 2-year-old car costs $18,000, what will be the value of the car when it is 6 years old?

A) $600   B) $5,400

C) $6,000   D) $54,000

17. If a boat travels upstream at 16 km/h and downstream at 20 km/h, how fast does the boat travel in still water?

A) 5 km/h   B) 18 km/h

C) 22 km/h   D) 36 km/h

STOP

This is the end of the test. If you finish before time is up, check your work.

LESSON 93 Factoring Polynomials Using GCFs

Multiply. Review Lessons 81 and 82 if needed.

1. $(3x^2)(2x^4)$

2. $2x^3(x^2 - 3x - 4)$

3. $(x + 5)(x - 3)$

4. $(x + 2)(x^2 + 5x - 6)$

☐ **BASIC DEFINITIONS** ···

A **factor** is a number or expression that is multiplied by another number or expression to yield a product. For example, 2 and 4 are factors of 8 because $2 \times 4 = 8$. Similarly, $(x + 2)$ and $(x - 2)$ are factors of $x^2 - 4$ because $(x + 2)(x - 2) = x^2 - 4$.

Factorization (also called **factoring** or **to factor**) is writing a number or expression as a product of factors. For example, we can factor 8 as 2×4 and $x^2 - 4$ as $(x + 2)(x - 2)$.

☐ **FINDING GCFs OF POLYNOMIALS** ···

The **greatest common factor** (GCF) of a polynomial is the largest monomial that divides (is a factor of) each term of the polynomial.

To find the GCF of a polynomial, 1) find the GCF of the coefficients, 2) find the GCF of the variables by taking the lowest power of each variable that is common to all the terms, and then 3) multiply the GCFs together.

➜ **EXAMPLE** Find the GCF.

a. $3x^5 + 6x^4 + 18x$ ⟹ GCF(3, 6, 18) = 3 and GCF(x^5, x^4, x) = x, so GCF = $3x$.

b. $2x^4y^3 + x^3y^2 + 4x^2$ ⟹ GCF(2, 1, 4) = 1 and GCF(x^4y^3, x^3y^2, x^2) = x^2, so GCF = x^2. Notice that y cannot be a common factor since it is not in every term.

➜ **TRY IT** Find the GCF.

5. $5x + 5$

6. $4x^2 - 6x$

7. $8x^3y^2 + 6x^2y^3$

☐ **FACTORING OUT GCFs** ···

Factoring a polynomial means writing it as a product of two or more polynomials. When a polynomial has a GCF other than 1, you can apply the distributive property in reverse to factor out the GCF and write the polynomial as a product of the GCF and its remaining factors. Notice that factoring is simply the reverse of multiplying.

Multiplying ⟹
$$a(b + c) = ab + ac$$
⟸ Factoring

➔ **EXAMPLE** Factor out the GCF.

a. $3x^5 + 6x^4 + 18x = 3x(x^4 + 2x^3 + 6)$ Factor out the GCF $3x$.

b. $2x^4y^3 + x^3y^2 + 4x^2 = x^2(2x^2y^3 + xy^2 + 4)$ Factor out the GCF x^2.

➔ **TRY IT** Factor out the GCF.

8. $5x + 5$ 　　　　　　 9. $4x^2 - 6x$ 　　　　　　 10. $8x^3y^2 + 6x^2y^3$

☐ **CHECKING BY MULTIPLYING** ···

You can check your factoring by multiplying the factors to see if you get the original polynomial.

➔ **TRY IT** Factored correctly? Check by multiplying.

11. $4x^3 - 8x = 4x(x^2 - 2)$ 　　　　　　 12. $10x^2y - 5xy + 5y = 5y(2x^2 - x)$

☐ **EXERCISE YOUR SKILLS** ···

Factor out the GCF. Check by multiplying.

13. $3x + 6$ 　　　　　　　　　　 14. $14x^2 - 7$

15. $18x^5 + 12x^2$ 　　　　　　　 16. $3x^2 - 15x - 9$

17. $12x^3 + 6x^2 - 8x$ 　　　　　 18. $28x^4 + 14x^3 + 21x^2$

19. $2x^2y + y^2 - 5y$ 　　　　　　 20. $4x^3y^3 + 8x^2y^2 - 16xy$

EXTRA Factor out the GCF. Check by multiplying.

21. $9x - 12$ 　　　　　　　　　　 22. $x^2 + 5x$

23. $16x^3 - 20x$ 　　　　　　　　 24. $2x^2 - 8x + 4$

25. $2x^4 + x^3 - 2x^2$ 　　　　　　 26. $25x^5 + 20x^3 + 10x^2$

27. $14x^2y - 7xy + 28x$ 　　　　　 28. $7x^4y^2 + 6x^3y - x^2y^2$

LESSON 94 Factoring Polynomials by Grouping

☐ **REFRESH YOUR SKILLS** ··

Factor out the GCF. Review Lesson 93 if needed.

1. $3x^3 - 9x^2$

2. $4x^4 + 6x^3 - 12x$

☐ **FACTORING OUT COMMON BINOMIALS** ···

You can factor out a common binomial factor from a polynomial just as you factor out the GCF from a polynomial. Simply apply the distributive property in reverse.

➜ **EXAMPLE** Factor out the common binomial.

$$4x(x - 2) + 3(x - 2) = (x - 2)(4x + 3)$$ $(x - 2)$ is common, so factor it out.

➜ **TRY IT** Factor out the common binomial.

3. $x(x + 2) + 3(x + 2)$

4. $4x^3(2x^2 - 7) - 3(2x^2 - 7)$

☐ **FACTORING 4-TERM POLYNOMIALS BY GROUPING** ···

Sometimes you can factor a 4-term polynomial by grouping and factoring out a binomial.

➜ **EXAMPLE** Factor by grouping.

$$
\begin{aligned}
3x^3 - 9x^2 + 2x - 6 &= (3x^3 - 9x^2) + (2x - 6) && \text{Group the terms.}\\
&= 3x^2(x - 3) + 2(x - 3) && \text{Factor out the GCF from each group.}\\
&= (x - 3)(3x^2 + 2) && \text{Factor out the common binomial.}
\end{aligned}
$$

➜ **TRY IT** Factor by grouping.

5. $x^3 + 2x^2 + 4x + 8$

6. $2x^3 + 10x^2 - 3x - 15$

When a polynomial has a GCF other than 1, factor out the GCF first. Then the remaining polynomial will be easier to factor.

➜ **EXAMPLE** Factor out the GCF first, then factor by grouping.

$$
\begin{aligned}
4x^4 + 6x^3 - 8x^2 - 12x &= 2x[2x^3 + 3x^2 - 4x - 6] && \text{Factor out the GCF.}\\
&= 2x[x^2(2x + 3) - 2(2x + 3)] && \text{Factor by grouping.}\\
&= 2x(2x + 3)(x^2 - 2)
\end{aligned}
$$

➜ **TRY IT** Factor out the GCF first, then factor by grouping.

7. $6x^3 - 8x^2 + 18x - 24$

8. $3x^6 + 6x^4 + 12x^3 + 24x$

Factor by grouping. Check by multiplying.

9. $x^3 + 4x^2 + x + 4$

10. $x^3 - 2x^2 + x - 2$

11. $2x^3 + 4x^2 - 7x - 14$

12. $3x^3 - 15x^2 - 2x + 10$

13. $2x^3 - 3x^2 + 8x - 12$

14. $5x^3 - 7x^2 + 5x - 7$

15. $30x^4 - 25x^3 - 12x + 10$

16. $14x^5 + 4x^3 + 21x^2 + 6$

Factor out the GCF first, then factor by grouping. Check by multiplying.

17. $8x^3 + 4x^2 + 8x + 4$

18. $10x^3 - 10x^2 + 5x - 5$

19. $6x^4 + 3x^3 - 10x^2 - 5x$

20. $2x^4 + 6x^3 - 4x^2 - 12x$

EXTRA Factor as much as possible. Check by multiplying.

21. $2x^2 - 5x$

22. $3x^2 + 9x - 6$

23. $x^2(x - 2) - 7(x - 2)$

24. $x^3(4x + 5) + (4x + 5)$

25. $x^3 - x^2 - 3x + 3$

26. $5x^3 - 2x^2 + 5x - 2$

27. $2x^4 + x^3 + 14x + 7$

28. $5x^5 + 20x^3 - x^2 - 4$

29. $3x^3 + 3x^2 + 6x + 6$

30. $12x^3 - 60x^2 - 4x + 20$

31. $3x^3 + 6x^2 - 15x - 30$

32. $14x^3 - 70x^2 - 2x + 10$

33. $12x^5 - 4x^4 + 9x^3 - 3x^2$

34. $20x^4 - 8x^3 + 30x^2 - 12x$

LESSON 95 Factoring Simple Quadratics

☐ **FACTORING SIMPLE QUADRATICS WITH POSITIVE COEFFICIENTS** ·······················

Consider multiplying two simple binomials $x + m$ and $x + n$. As shown on the right, their product will be a trinomial of the form $x^2 + bx + c$. Now think about factoring a trinomial of the form $x^2 + bx + c$. If we find m and n such that $b = m + n$ and $c = mn$, we can factor the trinomial as $(x + m)(x + n)$.

$$(x + m)(x + n)$$
$$= x^2 + nx + mx + mn$$
$$= x^2 + (n + m)x + mn$$
$$= x^2 + bx + c$$

➔ **TRY IT** Find the values of b and n.

1. $x^2 + bx + 6 = (x + 3)(x + n)$

2. $x^2 + bx + 8 = (x + 2)(x + n)$

Here are the steps to factor $x^2 + bx + c$ as $(x + m)(x + n)$.

➔ **EXAMPLE** Factor.

① $x^2 + 7x + 12 = (x \qquad)(x \qquad)$

② $c = mn \qquad m + n = b$
$12 = 1 \times 12 \quad \rightarrow \quad 1 + 12 = 13$
$12 = 2 \times 6 \quad \rightarrow \quad 2 + 6 = 8$
$12 = 3 \times 4 \quad \rightarrow \quad 3 + 4 = 7 \checkmark$

1. Set up two blank parentheses.
2. List all the factor pairs of c and choose the pair that adds up to b. We list all the factor pairs of 12 and choose $12 = 3 \times 4$ because $3 + 4 = 7$.
3. Place the factors in the parentheses.
4. Check by multiplying the factors.

③ $x^2 + 7x + 12 = (x + 3)(x + 4)$

➔ **TRY IT** Factor.

3. $x^2 + 3x + 2$

4. $x^2 + 7x + 10$

☐ **FACTORING SIMPLE QUADRATICS WITH NEGATIVE COEFFICIENTS** ·······················

Note that you may need to consider negative factors. If c is positive, m and n have the same sign. If c is negative, m and n have opposite signs. Study each example carefully.

➔ **EXAMPLE** Factor.

① $x^2 - 6x + 8 = (x \qquad)(x \qquad)$

② $c = mn \qquad m + n = b$
$8 = 2 \times 4 \quad \rightarrow \quad 2 + 4 = 6$
$8 = -2 \times -4 \quad \rightarrow \quad -2 - 4 = -6 \checkmark$
$\ldots$

③ $x^2 - 6x + 8 = (x - 2)(x - 4)$

➔ **EXAMPLE** Factor.

① $x^2 - 5x - 6 = (x \qquad)(x \qquad)$

② $c = mn \qquad m + n = b$
$-6 = -1 \times 6 \quad \rightarrow \quad -1 + 6 = 5$
$-6 = 1 \times -6 \quad \rightarrow \quad 1 - 6 = -5 \checkmark$
$\ldots$

③ $x^2 - 5x - 6 = (x + 1)(x - 6)$

➔ **TRY IT** Factor.

5. $x^2 - 3x + 2$

6. $x^2 + 3x - 10$

Find the values of b and n.

7. $x^2 + bx + 5 = (x + 5)(x + n)$ 8. $x^2 + bx - 6 = (x - 2)(x + n)$

9. $x^2 + bx - 12 = (x + 3)(x + n)$ 10. $x^2 + bx + 20 = (x - 4)(x + n)$

Factor. Check by multiplying.

11. $x^2 - x - 2$ 12. $x^2 + x - 2$

13. $x^2 + 7x + 6$ 14. $x^2 + 6x + 5$

15. $x^2 - 2x - 15$ 16. $x^2 + 9x + 14$

17. $x^2 - 9x + 20$ 18. $x^2 + 4x - 12$

19. $x^2 + 10x + 24$ 20. $x^2 - 12x + 35$

EXTRA Factor as much as possible. Check by multiplying.

21. $x^2 + x - 6$ 22. $x^2 - x - 6$

23. $x^2 + 4x + 3$ 24. $x^2 + 2x - 3$

25. $x^2 - 7x + 6$ 26. $x^2 - 5x + 6$

27. $x^2 + 2x - 8$ 28. $x^2 - 2x - 8$

29. $x^2 + 7x + 12$ 30. $x^2 - 4x - 12$

31. $x^2 + 9x + 18$ 32. $x^2 - 9x + 18$

33. $x^2 + 11x + 30$ 34. $x^2 - 11x + 30$

LESSON 96 Factoring Simple Quadratics

☐ **REFRESH YOUR SKILLS** ···

Factor out the GCF. Review Lesson 93 if needed.

1. $2x^2 - 6x$

2. $8x^2 + 2x + 10$

Factor. Review Lesson 95 if needed.

3. $x^2 + 4x + 3$

4. $x^2 - 2x - 8$

☐ **FACTORING SIMPLE QUADRATICS WITH COMMON FACTORS** ···

The technique you've just used to factor a trinomial is called **trial and error** because you try different combinations of factors until you find the right combination that will correctly factor the trinomial. It is also called **unFOILing** or **reverse FOIL** because it is literally the reverse process of multiplying two binomials using the FOIL method.

As always, when a polynomial has a GCF other than 1, factor out the GCF first. Then the remaining polynomial will be easier to factor.

➔ **EXAMPLE** Factor out the GCF first, then factor further.

$$3x^2 - 9x - 30 = 3(x^2 - 3x - 10) \qquad \text{Factor out the GCF.}$$
$$= 3(x + 2)(x - 5) \qquad \text{Factor by trial and error: } -10 = 2 \times -5 \text{ and } 2 - 5 = -3.$$

➔ **TRY IT** Factor out the GCF first, then factor further.

5. $2x^2 + 14x + 20$

6. $5x^2 + 5x - 60$

☐ **EXERCISE YOUR SKILLS** ···

Factor. Check by multiplying.

7. $x^2 - x - 6$

8. $x^2 - 7x + 12$

9. $x^2 + 4x - 32$

10. $x^2 - 5x - 36$

11. $x^2 - 10x + 21$

12. $x^2 + 13x + 40$

13. $x^2 + 10x + 24$

14. $x^2 + 4x - 45$

Factor out the GCF first, then factor further. Check by multiplying.

15. $3x^2 + 3x - 18$

16. $2x^2 + 12x + 16$

17. $4x^2 + 4x - 80$

18. $7x^2 - 49x + 70$

19. $2x^2 - 10x - 28$

20. $9x^2 + 90x + 81$

21. $7x^2 + 63x + 56$

22. $4x^2 - 32x + 60$

EXTRA Factor as much as possible. Check by multiplying.

23. $x^2 - x - 2$

24. $x^2 + x - 6$

25. $x^2 + 5x + 6$

26. $x^2 + 4x - 5$

27. $x^2 - 9x + 14$

28. $x^2 - 7x + 12$

29. $x^2 - x - 30$

30. $x^2 + x - 56$

31. $x^2 - 7x - 18$

32. $x^2 + 5x - 24$

33. $x^2 + 9x + 20$

34. $x^2 + 14x + 48$

35. $x^2 - 11x + 28$

36. $x^2 - 12x + 27$

37. $4x^2 - 20x - 96$

38. $3x^2 - 12x - 36$

39. $3x^2 - 27x + 54$

40. $2x^2 + 4x - 70$

41. $4x^2 - 24x + 32$

42. $3x^2 + 15x + 18$

43. $7x^3 - 35x^2 + 42x$

44. $4x^3 + 16x^2 - 48x$

LESSON 97 Factoring Quadratics

☐ **REFRESH YOUR SKILLS** ···

Factor. Review Lesson 95 if needed.

1. $x^2 + 9x + 18$

2. $x^2 + 5x - 36$

☐ **FACTORING QUADRATICS BY TRIAL AND ERROR** ···

We can factor a trinomial of the form $ax^2 + bx + c$ in the same way we factor a trinomial of the form $x^2 + bx + c$. As shown on the right, p and q are factors of a while m and n are factors of c. So we just need to find a combination of factors of a and c such that the outer and inner products add up to the middle term bx.

$(px + m)(qx + n)$
$= pqx^2 + pnx + mqx + mn$
$= pqx^2 + (pn + qm)x + mn$
$= ax^2 + bx + c$

➔ **TRY IT** Find the values of b and n.

3. $2x^2 + bx + 3 = (x + 3)(2x + n)$

4. $3x^2 + bx - 8 = (x - 2)(3x + n)$

5. $6x^2 + bx + 6 = (2x - 3)(3x + n)$

6. $12x^2 + bx - 20 = (3x + 4)(4x + n)$

Here are the steps to factor $ax^2 + bx + c$ as $(px + m)(qx + n)$.

➔ **EXAMPLE** Factor.

① $4x^2 + 4x - 3 = (x \quad)(4x \quad)$
   OR $(2x \quad)(2x \quad)$

②

$c = mn$	$(px + m)(qx + n)$	middle term
1×-3	$(x + 1)(4x - 3)$	$-3x + 4x = x$
	$(2x + 1)(2x - 3)$	$-6x + 2x = -4x$
-1×3	$(x - 1)(4x + 3)$	$3x - 4x = -x$
	$(2x - 1)(2x + 3)$	$6x - 2x = 4x$ ✓
3×-1	...	

1. Set up two blank parentheses for each factor pair of a so that the first term is ax^2. We start with two possible factorizations because $4 = 1 \times 4$ and $4 = 2 \times 2$.

2. Place each factor pair of c into each possible factorization and find the middle term.

3. Choose a factorization that produces the correct middle term bx.

4. Check by multiplying the factors.

③ $4x^2 + 4x - 3 = (2x - 1)(2x + 3)$

➔ **TRY IT** Factor. Notice that there are three possible factorizations in the second problem.

7. $8x^2 - 18x - 5 = (x \quad)(8x \quad)$
   OR $(2x \quad)(4x \quad)$

8. $12x^2 + x - 6 = (x \quad)(12x \quad)$
   OR $(2x \quad)(6x \quad)$
   OR $(3x \quad)(4x \quad)$

Factor. Check by multiplying.

9. $2x^2 + 5x + 3$

10. $3x^2 - 16x + 5$

11. $7x^2 + 13x - 2$

12. $5x^2 + 16x + 3$

13. $8x^2 - 22x + 5$

14. $4x^2 + 13x - 12$

15. $6x^2 + 11x + 3$

16. $15x^2 - 4x - 4$

17. $12x^2 + 20x + 3$

18. $20x^2 - 21x - 5$

19. $18x^2 - 17x + 4$

20. $16x^2 + 16x - 21$

EXTRA Factor as much as possible. Check by multiplying.

21. $x^2 - 3x - 40$

22. $x^2 - 7x + 12$

23. $2x^2 + x - 1$

24. $5x^2 - 9x - 2$

25. $5x^2 - 2x - 3$

26. $3x^2 + 7x - 6$

27. $2x^2 + 11x + 9$

28. $3x^2 - 14x + 8$

29. $8x^2 - 10x - 3$

30. $6x^2 + 7x - 20$

31. $4x^2 + 16x + 15$

32. $10x^2 + 31x - 14$

33. $12x^2 + 7x - 10$

34. $20x^2 - 23x + 6$

35. $18x^2 + 39x + 20$

36. $16x^2 - 14x - 15$

LESSON 98 Factoring Quadratics

☐ REFRESH YOUR SKILLS

Factor by grouping. Review Lesson 94 if needed.

1. $x^3 + 3x^2 + x + 3$

2. $9x^3 + 12x^2 - 3x - 4$

☐ FACTORING QUADRATICS BY GROUPING

You can also factor a trinomial of the form $ax^2 + bx + c$ by grouping, or the **ac method**. The idea is simple: rewrite the trinomial as a 4-term polynomial by breaking up bx into two parts, then factor the 4-term polynomial by grouping.

$$ax^2 + bx + c$$
$$= ax^2 + rx + sx + c$$

➜ TRY IT Factor by grouping.

3. $x^2 - x + 2x - 2$

4. $4x^2 + 2x - 6x - 3$

To rewrite $ax^2 + bx + c$ as $ax^2 + rx + sx + c$, we just need to find r and s whose product is ac and whose sum is b. Why? Compare the coefficients in the equation on the right. As you can see, $r + s = b$ and $rs = (pn)(qm) = (pq)(mn) = ac$.

$$(px + m)(qx + n)$$
$$= pqx^2 + pnx + qmx + mn$$
$$= ax^2 + rx + sx + c$$
$$= ax^2 + bx + c$$

Here are the steps to factor $ax^2 + bx + c$ as $(px + m)(qx + n)$ by grouping.

➜ EXAMPLE Factor by grouping (the ac method).

① $4x^2 + 4x - 3 = 4x^2 + rx + sx - 3$

② $ac = rs \qquad\qquad r + s = b$
$-12 = 1 \times -12 \quad\rightarrow\quad 1 - 12 = -11$
$-12 = -1 \times 12 \quad\rightarrow\quad -1 + 12 = 11$
$-12 = 2 \times -6 \quad\rightarrow\quad 2 - 6 = -4$
$-12 = -2 \times 6 \quad\rightarrow\quad -2 + 6 = 4 \checkmark$
$\dots$

③ $4x^2 + 4x - 3 = 4x^2 - 2x + 6x - 3$

④ $\qquad\qquad\quad = 2x(2x - 1) + 3(2x - 1)$
$\qquad\qquad\quad = (2x - 1)(2x + 3)$

1. Rewrite the trinomial as a 4-term polynomial using r and s.
2. Find r and s whose product is ac and whose sum is b.
3. Plug the values of r and s into the 4-term polynomial.
4. Factor the 4-term polynomial by grouping.
5. Check by multiplying the factors.

➜ TRY IT Rewrite as a 4-term polynomial, then factor by grouping.

5. $2x^2 + 3x + 1$

6. $3x^2 + 5x - 2$

Factor by grouping. Check by multiplying.

7. $2x^3 + x^2 + 6x + 3$

8. $3x^3 - 2x^2 - 15x + 10$

9. $x^2 + 4x + 3x + 12$

10. $3x^2 + 2x + 15x + 10$

Factor by grouping. Check by multiplying.

11. $2x^2 - 5x + 2$

12. $3x^2 + 4x - 4$

13. $3x^2 + 8x + 5$

14. $2x^2 - 7x + 5$

15. $4x^2 - 4x - 3$

16. $5x^2 + 14x - 3$

17. $2x^2 + 13x + 21$

18. $16x^2 - 6x - 1$

19. $4x^2 + 21x + 20$

20. $12x^2 + 4x - 5$

EXTRA Factor as much as possible. Check by multiplying.

21. $5x^2 + 7x + 2$

22. $2x^2 - 3x - 9$

23. $2x^2 - 9x + 4$

24. $6x^2 + 5x + 1$

25. $6x^2 + 13x + 2$

26. $3x^2 - 11x + 10$

27. $8x^2 + 18x + 9$

28. $18x^2 - 9x - 2$

29. $15x^2 - 4x - 3$

30. $3x^2 - 19x + 20$

31. $2x^2 + 3x - 35$

32. $4x^2 - 8x - 21$

33. $12x^2 + 5x - 2$

34. $15x^2 + 19x + 6$

LESSON 99 Factoring Special Products

Be sure you know special product patterns. Multiply. Review Lesson 83 if needed.

1. $(x + 1)^2$
2. $(x - 2)^2$
3. $(x + 3)(x - 3)$

□ **FACTORING SPECIAL PRODUCTS** ···

You can use special product patterns to factor certain polynomials more quickly.

Factoring a perfect square trinomial:

$$a^2 + 2ab + b^2 = (a + b)^2 \quad \Rightarrow \quad x^2 + 6x + 9 = x^2 + 2 \cdot x \cdot 3 + 3^2 = (x + 3)^2$$

$$a^2 - 2ab + b^2 = (a - b)^2 \quad \Rightarrow \quad 4x^2 - 4x + 1 = (2x)^2 - 2 \cdot 2x \cdot 1 + 1^2 = (2x - 1)^2$$

Factoring a difference of squares:

$$a^2 - b^2 = (a + b)(a - b) \quad \Rightarrow \quad 9x^2 - 25 = (3x)^2 - 5^2 = (3x + 5)(3x - 5)$$

The patterns above are worth memorizing because they occur so frequently in algebra. Write them down in your notebook several times if you have not memorized them yet. Familiarize yourself with these patterns enough to work out the problems mentally.

➜ **EXAMPLE** Perfect square

$4x^2 + 4x + 1$

$= (2x)^2 + 2 \cdot 2x \cdot 1 + 1^2$

$= (2x + 1)^2$

➜ **TRY IT** Factor.

4. $x^2 + 4x + 4$

5. $x^2 + 14x + 49$

6. $16x^2 + 8x + 1$

7. $9x^2 + 30x + 25$

➜ **EXAMPLE** Perfect square

$9x^2 - 12x + 4$

$= (3x)^2 - 2 \cdot 3x \cdot 2 + 2^2$

$= (3x - 2)^2$

➜ **TRY IT** Factor.

8. $x^2 - 2x + 1$

9. $x^2 - 10x + 25$

10. $36x^2 - 12x + 1$

11. $16x^2 - 24x + 9$

➜ **EXAMPLE** Difference of squares

$25x^2 - 16$

$= (5x)^2 - 4^2$

$= (5x + 4)(5x - 4)$

➜ **TRY IT** Factor.

12. $x^2 - 16$

13. $x^2 - 64$

14. $4x^2 - 1$

15. $49x^2 - 4$

Factor using special product patterns. Check by multiplying.

16. $x^2 - 4$ **17.** $x^2 - 6x + 9$

18. $x^2 + 8x + 16$ **19.** $x^2 - 100$

20. $x^2 - 14x + 49$ **21.** $x^2 + 10x + 25$

22. $9x^2 - 12x + 4$ **23.** $4x^2 + 36x + 81$

24. $16x^2 + 24x + 9$ **25.** $36x^2 - 49$

26. $64x^2 - 9$ **27.** $25x^2 - 60x + 36$

EXTRA Factor using special product patterns. Check by multiplying.

28. $x^2 - 4x + 4$ **29.** $x^2 + 12x + 36$

30. $x^2 - 36$ **31.** $x^2 - 20x + 100$

32. $x^2 + 18x + 81$ **33.** $x^2 - 25$

34. $x^2 - 24x + 144$ **35.** $x^2 - 64$

36. $4x^2 - 4x + 1$ **37.** $64x^2 - 80x + 25$

38. $4x^2 - 81$ **39.** $36x^2 + 12x + 1$

40. $4x^2 - 28x + 49$ **41.** $25x^2 - 36$

42. $25x^2 + 30x + 9$ **43.** $9x^2 - 48x + 64$

LESSON 100 Factoring Quadratics in Any Form

☐ **REFRESH YOUR SKILLS** ···

Factor when the leading coefficient is 1. Review Lesson 95 if needed.

1. $x^2 + x - 2$

2. $x^2 + 9x + 14$

Factor when the leading coefficient is not 1. Review Lessons 97 and 98 if needed.

3. $2x^2 - x - 10$

4. $8x^2 + 26x + 15$

Factor using special product patterns. Review Lesson 99 if needed.

5. $x^2 + 4x + 4$

6. $36x^2 - 49$

☐ **FACTORING OUT −1** ···

When the leading coefficient of a polynomial is negative, factor out −1 first and then factor the remaining polynomial as usual. The example below factors out −1 along with the GCF.

➔ **EXAMPLE** Factor out −1 first, then factor further.

a. $-x^2 - x + 2$ $\quad = -(x^2 + x - 2)$ $\qquad$ Factor out −1.

$\qquad\qquad\qquad = -(x - 1)(x + 2)$ $\qquad$ Factor by trial and error or by grouping.

b. $-6x^2 + 3x + 30$ $\quad = -3(2x^2 - x - 10)$ $\qquad$ Factor out −1 along with the GCF 3.

$\qquad\qquad\qquad\quad = -3(x + 2)(2x - 5)$ $\qquad$ Factor by trial and error or by grouping.

➔ **TRY IT** Factor out −1 first, then factor further.

7. $-x^2 - 2x + 24$

8. $-20x^2 - 60x - 25$

☐ **EXERCISE YOUR SKILLS** ···

Factor. Use any method you prefer. Check by multiplying.

9. $x^2 + 3x - 10$

10. $x^2 - 7x + 12$

11. $x^2 - 4$

12. $2x^2 + 7x - 4$

13. $5x^2 - 8x + 3$

14. $9x^2 - 6x + 1$

Factor out -1 first, then factor further. Check by multiplying.

15. $-x^2 + 10x - 25$

16. $-16x^2 + 9$

17. $-3x^2 - 10x - 3$

18. $-14x^2 + 17x + 6$

19. $-3x^2 + 24x - 48$

20. $-6x^2 + 32x + 24$

EXTRA Factor as much as possible. Check by multiplying.

21. $x^2 + 6x + 8$

22. $x^2 - 4x + 4$

23. $x^2 - 3x - 28$

24. $x^2 + 3x - 18$

25. $x^2 - 12x + 35$

26. $x^2 + 8x + 15$

27. $5x^2 - 13x - 6$

28. $3x^2 - 16x - 12$

29. $7x^2 + 18x + 8$

30. $4x^2 - 25$

31. $16x^2 - 8x + 1$

32. $8x^2 + 18x + 9$

33. $6x^2 - 11x - 10$

34. $15x^2 + 14x - 8$

35. $2x^2 + 8x - 42$

36. $6x^2 + 12x + 6$

37. $15x^2 + 65x + 20$

38. $21x^2 + 35x - 14$

39. $80x^2 - 36x + 4$

40. $24x^2 + 2x - 12$

41. $-x^2 + 36$

42. $-5x^2 - 18x + 8$

43. $-8x^2 + 30x - 25$

44. $-36x^2 - 48x - 15$

LESSON 101 Factoring Polynomials Completely

☐ **REFRESH YOUR SKILLS** ┈┈

Redo the examples you have studied earlier.

1. Explain how to factor out the GCF from $3x^5 + 6x^4 + 18x$. Review Lesson 93 if needed.

2. Explain how to factor $3x^3 - 9x^2 + 2x - 6$ by grouping. Review Lesson 94 if needed.

3. Explain how to factor $4x^2 + 4x - 3$ by trial and error or by grouping. Review Lessons 97 and 98 if needed.

☐ **FACTORING POLYNOMIALS COMPLETELY** ┈┈┈┈┈┈┈┈┈┈┈┈┈┈┈┈┈┈┈┈┈┈┈┈┈┈┈┈┈┈┈┈┈

So far, you have learned various methods for factoring polynomials. To factor polynomials of any form, you first need to identify the type of polynomial and then decide which method(s) to use. Here is a general strategy. When you factor a polynomial, try these steps.

> 1. Factor out the GCF first (including −1 if the leading coefficient is negative).
> 2. If it is a special product, factor by following the pattern.
> 3. If it is a trinomial, factor by trial and error or by grouping.
> 4. If it has more than three terms, factor by grouping.
> 5. Check each factor to see if you can factor it further. If so, factor it again.

Let's see how to factor polynomials completely using the strategy above. We say a polynomial is factored completely when it cannot be factored any more.

➜ **EXAMPLE** Factor completely.

$$2x^4 - 32$$
① $= 2(x^4 - 16)$
② $= 2(x^2 + 4)(x^2 - 4)$
② $= 2(x^2 + 4)(x + 2)(x - 2)$

➜ **TRY IT** Factor completely.

4. $x^4 - 81$

5. $4x^3 - 100x$

➜ **EXAMPLE** Factor completely.

$$-x^5 + x^3 - 3x^2 + 3$$
① $= -(x^5 - x^3 + 3x^2 - 3)$
  $= -[x^3(x^2 - 1) + 3(x^2 - 1)]$
④ $= -(x^2 - 1)(x^3 + 3)$
② $= -(x + 1)(x - 1)(x^3 + 3)$

➜ **TRY IT** Factor completely.

6. $x^3 + x^2 - 9x - 9$

7. $-2x^3 - x^2 + 8x + 4$

Factor out the GCF. Check by multiplying.

8. $6x^2 + 10x - 6$ **9.** $25x^4 + 10x^3 + 15x^2$

Factor using special product patterns. Check by multiplying.

10. $x^2 - 10x + 25$ **11.** $x^2 - 36$

Factor by trial and error or by grouping. Check by multiplying.

12. $x^2 - 9x + 18$ **13.** $12x^2 + 17x + 6$

Factor by grouping. Check by multiplying.

14. $6x^3 - 18x^2 - x + 3$ **15.** $14x^3 + 7x^2 - 2x - 1$

Factor completely. Check by multiplying.

16. $8x^2 - 2x - 6$ **17.** $60x^2 - 9x - 6$

18. $x^3 - 49x$ **19.** $-8x^3 - 8x^2 - 2x$

20. $3x^4 - 48$ **21.** $x^3 + 4x^2 - 9x - 36$

EXTRA Factor completely. Check by multiplying.

22. $x^2 + 3x - 40$ **23.** $10x^2 - x - 3$

24. $9x^2 + 12x + 4$ **25.** $4x^2 - 81$

26. $5x^2 - 15x - 20$ **27.** $-18x^2 + 21x - 6$

28. $3x^3 + 12x^2 + 12x$ **29.** $x^3 - 5x^2 - 4x + 20$

30. $x^3 - 25x$ **31.** $-10x^3 + 2x^2 - 15x + 3$

LESSON 102 Catch Up and Review!

Catch up if you are behind. Use the review problems below to make sure you're on track.

LESSON 93 Factor out the GCF.

1. $3x^2 - 6$

2. $8x^5 + 6x^2 + 4x$

3. $4xy - 8y$

4. $18x^3y^2 + 27x^2y^3$

LESSON 94 Factor by grouping.

5. $x^3 - 5x^2 + x - 5$

6. $x^4 - 5x^3 - 3x + 15$

7. $2x^3 + x^2 + 8x + 4$

8. $8x^3 + 6x^2 - 12x - 9$

LESSONS 95 Factor when the leading coefficient is 1.

9. $x^2 + 6x + 8$

10. $x^2 + 5x - 6$

11. $x^2 - 8x + 15$

12. $x^2 - 4x - 12$

LESSONS 97–98 Factor when the leading coefficient is not 1.

13. $2x^2 + x - 1$

14. $3x^2 - 4x - 4$

15. $6x^2 + 11x + 3$

16. $20x^2 - 23x + 6$

LESSON 99 Factor using special product patterns.

17. $x^2 - 12x + 36$

18. $x^2 + 10x + 25$

19. $x^2 - 16$

20. $9x^2 - 121$

LESSON 100 Factor out -1 first, then factor further.

21. $-x^2 + 2x + 15$

22. $-x^2 + 14x - 49$

23. $-12x^2 + 12x - 3$

24. $-21x^2 - 35x + 14$

LESSON 101 Factor completely.

25. $9x^4 - 4x^2$

26. $2x^3 + 8x^2 + 5x + 20$

27. $-2x^4 + 162$

28. $3x^3 - 4x^2 - 75x + 100$

□ **MIXED REVIEW: PRE-ALGEBRA** ··

Brush up on the topics covered in Pre-Algebra.

29. The mean is the average. To find the mean of a data set, divide the sum of the values by the number of values in the set. Find the mean of the data set {3, 4, 5, 2, 3, 7, 5, 9, 3, 7}.

30. The median is the middle value. To find the median of a data set, order the values in the set and find the middle value. If there are two middle values, add them and divide by 2. Find the median of the same data set above.

31. The mode is the most frequent value. To find the mode of a data set, simply find the value that occurs most frequently in the set. A data set can have no mode (no values repeated), one mode, or multiple modes. Find the mode(s) of the same data set above.

32. The circle graph shows favorite sports of 200 middle school students. How many students answered that they like soccer the most?

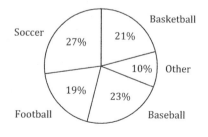

33. The dot plot shows the daily high temperatures in Celsius of a city over 15 days. What is the median temperature?

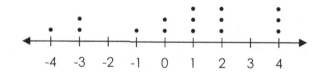

LESSON 103 Solving Quadratics by Taking Square Roots

☐ **REFRESH YOUR SKILLS** ···

Evaluate. Review Lesson 1 if needed.   Simplify. Review Lessons 64 and 65 if needed.

1. 3^2 2. $(-3)^2$ 3. $\sqrt{12}$ 4. $\sqrt{x^2}$

☐ **SOLVING QUADRATICS BY TAKING SQUARE ROOTS** ··

A **quadratic equation** is an equation that can be written in the standard form $ax^2 + bx + c = 0$, where a, b, and c are real numbers and $a \neq 0$. A solution to a quadratic equation is called a **root**. Solving a quadratic equation means finding its roots.

Let's start with a simple quadratic equation, $x^2 = 9$. You can easily see that the roots of this equation are $x = 3$ and $x = -3$ because both numbers are equal to 9 when squared. This example illustrates the **square root property** shown on the right. The notation $\pm$ is read "plus or minus" and means that either sign may be used. That is, $x = \pm\sqrt{k}$ means either $x = +\sqrt{k}$ or $x = -\sqrt{k}$.

> *For any real number k,*
>
> *if $x^2 = k$, then $x = \pm\sqrt{k}$*

➜ **EXAMPLE** Solve using the square root property.

$x^2 = 18$

$x = \pm\sqrt{18}$

$x = \pm 3\sqrt{2}$

Apply the square root property by taking the square root of each side and adding ± to the side with the number. Then simplify the radical.

➜ **TRY IT** Solve.

5. $x^2 = 25$

6. $x^2 = 40$

You can use the square root property to solve a quadratic equation of the form $ax^2 + c = 0$. This process of solving quadratic equations is known as taking or extracting square roots.

➜ **EXAMPLE** Solve by taking square roots.

$x^2 - 4 = 0$

$x^2 = 4$ Isolate the squared term.

$x = \pm\sqrt{4}$ Apply the square root property.

$x = \pm 2$ Simplify the radical.

➜ **TRY IT** Solve.

7. $x^2 - 6 = 0$

8. $x^2 - 4 = 28$

➜ **EXAMPLE** Solve by taking square roots.

$2x^2 - 9 = 7$

$2x^2 = 16$

$x^2 = 8$ Isolate the squared term.

$x = \pm\sqrt{8}$ Apply the square root property.

$x = \pm 2\sqrt{2}$ Simplify the radical.

➜ **TRY IT** Solve.

9. $4x^2 = 20$

10. $5x^2 + 7 = 142$

Solve by taking square roots. Check your solutions.

11. $x^2 = 8$ **12.** $2x^2 = 32$

13. $-x^2 = -54$ **14.** $x^2 - 27 = 0$

15. $x^2 - 8 = 40$ **16.** $2x^2 - 100 = 0$

17. $3x^2 + 17 = 71$ **18.** $5x^2 - 42 = 13$

19. $-3x^2 = 108 - 4x^2$ **20.** $4x^2 - 12 = 2x^2 + 12$

EXTRA Solve by taking square roots. Check your solutions.

21. $x^2 = 49$ **22.** $5x^2 = 100$

23. $-4x^2 = -172$ **24.** $x^2 - 121 = 0$

25. $x^2 + 9 = 13$ **26.** $6x^2 - 216 = 0$

27. $2x^2 - 19 = 45$ **28.** $7x^2 + 11 = 74$

29. $36 - 9x^2 = 27$ **30.** $2x^2 - 14 = 148$

31. $x^2 + 85 = 2x^2 + 34$ **32.** $3x^2 + 16 = 6x^2 + 10$

CHALLENGE Solve. (*Hint*: Multiply and simplify first.)

33. $(x + 3)(x - 3) = 5$ **34.** $(2x + 1)(2x - 1) = 23$

35. $3(x + 4)(x - 4) = 18$ **36.** $(3x - 1)(x + 3) = 8x$

37. $(3x + 5)(3x - 5) = (x + 1)(x - 1)$ **38.** $(x + 2)(x - 2) = (2x + 7)(2x - 7)$

LESSON 104 Solving Quadratics by Taking Square Roots

☐ **REFRESH YOUR SKILLS** ···

Solve. Review Lessons 3 and 103 if needed.

1. $2x + 3 = 9$

2. $2x^2 - 9 = 7$

☐ **SOLVING QUADRATICS BY TAKING SQUARE ROOTS** ···

You can also solve a quadratic equation of the form $a(px + q)^2 + r = 0$ using the square root property. The key is to isolate the squared term first.

➜ **EXAMPLE** Solve by taking square roots.

$(x - 5)^2 - 9 = 0$	
$(x - 5)^2 = 9$	Isolate the squared term.
$x - 5 = \pm\sqrt{9}$	Apply the square root property.
$x - 5 = \pm 3$	Simplify the radical.
$x = 5 \pm 3$	Solve for x.
$x = 8, x = 2$	Separate the solutions.

➜ **TRY IT** Solve.

3. $(x - 9)^2 = 4$

4. $(x + 5)^2 - 81 = 0$

➜ **EXAMPLE** Solve by taking square roots.

$(2x - 8)^2 - 24 = 0$	
$(2x - 8)^2 = 24$	Isolate the squared term.
$2x - 8 = \pm\sqrt{24}$	Apply the square root property.
$2x - 8 = \pm 2\sqrt{6}$	Simplify the radical.
$2x = 8 \pm 2\sqrt{6}$	
$x = 4 \pm \sqrt{6}$	Solve for x.

➜ **TRY IT** Solve.

5. $(3x - 5)^2 = 16$

6. $(4x + 12)^2 - 32 = 0$

➜ **EXAMPLE** Solve by taking square roots.

$2(3x + 1)^2 - 5 = 7$	
$2(3x + 1)^2 = 12$	
$(3x + 1)^2 = 6$	Isolate the squared term.
$3x + 1 = \pm\sqrt{6}$	Apply the square root property.
$x = \dfrac{-1 \pm \sqrt{6}}{3}$	Solve for x.

➜ **TRY IT** Solve.

7. $2(5x - 1)^2 = 20$

8. $5(4x + 3)^2 - 10 = 0$

As shown in the examples above, the plus or minus symbol is often used to condense the two solutions into one. You could separate the solutions and list them individually.

Solve by taking square roots. Check your solutions.

9. $(x + 5)^2 = 90$

10. $(x - 1)^2 - 5 = 0$

11. $(x - 7)^2 + 5 = 54$

12. $(x + 1)^2 - 78 = 72$

13. $3(x - 1)^2 = 75$

14. $(4x - 3)^2 = 25$

15. $3(x - 4)^2 - 7 = 20$

16. $5(x + 2)^2 - 12 = 53$

17. $(2x + 3)^2 - 6 = 0$

18. $(5x - 2)^2 - 45 = 0$

19. $2(3x - 1)^2 - 16 = 0$

20. $6(3x + 5)^2 - 96 = 0$

EXTRA Solve by taking square roots. Check your solutions.

21. $x^2 + 4 = 16$

22. $3x^2 - 27 = 0$

23. $(x - 3)^2 = 20$

24. $(9x - 5)^2 = 0$

25. $4(x + 1)^2 = 36$

26. $(x - 4)^2 - 48 = 0$

27. $(2x + 6)^2 - 28 = 0$

28. $3(x + 4)^2 - 12 = 78$

29. $4(x - 7)^2 - 10 = 54$

30. $2(4x + 1)^2 - 24 = 0$

CHALLENGE Solve. (*Hint*: Factor the left side.)

31. $x^2 + 2x + 1 = 5$

32. $x^2 - 6x + 9 = 7$

33. $x^2 - 10x + 25 = 9$

34. $x^2 + 12x + 36 = 8$

35. $4x^2 + 4x + 1 = 49$

36. $4x^2 - 12x + 9 = 25$

LESSON 105 Solving Quadratics by Factoring

☐ **REFRESH YOUR SKILLS** ⋯⋯⋯⋯⋯⋯⋯⋯⋯⋯⋯⋯⋯⋯⋯⋯⋯⋯⋯⋯⋯⋯⋯⋯⋯⋯⋯⋯⋯⋯⋯⋯⋯⋯⋯⋯⋯

Solve. Review Lessons 3 and 103 if needed.

1. $x - 3 = 5$

2. $(x - 5)^2 - 9 = 0$

Factor as the product of two binomials. Review Lesson 95 if needed.

3. $x^2 - 6x + 8$

4. $x^2 + 7x + 12$

☐ **SOLVING QUADRATICS BY FACTORING** ⋯⋯⋯⋯⋯⋯⋯⋯⋯⋯⋯⋯⋯⋯⋯⋯⋯⋯⋯⋯⋯⋯⋯⋯⋯⋯⋯⋯⋯

When one side of a quadratic equation is factored as a product of linear factors and the other side is 0, we can solve the equation easily using the **zero product property** shown on the right.

> *For any real numbers a and b,*
>
> *if* $ab = 0$, *then* $a = 0$ *or* $b = 0$.

➔ **EXAMPLE** Solve the factored form.

$$(x + 1)(x - 4) = 0$$

Use the zero product property:

$x + 1 = 0$ or $x - 4 = 0$

$x = -1$ or $x = 4$

The solutions (roots) are $x = -1$ and $x = 4$.

➔ **TRY IT** Solve.

5. $x(x - 5) = 0$

6. $(x + 2)(x + 3) = 0$

Here are the steps to solve a quadratic equation by factoring.

➔ **EXAMPLE** Solve by factoring.

$$x^2 + 5x - 10 = 2x$$

① $x^2 + 3x - 10 = 0$

② $(x - 2)(x + 5) = 0$

③ $x - 2 = 0$ or $x + 5 = 0$

④ $x - 2, x = -5$

1. Move all the terms to one side and make the other side 0.
2. Factor the quadratic polynomial.
3. Apply the zero product property by setting each factor equal to zero.
4. Solve each equation individually.
5. Check the solutions.

➔ **TRY IT** Solve by factoring.

7. $x^2 + 3x + 2 = 0$

8. $x^2 + 3x - 4 = 0$

9. $x^2 + 6 = 5x$

10. $x^2 - 7x = 6x - 40$

Solve by factoring. Check your solutions.

11. $x^2 - x - 2 = 0$

12. $x^2 - 5x + 6 = 0$

13. $x^2 + 8x + 12 = 0$

14. $x^2 - 7x + 6 = 0$

15. $x^2 + 4x + 3 = 0$

16. $x^2 + x - 12 = 0$

17. $x^2 + x = 6$

18. $x^2 + 8 = 6x$

19. $x^2 + 2x = 6x + 5$

20. $x^2 - x + 14 = -10x$

EXTRA Solve by factoring. Check your solutions.

21. $x^2 + x - 2 = 0$

22. $x^2 + 4x + 4 = 0$

23. $x^2 - x - 6 = 0$

24. $x^2 - 9x + 8 = 0$

25. $x^2 - 6x + 9 = 0$

26. $x^2 + 3x - 10 = 0$

27. $x^2 - 7x + 10 = 0$

28. $x^2 - 7x + 12 = 0$

29. $x^2 + 5x - 36 = 0$

30. $x^2 + 12x + 32 = 0$

31. $x^2 = 2x + 15$

32. $2x = 8 - x^2$

33. $x^2 + 4 = -5x$

34. $x^2 + 9x = -18$

35. $x^2 + 3x = 10$

36. $x^2 + 40 = 13x$

37. $x^2 = 10x - 16$

38. $x^2 + 8x + 9 = 2$

LESSON 106 Solving Quadratics by Factoring

☐ REFRESH YOUR SKILLS

Solve by factoring. Review Lesson 105 if needed.

1. $x^2 + 7x + 10 = 0$

2. $x^2 - 2x - 8 = 0$

Factor as the product of two binomials. Review Lessons 97 and 98 if needed.

3. $7x^2 + 5x - 2$

4. $6x^2 + 7x - 3$

Factor completely. Review Lesson 101 if needed.

5. $x^3 - 25x$

6. $x^3 - 5x^2 - 4x + 20$

☐ SOLVING QUADRATICS BY FACTORING

You can use factoring to solve quadratic equations with a leading coefficient greater than 1. Here is an example. Refer to the steps in the previous lesson.

➔ EXAMPLE Solve by factoring.

① $4x^2 + 4x - 3 = 0$

② $(2x - 1)(2x + 3) = 0$

③ $2x - 1 = 0$ or $2x + 3 = 0$

④ $x = 1/2, x = -3/2$

➔ TRY IT Solve by factoring.

7. $2x^2 + 13x + 6 = 0$

8. $6x^2 + 7x - 20 = 0$

☐ APPLYING THE ZERO PRODUCT PROPERTY

Here is a tricky example. The equation appears factored but is not equal to zero. Remember, the equation must be set equal to zero to use the zero product property.

➔ EXAMPLE Solve by factoring.

$(x + 4)(2x - 1) = 11$

① $2x^2 + 7x - 15 = 0$

② $(2x - 3)(x + 5) = 0$

③ $2x - 3 = 0$ or $x + 5 = 0$

④ $x = 3/2, x = -5$

➔ TRY IT Solve by factoring.

9. $(x + 2)(x - 1) = 28$

10. $(x - 2)(4x - 5) = 7$

The zero product property applies to a product of two or more factors. If the product is zero, at least one of the factors must be zero. See below how the cubic equation is solved.

→ **EXAMPLE** Solve by factoring.

$$4x^3 = 16x^2 - 12x$$

① $\quad 4x^3 - 16x^2 + 12x = 0$

$\quad\quad 4x(x^2 - 4x + 3) = 0$

② $\quad 4x(x-1)(x-3) = 0$

③ $\quad x = 0 \text{ or } x - 1 = 0 \text{ or } x - 3 = 0$

④ $\quad x = 0, x = 1, x = 3$

→ **TRY IT** Solve by factoring.

11. $x^3 - 3x^2 + 2x = 0$

12. $4x^3 + 18x^2 - 10x = 0$

□ **EXERCISE YOUR SKILLS** ···

Solve by factoring. Check your solutions.

13. $5x^2 + 4x - 1 = 0$

14. $4x^2 - 13x - 12 = 0$

15. $4x^2 - 49 = 0$

16. $6x^2 + 11x + 3 = 0$

17. $(x - 3)(x - 5) = -1$

18. $7x(x + 7) = 6(x - 1)$

19. $x^3 + 6x^2 + 9x = 0$

20. $-2x^3 - x^2 + x = 0$

EXTRA Solve by factoring. Check your solutions.

21. $5x^2 - 9x - 2 = 0$

22. $3x^2 + 7x - 6 = 0$

23. $15x^2 - 4x - 4 = 0$

24. $12x^2 - 20x + 3 = 0$

25. $8x^2 - 22x + 5 = 0$

26. $9x^2 - 24x + 16 = 0$

27. $x^2 + 28 = 11x$

28. $2x^2 = 5(x + 5)$

29. $x(x + 2) = 3x$

30. $(x - 2)(x + 6) = 5x + 8$

31. $x^3 - 16x = 0$

32. $8x^3 + 8x^2 + 2x = 0$

LESSON 107 Solving Quadratics by Completing the Square

□ **REFRESH YOUR SKILLS** ....

Factor as the square of a binomial. Review Lesson 99 if needed.

1. $x^2 + 4x + 4$

2. $x^2 - 6x + 9$

Solve by taking square roots. Review Lesson 104 if needed.

3. $(x - 7)^2 = 4$

4. $(x + 3)^2 = 8$

□ **COMPLETING THE SQUARE** ....

Completing the square is the process of adding a constant c to an expression of the form $x^2 + bx$ to make it a perfect square trinomial. To complete the square, you need to add the square of half the coefficient of x. See the example below. You'll find it's easier than it sounds!

$$x^2 + bx + \left(\frac{b}{2}\right)^2 = \left(x + \frac{b}{2}\right)^2$$

➜ **EXAMPLE** Complete the square, then factor.

$x^2 - 8x + c$ The coefficient of x is −8, and
$\quad 2 \cdot x \cdot -4$ the square of half of −8 is 16.

$= x^2 - 8x + 16$ 16 completes the square.

$= (x - 4)^2$ Factor.

➜ **TRY IT** Find the values of c and d.

5. $x^2 + 2x + c = (x + d)^2$

6. $x^2 - 4x + c = (x + d)^2$

□ **SOLVING QUADRATICS BY COMPLETING THE SQUARE** ....

You can solve any quadratic equation by completing the square. Here are the steps.

➜ **EXAMPLE** Solve by completing the square.

① $x^2 + 4x - 12 = 0$

② $x^2 + 4x = 12$

③ $x^2 + 4x + 4 = 12 + 4$

④ $(x + 2)^2 = 16$

$\quad x + 2 = \pm 4$

⑤ $x = 2, x = -6$

1. Make sure the leading coefficient is 1.
2. Move the constant to the right side of the equation.
3. Complete the square by adding the square of half the coefficient of x to both sides.
4. Factor the left side as the square of a binomial, and simplify the right side.
5. Solve the equation by taking the square root of each side.
6. Check the solutions.

➜ **TRY IT** Solve by completing the square.

7. $x^2 + 2x - 3 = 0$

8. $x^2 - 6x + 4 = 0$

□ **EXERCISE YOUR SKILLS** ···

Complete the square, then factor as the square of a binomial.

9. $x^2 + 6x$ | **10.** $x^2 - 10x$

Solve by completing the square.

11. $x^2 - 4x - 6 = 0$ **12.** $x^2 + 2x - 8 = 0$

13. $x^2 - 6x - 9 = 0$ **14.** $x^2 + 8x + 7 = 0$

15. $x^2 - 20x - 21 = 0$ **16.** $x^2 + 12x + 20 = 0$

17. $x^2 - 18x + 74 = 0$ **18.** $x^2 - 10x + 15 = 0$

19. $x^2 + 9x = 5x + 5$ **20.** $x^2 + 10x = 16x - 8$

EXTRA Solve by completing the square.

21. $x^2 + 2x - 1 = 0$ **22.** $x^2 - 6x - 7 = 0$

23. $x^2 - 8x - 5 = 0$ **24.** $x^2 + 4x - 8 = 0$

25. $x^2 + 6x + 4 = 0$ **26.** $x^2 + 8x + 12 = 0$

27. $x^2 + 10x - 56 = 0$ **28.** $x^2 - 16x + 10 = 0$

29. $x^2 - 12x - 28 = 0$ **30.** $x^2 + 18x - 9 = 0$

31. $x^2 - 10x + 9 = 16$ **32.** $x^2 - 14x - 12 = 20$

33. $x^2 + 15x - 3 = 13x$ **34.** $x^2 - 10x = 18 - 4x$

35. $x^2 - 14x + 16 = 25 - 6x$ **36.** $x^2 + 18x + 52 = 12 + 2x$

LESSON 108 Solving Quadratics by Completing the Square

☐ **REFRESH YOUR SKILLS** ⋯⋯⋯⋯⋯⋯⋯⋯⋯⋯⋯⋯⋯⋯⋯⋯⋯⋯⋯⋯⋯⋯⋯⋯⋯⋯⋯⋯⋯⋯⋯⋯

Complete the square, then factor as the square of a binomial. Review Lesson 107 if needed.

1. $x^2 + 2x$

2. $x^2 - 8x$

Solve by completing the square. Review Lesson 107 if needed.

3. $x^2 + 4x - 7 = 0$

4. $x^2 - 6x - 15 = 0$

☐ **SOLVING QUADRATICS BY COMPLETING THE SQUARE** ⋯⋯⋯⋯⋯⋯⋯⋯⋯⋯⋯⋯⋯⋯⋯⋯⋯⋯⋯⋯

If the leading coefficient is not 1, simply divide both sides by the leading coefficient to make it 1 before completing the square. Refer to the steps in the previous lesson.

➡ **EXAMPLE** Solve by completing the square.

$$2x^2 - 6x - 4 = 0$$

① $x^2 - 3x - 2 = 0$

② $x^2 - 3x = 2$

③ $x^2 + 2 \cdot x \cdot -\dfrac{3}{2} + \left(-\dfrac{3}{2}\right)^2 = 2 + \left(-\dfrac{3}{2}\right)^2$

④ $\left(x - \dfrac{3}{2}\right)^2 = \dfrac{17}{4}$

$x - \dfrac{3}{2} = \pm \dfrac{\sqrt{17}}{2}$

⑤ $x = \dfrac{3 \pm \sqrt{17}}{2}$

$$5x^2 + 2x - 1 = 0$$

① $x^2 + \dfrac{2}{5}x - \dfrac{1}{5} = 0$

② $x^2 + \dfrac{2}{5}x = \dfrac{1}{5}$

③ $x^2 + 2 \cdot x \cdot \dfrac{1}{5} + \left(\dfrac{1}{5}\right)^2 = \dfrac{1}{5} + \left(\dfrac{1}{5}\right)^2$

④ $\left(x + \dfrac{1}{5}\right)^2 = \dfrac{6}{25}$

$x + \dfrac{1}{5} = \pm \dfrac{\sqrt{6}}{5}$

⑤ $x = \dfrac{-1 \pm \sqrt{6}}{5}$

➡ **TRY IT** Solve by completing the square.

5. $x^2 - 3x - 1 = 0$

6. $x^2 + 5x + 2 = 0$

7. $2x^2 + 2x - 1 = 0$

8. $5x^2 + 6x - 7 = 0$

Complete the square, then factor as the square of a binomial.

9. $x^2 - x$

10. $x^2 + \dfrac{2}{3}x$

Solve by completing the square.

11. $x^2 - x - 1 = 0$

12. $x^2 + 3x - 3 = 0$

13. $x^2 + 7x + 10 = 0$

14. $x^2 + 9x + 15 = 0$

15. $4x^2 + 8x - 3 = 0$

16. $2x^2 + 10x - 12 = 0$

17. $5x^2 - 5x - 30 = 0$

18. $3x^2 + 2x - 6 = 0$

19. $3x^2 - 6x - 9 = 0$

20. $5x^2 - 6x - 3 = 0$

EXTRA Solve by completing the square.

21. $x^2 - 4x - 6 = 0$

22. $x^2 + 2x - 8 = 0$

23. $x^2 + x - 1 = 0$

24. $x^2 - 5x - 4 = 0$

25. $3x^2 - 3x - 9 = 0$

26. $4x^2 - 8x + 1 = 0$

27. $5x^2 - 2x - 3 = 0$

28. $2x^2 - 3x - 2 = 0$

29. $2x^2 + x - 4 = 0$

30. $4x^2 - 2x - 3 = 0$

31. $x^2 - 2x + 1 = 6 - x$

32. $x^2 + 4 = 9x - 5$

CHALLENGE Solve by completing the square. Don't forget to rationalize the denominator.

33. $7x^2 = x^2 + 12x - 3$

34. $9x^2 - 3x + 2 = 3x + 7$

LESSON 109 Solving Quadratics by the Quadratic Formula

☐ REFRESH YOUR SKILLS ··

Solve by completing the square. Review Lessons 107 and 108 if needed.

1. $x^2 - 4x - 10 = 0$

2. $x^2 + 5x + 5 = 0$

3. $4x^2 - 8x + 1 = 0$

4. $3x^2 - 18x - 9 = 0$

☐ **SOLVING QUADRATICS BY THE QUADRATIC FORMULA** ·····························

If a quadratic equation is in standard form, you can find its roots using the **quadratic formula** shown on the right. Simply plug a, b, and c into the formula and simplify, then you have the roots! The quadratic formula is important because it lets you solve any quadratic equation. Familiarize yourself with the formula by writing it on your notebook multiple times. (You will learn where the quadratic formula comes from in the next lesson.)

> *The roots of $ax^2 + bx + c = 0$ are*
> $$x = \frac{-b \pm \sqrt{b^2 - 4ac}}{2a}$$

To solve a quadratic equation by the quadratic formula, first write the equation in standard form to identify a, b, and c. Then plug them into the formula and simplify.

➔ **EXAMPLE** Solve by the quadratic formula.

$5x^2 + 2x - 1 = 0 \quad a = 5, b = 2, c = -1$

$x = \dfrac{-2 \pm \sqrt{2^2 - 4 \cdot 5 \cdot (-1)}}{2 \cdot 5}$

$= \dfrac{-2 \pm \sqrt{24}}{10}$

$= \dfrac{-1 \pm \sqrt{6}}{5}$ Simplify.

➔ **TRY IT** Solve by the quadratic formula.

5. $x^2 - x - 2 = 0$

6. $x^2 + 7x + 9 = 0$

7. $4x^2 - 9x + 5 = 0$

If a term is missing, use 0 as its coefficient.

➔ **EXAMPLE** Solve by the quadratic formula.

$x^2 - 24 = 0 \quad\quad a = 1, b = 0, c = -24$

$x = \dfrac{-0 \pm \sqrt{0^2 - 4 \cdot 1 \cdot (-24)}}{2 \cdot 1}$

$= \dfrac{\pm\sqrt{96}}{2} = \pm 2\sqrt{6}$

➔ **TRY IT** Solve by the quadratic formula.

8. $x^2 - 7 = 0$

9. $4x^2 - 3x = 0$

Solve by the quadratic formula.

10. $x^2 - 8 = 0$

11. $x^2 - 5x + 2 = 0$

12. $x^2 + 4x + 2 = 0$

13. $x^2 - 2x - 3 = 0$

14. $x^2 + 8x + 6 = 0$

15. $x^2 - 6x + 9 = 0$

16. $7x^2 - 3x = 0$

17. $6x^2 - 7x + 2 = 0$

18. $5x^2 - 5x - 1 = 0$

19. $4x^2 + 6x + 1 = 0$

EXTRA Solve by the quadratic formula.

20. $x^2 - 9x = 0$

21. $x^2 + 7x + 6 = 0$

22. $x^2 - x - 4 = 0$

23. $x^2 - 3x - 5 = 0$

24. $x^2 + 5x + 6 = 0$

25. $x^2 + 6x + 4 = 0$

26. $x^2 - 7x + 4 = 0$

27. $x^2 - 3x - 3 = 0$

28. $x^2 + 2x - 6 = 0$

29. $x^2 - 9x + 8 = 0$

30. $5x^2 - 25 = 0$

31. $2x^2 + 8x + 8 = 0$

32. $2x^2 - 9x + 7 = 0$

33. $3x^2 + 7x - 6 = 0$

34. $5x^2 - 11x + 6 = 0$

35. $12x^2 - 20x + 3 = 0$

36. $3x^2 + 12x + 10 = 0$

37. $2x^2 + 13x + 15 = 0$

LESSON 110 Solving Quadratics by the Quadratic Formula

☐ **REFRESH YOUR SKILLS** ···

Solve by completing the square. Review Lessons 107 and 108 if needed.

1. $x^2 + 2x - 3 = 0$

2. $x^2 + 8x + 10 = 0$

3. $2x^2 + 6x - 2 = 0$

4. $5x^2 - 2x - 3 = 0$

Solve by the quadratic formula. Review Lesson 109 if needed.

5. $x^2 - 2x - 4 = 0$

6. $x^2 + 5x + 3 = 0$

7. $2x^2 - 3x - 2 = 0$

8. $4x^2 - 2x - 1 = 0$

☐ **DERIVING THE QUADRATIC FORMULA** ··

The quadratic formula is derived by completing the square on the standard form of a quadratic equation. Let's see how it is done. Refer to the steps in Lesson 107.

$$5x^2 + 2x - 1 = 0 \qquad\qquad ax^2 + bx + c = 0$$

① $x^2 + \dfrac{2}{5}x - \dfrac{1}{5} = 0$ ① $x^2 + \dfrac{b}{a}x + \dfrac{c}{a} = 0$

② $x^2 + \dfrac{2}{5}x = \dfrac{1}{5}$ ② $x^2 + \dfrac{b}{a}x = -\dfrac{c}{a}$

③ $x^2 + 2 \cdot x \cdot \dfrac{1}{5} + \left(\dfrac{1}{5}\right)^2 = \dfrac{1}{5} + \left(\dfrac{1}{5}\right)^2$ ③ $x^2 + 2 \cdot x \cdot \dfrac{b}{2a} + \left(\dfrac{b}{2a}\right)^2 = -\dfrac{c}{a} + \left(\dfrac{b}{2a}\right)^2$

④ $\left(x + \dfrac{1}{5}\right)^2 = \dfrac{6}{25}$ ④ $\left(x + \dfrac{b}{2a}\right)^2 = \dfrac{-4ac + b^2}{4a^2}$

$x + \dfrac{1}{5} = \pm\dfrac{\sqrt{6}}{5}$ $x + \dfrac{b}{2a} = \pm\dfrac{\sqrt{b^2 - 4ac}}{2a}$

⑤ $x = \dfrac{-1 \pm \sqrt{6}}{5}$ ⑤ $x = \dfrac{-b \pm \sqrt{b^2 - 4ac}}{2a}$

The quadratic formula is one of the most important formulas that you will learn in Algebra. Write the formula down in your notebook several times and try to memorize it if you have not already done so.

Solve by the quadratic formula. Remember that a quadratic equation must be in standard form to use the quadratic formula.

9. $x^2 - x - 5 = 0$

10. $x^2 - 2x - 1 = 0$

11. $x^2 - 9x + 14 = 0$

12. $x^2 + 4x - 2 = 0$

13. $5x^2 - 2x - 3 = 0$

14. $2x^2 + x - 2 = 0$

15. $3x^2 + 6x - 5 = 0$

16. $4x^2 + 10x + 5 = 0$

17. $x^2 + 7x - 5 = 2x$

18. $x^2 + 5x - 1 = 6x^2$

19. $x^2 + 7x = 3x + 12$

20. $3x^2 + 9x + 3 = x - 2$

EXTRA Solve by the quadratic formula.

21. $x^2 + 8x + 2 = 0$

22. $x^2 - x - 10 = 0$

23. $x^2 + 6x + 4 = 0$

24. $x^2 - 6x - 16 = 0$

25. $5x^2 - 5x + 1 = 0$

26. $4x^2 - 11x + 6 = 0$

27. $3x^2 + 2x - 2 = 0$

28. $4x^2 + 8x - 1 = 0$

29. $6x^2 - 7x - 3 = 0$

30. $2x^2 - 13x - 7 = 0$

31. $x^2 + 4x = 2x + 8$

32. $x^2 - 2x + 1 = 8$

33. $3x^2 + 4x = 4$

34. $3x - 2 = -9x^2$

35. $2x^2 + x = 9x - 5$

36. $4x^2 - 10x + 1 = 2x$

LESSON 111 Solving Quadratics Using Any Method

☐ **REFRESH YOUR SKILLS** ··

Solve using the specified method. Review Lessons 104, 105, 107 and 109 if needed.

1. By taking square roots:

$$(x - 5)^2 - 9 = 0$$

2. By factoring:

$$x^2 + 3x - 10 = 0$$

3. By completing the square:

$$x^2 + 4x - 12 = 0$$

4. By the quadratic formula:

$$5x^2 + 2x - 1 = 0$$

☐ **CHOOSING A METHOD FOR SOLVING QUADRATICS** ··

Now you know four different methods for solving quadratic equations. Then the question arises, which one is best to use? The answer is, whichever easier for you! You could use the quadratic formula for all quadratic equations, but you'll often find it simpler and faster to use other methods once you get used to them.

Here is an example of solving one equation in three different ways. Which do you find the easiest?

➔ **EXAMPLE** Solve $x^2 + 2x = 3$ using the specified method.

By factoring:	By completing the square:	By the quadratic formula:
$x^2 + 2x = 3$	$x^2 + 2x = 3$	$x^2 + 2x = 3$
$x^2 + 2x - 3 = 0$	$x^2 + 2x + 1 = 3 + 1$	$x^2 + 2x - 3 = 0$
$(x - 1)(x + 3) = 0$	$(x + 1)^2 = 4$	$x = \dfrac{-2 \pm \sqrt{2^2 - 4 \cdot 1 \cdot (-3)}}{2 \cdot 1}$
$x = 1, x = -3$	$x + 1 = \pm 2$	
	$x = 1, x = -3$	$x = 1, x = -3$

For the standard form $ax^2 + bx + c = 0$, it is often best to solve by taking square roots when $b = 0$, by completing the square when $a = 1$ and b is even, and by factoring when the quadratic expression is easily factorable.

➔ **TRY IT** Choose a method, then solve. Explain your choice.

5. $x^2 + 3x + 1 = 0$

6. $x^2 - x - 2 = 0$

7. $x^2 + 2x - 4 = 0$

8. $3x^2 - 12 = 0$

9. $3x^2 - 5x - 2 = 0$

10. $4x^2 + 4x - 5 = 0$

Solve by taking square roots.

11. $2x^2 + 15 = 31$ **12.** $(x + 2)^2 - 11 = 0$

Solve by factoring.

13. $x^2 + x - 6 = 0$ **14.** $2x^2 - 5x + 2 = 0$

Solve by completing the square.

15. $x^2 - 4x - 4 = 0$ **16.** $x^2 + 12x + 16 = 0$

Solve by the quadratic formula.

17. $x^2 - 7x + 5 = 0$ **18.** $9x^2 + 6x - 1 = 0$

Solve. Use any method you prefer.

19. $x^2 + 8x - 2 = 0$ **20.** $(x - 2)^2 - 12 = 0$

21. $x^2 + 7x + 12 = 0$ **22.** $5x^2 - 10x - 4 = 0$

EXTRA Solve. Use any method you prefer.

23. $x^2 - 6 = 0$ **24.** $x^2 + 3x - 9 = 0$

25. $x^2 + 3x - 4 = 0$ **26.** $x^2 - 9 = 11$

27. $x^2 - 7x + 9 = 0$ **28.** $x^2 - 2x - 15 = 0$

29. $x^2 - 4x - 3 = 0$ **30.** $x^2 + 10x - 2 = 0$

31. $2x^2 + 8x + 7 = 0$ **32.** $4(2x - 1)^2 - 36 = 0$

LESSON 112 Number of Solutions to Quadratic Equations

☐ **REFRESH YOUR SKILLS** ···

Solve by factoring. Review Lessons 105 and 106 if needed.

1. $x^2 + 3x + 2 = 0$

2. $2x^2 + 3x - 2 = 0$

Solve by completing the square. Review Lessons 107 and 108 if needed.

3. $x^2 + 2x - 3 = 0$

4. $5x^2 + 2x - 1 = 0$

Solve by the quadratic formula. Review Lesson 109 if needed.

5. $x^2 - 5x + 2 = 0$

6. $3x^2 + 7x + 2 = 0$

☐ **CLASSIFYING SOLUTIONS TO QUADRATIC EQUATIONS** ···

A quadratic equation may have two solutions, one solution, or no solution. We can determine the number of solutions to a quadratic equation using the **discriminant**, $b^2 - 4ac$, which is the expression inside the radical in the quadratic formula.

If $b^2 - 4ac > 0$, there are two solutions. If $b^2 - 4ac = 0$, there is one solution. If $b^2 - 4ac < 0$, there is no solution because we cannot take the square root of a negative number.

$$D = b^2 - 4ac$$
$$D > 0 \rightarrow two\ roots$$
$$D = 0 \rightarrow one\ root$$
$$D < 0 \rightarrow no\ roots$$

➔ **EXAMPLE** Determine the number of solutions.

$x^2 - 9 = 0$

$D = 0^2 - 4 \cdot 1 \cdot (-9)$

$= 36 > 0$

The discriminant is positive, so there are two solutions.

$x^2 + 2x + 1 = 0$

$D = 2^2 - 4 \cdot 1 \cdot 1$

$= 0$

The discriminant is 0, so there is one solution.

$x^2 + 9 = 0$

$D = 0^2 - 4 \cdot 1 \cdot 9$

$= -36 < 0$

The discriminant is negative, so there is no solution.

➔ **TRY IT** Find the discriminant, then determine the number of solutions. Do not solve.

7. $x^2 - 4x + 7 = 0$

8. $x^2 + 3x - 5 = 0$

9. $4x^2 + 3x + 1 = 0$

10. $9x^2 + 12x + 4 = 0$

Find the discriminant, then determine the number of solutions. Do not solve.

11. $x^2 - 4x + 4 = 0$ **12.** $x^2 - 6x + 11 = 0$

13. $7x^2 - 5x + 2 = 0$ **14.** $5x^2 + 7x - 6 = 0$

Solve. Use any method you prefer.

15. $x^2 + 2x - 1 = 0$ **16.** $x^2 + 3x + 9 = 0$

17. $x^2 + 5x + 2 = 0$ **18.** $x^2 - 8x + 16 = 0$

19. $2x^2 - 5x + 7 = 0$ **20.** $3x^2 + 2x - 8 = 0$

21. $16x^2 - 49 = 0$ **22.** $2x^2 + 6x + 5 = 0$

EXTRA Solve. Use any method you prefer.

23. $x^2 + 2x - 8 = 0$ **24.** $x^2 - 5x + 10 = 0$

25. $x^2 + 6x + 9 = 0$ **26.** $x^2 - 20 = 0$

27. $x^2 - 8x + 15 = 0$ **28.** $x^2 + 10x + 4 = 0$

29. $x^2 - 4x + 13 = 0$ **30.** $x^2 - 14x + 49 = 0$

31. $7x^2 - 2x - 1 = 0$ **32.** $4x^2 - 4x + 3 = 0$

33. $4x^2 - 28 = 0$ **34.** $5x^2 + 8x + 2 = 0$

35. $3x^2 - 8x + 4 = 0$ **36.** $4x^2 + 9x + 3 = 0$

37. $14x^2 - 9x + 1 = 0$ **38.** $25x^2 + 20x + 4 = 0$

LESSON 113 Applications of Quadratic Equations

☐ **REFRESH YOUR SKILLS** ···

Explain how to solve each problem using the general strategy of solving word problems: 1) define a variable, 2) set up an equation to model the given situation, 3) solve the equation as usual, and then 4) answer what's being asked. Review Lesson 9 if needed.

1. The sum of three consecutive even integers is 12. Find the integers.

2. The length of a rectangle is twice its width. The perimeter is 18 feet. Find the dimensions of the rectangle.

Use the Pythagorean Theorem to find the missing side. Leave your answers in simplest radical form, if applicable. Review Lesson 69 if needed.

3.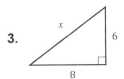

4.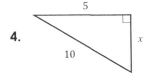

☐ **SOLVING QUADRATIC EQUATION WORD PROBLEMS** ···

So far, you have worked on word problems involving linear equations. Using the same strategy, you can also solve word problems involving quadratic equations. Study each example below. Notice that an equation that models the given situation is now quadratic, not linear.

➜ **EXAMPLE** Numbers

The product of two positive consecutive even integers is 80. Find the integers.

1. Let x = the first even integer
2. $x + 2$ = the second even integer
   The product is 80, so $x(x + 2) = 80$.
3. Solve by factoring or by completing the square, and you get $x = 8$ or $x = -10$.
4. The two positive integers are 8 and 10.

➜ **EXAMPLE** Pythagorean Theorem

The diagonal of a square measures $5\sqrt{2}$ cm. Find the length of each side.

1. Let x = the side length of the square
2. Applying the Pythagorean Theorem gives $x^2 + x^2 = (5\sqrt{2})^2$.
3. Solve by taking the square root of each side, and you get $x = 5$ or $x = -5$.
4. The (positive) length of each side is 5.

➜ **TRY IT** Solve.

5. The product of two positive consecutive even integers is 168. Find the integers.

6. The difference between two positive integers is 5. Their product is 84. Find the integers.

➜ **TRY IT** Solve.

7. The diagonal of a square measures $9\sqrt{2}$ cm. Find the length of each side.

8. The hypotenuse of a right triangle is 2 inches longer than one leg and 4 inches longer than the other leg. Find the dimensions of the triangle.

→ **EXAMPLE** Geometry

The area of a rectangle is 75 cm². Its length is 5 cm longer than twice its width. Find the dimensions of the rectangle.

1. Let x = the width of the rectangle
2. $2x + 5$ = the length of the rectangle
   The area is 75, so $x(2x + 5) = 75$.
3. Solve by factoring or by the quadratic formula, and you get $x = 5$ or $x = -15/2$.
4. The width is 5 cm, and the length is 15 cm.

→ **TRY IT** Solve.

9. The area of a rectangle is 96 cm². Its length is 4 cm longer than its width. Find the dimensions of the rectangle.

10. The area of a rectangle is 90 ft². Its length is 3 feet shorter than three times its width. Find the dimensions of the rectangle.

☐ **EXERCISE YOUR SKILLS** ···

For each problem, 1) define a variable, 2) set up an equation, 3) solve the equation, and 4) answer what's being asked. Show your work in your notebook.

11. The sum of the squares of two consecutive positive integers is 61. Find the integers.

12. The sum of two positive integers is 10. The sum of their squares is 58. Find the integers.

13. The difference between two positive integers is 3. The sum of the smaller and the square of the larger is 39. Find the integers.

14. A rectangle has a diagonal of 13 cm and a width of 5 cm. Find the height of the rectangle.

15. The hypotenuse of a right triangle is 1 cm longer than one leg and 2 cm longer than the other leg. Find the dimensions of the triangle.

16. The area of a rectangle is 65 square feet. Its length is 2 feet shorter than three times its width. Find the dimensions of the rectangle.

17. A rectangle has a perimeter of 36 inches and an area of 80 square inches. Find the dimensions of the rectangle.

18. An isosceles right triangle, a right triangle with two legs equal in length, has a hypotenuse of $4\sqrt{2}$ feet. Find the perimeter of the triangle.

CHALLENGE Solve.

19. A rectangle has a width of 5 cm and a height of 4 cm. A strip of uniform width is added around the rectangle to increase its area by 36 cm². What is the width of the strip?

20. Two cars left an intersection at the same time. Car A traveled north and car B traveled east. When car A traveled 20 miles, the distance between the two cars was 10 miles more than the distance traveled by car B. How far did car B travel?

LESSON 114 Catch Up and Review!

Catch up if you are behind. Use the review problems below to make sure you're on track.

LESSONS 103–104 Solve by taking square roots.

1. $x^2 - 45 = 0$

2. $(x - 1)^2 - 16 = 0$

3. $(9x - 5)^2 - 8 = 0$

4. $3(2x - 1)^2 - 3 = 15$

LESSON 105–106 Solve by factoring.

5. $x^2 - 5x + 6 = 0$

6. $x^2 - 25 = 0$

7. $4x^2 + 8x + 3 = 0$

8. $5x^2 - 9x - 2 = 0$

LESSON 107–108 Solve by completing the square.

9. $x^2 - 4x - 10 = 0$

10. $x^2 + 6x - 11 = 0$

11. $3x^2 + 2x - 3 = 0$

12. $3x^2 + 18x + 15 = 0$

LESSON 109–110 Solve by the quadratic formula.

13. $x^2 - x - 8 = 0$

14. $x^2 + 3x + 1 = 0$

15. $5x^2 + 2x - 2 = 0$

16. $3x^2 - x - 4 = 0$

LESSONS 111–112 Solve. Use any method you prefer.

17. $x^2 + 12x + 36 = 0$

18. $4x^2 - 64 = 0$

19. $2x^2 + 8x + 7 = 0$

20. $6x^2 + 8x + 5 = 0$

21. The sum of the squares of two consecutive even positive integers is 100. Find the integers.

22. The diagonal of a square measures $3\sqrt{2}$ cm. Find the length of each side.

23. The area of a rectangle is 60 cm². Its length is 7 cm shorter than its width. Find the dimensions of the rectangle.

☐ **MIXED REVIEW: PRE-ALGEBRA** ···

Brush up on the topics covered in Pre-Algebra.

24. A set is a collection of things called elements. A Venn diagram is a diagram that shows the relationships among sets. Venn diagrams are useful when performing set operations. Below are four basic set operations. In each Venn diagram, shade the region(s) representing the result of the indicated operation.

Union	Intersection	Complement	Difference
$A \cup B$	$A \cap B$	A^C	$A - B$
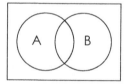	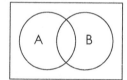	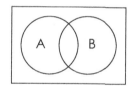	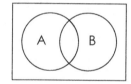
The set of all elements that are either in A or in B.	The set of elements that are both in A and in B.	The set of elements that are not in A	The set of elements that are in A but not in B

25. Given A = {1, 2, 3, 4} and B = {3, 4, 5, 6}, find A − (A ∩ B).

26. True or false? { 1, 3 } is a subset of { 2, 3, 5 }.

27. True or false? An empty set is a subset of every set.

28. List all the possible outcomes of tossing a coin and rolling a die.

29. How many outfits are possible with 5 shirts and 4 pairs of pants?

LESSON 115 Graphing Parabolas by Plotting Points

☐ **REFRESH YOUR SKILLS** ···

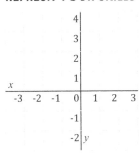

1. Find the ordered-pair solutions of $y = x + 1$ that correspond to $x = -3$, 0, and 2. Review Lesson 14 if needed.

2. Graph $y = x + 1$ by plotting the three ordered-pair solutions above and then drawing a line through them. Review Lesson 14 if needed.

☐ **GRAPHING PARABOLAS BY PLOTTING POINTS** ·····························

A **quadratic function** is a function that can be written in the standard form $y = ax^2 + bx + c$, where $a \neq 0$. The graph of a quadratic function is a U-shaped curve called a **parabola**.

> Standard form
>
> $$ax^2 + bx + c = 0$$

To graph a quadratic function, first plot as many points as necessary to recognize the shape of its graph. Then connect the plotted points with a smooth U-shaped curve.

➔ **EXAMPLE** Graph $y = x^2 - 4x + 1$.

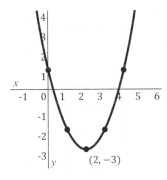

1. Plot as many points as possible: (0, 1), (1, −2), (2, −3), (3, −2), (4, 1)
2. Connect the points with a smooth curve.

➔ **TRY IT 3.** Graph $y = x^2 - 2$.

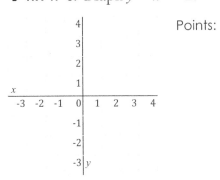

Points:

☐ **IDENTIFYING FEATURES OF PARABOLAS FROM GRAPHS** ·······························

A parabola opens upward if the leading coefficient a is positive, and it opens downward if the leading coefficient a is negative. The lowest or highest point of the parabola is the **vertex**. The vertical line that passes through the vertex and divides the parabola into two symmetric parts is the **axis of symmetry**.

➔ **EXAMPLE** Features of $y = -x^2 - 2x + 3$

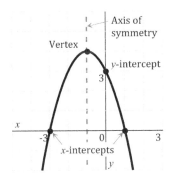

The vertex is at (−1, 4).

The axis of symmetry is $x = -1$.

The y-intercept is 3.

The x-intercepts are −3 and 1.

➔ **TRY IT 4.** Identify the features.

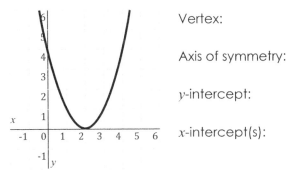

Vertex:

Axis of symmetry:

y-intercept:

x-intercept(s):

Graph by plotting the points for the given *x*-values. Then identify the vertex and axis of symmetry.

5. $y = x^2$

for $x = -2, -1, 0, 1, 2$

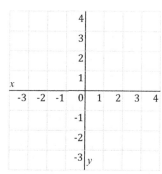

6. $y = x^2 - 3$

for $x = -2, -1, 0, 1, 2$

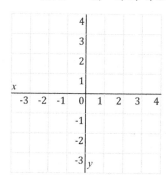

7. $y = x^2 + 2x$

for $x = -3, -2, -1, 0, 1$

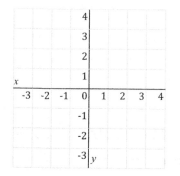

8. $y = -x^2$

for $x = -2, -1, 0, 1, 2$

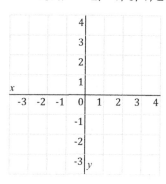

9. $y = -x^2 + 2$

for $x = -2, -1, 0, 1, 2$

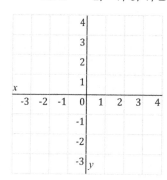

10. $y = -x^2 + 2x$

for $x = -1, 0, 1, 2, 3$

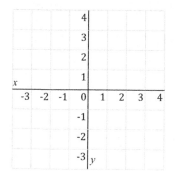

11. $y = x^2 - 2x + 1$

for $x = -1, 0, 1, 2, 3$

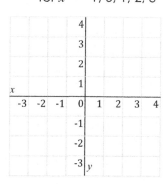

12. $y = \frac{1}{4}x^2$

for $x = -4, -2, 0, 2, 4$

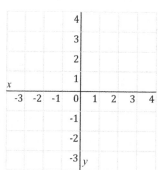

13. $y = -2x^2 + 4$

for $x = -2, -1, 0, 1, 2$

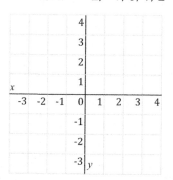

□ **ABOUT DIRECTIONS OF PARABOLAS** ···

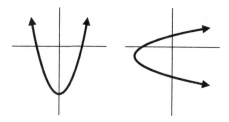

Parabolas can be either vertical or horizontal. The graphs of quadratic functions are vertical parabolas. In this workbook, we are talking about vertical parabolas only, as graphs of quadratic functions. You'll learn about horizontal parabolas in Algebra 2.

LESSON 116 Graphing Parabolas Using the Vertex Formula

☐ **REFRESH YOUR SKILLS**

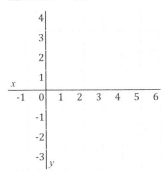

1. Graph $y = x^2 - 4x + 1$ by plotting as many points as necessary to recognize the shape of its graph. Review Lesson 115 if needed.

2. Identify the axis of symmetry and vertex from your graph. Review Lesson 115 if needed.

☐ **FINDING VERTICES OF PARABOLAS USING THE VERTEX FORMULA**

To find the vertex of a parabola without graphing, first find the axis of symmetry, or the x-value of the vertex, using the **vertex formula** shown on the right. Then find the y-value of the vertex by plugging the x-value into the given function. (You will learn where the vertex formula comes from in a later lesson.)

> Given $y = ax^2 + bx + c$,
>
> the axis of symmetry is $x = -\dfrac{b}{2a}$

→ **EXAMPLE** Find the vertex of $y = -x^2 - 2x + 3$.

1. Find the x-value using the vertex formula.
$$x = -\frac{b}{2a} = -\frac{-2}{2(-1)} = -1$$

2. Find the y-value using the x-value.
$$y = -(-1)^2 - 2(-1) + 3 = 4$$

3. The vertex is $(-1, 4)$, and the axis of symmetry is $x = -1$.

→ **TRY IT** Find the vertex.

3. $y = x^2 - 2x + 1$

4. $y = -x^2 + 6x - 5$

5. $y = \frac{1}{2}x^2 + 4x - 2$

☐ **GRAPHING PARABOLAS USING THE VERTEX FORMULA**

You can graph any parabola by plotting enough points to recognize its U-shape. However, you know that all parabolas are symmetric and their axis of symmetry passes through their vertex. That means you can graph a parabola faster by plotting the vertex and points on each side of the vertex.

→ **EXAMPLE** Graph $y = -x^2 - 2x + 3$.

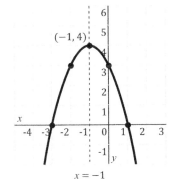

1. Plot the vertex. The vertex is $(-1, 4)$, as found above.
2. Plot some points on one side of the vertex. The y-intercept is often used because it is easy to find by setting $x = 0$. We plot two points $(0, 3)$ and $(1, 0)$.
3. Reflect the points from Step 2 across the axis of symmetry. The points reflected across $x = -1$ are $(-2, 3)$ and $(-3, 0)$.
4. Draw a parabola through the plotted points.

➜ **TRY IT 6.** Graph $y = x^2 - 6x + 8$.

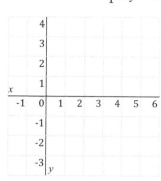

Vertex:

Axis of symmetry:

Points on one side:

Points reflected:

➜ **TRY IT 7.** Graph $y = -\frac{1}{4}x^2 - x$.

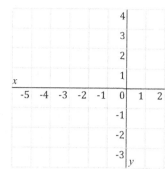

Vertex:

Axis of symmetry:

Points on one side:

Points reflected:

☐ **EXERCISE YOUR SKILLS** ··

Find the axis of symmetry, vertex, and y-intercept.

8. $y = x^2 + 8x$

9. $y = x^2 + 6x + 5$

10. $y = -x^2 + 4$

11. $y = -x^2 + 8x - 7$

12. $y = 3x^2 - 6x + 1$

13. $y = -\frac{1}{2}x^2 - 2x + 2$

Graph by plotting the vertex and two additional points on each side of the vertex. Use the y-intercept when possible.

14. $y = x^2 + 2x$

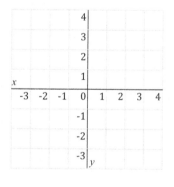

15. $y = x^2 + 4x + 3$

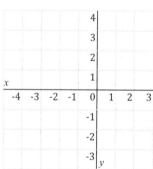

16. $y = \frac{1}{2}x^2 - 2x - 2$

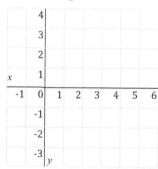

17. $y = -x^2 - 4x$

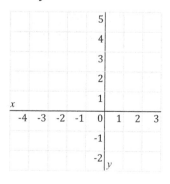

18. $y = -x^2 + 2x - 1$

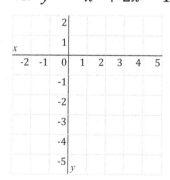

19. $y = -2x^2 + 4x$

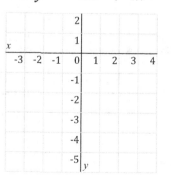

LESSON 117 Graphing Parabolas in Vertex Form

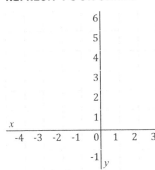

1. Find the axis of symmetry, vertex, and y-intercept of $y = -x^2 - 2x + 3$ without graphing. Review Lesson 116 if needed.

2. Graph $y = -x^2 - 2x + 3$ by plotting the vertex and two additional points on each side of the vertex. Review Lesson 116 if needed.

☐ **FINDING VERTICES OF PARABOLAS IN VERTEX FORM**

Any quadratic function $y = ax^2 + bx + c$ can be written in the form $y = a(x - h)^2 + k$. This is called the **vertex form** of the quadratic function because the point (h, k) is the vertex of its graph. The point (h, k) is the vertex because y has a minimum or maximum value of k when x is h.

To find the vertex of a parabola in vertex form, simply identify h and k from the given function.

> Vertex form
>
> $$y = a(x - h)^2 + k$$
>
> Vertex: (h, k)
>
> Axis of symmetry: $x = h$

➔ **EXAMPLE** Find the vertex of $y = (x + 2)^2$.

1. Find h and k. Here $h = -2$ and $k = 0$.
2. Find the vertex (h, k). The vertex is $(-2, 0)$, and the axis of symmetry is $x = -2$.
3. In addition, without graphing, we know:
    - The parabola opens upward ($a = 1 > 0$).
    - The y-intercept is 4 ($y = 4$ when $x = 0$).
    - The x-intercept is -2 ($x = -2$ when $y = 0$).

➔ **TRY IT** Find the vertex.

3. $y = x^2 + 3$

4. $y = (x - 1)^2$

5. $y = (x + 4)^2 - 2$

☐ **GRAPHING PARABOLAS IN VERTEX FORM**

You can graph a parabola in vertex form the same way you did before, but now the vertex is given as (h, k) and the axis of symmetry as $x = h$.

➔ **EXAMPLE** Graph $y = (x + 2)^2$.

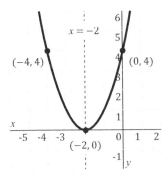

1. Plot the vertex: $(-2, 0)$.
2. Plot a point on one side: $(0, 4)$.
3. Reflect $(0, 4)$ across $x = -2$, then plot $(-4, 4)$.
4. Draw a parabola through the points.

➔ **TRY IT 6.** Graph $y = (x - 2)^2 - 1$.

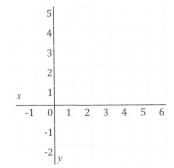

Vertex:

Axis of symmetry:

Point on one side:

Point reflected:

Find the axis of symmetry, vertex, and *y*-intercept.

7. $y = x^2 + 5$　　　　　　　　　　**8.** $y = -x^2 - 7$

9. $y = (x - 4)^2$　　　　　　　　　　**10.** $y = -(x + 3)^2$

11. $y = 3(x + 1)^2 - 5$　　　　　　　**12.** $y = -\frac{1}{4}(x - 2)^2 + 3$

Graph by plotting the vertex and one additional point on each side of the vertex. Use the *y*-intercept when possible.

13. $y = x^2 - 2$

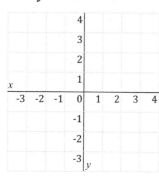

14. $y = (x - 3)^2$

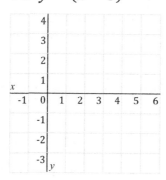

15. $y = (x + 2)^2 - 1$

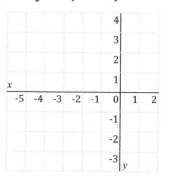

16. $y = -x^2 + 1$

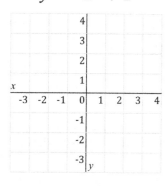

17. $y = -(x - 2)^2$

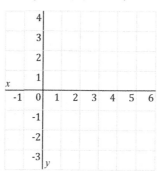

18. $y = -(x + 1)^2 + 3$

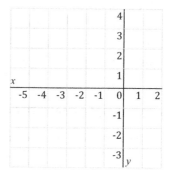

19. $y = -4(x + 1)^2 + 2$

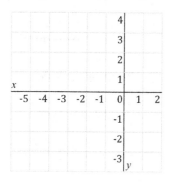

20. $y = 2(x - 2)^2 - 2$

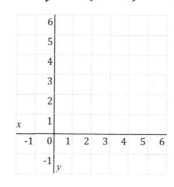

21. $y = -\frac{1}{3}(x - 3)^2 + 2$

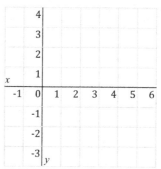

LESSON 118 Graphing Parabolas in Intercept Form

1. Find the axis of symmetry, vertex, and y-intercept of $y = (x + 2)^2$. Review Lesson 117 if needed.

2. Graph $y = (x + 2)^2$ by plotting the vertex, the y-intercept, and its reflection point. Review Lesson 117 if needed.

☐ FINDING VERTICES OF PARABOLAS IN INTERCEPT FORM

A quadratic function $y = ax^2 + bx + c$ can also be written in the form $y = a(x - p)(x - q)$. This is called the **intercept form**, or **factored form**, of the quadratic function because p and q are the x-intercepts of its graph. The values p and q are the x-intercepts, or **zeros**, because y is 0 when x is p or q.

> Intercept form
> $$y = a(x - p)(x - q)$$
> Axis of symmetry: $x = \dfrac{p + q}{2}$

What is the vertex of a parabola in intercept form? Parabolas are symmetric, so the x-value of the vertex is halfway between the two x-intercepts. Its y-value can be found by plugging the x-value into the given function.

➔ **EXAMPLE** Find the vertex of $y = -x(x - 4)$.

1. Find the x-intercepts. Here $p = 0$ and $q = 4$.
2. Find the x-value of the vertex.
$$x = \frac{p + q}{2} = \frac{0 + 4}{2} = 2$$
3. Find the y-value using the x-value.
$$y = -2(2 - 4) = 4$$
4. The vertex is (2, 4), and the axis of symmetry is $x = 2$.

➔ **TRY IT** Find the vertex.

3. $y = x(x - 2)$

4. $y = (x + 1)(x - 3)$

5. $y = -\frac{1}{4}(x + 4)(x - 4)$

☐ GRAPHING PARABOLAS IN INTERCEPT FORM

You can graph a parabola in intercept form by plotting the vertex and x-intercepts.

➔ **EXAMPLE** Graph $y = -x(x - 4)$.

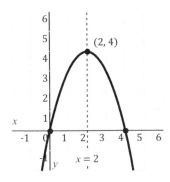

1. Plot the x-intercepts: (0, 0) and (4, 0).
2. Plot the vertex: (2, 4).
3. Draw a parabola through the points.

➔ **TRY IT 6.** Graph $y = (x + 1)(x + 3)$.

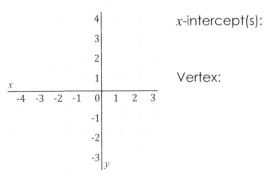

x-intercept(s):

Vertex:

Find the vertex, *y*-intercept, and *x*-intercepts (zeros).

7. $y = x(x - 4)$

8. $y = -x(x + 2)$

9. $y = (x + 1)(x - 5)$

10. $y = -(x - 1)(x - 7)$

11. $y = 2(x - 1)(x + 3)$

12. $y = -\frac{1}{2}(x + 2)(x + 6)$

Graph by plotting the vertex and *x*-intercepts.

13. $y = x(x - 4)$

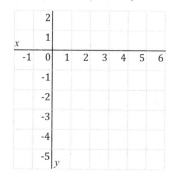

14. $y = (x + 1)(x - 3)$

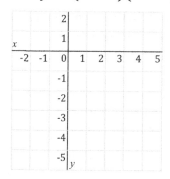

15. $y = (x - 2)(x - 6)$

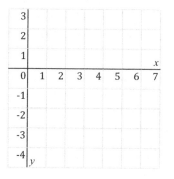

16. $y = -x(x + 2)$

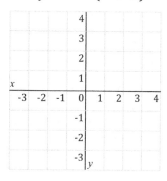

17. $y = -(x - 1)(x + 1)$

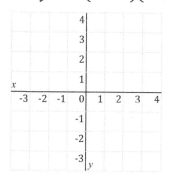

18. $y = -(x + 1)(x + 5)$

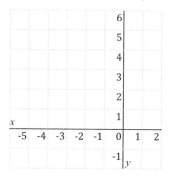

19. $y = -\frac{1}{4}x(x + 4)$

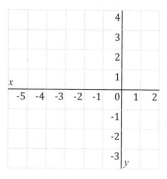

20. $y = \frac{1}{3}(x - 2)(x + 4)$

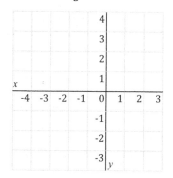

21. $y = 4(x - 1)(x - 3)$

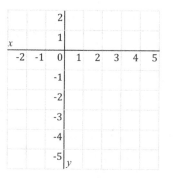

LESSON 119 Graphing Parabolas in Standard Form

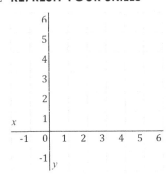

1. Find the vertex, y-intercept, and x-intercepts of $y = -x(x - 4)$. Review Lesson 118 if needed.

2. Graph $y = -x(x - 4)$ by plotting the vertex and x-intercepts. Review Lesson 118 if needed.

☐ **CONVERTING STANDARD FORM TO VERTEX FORM**

To convert a quadratic function from standard form to vertex form, use the strategy of completing the square.

➜ **EXAMPLE** Convert to vertex form.

a. $y = x^2 - 4x + 3$
   $= x^2 - 4x + \mathbf{4} - \mathbf{4} + 3$
   $= (x - 2)^2 - \mathbf{4} + 3$
   $= (x - 2)^2 - 1$

b. $y = -3x^2 + 6x + 1$
   $= -3(x^2 - 2x) + 1$
   $= -3(x^2 - 2x + \mathbf{1} - \mathbf{1}) + 1$
   $= -3(x^2 - 2x + \mathbf{1}) + \mathbf{3} + 1$
   $= -3(x - 1)^2 + 4$

Pull −1 out.
−3 × −1 = 3

➜ **TRY IT** Convert to vertex form.

3. $y = x^2 + 2x - 3$

4. $y = -2x^2 - 8x - 3$

Notice that the vertex formula $-b/2a$ results from completing the square on the standard form of a quadratic function. Try yourself converting the standard form $y = ax^2 + bx + c$ to the vertex form $y = a(x - h)^2 + k$. Review Lessons 110 and 116 if needed.

☐ **CONVERTING STANDARD FORM TO INTERCEPT FORM**

To convert a quadratic function from standard form to intercept form, simply factor the function.

➜ **EXAMPLE** Convert to intercept form.

a. $y = x^2 - 4x + 3$
   $= (x - 1)(x - 3)$

b. $y = -3x^2 + 3x + 6$
   $= -3(x^2 - x - 2)$
   $= -3(x + 1)(x - 2)$

➜ **TRY IT** Convert to intercept form.

5. $y = x^2 + 2x - 3$

6. $y = -2x^2 + 2x + 12$

In general, when graphing a parabola, we plot its key points like the vertex and intercepts.

To graph a parabola in standard form, find the vertex and axis of symmetry by using the vertex formula or by converting to vertex form. Find the x-intercepts, if they exist, by converting to intercept form. Find the y-intercept by setting $x = 0$. Then plot the key points and graph the parabola.

➔ EXAMPLE Graph $y = x^2 - 4x + 3$.

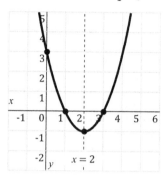

The vertex form is
$y = (x - 2)^2 - 1$, so
the vertex is $(2, -1)$.

The intercept form is
$y = (x - 1)(x - 3)$, so
the x-intercepts are
1 and 3.

The y-intercept is 3.

➔ TRY IT 7. Graph $y = x^2 + 2x - 3$.

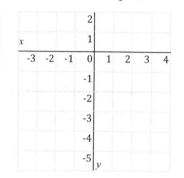

Vertex:

x-intercepts:

y-intercept:

Convert to vertex form and to intercept form.

8. $y = x^2 - 9$

9. $y = x^2 - 6x + 9$

10. $y = x^2 - 2x - 8$

11. $y = -x^2 - 4x + 5$

12. $y = 3x^2 + 6x - 9$

13. $y = -2x^2 + 12x - 10$

14. $y = \frac{1}{5}x^2 - 2x$

15. $y = -\frac{1}{2}x^2 + 2x + 16$

Graph by plotting the vertex and one additional point on each side of the vertex. Use the intercepts when possible.

16. $y = x^2 + 6x + 8$

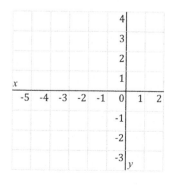

17. $y = 2x^2 - 8x + 6$

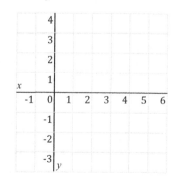

18. $y = -\frac{1}{2}x^2 + 2$

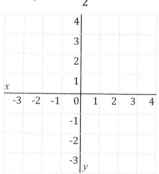

LESSON 120 Graphing Parabolas in All Forms

□ **REFRESH YOUR SKILLS**

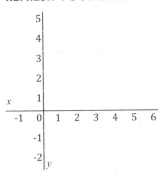

1. Convert $y = x^2 - 4x + 3$ to vertex form and to intercept form. Review Lesson 119 if needed.

2. Graph $y = x^2 - 4x + 3$ by plotting the vertex and intercepts. Review Lesson 119 if needed.

□ **IDENTIFYING FEATURES OF PARABOLAS FROM EQUATIONS**

Let's review three ways of writing a quadratic function. These three forms are equivalent to each other, and yet each form tells us something different about the function's graph.

Vertex form	Intercept form	Standard form
$y = a(x - h)^2 + k$	$y = a(x - p)(x - q)$	$y = ax^2 + bx + c$
Vertex: (h, k)	x-intercepts: p and q	y-intercept: c
Axis of symmetry: $x = h$	Axis of symmetry: $x = \dfrac{p+q}{2}$	Axis of symmetry: $x = -\dfrac{b}{2a}$

As you have learned so far, there are different ways to find the key points, like the vertex and intercepts, of a parabola. Use whichever method you find easier to work with. The example below finds them by converting between the three forms.

➔ **EXAMPLE** Find the vertex and intercepts.

$y = x^2 + 4x$ y-intercept: 0

$= x(x + 4)$ x-intercepts: 0, −4

$= (x + 2)^2 - 4$ Vertex: (−2, −4)

➔ **TRY IT** Find the vertex and intercepts.

3. $y = x^2 - 2x - 3$

4. $y = -x^2 + 8x - 7$

When a parabola is given in vertex form, you can also find the x-intercepts by setting $y = 0$ and solving the resulting quadratic equation by taking square roots. As shown below, you'll find the same x-intercepts as in the example above.

➔ **EXAMPLE** Find the x-intercepts.

$(x + 2)^2 - 4 = 0$ Set $y = 0$.

$(x + 2)^2 = 4$ Solve for x by taking square roots.

$x + 2 = \pm 2$

$x = 0, x = -4$ x-intercept: 0, −4

➔ **TRY IT** Find the x-intercepts.

5. $y = (x + 3)^2 - 9$

6. $y = -2(x - 1)^2 + 8$

☐ **GRAPHING PARABOLAS IN ALL FORMS** ··

You can graph a parabola in any form by plotting its key points, as you did in the previous lessons.

Note, though, that not all parabolas have x-intercepts, or zeros. If a parabola opens upward and its vertex is above the x-axis, there will be no x-intercepts. Similarly, if a parabola opens downward and its vertex is below the x-axis, there will be no x-intercepts.

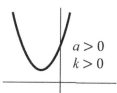
$a > 0$
$k > 0$

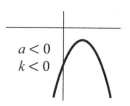
$a < 0$
$k < 0$

➔ **EXAMPLE** Graph $y = x^2 + 4x + 5$.

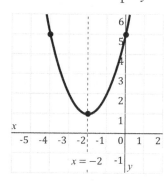

The vertex form is $y = (x + 2)^2 + 1$, so the vertex is at $(-2, 1)$.

No x-intercepts because the graph is above the x-axis.

The y-intercept is 5.

➔ **TRY IT 7.** Graph $y = -x^2 + 2x - 2$.

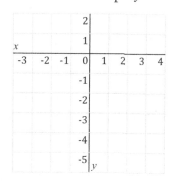

Vertex:

x-intercept(s):

y-intercept:

☐ **EXERCISE YOUR SKILLS** ··

Find the vertex, y-intercept, and x-intercepts (if any).

8. $y = (x + 2)^2 - 4$

9. $y = -2(x - 1)^2 - 3$

10. $y = 4(x + 1)(x + 3)$

11. $y = -(x + 1)(x - 5)$

12. $y = x^2 - 4$

13. $y = -x^2 + 6x - 9$

14. $y = 3x^2 + 6x + 4$

15. $y = \frac{1}{2}x^2 - 4x + 6$

Graph by plotting the vertex and one additional point on each side of the vertex. Use the intercepts when possible.

16. $y = (x - 1)^2 - 4$

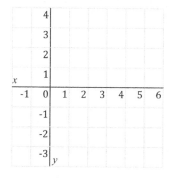

17. $y = -x(x - 2)$

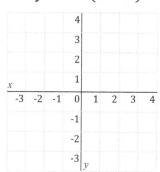

18. $y = x^2 - 6x + 5$

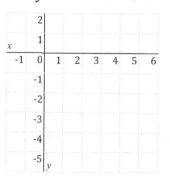

LESSON 121 Finding Equations of Parabolas

☐ **REFRESH YOUR SKILLS** ···

Find the vertex, y-intercept, and x-intercepts (if any). Review Lesson 120 if needed.

1. $y = (x + 3)^2 - 1$ **2.** $y = -(x - 5)^2$

3. $y = (x + 1)(x - 3)$ **4.** $y = -3x(x - 2)$

5. $y = 2x^2 - 8x + 6$ **6.** $y = 3x^2 + 6x + 5$

☐ **FINDING EQUATIONS OF PARABOLAS FROM VERTEX AND A POINT** ······················

To find an equation of a parabola given its vertex and a point on the parabola, write the vertex form using the vertex. Then find the leading coefficient using the point.

➔ **EXAMPLE** Find an equation of the parabola with the vertex at $(2, 1)$ and a point at $(3, 4)$.

$y = a(x - 2)^2 + 1$	Vertex form
$4 = a(3 - 2)^2 + 1$	Plug in (3, 4).
$4 = a + 1; \ a = 3$	Solve for a.
$y = 3(x - 2)^2 + 1$	Answer
$y = 3x^2 - 12x + 13$	Standard form

➔ **TRY IT** Find an equation of each parabola given its vertex and a point.

7. Vertex $(1, 1)$; Point $(2, 2)$

8. Vertex $(3, -9)$; Point $(5, -1)$

☐ **FINDING EQUATIONS OF PARABOLAS FROM ZEROS AND A POINT** ······················

To find an equation of a parabola given its zeros (x-intercepts) and a point on the parabola, write the intercept form using the zeros. Then find the leading coefficient using the point.

➔ **EXAMPLE** Find an equation of the parabola with the zeros at 1 and 5 and a point at $(2, 3)$.

$y = a(x - 1)(x - 5)$	Intercept form
$3 = a(2 - 1)(2 - 5)$	Plug in (2, 3).
$3 = -3a; \ a = -1$	Solve for a.
$y = -(x - 1)(x - 5)$	Answer
$y = -x^2 + 6x - 5$	Standard form

➔ **TRY IT** Find an equation of each parabola given its zeros and a point.

9. $x = 3$ and $x = 7$; Point $(4, -3)$

10. $x = 0$ and $x = 4$; Point $(3, 9)$

☐ **FINDING EQUATIONS OF PARABOLAS FROM GRAPHS** ···

To find an equation of a parabola given its graph, first identify the key points from the graph. Then use either strategy shown above.

→ EXAMPLE Find an equation of the parabola.

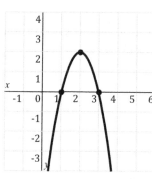

Write the vertex form or the intercept form.
$y = a(x - 1)(x - 3)$

Then use any point to find a. Plug in (2, 2), and you get $a = -2$.

So its equation is
$y = -2(x - 1)(x - 3)$

→ TRY IT 11. Find an equation of the parabola.

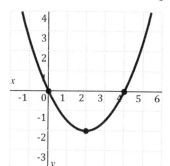

Vertex form or intercept form:

Value of a:

Equation:

□ **EXERCISE YOUR SKILLS** ···

Find an equation of each parabola in standard form.

12. A parabola has vertex (−2, 3) and passes through (0, 7).

13. A parabola has vertex (0, 9) and passes through (2, 5).

14. A parabola has vertex (0, −6) and passes through (3, −3).

15. A parabola has zeros at $x = 1$ and $x = 5$ and passes through (0, 5).

16. A parabola has zeros at $x = 0$ and $x = 3$ and passes through (1, 4).

17. A parabola has zeros at $x = -4$ and $x = 4$ and passes through (3, 7).

18. A parabola has zeros at $x = 4$ and $x = -8$ and passes through (2, −5).

Find an equation of each parabola in standard form.

19.

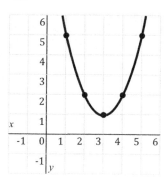

20.

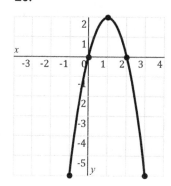

21.

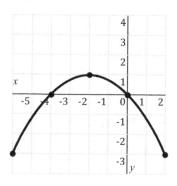

LESSON 122 Transforming Parabolas

☐ **GRAPHING PARABOLAS USING TRANSFORMATIONS** ·································

A **function family** is a group of functions with similar characteristics. The family of linear functions includes functions whose graph is a line. The family of quadratic functions includes functions whose graph is a parabola. A **parent function** is the most basic form of a function family. The parent function of the family of linear functions is $y = x$. The parent function of the family of quadratic functions is $y = x^2$.

For linear and quadratic functions, the graph of any function can be obtained from the graph of the parent function by translations (shifts), reflections (flips), and scaling (stretches or shrinks). In other words, instead of plotting points, you can graph any parabola by transforming $y = x^2$.

To graph $y = (x - h)^2 + k$, shift $y = x^2$ horizontally h units and vertically k units so that the transformed parabola has a vertex at (h, k).

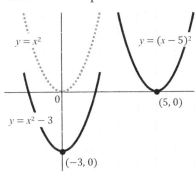

→ **EXAMPLE** Graph.

$y = x^2 - 3$
Shift $y = x^2$ down 3 units.

$y = (x - 5)^2$
Shift $y = x^2$ right 5 units.

→ **TRY IT** Describe how to graph.

1. $y = x^2 + 3$

2. $y = (x + 2)^2$

3. $y = (x - 1)^2 - 4$

To graph $y = -x^2$, flip $y = x^2$ over the x-axis. To graph $y = -(x - h)^2 + k$, flip $y = x^2$ over the x-axis and then shift horizontally h units and vertically k units.

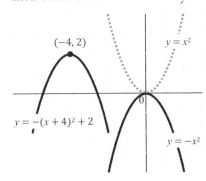

→ **EXAMPLE** Graph.

$y = -x^2$
Flip $y = x^2$ over the x-axis.

$y = -(x + 4)^2 + 2$
Flip $y = x^2$ over the x-axis, shift left 4 units, and shift up 2 units.

→ **TRY IT** Describe how to graph.

4. $y = -x^2 + 1$

5. $y = -(x - 3)^2$

6. $y = -(x + 2)^2 - 5$

To graph $y = ax^2$, scale $y = x^2$ by a. If $|a| < 1$, the parabola becomes wider than $y = x^2$ because the y-values are smaller for the same x-values. If $|a| > 1$, the parabola becomes skinnier (taller).

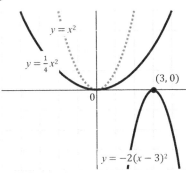

→ **EXAMPLE** Graph.

$y = \frac{1}{4}x^2$
Scale $y = x^2$ by 1/4.

$y = -2(x - 3)^2$
Scale $y = x^2$ by 2, flip over the x-axis, and shift right 3 units.

→ **TRY IT** Describe how to graph.

7. $y = 3x^2$

8. $y = \frac{1}{2}x^2 + 4$

9. $y = -4(x - 1)^2 + 2$

☐ **FINDING EQUATIONS OF TRANSFORMED PARABOLAS** ···

To find an equation of a transformed parabola, identify a, h, and k and write the vertex form.

➜ **EXAMPLE** Find an equation of the parabola obtained by scaling $y = x^2$ by 2, flipping over the x-axis, shifting left 3 units, and shifting up 1 unit.

$y = a(x - h)^2 + k$ Start with the vertex form.

$y = -2(x + 3)^2 + 1$ Find a, h, and k.

- $a = -2$ because the graph is scaled by 2 and flipped over the x-axis.
- $h = -3$ and $k = 1$ because the vertex is at $(-3, 1)$ after shifting.

➜ **TRY IT** Find an equation of each parabola obtained by transforming $y = x^2$ as described.

10. Flip over the x-axis, then shift right 1 unit and down 4 units.

11. Scale by 3, then shift left 2 units and up 3 units.

☐ **EXERCISE YOUR SKILLS** ···

Describe how you would transform $y = x^2$ to graph each parabola.

12. $y = x^2 + 1$

13. $y = (x + 5)^2 - 3$

14. $y = -(x - 3)^2$

15. $y = 2(x - 1)^2 + 5$

Graph by transforming $y = x^2$. Then describe your transformations.

16. $y = -x^2 + 2$

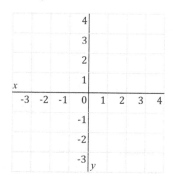

17. $y = \frac{1}{2}(x + 2)^2$

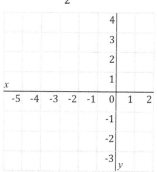

18. $y = 4(x - 3)^2 - 2$

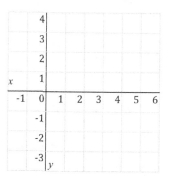

Find an equation of each parabola obtained by transforming $y = x^2$ as described.

19. Shift right 4 units and up 2 units.

20. Flip over the x-axis and shift up 4 units.

21. Scale by 2 and shift right 3 units.

22. Scale by 3 and flip over the x-axis.

LESSON 123 Applications of Quadratic Functions

☐ **REFRESH YOUR SKILLS** ···

Find the vertex, y-intercept, and x-intercept(s). Review Lesson 120 if needed.

1. $y = x^2 - 9$

2. $y = -x^2 + 16$

3. $y = x^2 + 4x + 4$

4. $y = -x^2 - 2x + 8$

5. $y = 2x^2 - 4x - 6$

6. $y = -5x^2 + 20x$

☐ **SOLVING PROJECTILE MOTION PROBLEMS** ···

One common application of quadratic functions is projectile motion. **Projectile motion** is the motion of an object dropped, thrown straight up, or thrown straight down. Projectile motion problems ask you to answer questions about an object in projectile motion, such as how high it rises, when it reaches a certain height, how long it takes to land, and so on.

➔ **EXAMPLE** Object thrown up into the air

A ball is thrown straight up from a height of 128 feet with an initial speed of 32 feet per second. Its height h, in feet, after t seconds is given by the function $h(t) = -16t^2 + 32t + 128$. Determine a) what is the maximum height reached by the ball, b) when the ball hits the ground, and c) when the ball reaches a height of 80 feet.

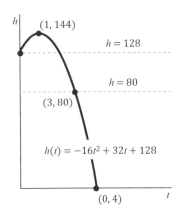

a. We need to find the vertex of the parabola.
   Convert $h(t)$ to vertex form, and you get $h(t) = -16(t - 1)^2 + 144$.
   So the ball reaches its maximum height of 144 feet after 1 second.

b. We need to find t when $h = 0$.
   Solve $-16t^2 + 32t + 128 = 0$, and you get $t = -2$ or $t = 4$.
   So the ball hits the ground after 4 seconds.

c. We need to find t when $h = 80$.
   Solve $-16t^2 + 32t + 128 = 80$, and you get $t = -1$ or $t = 3$.
   So the ball reaches a height of 80 feet after 3 seconds.

➔ **TRY IT** Solve.

7. A ball is thrown straight up from a height of 160 feet with an initial speed of 48 feet per second. Its height h, in feet, after t seconds is given by $h(t) = -16t^2 + 48t + 160$.

   a. When does the ball reach its maximum height?
   b. What is the maximum height reached by the ball?
   c. When will the ball hit the ground?
   d. When will the ball be at a height of 160 feet again?

➔ **EXAMPLE** Object dropped

A ball is dropped from a height of 122.5 meters, and the function $h(t) = -4.9t^2 + 122.5$ gives its height h, in meters, after t seconds. Determine a) how long the ball takes to hit the ground and b) when the ball reaches a height of 44.1 meters.

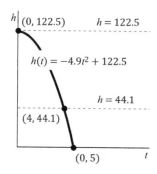

a. We need to find t when $h = 0$.
   Solve $-4.9t^2 + 122.5 = 0$, and you get $t = -5$ or $t = 5$.
   So the ball hits the ground after 5 seconds.

b. We need to find t when $h = 44.1$.
   Solve $-4.9t^2 + 122.5 = 44.1$, and you get $t = -4$ or $t = 4$.
   So the ball reaches a height of 44.1 meters after 4 seconds.

➔ **TRY IT** Solve.

8. A ball is dropped from a height of 64 feet. Its height h, in feet, after t seconds is given by $h(t) = -16t^2 + 64$.

   a. When will the ball hit the ground?
   b. When will the ball reach a height of 48 feet?

☐ **EXERCISE YOUR SKILLS** ···

Solve. Round your answers to the nearest tenth if necessary.

9. A ball is thrown vertically upwards from the top of a building of height 24.5 meters with an initial speed of 19.6 meters per second. Its height h, in meters, after t seconds is given by $h(t) = -4.9t^2 + 19.6t + 24.5$.

   a. When does the ball reach its maximum height?
   b. How much higher does the ball rise above the top of the building?
   c. How long will the ball be in the air before it hits the ground?

10. A golf ball is hit from ground level with an initial speed of 96 feet per second. Its height h, in feet, after t seconds is given by $h(t) = -16t^2 + 96t$.

   a. When does the ball reach its maximum height?
   b. How high will the ball rise before it starts falling?
   c. How long will it take for the ball to hit the ground?
   d. When will the ball reach a height of 80 feet?

11. The average number of patrons using the computer room in a local library is modeled by the function $f(t) = -t^2 + 8t + 4$, where t represents the number of hours since 9 a.m.

   a. At what hour of the day is the computer room most crowded?
   b. On average, how many patrons are using the computer room at 3 p.m.?

LESSON 124 Catch Up and Review!

Catch up if you are behind. Use the review problems below to make sure you're on track.

LESSON 116 Use the vertex formula to find the vertex, then graph.

1. $y = x^2 - 2x$

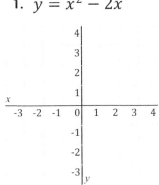

2. $y = -x^2 - 4x - 2$

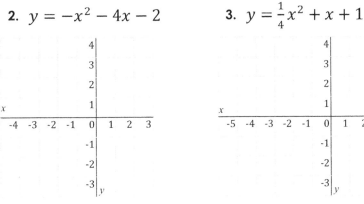

3. $y = \frac{1}{4}x^2 + x + 1$

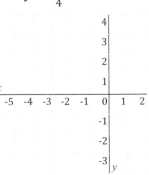

LESSON 117 Find the vertex and y-intercept, then graph.

4. $y = -x^2 + 2$

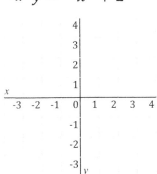

5. $y = (x - 1)^2 - 2$

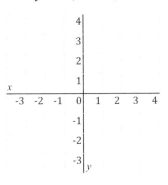

6. $y = -\frac{1}{2}(x + 2)^2 + 1$

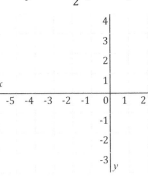

LESSON 118 Find the vertex and intercepts, then graph.

7. $y = (x + 1)(x + 3)$

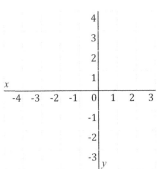

8. $y = -3x(x - 2)$

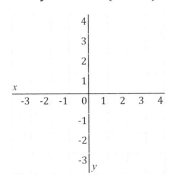

9. $y = \frac{1}{3}(x + 2)(x - 4)$

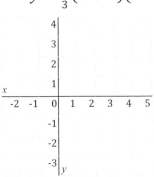

LESSONS 119–120 Find the vertex, y-intercept, and x-intercepts (if any).

10. $y = (x + 1)^2 + 3$

11. $y = -(x + 2)(x - 4)$

12. $y = x^2 - 6x + 9$

13. $y = -x^2 + 4x - 5$

ESSON 121 Find an equation of each parabola in standard form.

14.

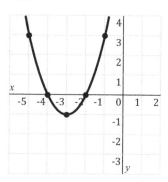

15.

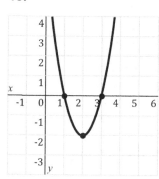

16.

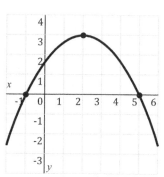

LESSON 122 Find an equation of each parabola obtained by transforming $y = x^2$ as described.

17. Shift left 3 units and up 4 units.

18. Shift right 2 units and down 5 units.

19. Scale by 4 and shift right 1 unit.

20. Flip over the x-axis and shift up 6 units.

LESSON 123 Solve.

21. A golf ball is hit from the ground with an initial speed of 128 feet per second. Its height h, in feet, after t seconds is given by the function $h(t) = -16t^2 + 128t$. What is the maximum height reached by the ball?

☐ **MIXED REVIEW: PRE-ALGEBRA** ···

Brush up on the topics covered in Pre-Algebra.

22. The factorial $n!$ is defined as the product $n \cdot (n - 1) \cdot (n - 2) \cdot \ldots \cdot 3 \cdot 2 \cdot 1$. Evaluate $10!/8!$. Do not use a calculator.

23. You pick 3 toppings out of 10 for a pizza. Is this a permutation or a combination?

24. In how many different ways can you arrange 4 books on a shelf?

LESSON 125 Simplifying Rational Expressions

☐ **REFRESH YOUR SKILLS** ....

Factor completely. Review Lesson 101 if needed.

1. $x^2 - 3x - 10$
2. $3x^2 + 7x - 6$

3. $x^3 - 81x$
4. $x^3 + 4x^2 - 4x - 16$

☐ **FINDING EXCLUDED VALUES OF RATIONAL EXPRESSIONS** ....

A **rational expression** is a fraction whose numerator and denominator are polynomials. The **domain of a rational expression** is all real numbers except those that make the denominator zero, because rational expressions are undefined when the denominator is zero.

To determine the values to exclude from the domain of a rational expression, set the denominator equal to zero and solve the resulting equation.

➜ **EXAMPLE** Find the excluded values.

$\dfrac{2x^2 + 5x - 3}{x^2 + x - 6}$ Original expression

$x^2 + x - 6 = 0$ Set the denominator = 0,
$(x - 2)(x + 3) = 0$ then solve for x.
$x = 2, x = -3$

Excluded values: 2 and −3

➜ **TRY IT** Find the excluded values.

5. $\dfrac{x - 3}{x^2 - 9}$

6. $\dfrac{x^2 - 4x + 4}{x^2 + 4x - 12}$

☐ **SIMPLIFYING RATIONAL EXPRESSIONS** ....

A rational expression is simplified when its numerator and denominator have no common factors other than one. To simplify a rational expression, factor the numerator and denominator completely and then cancel common factors. Be sure to use the original denominator when finding excluded values. Let's see how to simplify the example above.

➜ **EXAMPLE** Simplify. State any excluded values.

$$\frac{2x^2 + 5x - 3}{x^2 + x - 6} = \frac{(2x - 1)(x + 3)}{(x - 2)(x + 3)} = \frac{(2x - 1)\cancel{(x + 3)}}{(x - 2)\cancel{(x + 3)}} = \frac{2x - 1}{x - 2} \, for \, x \neq 2, -3$$

➜ **TRY IT** Simplify. State any excluded values.

7. $\dfrac{x^2 - 8x + 12}{x^2 + 5x - 14}$

8. $\dfrac{2x^2 + x}{2x^2 + 11x + 5}$

Find the excluded values.

9. $\dfrac{x}{2x^2 - 8x}$

10. $\dfrac{x + 2}{x^2 - x - 6}$

Simplify. State any excluded values.

11. $\dfrac{4x^4}{16x^2}$

12. $\dfrac{5x}{5x^2 + 10x}$

13. $\dfrac{9 - x}{x^2 - 9x}$

14. $\dfrac{x - 5}{-2x^2 + 10x}$

15. $\dfrac{x + 4}{x^2 + 5x + 4}$

16. $\dfrac{x + 3}{2x^2 + x - 15}$

17. $\dfrac{x^2 + 3x - 10}{x^2 + 2x - 15}$

18. $\dfrac{4x^2 - 3x - 1}{x^2 + 7x - 8}$

EXTRA Simplify. State any excluded values.

19. $\dfrac{15x^5}{20x^4}$

20. $\dfrac{x + 5}{x^2 - 25}$

21. $\dfrac{x^2}{x^2 + 4x}$

22. $\dfrac{x + 4}{x^2 - x - 20}$

23. $\dfrac{x^2 - 4x + 4}{x^2 + 4x - 12}$

24. $\dfrac{x^2 - 16}{x^2 + 3x - 4}$

25. $\dfrac{2x^2 + 5x + 2}{3x^2 + 4x - 4}$

26. $\dfrac{-x^3 - 9x^2 - 14x}{3x^2 + 15x - 42}$

LESSON 126 Multiplying and Dividing Rational Expressions

☐ **REFRESH YOUR SKILLS** ··

Evaluate. Review Pre Algebra if you have difficulty solving these problems.

1. $\dfrac{3}{5} \times \dfrac{5}{9}$
2. $\dfrac{3}{8} \times 2$
3. $\dfrac{5}{8} \div \dfrac{3}{4}$
4. $\dfrac{4}{5} \div 8$

☐ **MULTIPLYING RATIONAL EXPRESSIONS** ··

To multiply rational expressions, factor each numerator and denominator completely and cancel common factors. Then multiply what's left. Be sure to exclude from the domain the values that make the original denominators zero. In the example below, we need to exclude 0 and 2 from the domain because they make x^2 and $4 - 2x$ zero.

➔ **EXAMPLE** Multiply. State any excluded values.

$$\dfrac{2}{x^2} \cdot \dfrac{x^3 - 2x^2}{4 - 2x} = \dfrac{2}{x^2} \cdot \dfrac{x^2(x-2)}{2(2-x)} = \dfrac{\cancel{2}}{\cancel{x^2}} \cdot \dfrac{\cancel{x^2}(x-2)}{\cancel{2}(2-x)} = \dfrac{x-2}{2-x} = -1 \; for \; x \neq 0, 2$$

➔ **TRY IT** Multiply. State any excluded values.

5. $\dfrac{x^2 + 4x - 5}{x^2 + 5x} \cdot \dfrac{x^2}{x^2 - 1}$

6. $\dfrac{2x^2 + 13x - 7}{x - 5} \cdot \dfrac{x - 5}{x + 7}$

☐ **DIVIDING RATIONAL EXPRESSIONS** ···

To divide rational expressions, multiply the dividend (the first fraction) by the reciprocal of the divisor (the second fraction). Be careful when finding excluded values. First, we need to exclude the values that make the original denominators zero. In addition, we need to exclude the values that make the numerator of the divisor zero because the whole expression is undefined when the divisor is zero. In the example below, we need to exclude 0 and -1 from the domain because they make $x^2 + x$ and $x + 1$ zero. We also need to exclude 2 because it makes $x - 2$ zero.

➔ **EXAMPLE** Divide. State any excluded values.

$$\dfrac{x^2 - 4}{x^2 + x} \div \dfrac{x - 2}{x + 1} = \dfrac{x^2 - 4}{x^2 + x} \cdot \dfrac{x + 1}{x - 2} = \dfrac{(x+2)(x-2)}{x(x+1)} \cdot \dfrac{x+1}{x-2} = \dfrac{x+2}{x} \; for \; x \neq 0, -1, 2$$

➔ **TRY IT** Divide. State any excluded values.

7. $\dfrac{x^2 - 6x}{x + 9} \div \dfrac{x - 6}{2x + 18}$

8. $\dfrac{x}{x^2 - 9} \div \dfrac{5x - 3}{5x^2 + 12x - 9}$

☐ **EXERCISE YOUR SKILLS** ···

Multiply. State any excluded values.

9. $\dfrac{8}{9x^2} \cdot \dfrac{3x^3}{4}$

10. $\dfrac{x+1}{x-5} \cdot \dfrac{5-x}{5x+5}$

11. $\dfrac{x^2-6x+9}{x^2+3x} \cdot \dfrac{2x}{x-3}$

12. $\dfrac{x^2-6x-16}{2x^2+5x} \cdot \dfrac{2x+5}{6x+12}$

13. $\dfrac{x-4}{x^2-9} \cdot \dfrac{5x^2+16x+3}{5x^2-19x-4}$

14. $\dfrac{2x^2-7x+6}{2x^3-3x^2-2x+3} \cdot \dfrac{x^2-x}{7x-14}$

Divide. State any excluded values. (*Hint:* Just as the reciprocal of a number is 1 over the number, the reciprocal of an expression is 1 over the expression.)

15. $\dfrac{12x}{5} \div \dfrac{6x^2}{10}$

16. $\dfrac{x+2}{x+5} \div \dfrac{x-2}{3x+15}$

17. $\dfrac{x^2+6x+9}{8x} \div \dfrac{x+3}{24x^2}$

18. $\dfrac{x^2+11x+28}{x^2+3x-28} \div (x+4)$

19. $\dfrac{2x^2+x-21}{2x+7} \div (x^2+4x-21)$

20. $\dfrac{x-8}{3x^2+20x+25} \div \dfrac{40-5x}{9x^2-25}$

EXTRA Multiply or divide. State any excluded values.

21. $\dfrac{3}{5x^2} \cdot \dfrac{5x}{18}$

22. $\dfrac{7}{2x^2} \div \dfrac{14}{5x^3}$

23. $\dfrac{x^2-4}{x+2} \cdot \dfrac{x+1}{x-2}$

24. $\dfrac{x^2+2x-8}{x+4} \div (x^2+3x-10)$

25. $\dfrac{x^2-6x+9}{x^2-2x+1} \cdot \dfrac{x-1}{x-3}$

26. $\dfrac{x^2-3x-10}{2x^2-4x-30} \div \dfrac{x-3}{4x^2-36}$

LESSON 127 Adding and Subtracting Rational Expressions

☐ **REFRESH YOUR SKILLS** ···

Evaluate. Review Pre-Algebra if you have difficulty solving these problems.

1. $\dfrac{3}{5} + \dfrac{2}{5}$
2. $\dfrac{7}{9} - \dfrac{1}{9}$
3. $\dfrac{1}{3} + \dfrac{1}{2}$
4. $\dfrac{5}{6} - \dfrac{4}{9}$

☐ **ADDING AND SUBTRACTING RATIONAL EXPRESSIONS WITH LIKE DENOMINATORS** ·······················

To add or subtract rational expressions with like denominators, simply add or subtract their numerators and keep the common denominator. Then simplify as needed. Be sure to exclude from the domain the values that make the original denominators zero.

➜ **EXAMPLE** Add. State any excluded values.

$$\frac{x^2 + 6x}{x + 3} + \frac{9}{x + 3} = \frac{x^2 + 6x + 9}{x + 3} = \frac{(x + 3)^2}{x + 3} = x + 3 \; for \; x \neq -3$$

➜ **TRY IT** Add or subtract. State any excluded values.

5. $\dfrac{x + 1}{2x + 3} + \dfrac{3x + 5}{2x + 3}$

6. $\dfrac{2x + 5}{x^2 + 3x - 10} - \dfrac{x + 7}{x^2 + 3x - 10}$

☐ **FINDING THE LCM OF POLYNOMIALS** ··

To find the **least common multiple** (LCM) of two polynomials, first factor each polynomial completely and then find the product of the highest power of each factor.

➜ **EXAMPLE** Find the LCM.

$3x^2 - 27$ and $x^2 + 6x + 9$

Factor each completely.

$3(x + 3)(x - 3)$ and $(x + 3)^2$

Find the product of the highest power of each factor.

$LCM = 3(x + 3)^2(x - 3)$

➜ **TRY IT** Find the LCM.

7. $x + 1$ and $x - 5$

8. $x^2 + x$ and $x^2 + 2x + 1$

9. $x^2 - 16$ and $3x^2 + 10x - 8$

☐ **ADDING AND SUBTRACTING RATIONAL EXPRESSIONS WITH UNLIKE DENOMINATORS** ·····················

To add or subtract rational expressions with unlike denominators, first factor each denominator to find the **least common denominator** (LCD). Next, rewrite each fraction using the LCD as the denominator. Then add or subtract just as with rational expressions having like denominators. Remember, the LCD is the least common multiple (LCM) of the denominators.

→ **EXAMPLE** Subtract. State any excluded values.

$$\frac{x}{2x-4}-\frac{2}{x^2-2x}=\frac{x}{2(x-2)}-\frac{2}{x(x-2)}=\frac{x\cdot x}{2(x-2)\cdot x}-\frac{2\cdot 2}{x(x-2)\cdot 2}\quad LCD=2x(x-2)$$

$$=\frac{x^2-4}{2x(x-2)}=\frac{(x+2)(x-2)}{2x(x-2)}=\frac{x+2}{2x}\,for\;x\neq 0,2$$

→ **TRY IT** Add or subtract. State any excluded values.

10. $\dfrac{x+2}{x}-\dfrac{x+6}{x+4}$

11. $\dfrac{x^2-9x}{x^2+2x-3}+\dfrac{9}{x+3}$

☐ **EXERCISE YOUR SKILLS** ···

Add or subtract. State any excluded values.

12. $\dfrac{x^2}{x+2}-\dfrac{4}{x+2}$

13. $\dfrac{2x-5}{x^2+5x-14}+\dfrac{x-1}{x^2+5x-14}$

14. $\dfrac{x+4}{x+5}-\dfrac{x-1}{x}$

15. $\dfrac{x^2+8}{x^2-2x-8}+\dfrac{2}{x+2}$

16. $\dfrac{x}{x-3}-\dfrac{5x+6}{x^2+x-12}$

17. $\dfrac{x^2+5x+1}{6x^2+x-1}+\dfrac{x}{2x+1}$

EXTRA Add or subtract. State any excluded values.

18. $\dfrac{x-1}{x+2}+\dfrac{x+5}{x+2}$

19. $\dfrac{x^3}{x^4-16}-\dfrac{4x}{x^4-16}$

20. $\dfrac{x}{x^2+10x+25}-\dfrac{1}{x+5}$

21. $\dfrac{x-5}{x-6}+\dfrac{x-15}{x^2-3x-18}$

22. $\dfrac{5-x}{x^2-2x-15}+\dfrac{x-2}{x+3}$

23. $\dfrac{1}{2x+1}+\dfrac{x-2}{2x^2+7x+3}$

LESSON 128 Solving Rational Equations

☐ **REFRESH YOUR SKILLS** ···

Solve by clearing fractions first. Review Lesson 5 if needed.

1. $\dfrac{3}{4}x - \dfrac{1}{4} = \dfrac{1}{2}$

2. $\dfrac{3}{10}x + \dfrac{2}{5} = \dfrac{1}{2}$

☐ **SOLVING RATIONAL EQUATIONS RESULTING IN LINEAR EQUATIONS** ····················

A **rational equation** is an equation containing rational expressions. To solve a rational equation, find the least common denominator (LCD) of all denominators in the equation. Next, clear the fractions by multiplying both sides of the equation by the LCD. Then solve the resulting equation.

➔ **EXAMPLE** Solve. Check for excluded values.

$$\frac{1}{x} = \frac{1}{2x} + \frac{1}{x^2}$$

Excluded: $x \neq 0$
LCD $= 2x^2$

$$2x^2 \cdot \frac{1}{x} = 2x^2 \left(\frac{1}{2x} + \frac{1}{x^2} \right)$$

Multiply both sides by the LCD, $2x^2$.

$2x = x + 2$ Solve for x.

$x = 2$ It's valid $(x \neq 0)$.

➔ **TRY IT** Solve. Check for excluded values.

3. $\dfrac{5}{x^2} + \dfrac{4}{x} = \dfrac{9}{x}$

4. $\dfrac{7}{x-5} = \dfrac{5}{x-3}$

☐ **SOLVING RATIONAL EQUATIONS RESULTING IN QUADRATIC EQUATIONS** ··············

In our example below, the resulting equation is quadratic and can be solved by factoring.

➔ **EXAMPLE** Solve. Check for excluded values.

$$\frac{3}{x} = \frac{1}{2} + \frac{3}{x^2 + x}$$

Original equation

$6(x + 1) = x(x + 1) + 6$

$x^2 - 5x = 0$ Simplify.

$$\frac{3}{x} = \frac{1}{2} + \frac{3}{x(x+1)}$$

Excluded: $x \neq 0, -1$
LCD $= 2x(x + 1)$

$x(x - 5) = 0$ Factor.

$x = 0$ or $x = 5$ Potential solutions

$$2x(x+1) \cdot \frac{3}{x} = 2x(x+1) \left(\frac{1}{2} + \frac{3}{x(x+1)} \right)$$

$x \neq 0$, so $x = 5$ Exclude 0.

Notice that, in the example above, one of the solutions, $x = 0$, is an excluded value because it makes the denominators x and $x^2 + x$ zero. Such a solution is called an extraneous solution. An **extraneous solution** is a value that satisfies a transformed equation but does not satisfy the original equation. So be sure to check and reject any extraneous solutions when solving rational equations. The example above has only one solution, $x = 5$.

➜ **TRY IT** Solve. Check for extraneous solutions.

5. $\dfrac{1}{4x} - \dfrac{1}{6x} = \dfrac{x}{3}$

6. $\dfrac{x}{x+5} = \dfrac{2}{x} - \dfrac{5}{x+5}$

☐ **EXERCISE YOUR SKILLS** ···

Solve. Check for extraneous solutions.

7. $\dfrac{1}{2x} + \dfrac{1}{4} = \dfrac{2}{x}$

8. $\dfrac{5}{x+6} - \dfrac{2}{x} = 0$

9. $\dfrac{1}{2x-5} = \dfrac{3}{x}$

10. $\dfrac{4}{x-7} = \dfrac{2}{x-9}$

11. $\dfrac{2}{x} = \dfrac{1}{5x} + \dfrac{9}{x^2}$

12. $\dfrac{x}{x-2} - \dfrac{x-2}{x+3} = \dfrac{1}{x+3}$

13. $\dfrac{5}{x} + \dfrac{x}{x-8} = \dfrac{1}{x}$

14. $\dfrac{x}{x-1} - \dfrac{5}{x} = \dfrac{1}{x^2-x}$

EXTRA Solve. Check for extraneous solutions.

15. $\dfrac{1}{2} - \dfrac{1}{x} = \dfrac{1}{4}$

16. $\dfrac{1}{x+2} = \dfrac{2}{x-4}$

17. $\dfrac{5}{3x-2} = \dfrac{3}{x-2}$

18. $\dfrac{x+7}{x^2-9} = \dfrac{1}{x-3} + \dfrac{2}{x+3}$

19. $\dfrac{x}{3} - \dfrac{1}{x} = \dfrac{2}{3}$

20. $\dfrac{x}{x+6} - \dfrac{1}{x} = \dfrac{2}{x}$

21. $\dfrac{x}{2} - \dfrac{3}{x} = \dfrac{x+9}{x}$

22. $\dfrac{x}{2x+1} + \dfrac{1}{x+3} = \dfrac{1}{3}$

LESSON 129 Solving Rational Equations

☐ **REFRESH YOUR SKILLS** ⋯⋯⋯⋯⋯⋯⋯⋯⋯⋯⋯⋯⋯⋯⋯⋯⋯⋯⋯⋯⋯⋯⋯⋯⋯⋯⋯⋯⋯⋯⋯⋯⋯⋯

Determine the number of solutions. Explain your answers. Review Lesson 8 if needed.

1. $2 - 5x = x - 6x + 8$

2. $3(x - 1) + 4 = 3x + 1$

Use the discriminant to determine the number of solutions. Review Lesson 112 if needed.

3. $x^2 + 5x - 5 = 0$

4. $4x^2 + 3x + 1 = 0$

Solve. Check for extraneous solutions. Review Lesson 128 if needed.

5. $\dfrac{2}{x - 3} = \dfrac{1}{x + 1}$

6. $\dfrac{1}{x} - \dfrac{x}{x + 3} = \dfrac{1}{x^2 + 3x}$

☐ **SOLVING RATIONAL EQUATIONS WITH NO OR INFINITE SOLUTIONS** ⋯⋯⋯⋯⋯⋯⋯⋯⋯⋯⋯⋯⋯⋯

As you already know, some equations may have infinitely many solutions and other equations may have no solution at all.

➜ **EXAMPLE** Infinitely many solutions

$\dfrac{1}{x} = \dfrac{1}{x + 1} + \dfrac{1}{x^2 + x}$ Excluded: $x \neq 0, -1$
                             LCD $= x(x + 1)$

$x + 1 = x + 1$ Multiply both sides
                   by $x(x + 1)$, then
$0x = 0$ solve for x.

All x but 0 and −1

➜ **EXAMPLE** No solution

$\dfrac{1}{x} = \dfrac{1}{x - 1} + \dfrac{2}{x^2 - x}$ Excluded: $x \neq 0, 1$
                             LCD $= x(x - 1)$

$x - 1 = x + 2$ Multiply both sides
                   by $x(x - 1)$, then
$0x = 3$ solve for x.

No solution

Sometimes there is no solution because there is no potential solution at all or because all potential solutions are extraneous.

➜ **EXAMPLE** No potential solution

$\dfrac{1}{x} = \dfrac{x}{x + 1} + \dfrac{2}{x^2 + x}$ Excluded: $x \neq 0, -1$
                             LCD $= x(x + 1)$

$x + 1 = x^2 + 2$

$x^2 - x + 1 = 0$ $b^2 - 4ac = -3 < 0$

No solution

➜ **EXAMPLE** No non-extraneous solution

$\dfrac{3 - x}{x - 1} - \dfrac{2}{x} = \dfrac{2}{x^2 - x}$ Excluded: $x \neq 0, 1$
                             LCD $= x(x - 1)$

$x(3 - x) - 2(x - 1) = 2$

$x^2 - x = 0$

$x = 0, x = 1$ All extraneous

No solution

→ **TRY IT** Solve.

7. $\dfrac{1}{x-2} = \dfrac{1}{x}$

8. $\dfrac{1}{x} = \dfrac{1}{3x} + \dfrac{x+4}{6x}$

9. $\dfrac{x+1}{x} - \dfrac{3}{2x} = \dfrac{2x-1}{2x}$

10. $\dfrac{1}{x-2} + \dfrac{2}{x+1} = \dfrac{x}{x-2}$

☐ **EXERCISE YOUR SKILLS** ···

Solve. Check for extraneous solutions.

11. $\dfrac{1}{3x+5} = \dfrac{2}{x}$

12. $\dfrac{x}{2} + \dfrac{8}{x} = \dfrac{x+6}{x}$

13. $\dfrac{5}{3x-2} = \dfrac{3}{x-2}$

14. $\dfrac{x^2+8}{x^2} = \dfrac{6}{x} - \dfrac{1}{x^2}$

15. $\dfrac{x-2}{x+3} = \dfrac{2}{x-2} - \dfrac{5}{x+3}$

16. $\dfrac{x-7}{x^2+5x+4} = \dfrac{4}{x+1} - \dfrac{5}{x+4}$

17. $\dfrac{1}{x+4} = \dfrac{2x-3}{2x^2+7x-4}$

18. $\dfrac{x-1}{x+4} = \dfrac{1}{x+4} + \dfrac{6}{x-1}$

EXTRA Solve. Check for extraneous solutions.

19. $\dfrac{4}{x-5} = \dfrac{5}{x-3}$

20. $\dfrac{4}{x+2} - \dfrac{1}{2} = \dfrac{3}{x+4}$

21. $\dfrac{x}{5x-8} - \dfrac{2}{x} = 0$

22. $\dfrac{1}{x^2+5x} + \dfrac{2}{x} = \dfrac{x+6}{x^2+5x}$

23. $\dfrac{x}{2x+1} = \dfrac{1}{3} - \dfrac{1}{x+3}$

24. $\dfrac{x}{x+2} = \dfrac{1}{x+5} - \dfrac{6}{x^2+7x+10}$

LESSON 130 Applications of Rational Equations

☐ **REFRESH YOUR SKILLS** ··

Solve. Check for extraneous solutions. Review Lessons 128 and 129 if needed.

1. $\dfrac{1}{3} = \dfrac{5}{6} + \dfrac{1}{x}$

2. $\dfrac{x}{6} + \dfrac{6}{x} = 2$

3. $\dfrac{1}{2x} + \dfrac{x-1}{4x} = \dfrac{3}{x}$

4. $\dfrac{x}{x+1} = \dfrac{2}{x} - \dfrac{3}{x+1}$

☐ **SOLVING WORK PROBLEMS** ···

Suppose you can paint a room in 4 hours. How much of the room can you paint in 3 hours? Your work rate is 1/4 of the room per hour, so you can paint 3/4 of the room in 3 hours. This example illustrates the relationship between work, rate, and time.

$$\frac{1\ room}{4\ hrs} \times 3\ hrs = \frac{3}{4}\ room \quad \Longrightarrow \quad \boxed{work\ rate \times time\ worked = work\ completed}$$

Now suppose your sister can paint the room in 2 hours. You can paint 1/4 of the room in one hour, and she can paint 1/2 of the room in one hour. Together, you and your sister can paint 3/4 of the room in one hour. This example shows that you can add the individual work rates to find the combined work rate.

$$\frac{1}{4}\ room/hr + \frac{1}{2}\ room/hr = \frac{3}{4}\ room/hr \quad \Longrightarrow \quad \boxed{rate_A + rate_B = rate_{A\ \&\ B}}$$

A typical work problem involves multiple machines or people working together to complete a task. Here are three examples. As always with word problems, we follow the steps: 1) define a variable, 2) set up an equation to model the given situation, 3) solve the equation as usual, and then 4) answer what's being asked. Study each example carefully.

➔ **EXAMPLE** Working together

Pipe A can drain a pool in 2 hours. Pipe B can drain the pool in 6 hours. How long will it take to drain the pool when both pipes are used?

1. Let x = time to drain the pool together
2. Rate of A + rate of B = rate of A & B
   $\dfrac{1}{2} + \dfrac{1}{6} = \dfrac{1}{x}$ pool/hour
3. Solve for x, and you get $x = 3/2$.
4. It will take 1.5 hours.

➔ **TRY IT** Solve.

5. Pipe A can fill a tank in 2 hours. Pipe B can fill the tank in 3 hours. How long will it take to fill the tank if both pipes are used?

6. Mark can mow the lawn by himself in 30 minutes. Liam can mow the lawn in 45 minutes. How long will it take to mow the lawn if they work together?

→ **EXAMPLE** Working alone

Joe and Paul can paint a fence together in 4 hours. Joe alone can paint the fence in 6 hours. How long will it take Paul to paint the fence alone?

1. Let x = time taken by Paul
2. Rate of Joe + rate of Paul = rate of both
   $$\frac{1}{6} + \frac{1}{x} = \frac{1}{4} \; fence/hour$$
3. Solve for x, and you get $x = 12$.
4. It will take Paul 12 hours.

→ **EXAMPLE** Working alone

Two pipes A and B together can fill a pool in 2 hours. If used alone, pipe B takes 3 hours longer than pipe A. How long will pipe B take to fill the pool by itself?

1. Let x = time taken by pipe A
2. $x + 3$ = time taken by pipe B
   Rate of A + rate of B = rate of A & B
   $$\frac{1}{x} + \frac{1}{x + 3} = \frac{1}{2} \; pool/hour$$
3. Solve for x, and you get $x = 3$.
4. Pipe B alone will take 6 hours.

→ **TRY IT** Solve.

7. Jack can mow the yard in 3 hours alone. If Julie helps him, they can mow the yard in 1 hour. How long will it take Julie to mow the yard alone?

8. Two pipes A and B together can fill a pool in 2 hours. If used alone, pipe A takes 4 hours. How long will pipe B take to fill the pool by itself?

→ **TRY IT** Solve.

9. Laura can finish a certain task 6 hours faster than Brian can. Together, they can finish the task in 4 hours. How long will it take Brian to do it alone?

10. Liam can paint three times as fast as Alex. Working together, they can paint a house in 6 hours. How long will it take Liam to paint the house alone?

☐ **EXERCISE YOUR SKILLS** ···

For each problem, 1) define a variable, 2) set up an equation, 3) solve the equation, and 4) answer what's being asked. Show your work in your notebook.

11. Paul can paint a small house in 8 hours. Alex can paint the house in 12 hours. How long will it take to paint the house if they work together?

12. Sam can complete a certain task in 40 minutes. Ella can do it in 1 hour, and Adam can do it in 2 hours. How long will it take to complete the task if they work together?

13. Jerry's dad can assemble a computer by himself in 3 hours. If Jerry helps his dad, it takes 2 hours. How long will it take Jerry to assemble the computer alone?

14. Alex can clean the house in 1 hour. Working together, Alex and Jennifer can clean the house in just 20 minutes. How long will it take Jennifer alone to clean the house?

15. Pipe A can fill a pool twice as fast as pipe B. When both pipes are open, they fill the pool in 2 hours. How long will it take pipe A to fill the pool alone?

LESSON 131 Catch Up and Review!

Catch up if you are behind. Use the review problems below to make sure you're on track.

LESSON 101 Factor completely.

1. $x^2 + 2x - 8$

2. $2x^2 - 9x + 4$

3. $x^3 - 25x$

4. $x^3 - 5x^2 - 4x + 20$

LESSON 125 Simplify. State any excluded values.

5. $\dfrac{3x^5}{9x^2}$

6. $\dfrac{2x + 8}{x^2 + 4x}$

7. $\dfrac{2x^2 - x - 15}{x^2 + 6x - 27}$

8. $\dfrac{2x^3 - x^2 - 18x + 9}{2x^3 - 7x^2 + 3x}$

LESSON 126 Multiply or divide. State any excluded values.

9. $\dfrac{x^2 - x - 6}{x + 5} \cdot \dfrac{x + 5}{4x + 8}$

10. $\dfrac{1}{8x^2 - 64x} \cdot \dfrac{6x^3 - 48x^2}{x - 1}$

11. $\dfrac{x^2 + 4x - 5}{x - 1} \div (x^2 + 6x + 5)$

12. $\dfrac{x^2 - 3x - 10}{2x^2 - 4x - 30} \div \dfrac{x - 3}{4x^2 - 36}$

LESSON 127 Add or subtract. State any excluded values.

13. $\dfrac{4}{3x} + \dfrac{5}{3x}$

14. $\dfrac{x - 1}{x} - \dfrac{x + 4}{x + 5}$

15. $\dfrac{x}{x - 3} - \dfrac{5x + 6}{x^2 + x - 12}$

16. $\dfrac{5 - x}{x^2 - 2x - 15} + \dfrac{x - 2}{x + 3}$

LESSONS 128–129 Solve. Check for extraneous solutions.

17. $\dfrac{x+2}{x} + \dfrac{1}{5x} = \dfrac{2}{x}$

18. $\dfrac{2}{x} - \dfrac{x-7}{x^2} = \dfrac{1}{x}$

19. $\dfrac{x}{x+1} = \dfrac{2}{x} - \dfrac{3}{x+1}$

20. $\dfrac{x+4}{x+6} - \dfrac{9}{x^2+4x-12} = 2$

LESSON 130 Solve.

21. Pipe A can drain a tank in 20 minutes. Pipe B can drain the tank in 30 minutes. How long will it take to drain the tank if both pipes are left open?

22. Leah and Jose can paint a fence together in 3 hours. Leah alone can paint the fence in 5 hours. How long will it take Jose to paint the fence alone?

23. Sunny and Adam can mow the lawn in 20 minutes if they work together. If Sunny works twice as fast as Adam, how long will it take each of them to mow the lawn alone?

☐ **MIXED REVIEW: PRE-ALGEBRA** ···

Brush up on the topics covered in Pre-Algebra.

24. Probability is the likelihood of an event occurring. Probabilities are between 0 and 1. What is the probability of an event that is certain to occur?

25. Probability can be calculated by dividing the number of favorable outcomes by the number of total possible outcomes. A die is rolled. What are the possible outcomes?

26. Three coins are tossed. What is the probability of getting three heads?

27. A die is rolled twice. What is the probability of rolling the same numbers?

28. Two dice are rolled. What is the probability of rolling a sum of 8?

LESSON 132 Review: 1st Quarter

Let's review the topics covered in the first quarter.

LESSONS 3–8 & 38–40 Solve.

1. $4x + 3 = 7$

2. $9 - 2x \leq 15$

3. $3(2x + 3) = -2x - 7$

4. $-2 < 3(2 - x) + x \leq 8$

5. $|-3x + 1| + 4 = 5$

6. $|8 - 2x| + 3 > 7$

LESSONS 9–11 Solve

7. Cammy bought a shirt at $16.50. The price was 25% off the regular price. What was the regular price?

8. The length of a rectangle is twice its width. The perimeter is 24 feet. Find the dimensions of the rectangle.

9. Mike hiked around a circular mountain trail twice in a total of 4 hours. He walked the circle at 5 mph the first time and at 3 mph the second time. How long is the trail?

10. How much of a 5% acid solution must be added to 4 ounces of an 8% acid solution to produce a 6% acid solution?

11. Six pounds of candy costing $3 per pound is mixed with 4 pounds of candy costing $5 per pound. What is the price of the mixture per pound?

LESSONS 29–33 Solve.

12. $x - 2y = 8$
    $3x + 2y = 0$

13. $2x - y = 1$
    $5x - 4y = -5$

LESSONS 34–36 Solve

14. A boat traveled 36 km downstream in 1.5 hours. The return trip, going upstream, took 2 hours. Find the speed of the boat in still water and the speed of the current.

15. A 10% saline solution is to be mixed with a 30% saline solution to produce 10 gallons of an 18% saline solution. How much of each should be used?

16. Almonds sell for $4 a pound. Cereal sells for $2.40 a pound. A store wants to make 8 pounds of a mixture to sell for $3 per pound. How much of each should be used?

LESSONS 16–19 & 41–42 Graph.

17. $x = -2$

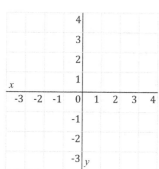

18. $x + 3y = 3$

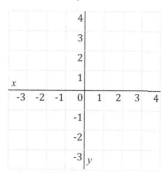

19. $y = |x + 1| - 1$

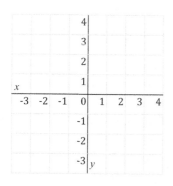

20. $y > -\frac{1}{2}x + 2$

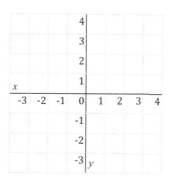

LESSONS 22–25 Find an equation of each line in slope-intercept form and in standard form. Use only integers and the smallest possible positive integer coefficient for x.

21. through $(2, 1)$ and $(-1, 7)$

22. perpendicular to $x + 5y = 2$, through $(1, 4)$

LESSON 133 Review: 2nd Quarter

Let's review the topics covered in the second quarter.

LESSONS 48–54 Identify as true or false. If false, explain why.

1. The relation $\{(2, 7), (3, -1), (3, 8), (5, 4)\}$ is not a function.

2. The function $y = x^2$ has a range of $0 \le y \le 4$ when the domain is $-2 < x < 2$.

3. Given $f(x) = 2x + 1$ and $g(x) = x^2 - 1$, $f(0) + g(-1)$ evaluates to -1.

4. The relation $\{(1, 2), (2, 4), (3, 6), (4, 8), (5, 10)\}$ represents a linear function.

5. The function $f(x) = (x - 1)^2$ has an average rate of change of 1 from $x = 0$ to $x = 1$.

6. The inverse of the function $f(x) = x - 5$ is $f^{-1}(x) = x + 5$.

LESSONS 56–57 Write a direct or inverse variation equation, then solve.

7. The amount of sales tax varies directly with the cost of the purchase. If the sales tax is $2.50 on a purchase of $50, what will be the sales tax on a purchase of $80?

8. The resale value of a car varies inversely with its age. If a 2-year-old car costs $15,000, what will be the value of the car when it is 5 years old?

LESSONS 58–60 Find the explicit formula and the recursive formula.

9. 2, 9, 16, 23, 30, ...

10. 3, 0, −3, −6, −9, ...

11. 6, 18, 54, 162, 486, ...

12. 2, 10, 50, 250, 1250, ...

LESSON 61 Solve. Round your answers to the nearest hundredth.

13. Carol put $5,000 in her savings account with a simple interest rate of 2% per year. What will be the balance of her account at the end of the 8th year?

14. A ball is dropped from a height of 20 meters. After the ball hits the floor, it rebounds to 60% of its previous height. How high will the ball rebound after its sixth bounce?

LESSONS 64–67 Simplify. Rationalize all denominators.

15. $\dfrac{12}{\sqrt{3}} + \sqrt{12}$

16. $\dfrac{\sqrt{27x^2y^3}}{\sqrt{3xy}}$

LESSON 68 Solve. Check for extraneous solutions.

17. $\sqrt{x+9} + 7 = 4$

18. $\sqrt{3x-7} = \sqrt{5-x}$

LESSON 69 Solve. Leave your answers in simplest radical form, if applicable.

19. A 12-foot ladder is leaning against a wall. The ladder reaches a height of 8 feet. How far is the bottom of the ladder from the wall?

LESSONS 71–74 & 77 Simplify using positive exponents.

20. $3x^{-5} \cdot 2x^3$

21. $\left(8x^{3/2}\right)^{2/3}$

LESSON 78 Write a function that models each situation, and then solve.

22. Melissa put $5,000 in her account that earns 3% interest compounded annually. What will be the balance of her account after five years?

LESSONS 80-86 Simplify. Write your answers in standard form.

23. $(2x+1)(x^2+3x-2)$

24. $(3x^2+8x+2) \div (3x-1)$

LESSON 134 Review: 3rd Quarter

Let's review the topics covered in the third quarter.

LESSON 93 Factor out the GCF.

1. $4x^2 - 8x - 4$

2. $12x^3 + 6x^2 - 8x$

LESSON 94 Factor by grouping.

3. $x^3 - 4x^2 + x - 4$

4. $x^3 + 2x^2 - 3x - 6$

5. $2x^3 - x^2 + 6x - 3$

6. $6x^3 - 4x^2 - 3x + 2$

LESSONS 95-97 Factor as the product of two binomials.

7. $x^2 + 3x + 2$

8. $x^2 - 2x - 8$

9. $2x^2 + 5x + 3$

10. $4x^2 + 15x - 4$

LESSON 99 Factor using special product patterns.

11. $x^2 + 4x + 4$

12. $x^2 - 6x + 9$

13. $25x^2 - 10x + 1$

14. $9x^2 - 16$

LESSON 101 Factor completely.

15. $4x^2 + 10x - 6$

16. $x^4 - 16$

17. $2x^3 - 50x$

18. $8x^4 + 2x^3 + 40x^2 + 10x$

LESSONS 103–104 Solve by taking square roots.

19. $4x^2 - 12 = 60$

20. $5(3x + 1)^2 - 20 = 0$

LESSON 105–106 Solve by factoring.

21. $x^2 + 3x - 10 = 0$

22. $3x^2 - 7x + 2 = 0$

LESSON 107–108 Solve by completing the square.

23. $x^2 - 4x - 8 = 0$

24. $2x^2 + 4x - 8 = 0$

LESSON 109–110 Solve by the quadratic formula.

25. $x^2 + 5x + 5 = 0$

26. $3x^2 - 8x + 2 = 0$

LESSONS 111–112 Solve. Use any method you prefer.

27. $(x - 1)^2 - 4 = 0$

28. $x^2 + 8x + 4 = 0$

29. $25x^2 - 9 = 0$

30. $2x^2 - x + 5 = 0$

LESSON 113 Solve.

31. The difference between two positive integers is 4. The sum of the larger and the square of the smaller is 34. Find the integers.

32. One leg of a right triangle is 14 cm longer than the shorter leg and 2 cm shorter than the hypotenuse. Find the dimensions of the triangle.

33. The area of a rectangle is 65 cm². Its length is 3 cm longer than twice its width. Find the dimensions of the rectangle.

LESSON 135 Review: 3rd Quarter

Let's review the topics covered in the third quarter.

LESSONS 116-119 Find the vertex, then graph. Use the intercepts when possible.

1. $y = (x - 1)^2 - 2$

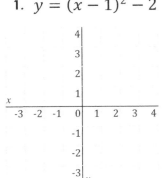

2. $y = -\frac{1}{2}(x + 2)(x - 2)$

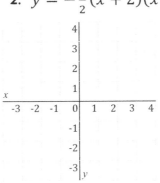

3. $y = x^2 - 6x + 8$

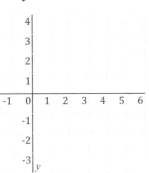

LESSON 120 Find the vertex, y-intercept, and x-intercepts (if any).

4. $y = (x - 2)^2 + 3$

5. $y = -4(x - 1)(x - 3)$

6. $y = -x^2 - 8x + 9$

7. $y = 2x^2 + 8x + 8$

LESSON 121 Find an equation of each parabola in standard form.

8. A parabola has vertex (2, –3) and passes through (5, 6).

9. A parabola has zeros at x = 2 and x = 6 and passes through (4, –2).

LESSON 122 Find an equation of each parabola obtained by transforming $y = x^2$ as described.

10. Shift left 5 units and down 2 units.

11 Scale by 3 and flip over the x-axis.

LESSON 123 Solve.

12. A ball is thrown vertically upwards from the top of a building of height 60 feet with an initial speed of 32 feet per second. Its height h, in feet, after t seconds is given by $h(t)$ = $-16t^2 + 32t + 60$. How much higher does the ball rise above the top of the building?

LESSONS 125–127 Simplify. State any excluded values.

13. $\dfrac{2x}{4x^2 + 10x}$

14. $\dfrac{x^2 + 9x + 20}{x^3 - 16x}$

15. $\dfrac{x^2 - 4}{x^2 + 3x + 2} \cdot \dfrac{x + 1}{x - 2}$

16. $\dfrac{x^3 - x^2 - 20x}{2x^2 + 10x + 8} \div \dfrac{x}{x + 1}$

17. $\dfrac{6x^2}{3x + 5} + \dfrac{10x}{3x + 5}$

18. $\dfrac{6}{x^2 - 9} + \dfrac{x}{x + 3} - \dfrac{1}{x - 3}$

LESSONS 128–129 Solve. Check for extraneous solutions.

19. $\dfrac{4}{x - 5} = \dfrac{2}{x + 2}$

20. $\dfrac{4}{x} + \dfrac{x}{4} = -2$

21. $\dfrac{x}{x + 3} = \dfrac{2}{x} - \dfrac{3}{x + 3}$

22. $\dfrac{1}{x - 4} + \dfrac{2}{x + 2} = \dfrac{3}{x + 5}$

LESSON 130 Solve.

23. Pipe A can fill a tank in 3 hours. Pipe B can fill the tank in 6 hours. How long will it take to fill the tank if both pipes are used?

24. Kyle can clean the yard in 45 minutes. Working together, Kyle and Susie can clean the yard in just 20 minutes. How long will it take Susie alone to clean the yard?

25. Machine A can print a magazine 10 minutes faster than machine B. When both machines are used, they can print the magazine in 12 minutes. How long will it take machine B to print the magazine alone?

LESSON 136 PSAT Practice

This is a timed practice test. Get a timer, a bubble answer sheet, and blank sheets of paper for your calculations. When you are ready, set the timer for **25 minutes** and begin. Do not use a calculator. Mark all your answers on the answer sheet. Only answers marked on the answer sheet can be scored. After the test, make sure you review what you missed.

1. $2m + 5 = 9 - m$

   $n + 4 = 3(n - 2)$

   According to the equations above, what is the value of $3m + 2n$?

   A) 9   B) 10

   C) 12   D) 14

2. If $32^2 \cdot 4^{-3} = 2^n$, what is the value of n ?

   A) 1   B) 2   C) 4   D) 7

3. Which of the following is equivalent to the expression $x^2 - 5x + 6$?

   A) $(x - 2)(x - 3)$ B) $(x - 2)(x + 3)$

   C) $(x - 6)(x + 1)$ D) $(x - 6)(x - 1)$

4. Which of the following is equivalent to the expression $x^6 - x^3 + x^2$?

   A) $x^3(x^3 - 1)$ B) $x^2(x^4 - x + 1)$

   C) $x^2(x^6 - x^3)$ D) $x(x^5 - x^3 + x^2)$

5. $(x^3)^{\frac{1}{p}} = \sqrt[3]{x}$

   If the equation above is true for all positive values of x, what is the value of p ?

   A) 1   B) 3   C) 6   D) 9

6. $x^2 + 3x - 10 = 0$

   If m and n are two solutions of the equation above, what is the value of $m + n$?

   A) -7 B) -3 C) 3   D) 7

7. $x^2 - 2x - 1 = 0$

   What are the solutions to the equation above?

   A) $1 \pm \sqrt{2}$ B) $-1 \pm \sqrt{2}$

   C) $\dfrac{1 \pm \sqrt{2}}{2}$ D) $\dfrac{-1 \pm 2\sqrt{2}}{2}$

8. $\dfrac{x^2 - 4}{x + 2} \cdot \dfrac{x + 1}{x - 2}$

   Which expression is equivalent to the expression above?

   A) $x + 1$ B) $x - 1$

   C) $x + 2$ D) $x - 2$

9. $\dfrac{x}{x + 5} = \dfrac{2}{x} - \dfrac{5}{x + 5}$

   What are all the values of x that satisfy the equation above?

   A) -5 B) 2

   C) 5   D) 2 and -5

Continue to the next page.

10. The function $f(x)$ is a linear function such that $f(2) = 4$ and $f(0) = -2$. Which of the following defines f?

A) $f(x) = x + 2$ B) $f(x) = 3x - 2$

C) $f(x) = 2x$ D) $f(x) = -x - 2$

11. Which of the following could be the equation of the graph shown below?

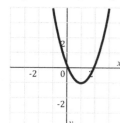

A) $y = x^2 - 1$

B) $y = x^2 + 2x$

C) $y = x^2 - 2x$

D) $y = -x^2 + 2x$

12. In an algebra test, Justin got $\frac{4}{5}$ of the problems correct and missed 5 problems. How many problems were in the test?

A) 10   B) 16   C) 20   D) 25

13. The scale on a map is 5 cm = 75 km. Two cities on the map are 3 cm apart. What is the actual distance between the two cities?

A) 0.2 km   B) 4.5 km

C) 20 km   D) 45 km

14. A rectangular garden has an area of 35 square feet. Its length is three feet shorter than twice its width. What is the perimeter of the garden?

A) 5   B) 7

C) 12   D) 24

15. A bakery sells pies by the slice or as whole pies. Each pie is cut into 8 slices. On a certain day, the bakery sold a total of 58 slices of pies, and 10 of them were sold by the slice. Which expression shows the number of pies sold as whole pies on that day?

A) $\dfrac{58 - 10}{8}$ B) $\dfrac{58 + 10}{8}$

C) $\dfrac{58}{8} - 10$ D) $\dfrac{58}{8} + 10$

16. $h(t) = -16t^2 + 32t + 128$

A ball is thrown straight up from a height of 128 feet with an initial speed of 32 feet per second. Its height h, in feet, after t seconds is given by the function above. Which of the following is an equivalent form of the function that displays the time the ball takes to hit the ground?

A) $h(t) = -16(t - 1)^2 + 144$

B) $h(t) = -16(t + 1)^2 + 144$

C) $h(t) = -16(t - 2)(t + 4)$

D) $h(t) = -16(t + 2)(t - 4)$

17. Pipe A can fill a tank in 2 hours. Pipe B can fill the tank in 3 hours. How long will it take to fill the tank if both pipes are used?

A) 1 hour   B) 1.2 hours

C) 2.5 hours   D) 5 hours

STOP

This is the end of the test. If you finish before time is up, check your work.

LESSON 137 PSAT Practice

This is a timed practice test. Get a timer, a bubble answer sheet, and blank sheets of paper for your calculations. When you are ready, set the timer for **25 minutes** and begin. Do not use a calculator. Mark all your answers on the answer sheet. Only answers marked on the answer sheet can be scored. After the test, make sure you review what you missed.

1. $|2x + 3| = 7$

   If a and b are the solutions to the equation above, what is the value of $|a + b|$?

   A) 0   B) 3   C) 7   D) 10

2. If $-1 \leq 2 - x < 4$, what is the greatest possible integer value of x ?

   A) 1   B) 2   C) 3   D) 5

3. $\sqrt{16x^4}$,

   If $x > 0$, which of the following is equivalent to the expression above?

   A) $2x$ B) $2x^2$ C) $4x$ D) $4x^2$

4. $x + 2y = 0$ and $2x + 3y = 2$

   If (p, q) is a solution to the system above, what is the value of $p + q$?

   A) -2 B) 1   C) 2   D) 6

5. $x^2 - 2x - 4k$

   If $x + 2$ is a factor of the expression above, what is the value of k ?

   A) -8 B) -2 C) 2   D) 8

6. $3x^2 - 8x - 3 = 0$

   If p and q are two solutions of the equation above, what is pq ?

   A) -9 B) -1 C) 1   D) 9

7. If $2^x \cdot 8^3 = 2^{10}$ and $\sqrt[3]{27^2} = 3^y$, what is the value of $y - x$?

   A) 1   B) 3

   C) 4   D) 5

8. $\dfrac{2}{x^2 - 1} + \dfrac{x}{x - 1} + \dfrac{1}{x + 1}$

   Which expression is equivalent to the expression above?

   A) $x - 1$ B) $x + 1$

   C) $\dfrac{x - 1}{x + 1}$ D) $\dfrac{x + 1}{x - 1}$

9. $\dfrac{5}{x} + \dfrac{x}{x - 3} = \dfrac{1}{x}$

   What are all the values of x that satisfy the equation above?

   A) -6 B) 2

   C) 3   D) 2 and -6

Continue to the next page.

10. Olivia has x one-dollar bills and y five-dollar bills totaling $20. Which of the following expresses the value of x in terms of y ?

A) $x = 20 - 5y$ B) $x = 5y - 20$

C) $x = \dfrac{20 - y}{5}$ D) $x = \dfrac{y - 20}{5}$

11. A monitor factory has a defect rate of 0.2%. An inspector checks 1,000 monitors. Which of the following is the best estimate for the number of monitors that will be found defective?

A) 1 B) 2 C) 10 D) 20

12. Joey's car uses 2 gallons of gas to travel 60 miles. This weekend Joey drove 210 miles at an average speed of 70 miles per hour. Approximately how many gallons of gas did Joey's car use this weekend?

A) 1.75 gallons B) 3 gallons

C) 3.5 gallons D) 7 gallons

13. In the xy-plane, a parabola has two x-intercepts at the points $(-1, 0)$ and $(3, 0)$. The vertex of the parabola occurs at the point $(p, -4)$. What is the value of p ?

A) -2 B) 1 C) 2 D) 4

14. $f(x) = ax^2 + x + 5$

Given the function above, what is the value of $f(-2)$ when $f(2) = 3$?

A) -7 B) -5 C) -1 D) 7

15. The table below shows some values of the function f. If the graph of f is a line, which of the following defines f ?

x	1	3	5	7
$f(x)$	3	7	11	15

A) $f(x) = 2x$ B) $f(x) = -x + 4$

C) $f(x) = 2x + 1$ D) $f(x) = x^2 + 2$

16. The graph of $y = ax^2 + bx + c$ is shown below. Which of the following must be true?

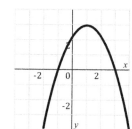

A) $a > 0$

B) $c < 0$

C) $ac < 0$

D) $ac > 0$

17. Machine A can finish a job in an hour. Machine B can finish the same job in x minutes. When both machines are used, they can finish the job in 20 minutes. What is the value of x ?

A) 1 hour B) 30 minutes

C) 20 minutes D) 15 minutes

STOP

This is the end of the test. If you finish before time is up, check your work.

LESSON 138 Measures of Center

☐ **FINDING MEASURES OF CENTER** ···

Statistics is the study of collecting, organizing, analyzing, and interpreting numerical data.

A **measure of center** is a value used in statistics to describe the center, or middle, of a data set. The common measures of center are **mean**, **median**, and **mode**.

The **mean** is the average. To find the mean of a data set, divide the sum of the values by the number of values in the set.

➔ **EXAMPLE** Find the mean.

3, 20, 3, 5, 3, 5, 6, 3

1. Find the sum of the values.
   3 + 20 + 3 + 5 + 3 + 5 + 6 + 3 = 48
2. Divide by the number of values.
   48 ÷ 8 = 6, so the mean is 6.

➔ **TRY IT** Find the mean.

1. 3, 6, 2, 5

2. 8, 5, 5, 6, 6, 2, 3, 9

The **median** is the middle value. To find the median of a data set, order the values in the set and find the middle value. If there are two middle values, add them and divide by 2.

➔ **EXAMPLE** Find the median.

3, 20, 3, 5, 3, 5, 6, 3

1. Order the values.
   3, 3, 3, 3, 5, 5, 6, 20
2. Find the middle value.
   (3 + 5) ÷ 2 = 4, so the median is 4.

➔ **TRY IT** Find the mean and median.

3. 3, 5, 4, 6, 8, 4

4. 4, 7, 5, 10, 6, 8, 9, 6, 8

The **mode** is the most frequent value. To find the mode of a data set, simply find the value that occurs most frequently in the set. Note that a data set can have no mode (no values repeated), one mode, or multiple modes.

➔ **EXAMPLE** Find the mode.

3, 20, 3, 5, 3, 5, 6, 3

1. Order the values.
   3, 3, 3, 3, 5, 5, 6, 20
2. Find the most frequent value.
   3 occurs most often, so the mode is 3.

➔ **TRY IT** Find the mean, median, and mode(s).

5. 1, 3, 4, 4, 0, 2, 4, 0, 1, 1

6. 12, 15, 17, 10, 19, 18, 14

☐ **IDENTIFYING OUTLIERS** ···

An **outlier** is a data value that is much greater or much less than the other data values in a data set. Identifying outliers is important because they can affect the measures of center.

→ **EXAMPLE** Identify the outlier, then describe how it affects the mean and median.

3, 20, 3, 5, 3, 5, 6, 3

1. 20 is much greater than the other values, so the outlier is 20.
2. When we remove the outlier, the mean decreases from 6 to 4. The median also decreases from 4 to 3.

→ **TRY IT** Identify the outlier, then describe how it affects the mean and median.

7. 9, 8, 39, 6, 8, 4, 5, 9

8. 47, 49, 52, 54, 57, 59, 10, 60

☐ **EXERCISE YOUR SKILLS** ···

Find the mean, median, and mode(s). Round to the nearest tenth, if necessary.

9. 0, 2, 0, 5, 3

10. 3, 4, 6, 7, 5, 2

11. 4, 8, 3, 7, 5, 6, 8, 7

12. 2, 3, 0, 5, 6, 7, 0, 5, 5, 9

13. 15, 12, 14, 15, 13, 15

14. 10, 14, 11, 12, 14, 15, 10, 13, 18

15. 101, 109, 107, 103, 105

16. 211, 113, 312, 114, 312, 210

Identify the outlier, then describe how it affects the mean and median.

17. 8, 4, 3, 72, 8, 5, 6, 7, 2, 9, 8

18. 54, 62, 5, 71, 56, 52, 60, 72

CHALLENGE These problems will require some thinking. Find the mystery data sets.

19. I am a data set of three whole numbers. My mean is 6, and my mode is 5. What are my numbers?

20. I am a data set of four whole numbers. My mean is 5, my median is 4.5, and my mode is 4. What are my numbers?

21. I am a data set of five whole numbers. My mean is 8, my median is 8, and my modes are 8 and 9. What are my numbers?

22. I am a data set of four whole numbers. My mean, median, and mode are all 4. My range, the difference between the highest and lowest values, is also 4. What are my numbers?

LESSON 139 Measures of Variation

Find the mean, median, and mode(s). Review Lesson 138 if needed.

1. 4, 1, 5, 2, 2

2. 4, 5, 3, 9, 5, 4, 8, 6

☐ **FINDING MEASURES OF VARIATION** ··

While a measure of center is a value that describes the center of a data set, a **measure of variation** is a value that describes the spread of a data set. The common measures of variation are **range**, **variance**, and **standard deviation**.

The **range** of a data set is the difference between the highest and lowest values in the set.

➔ **EXAMPLE** Find the range.

5, 8, 1, 10, 5, 7

1. The highest value is 10.
2. The lowest value is 1.
3. The range is 10 − 1 = 9.

➔ **TRY IT** Find the range.

3. 8, 10, 7, 8, 5, 10

4. 30, 20, 40, 25, 45

The **variance** of a data set is the average of the squared distances of each data value from the mean of the set. The **standard deviation** is the square root of the variance.

➔ **EXAMPLE** Find the variance and standard deviation.

5, 8, 1, 10, 5, 7

Distances of each data value:

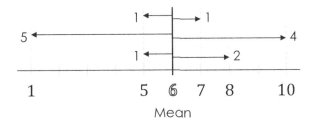

Mean

1. Find the mean. (5 + 8 + 1 + 10 + 5 + 7)/6 = 6
2. Find the squared distances of each data value from the mean.
   $|5 − 6|^2 = 1$, $|8 − 6|^2 = 4$, $|1 − 6|^2 = 25$,
   $|10 − 6|^2 = 16$, $|5 − 6|^2 = 1$, $|7 − 6|^2 = 1$
3. Find the variance, the average of the squared distances. (1 + 4 + 25 + 16 + 1 + 1)/6 = 8
4. Take the square root of the variance. Standard deviation = $\sqrt{8} \approx 2.8$

➔ **TRY IT** Find the mean, variance, and standard deviation. Round to the nearest tenth, if necessary. You may use a calculator.

5. 5, 5, 5, 5, 5, 5

6. 2, 4, 5, 5, 7, 7

7. 1, 2, 3, 7, 8, 9

8. 0, 1, 2, 5, 10, 12

☐ COMPARING STANDARD DEVIATIONS ···

The standard deviation of a data set measures how widely spread its data values are. The more spread out the data values are from the mean, the bigger the standard deviation will be. If all the data values are identical, the standard deviation is zero.

➜ **EXAMPLE** Suppose the data in problems 5 through 8 show the scores of four soccer teams during the season. What can you tell from the data?

All the data sets have a mean of 5, which means all the teams scored the same average number of goals per game. However, the standard deviations vary from 0 to 4.5. The lower the standard deviation is, the more the team scored consistently. The team with a standard deviation of 0 scored most consistently.

➜ **TRY IT 9.** Below are the quiz scores of two students. Whose scores appear to have the higher standard deviation? Find the standard deviations and verify your answer.

Mark: 90, 95, 90, 95, 100   Alex: 75, 80, 85, 100, 100

☐ EXERCISE YOUR SKILLS ···

Find the mean, median, mode, range, variance, and standard deviation. Round to the nearest tenth, if necessary. You may use a calculator.

10. 2, 6, 5, 6, 8, 3

11. 8, 10, 7, 8, 5, 10

12. 9, 2, 8, 7, 10, 7, 2, 11

13. 9, 5, 8, 10, 4, 11, 17, 8

14. 30, 20, 40, 25, 45

15. 45, 47, 42, 45, 47, 44

Below are the spelling test scores, over five practice tests, of four students in a class.

Logan: 100, 70, 80, 90, 100   Grace: 80, 80, 80, 80, 95

Emma: 80, 90, 90, 80, 80   Joshua: 60, 100, 50, 90, 100

16. Who has the highest mean score? Who has the lowest mean score?

17. Who has the highest range? Who has the smallest range?

18. Who has the highest standard deviation? Who has the lowest standard deviation?

19. Based on your analysis above, if you were the teacher of the class, who would be your first pick to represent the class in a spelling bee. Explain your reasoning.

LESSON 140 Box-and-Whisker Plots

☐ **FINDING FIVE-NUMBER SUMMARIES** ··

A **five-number summary** is a set of five values that provide information about a data set. It consists of the minimum, first quartile (Q1), median (second quartile or Q2), third quartile (Q3), and maximum. The first quartile is the median of the lower half of the data set. The third quartile is the median of the upper half of the data set. The **interquartile range** (IQR) is the difference between the first and third quartiles.

➜ **EXAMPLE** Find the five-number summary and interquartile range.

a. Given:

  10, 13, 7, 1, 8, 11, 4, 16, 2

Ordered:

  1, 2, 4, 7, 8, 10, 11, 13, 16
  Min Q1 Median Q3 Max

- Q1 is the median of {1, 2, 4, 7}.
- Q3 is the median of {10, 11, 13, 16}.
- Five-number summary: 1, 3, 8, 12, 16
- Interquartile range = 12 − 3 = 9

b. Given:

  15, 20, 12, 8, 14, 16, 15, 18

Ordered:

  8, 12, 14, 15, 15, 16, 18, 20
  Min Q1 Median Q3 Max

- Q1 is the median of {8, 12, 14, 15}.
- Q3 is the median of {15, 16, 18, 20}.
- Five-number summary: 8, 13, 15, 17, 20
- Interquartile range = 17 − 13 = 4

➜ **TRY IT** Find the five-number summary and interquartile range.

1. 1, 4, 7, 5, 0, 6

2. 5, 8, 2, 4, 9, 7, 5

3. 3, 4, 2, 7, 6, 3, 2, 5, 8

4. 12, 10, 15, 19, 14, 12, 13, 14, 11, 16

☐ **MAKING BOX-AND-WHISKER PLOTS** ··

A **box plot**, also called a **box and whisker plot**, is a way of graphically displaying a five-number summary on a number line. The left diagram below shows how a box plot represents five numbers. The right diagram shows the box plot of the first example above.

➜ **EXAMPLE** A box plot

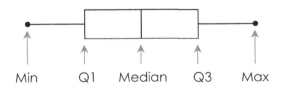

Min Q1 Median Q3 Max

➜ **EXAMPLE** The box plot of the example above

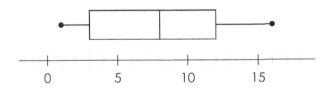

➜ **TRY IT** Find the five-number summary and interquartile range, then draw a box plot in your notebook.

5. 7, 9, 8, 4, 7, 9, 4, 9, 6, 7, 6, 10, 7

6. 38, 36, 30, 42, 44, 33, 31, 44, 35, 42

□ **INTERPRETING BOX-AND-WHISKER PLOTS** ···

Quartiles divide a data set into four parts, with approximately 25% of the data values in each part.

➔ **EXAMPLE** About what percent of the data is above 4, 6, and 8 respectively?

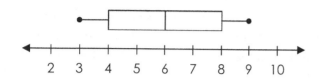

- Q1 is 4, so about 25% of the data is lower than 4, and about 75% of the data is above 4.
- Q2 is 6, so about 50% of the data is above 6.
- Q3 is 8, so above 25% of the data is above 8.

➔ **TRY IT 7.** Select all statements that correctly describe the given plot.

Ages of children at a toy store (years)

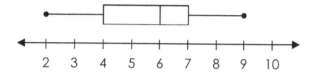

☐ The mean age is 6.

☐ The median age is 6.

☐ The interquartile range of the ages is 7.

☐ 25% of children are older than 7 years.

□ **EXERCISE YOUR SKILLS** ···

Find the five-number summary and interquartile range, then draw a box plot in your notebook.

8. 3, 2, 7, 5, 0, 6

9. 5, 8, 3, 4, 2, 6

10. 1, 3, 7, 4, 3, 5, 6

11. 9, 8, 6, 4, 7, 5, 10

12. 9, 14, 12, 8, 10, 10, 12

13. 19, 16, 17, 20, 17, 16, 17, 19, 14

14. 25, 25, 24, 26, 23, 20, 23, 24

15. 38, 42, 40, 34, 32, 44, 36, 32, 30, 40, 42

The box-and-whisker plots show the prices, in dollars, of magazines at two book stores.

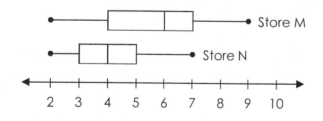

16. What is the median price at each store?

17. What is the interquartile range of the prices at each store?

18. What percent of the magazines at store M are above $4?

19. What percent of the magazines at store N are below $4?

20. What percent of the magazines at store M are not available at store N?

LESSON 141 Visualizing Data

☐ USING FREQUENCY TABLES

There are many ways to display data graphically. We'll take a look at some common ways.

A **frequency table** is a common way of organizing large amounts of data. It consists of three columns: category (or interval), tally, and frequency. The **frequency** is the total number of times that each category of data occurs. The frequency table on the right is from a survey of children on their favorite crayon color names.

Favorite crayon colors

Color name	Tally	Frequency
Pink Flamingo	⫴⫴⫴II	7
Inchworm	⫴⫴⫴IIII	9
Outer Space	IIII	4

➜ **TRY IT** Use the frequency table above to solve.

1. How many children were surveyed?

2. What percent of the children surveyed picked Inchworm as their favorite color name?

☐ USING DOT PLOTS

A **dot plot** uses dots above a number line to show how often a particular value occurs in a data set. Dot plots are usually used for small data sets. The dot plot on the right shows the data collected by rolling a die 12 times.

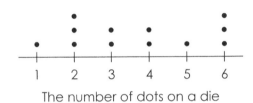

The number of dots on a die

➜ **TRY IT** Use the dot plot above to solve.

3. How many times did the die roll a number greater than 3?

4. Find the median, mode(s), and range of the data.

☐ USING STEM-AND-LEAF PLOTS

A **stem-and-leaf plot** shows numerical data arranged by place value. It splits each data value into two parts: a **stem** (the first digit or digits) and a **leaf** (the last digit). In the example on the right, the stem is the tens place value and the leaf is the ones place value. The plot shows the ages of members in a tennis club.

7, 9, 10, 10, 15, 17, 18, 23, 23, 27, 29

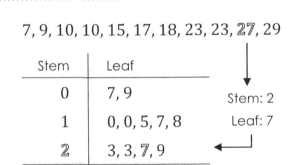

Stem	Leaf
0	7, 9
1	0, 0, 5, 7, 8
2	3, 3, 7, 9

Stem: 2
Leaf: 7

➜ **TRY IT** Use the stem-and-leaf plot above to solve.

5. How many members are older than 20?

6. Find the median, mode(s), and range of the data.

☐ USING BAR GRAPHS

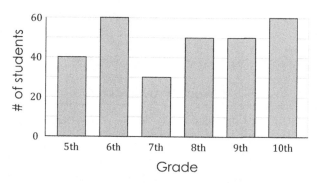

A **bar graph** or **bar chart** shows data using vertical or horizontal bars. The height or length of each bar represents the value or frequency of its corresponding category. Bar graphs are often used to display and compare data grouped into discrete categories. The bar graph on the left shows the number of students in each grade who own at least one pet.

➜ **TRY IT** Use the bar graph above to solve. Round to the nearest whole number, if necessary.

7. How many 7th graders own at least one pet?

8. How many students in total own at least one pet?

9. On average, how many students per grade own at least one pet?

☐ USING HISTOGRAMS

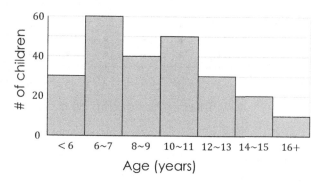

A **histogram** is a special type of bar graph where data are grouped into intervals of equal width. These intervals are consecutive and non-overlapping. A histogram is like a bar graph except that there are no gaps between bars because there are no gaps between intervals. The histogram on the left shows the ages of children who visited a city fair on a certain day.

➜ **TRY IT** Use the histogram above to solve.

10. What is the total number of children who visited the fair?

11. How many children below 10 years old visited the fair?

12. What percent of the children were between 12 and 13?

CHALLENGE Get a piece of paper. Draw each type of graph by making up your own data. Try to come up with real-life data such as quiz scores, heights over time, age distribution of a group, etc.

13. My frequency table shows:

14. My dot plot shows:

15. My stem-and-leaf plot shows:

16. My histogram shows:

Continued on the next page.

Below are the ages of members in a hiking club.

46 29 38 51 52 31 25 34 38 26 56 44 36 34 25

42 38 32 44 47 31 36 29 23 26 40 52 20 56 40

17. Complete the frequency table on the right.

18. How many members are in the club?

19. How many members are between 30 and 39?

20. What percent of the members are 40 and above?

Age group	# of members
20 ~ 29	
30 ~ 39	
40 ~ 49	
50 ~ 59	

The dot plot shows the number of hours students spent exercising in a certain week.

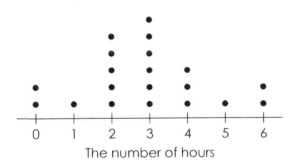

The number of hours

21. How many students spent at least 4 hours?

22. What are the median and mode of the data?

23. What is the mean number of hours spent exercising per student?

The stem-and-leaf plot shows the scores of a class on a science test.

Stem	Leaf
6	7, 8
7	0, 2, 9, 9
8	0, 4, 4, 5, 5, 6, 8
9	0, 2, 5, 6, 8
10	0, 0

24. How many students took the test?

25. What are the median and range of the scores?

26. How many students scored at least 80?

27. How many students scored less than 90?

The histogram shows the heights of the members in a jogging club.

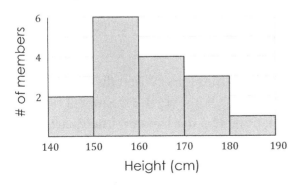

Height (cm)

28. How many members are in the club?

29. How many members are 160 cm and above?

30. What percent of the club are below 170 cm?

LESSON 142 Shapes of Distributions

☐ **REFRESH YOUR SKILLS** ···

Identify the outlier. Find the mean, median, interquartile range, and standard deviation with and without the outlier. Review Lessons 138, 139, and 140 if needed.

1. 2, 3, 3, 4, 5, 37

2. 12, 105, 110, 110, 110, 120

Use your calculations above to identify the following as true or false.

3. The outlier affects the mean more than it affects the median.

4. The outlier affects the interquartile range more than it affects the standard deviation.

☐ **IDENTIFYING SHAPES OF DISTRIBUTIONS** ···

One reason we display data graphically is to understand the shape of a distribution. A **left-skewed** distribution has a long left tail. A **right-skewed** distribution has a long right tail. A **symmetric** distribution is not skewed in any direction.

Skewed left (left-tailed)   Symmetric   Skewed right (right-tailed)

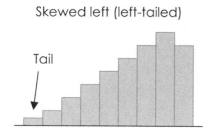
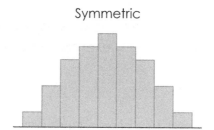
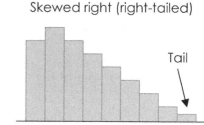

➜ **TRY IT 5.** Below are the number of goals scored per game for two soccer teams this year. Draw a dot plot for each data set, then describe the shape of each distribution.

Team A: 6, 7, 1, 4, 7, 4, 5, 5, 6, 2
5, 6, 6, 5, 6, 7, 3, 8, 0, 7

Team B: 2, 0, 1, 2, 6, 8, 3, 4, 3, 4
4, 5, 6, 5, 4, 5, 5, 3, 7, 3

☐ **CHOOSING APPROPRIATE MEASURES OF CENTER AND VARIATION** ································

The shape of a distribution is important in choosing the best measures of center and variation that describe the data set.

The mean and standard deviation are best used for symmetric distributions. When distributions are skewed or outliers are present, as shown in problems 1 through 4 above, the mean will be pulled toward the long tail and thus affect the standard deviation. The median and interquartile range (IQR) are better measures of center and variation for skewed distributions because they are less affected by skewness and outliers.

➜ **TRY IT 6.** What are the appropriate measures of center and variation for the number of goals scored per game by team A and team B on the previous page? Explain.

Team A: Team B:

□ **COMPARING DATA DISTRIBUTIONS** ···

➜ **TRY IT 7.** The dot plots show the number of miles two runners ran each day for 20 days. Which one has the higher center? Which one has the bigger spread?

 Runner A   Runner B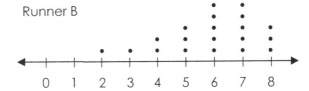

➜ **TRY IT 8.** Describe the shape of each distribution above. What are the appropriate measures of center and variation for each data set? Explain.

Runner A: Runner B:

□ **EXERCISE YOUR SKILLS** ···

Describe the shape of each distribution.

9.    10. 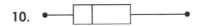   11.

12. 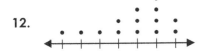   13.   14.

15. Shown below are the scores of a class on a science test. a) Draw a stem-and-leaf plot for the data. b) Describe the shape of the distribution. c) What are the appropriate measures of center and variation? Explain.

80	72	90	85	98
79	88	95	68	100
70	86	84	96	67
84	92	79	85	100

Continued on the next page.

16. The frequency table shows the heights of the members in a jogging club. a) Draw a histogram for the data. b) Describe the shape of the distribution. c) What are the appropriate measures of center and variation? Explain.

Height, h (cm)	Frequency
$140 \leq h < 150$	2
$150 \leq h < 160$	6
$160 \leq h < 170$	4
$170 \leq h < 180$	3
$180 \leq h < 190$	1

17. Two groups of students were surveyed about the average daily hours they spend online. Draw a dot plot for each data set, then describe the shape of each distribution.

Group A : 5, 4, 3, 6, 3, 4, 5, 6, 3, 5
4, 2, 7, 3, 1, 2, 5, 4, 6, 4

Group B: 3, 1, 7, 8, 2, 3, 1, 4, 2, 3
2, 4, 1, 2, 4, 5, 5, 2, 3, 6

18. Which of the two data sets above appears to have the higher mean? Which data set appears to have the higher standard deviation? What are the appropriate measures of center and variation for each data set? Explain.

Group A: Group B:

19. Find the five-number summary, then draw a box-and-whisker plot for each data set above.

Group A: Group B:

20. Find the mean, median, mode, range, and interquartile range for each data set above.

Group A: Group B:

LESSON 143 Scatter Plots

☐ **REFRESH YOUR SKILLS** ···

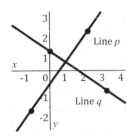

1. Find an equation of each line in slope-intercept form. Review Lesson 22 if needed.

2. Use your equations to find the value of y of each line when $x = 9$. Review Lesson 14 if needed.

☐ **READING SCATTER PLOTS** ···

A **scatter plot** is a graph that shows pairs of data plotted as points. Scatter plots are often used to identify the relationship between two data sets. The scatter plot on the right shows the experience in years and the hourly pay rate for 20 software engineers.

The relationship between two data sets is called their **correlation**. There are three types of correlation: positive, negative, and none. **Positive correlation** means that both sets of data values increase together. **Negative correlation** means that one set of data values increases as the other set decreases. For example, height and weight would likely have a positive correlation because taller people tend to be heavier. Altitude and temperature have a negative correlation because it gets colder as you go up.

➔ **TRY IT 3.** What type of correlation is shown in the plot above? What does it mean?

☐ **FINDING TREND LINES** ···

A **trend line**, or a **line of best fit**, is a line that best represents the data on a scatter plot. To find a trend line, draw a straight line as close as possible to all the points on a scatter plot.

➔ **EXAMPLE** Find a trend line and its equation.

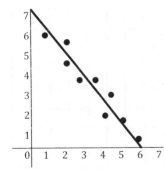

1. Draw a trend line that is closest to all the points.
2. Find its equation. The line passes through (0, 7) and (5, 1), so

$$y = -\frac{6}{5}x + 7$$

➔ **TRY IT 4.** Find a trend line and its equation.

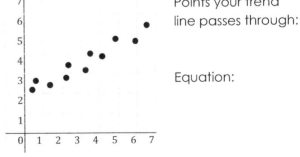

Points your trend line passes through:

Equation:

☐ **MAKING PREDICTIONS** ⋯⋯⋯⋯⋯⋯⋯⋯⋯⋯⋯⋯⋯⋯⋯⋯⋯⋯⋯⋯⋯⋯

We use trend lines to make predictions.

➔ **EXAMPLE** In the previous example, what will be the value of y when $x = 15$?

We can use the equation of the trend line to make predictions. Plug $x = 15$ into the equation, and you get $y = -11$. So we can predict that the value of y will be approximately -11 when $x = 15$.

➔ **TRY IT 5.** Find a trend line and its equation for the first scatter plot on the previous page. Use your equation to predict the hourly pay rate of a software engineer with 12 years of experience.

☐ **MAKING SCATTER PLOTS** ⋯⋯⋯⋯⋯⋯⋯⋯⋯⋯⋯⋯⋯⋯⋯⋯⋯⋯⋯⋯⋯

To make a scatter plot, simply plot the data as individual points on the coordinate plane.

➔ **TRY IT** The table shows the average monthly low temperature and jacket sales at a department store for the past 10 months. Make a scatter plot, draw a trend line, and answer each question.

Temperature (°F)	10	26	34	43	56	62	66	50	47	38
Jacket sales (k$)	4.5	3.0	3.5	2.4	0.9	1.0	0.4	1.3	2.0	2.0

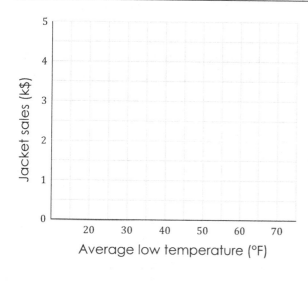

6. What type of correlation is shown in the plot?

7. Write an equation of your trend line in slope-intercept form.

8. Use your equation to predict jacket sales when the average low temperature is 20°F.

9. How would you describe the relationship between temperature and jacket sales?

☐ **EXERCISE YOUR SKILLS** ⋯⋯⋯⋯⋯⋯⋯⋯⋯⋯⋯⋯⋯⋯⋯⋯⋯⋯⋯⋯⋯

Identify the type of correlation.

10.

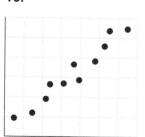

11.

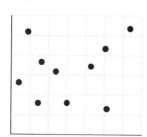

12.

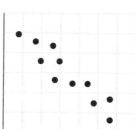

13.

Continued on the next page.

Draw a trend line and find its equation.

14.

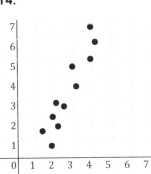

15.

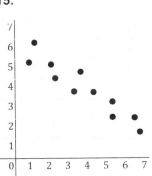

16.

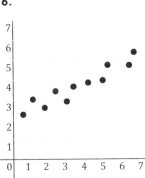

Predict the value of *y* when *x* = 30 in each scatter plot above.

17.

18.

19.

The table shows the math score and physics score of 10 middle school students. Make a scatter plot, draw a trend line, and answer each question.

Math score (%)	60	80	67	48	72	96	85	52	77	54
Physics score (%)	48	65	58	50	68	87	72	45	76	60

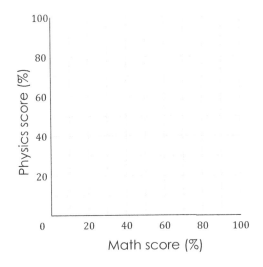

20. What type of correlation is shown in the plot?

21. Write an equation of your trend line in slope-intercept form.

22. Use your equation to predict the physics score of a student who scored 70 in the math test.

23. How would you describe the relationship between math score and physics score?

CHALLENGE Think of real-life examples of each type of correlation.

24. Examples of weak positive correlation:

25. Examples of strong positive correlation:

26. Examples of weak negative correlation:

27. Examples of strong negative correlation:

LESSON 144 Two-Way Frequency Tables

□ **READING TWO-WAY FREQUENCY TABLES** ···

Two-way frequency tables organize data based on
two categorical variables. For example, the table on
the right comes from a survey of 200 students.
According to the table, 80 male students have no pet.

	Pet(s)	No pet
Male	40	80
Female	32	48

Entries in a two-way frequency table are called **joint
frequencies**. The sum of the rows and columns are
called **marginal frequencies**. The marginal
frequencies in our example tell us that 40 + 32 = 72
students in the survey have a pet (or pets).

	Pet(s)	No pet	Total
Male	40	80	120
Female	32	48	80
Total	72	128	200

➔ **TRY IT** Use the tables above to solve.

1. How many female students have no pet?

2. How many male students are surveyed?

□ **READING TWO-WAY RELATIVE FREQUENCY TABLES** ·······························

Two-way relative frequency tables display
percentages or ratios rather than counts. The table on
the right shows relative frequencies for the whole
table above. Each entry in the table is divided by the
total count 200. According to the table, 40% of the
surveyed students are male students with no pet.

	Pet(s)	No pet	Total
Male	0.2	0.4	0.6
Female	0.16	0.24	0.4
Total	0.36	0.64	1.0

Two-way tables can also show relative frequencies for
rows or for columns. The table on the right is the
row-relative frequency table for the survey data above.
The entries in each row of the table are divided by the
total of the row. According to the table, 67% of the
surveyed male students have no pet.

	Pet(s)	No pet	Total
Male	0.33 (40/120)	0.67 (80/120)	1.0 (120/120)
Female	0.4 (32/80)	0.6 (48/80)	1.0 (80/80)
Total	0.36 (72/200)	0.64 (128/200)	1.0 (200/200)

➔ **TRY IT** Use the tables above to solve.

3. What percent of the surveyed students are female students with no pet?

4. What percent of the surveyed students have no pet?

5. What percent of the surveyed female students have a pet (or pets)?

☐ **MAKING TWO-WAY FREQUENCY TABLES** ···

Here is how you construct two-way frequency tables.

➜ **EXAMPLE** A survey of 50 students found that 25 students have a dog (or dogs), 20 students have a cat (or cats), and 8 students have both. Organize the results in a two-way frequency table.

1. Create a table using the two categories: cat(s) and dog(s).
2. Fill in the given values where appropriate. The given values are 50, 25, 20, and 8.
3. Calculate the missing values. For example, 50 – 20 = 30 students have no cat, and 25 – 8 students have a dog but no cat.

	Cat(s)	No cat	Total
Dog(s)	8 (Step 2)	17 (Step 3)	25 (Step 2)
No dog	12 (Step 3)	13 (Step 3)	25 (Step 3)
Total	20 (Step 2)	30 (Step 3)	50 (Step 2)

➜ **TRY IT 6.** A survey asked 25 students whether they use a computer or a tablet for their online learning. Fifteen students use a computer. Eighteen students use a tablet. Ten students use both. Organize the results in a two-way frequency table. Use your notebook.

☐ **MAKING TWO-WAY RELATIVE FREQUENCY TABLES** ···································

Now let's see how to construct two-way relative frequency tables.

➜ **EXAMPLE** Convert the two-way frequency table above into a two-way relative frequency table.

Simply divide each entry by the total count, 50. For example, 8/50 = 0.16 or 16% have both, and 13/50 = 0.26 or 26% have neither.

	Cat(s)	No cat	Total
Dog(s)	0.16		
No dog		0.26	
Total			1.0

➜ **TRY IT 7.** Complete the table.

➜ **EXAMPLE** Convert the two-way frequency table above into a column-relative frequency table.

Divide the entries in each column by the total of the column. For example, 8/20 = 0.4 or 40% of the cat owners have a dog (or dogs), and 13/30 = 0.43 or 43% of the non-cat owners have no dog.

	Cat(s)	No cat	Total
Dog(s)	0.4		
No dog		0.43	
Total	1.0	1.0	1.0

➜ **TRY IT 8.** Complete the table.

➜ **TRY IT 9.** Convert the two-way frequency table above into a row-relative frequency table by dividing the entries in each row by the total of the row. Use your notebook.

➜ **TRY IT 10.** Convert your table in problem 6 into a two-way relative frequency table, a row-relative frequency table, and a column-relative frequency table. Use your notebook.

Continued on the next page.

A survey asked a group of teens and adults whether they prefer online shopping or in-store shopping. Eighteen teens and 12 adults said they prefer online shopping. Nine teens and 21 adults said they prefer in-store shopping. Organize the results in a two-way frequency table. Then convert your table into a two-way relative frequency table, a row-relative frequency table, and a column-relative frequency table.

11. Two-way frequency table

	Online	In-store	Total
Teens			
Adults	12		
Total			

12. Two-way relative frequency table

	Online	In-store	Total
Teens			
Adults	0.2		
Total			1.0

13. Row-relative frequency table

	Online	In-store	Total
Teens			1.0
Adults	0.36		1.0
Total			1.0

14. Column-relative frequency table

	Online	In-store	Total
Teens			
Adults	0.4		
Total	1.0	1.0	1.0

Use the tables above to solve.

15. How many people participated in the survey?

16. How many teens participated in the survey?

17. How many adults prefer in-store shopping?

18. How many people prefer online shopping?

19. What percentage of the participants are teens?

20. What percentage of the teens prefer online shopping?

21. What percentage of the adults prefer in-store shopping?

22. Among the people who prefer online shopping, what percentage are teens?

23. Among the people who prefer in-store shopping, what percentage are teens?

LESSON 145 Catch Up and Review!

Catch up if you are behind. Use the review problems below to make sure you're on track.

LESSON 138 Find the mean, median, and mode(s).

1. 2, 3, 5, 1, 4

2. 18, 15, 14, 15, 16, 17, 12, 13

LESSON 139 Find the mean, range, and standard deviation.

3. 1, 5, 2, 3, 4

4. 7, 6, 1, 2, 5, 2, 5, 5, 3, 9

LESSON 140 Find the five-number summary and interquartile range, then draw a box plot.

5. 9, 12, 12, 8, 10, 15, 10

6. 35, 35, 30, 33, 34, 34, 36, 33

LESSON 141 Below are the scores of two students on their algebra quizzes. Draw a dot plot.

7. Ryan: 60, 70, 75, 80, 80, 85
85, 90, 90, 90, 95, 100

8. Logan: 75, 80, 80, 85, 85, 85
90, 90, 90, 90, 95, 95

LESSON 142 Describe the shape of each distribution above. Whose scores appear to have the greater standard deviation? What are the appropriate measures of center and variation? Explain.

9. Ryan's scores:

10. Logan's scores:

LESSON 143 Identify the type of correlation. Then draw a trend line and find its equation.

11.

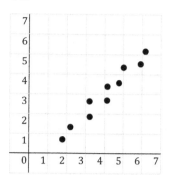

12.

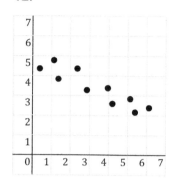

LESSON 144 Below are the results from a survey of restaurant customers. Complete the two-way frequency table, then convert it to a two-way relative frequency table.

13. Two-way frequency table

	Steak	Pasta	Total
Soup	40		
Salad		60	
Total		92	200

14. Two-way relative frequency table

	Steak	Pasta	Total
Soup	0.2		
Salad			
Total			1.0

☐ **MIXED REVIEW: PRE-ALGEBRA** ··

Brush up on the topics covered in Pre-Algebra.

Determine the best type of graph to use for each situation. Choose your answer from line graph, bar graph, circle graph, dot plot, and scatter plot.

15. What is the best type of graph for showing the percentage of four different types of insects found in a city park?

16. What is the best type of graph for showing changes in the monthly sales figures of a grocery store over the period of one year?

17. What is the best type of graph to use when comparing the number of students in each grade?

18. What is the best type of graph for showing the distribution of the algebra scores of the students in a class of 20 students?

19. What is the best type of graph to use when trying to find the correlation between temperature and ice cream sales?

LESSON 146 Theoretical and Experimental Probability

☐ **BASIC DEFINITIONS** ⋯⋯⋯⋯⋯⋯⋯⋯⋯⋯⋯⋯⋯⋯⋯⋯⋯⋯⋯⋯⋯⋯⋯⋯⋯⋯

The **probability** of an event is a measure of the likelihood that the event will occur. An **outcome** is the result of an experiment or activity. An **event** is a particular outcome or set of outcomes looked for. The specific sought-after outcomes for a certain event are called **favorable outcomes**.

The probability of event E is written as $P(E)$. It can be expressed as a fraction, a decimal, or a percent.

Probabilities are between 0 and 1. The probability of an impossible event is 0. The probability of a certain event is 1. The probability 0.5 means that the event is as likely as not to occur. Events with a probability closer to 1 are likely to occur. Events with a probability closer to 0 are unlikely to occur.

impossible   as likely as not   certain

| | | |
0   unlikely   0.5   likely   1.0

☐ **FINDING THEORETICAL PROBABILITIES** ⋯⋯⋯⋯⋯⋯⋯⋯⋯⋯⋯⋯⋯⋯⋯⋯⋯⋯⋯⋯

When a fair coin is tossed, we expect heads half the time. That is the **theoretical probability**, the probability that you expect to happen or that should happen in theory. Here is how to calculate theoretical probability.

$$P(E) = \frac{Number\ of\ favorable\ outcomes}{Total\ number\ of\ possible\ outcomes} \implies P(heads) = \frac{heads}{heads, tails} = 50\%$$

➜ **EXAMPLE** A die is rolled. Find P(odd).

- There are 6 possible outcomes:
  1, 2, 3, 4, 5, 6
- There are 3 favorable outcomes:
  1, 3, 5
- P(odd) = 3/6 = 1/2

➜ **TRY IT** A die is rolled. Find each probability.

1. P(at least 6)   2. P(less than 5)

3. P(3's multiple)   4. P(prime number)

☐ **FINDING EXPERIMENTAL PROBABILITIES** ⋯⋯⋯⋯⋯⋯⋯⋯⋯⋯⋯⋯⋯⋯⋯⋯⋯⋯

Suppose you toss a coin 10 times and get 8 heads and 2 tails. What is the probability of getting heads on your next toss? In theory, you expect a 50% chance of getting heads on any coin toss. In reality, however, your experiment indicates that you have an 80% chance. That is the **experimental probability**, the probability that actually happens in an experiment. The formula for experimental probability is very similar to the formula for theoretical probability.

$$P(E) = \frac{Number\ of\ times\ event\ E\ occurs}{Total\ number\ of\ trials} \implies P(heads) = \frac{8\ heads}{10\ tosses} = 80\%$$

➜ **EXAMPLE** You shot 25 free throws and made 15 of them. Find P(making the next shot).

$$P(\text{making the next shot}) = \frac{15\ shots\ made}{25\ free\ throws\ tried} = \frac{3}{5} = 0.6\ or\ 60\%$$

➜ TRY IT A spinner is spun 20 times. It landed on R six times, G ten times, and B four times.

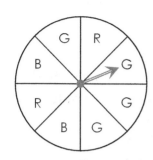

5. Theoretical P(R)

6. Experimental P(R)

7. Theoretical P(not B)

8. Experimental P(not B)

9. Theoretical P(B or G)

10. Experimental P(B or G)

□ **EXERCISE YOUR SKILLS** ···

Find the probability of each event as a fraction.

11. A letter is chosen at random from the alphabet. The letter is a vowel.

12. A month is randomly selected from a year. Its name starts with J or M.

An integer is chosen at random from 1 to 100. Find each probability as a percent.

13. P(9's multiple)

14. P(prime number ending with 1)

15. P(perfect square or perfect cube)

16. P(number whose cube root is negative)

Matt has a bag of black, white, clear, and blue marbles. He randomly drew a marble from the bag, recorded its color, and returned the marble in the bag. He repeated this experiment 30 times. A black marble was drawn 20 times, a white marble 4 times, and a clear marble 6 times. Find each probability as a fraction.

17. Experimental P(black)

18. Experimental P(blue)

19. Experimental P(not clear)

20. Experimental P(white or clear)

Matt's bag actually contained 18 black, 6 white, 10 clear, and 2 blue marbles. Find each probability as a fraction.

21. Theoretical P(black)

22. Theoretical P(blue)

23. Theoretical P(not clear)

24. Theoretical P(white or clear)

LESSON 147 Sample Spaces

☐ FINDING SAMPLE SPACES ···

A **sample space** is the set containing all possible outcomes of an experiment. To determine the sample space of an experiment, we list all the possible outcomes of the experiment.

➜ **EXAMPLE** Find the sample space.

a. Tossing a coin once

The sample space is {H, T}, where H stands for heads and T for tails.

b. Tossing a coin twice

There are 4 possible outcomes in the sample space: {HH, HT, TH, TT}.

➜ **TRY IT** Find the sample space.

1. Rolling a die

2. Tossing a coin three times

3. Tossing a coin and rolling a die

☐ FINDING SAMPLE SPACES USING TREE DIAGRAMS ··

You can use tree diagrams to find sample spaces. Tree diagrams are useful when you are organizing outcomes of an experiment that involves multiple stages.

➜ **EXAMPLE** Use a tree diagram to find the sample space of tossing a coin twice.

Tree diagram:

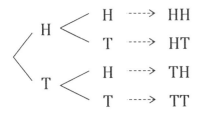

1st toss   2nd toss   Outcomes

The sample space is {HH, HT, TH, HH}.

➜ **TRY IT 4.** Use a tree diagram to find the sample space of tossing a coin three times.

☐ FINDING SAMPLE SPACES USING TABLES ···

When there are only two stages in an experiment, you can use two-way tables.

➜ **EXAMPLE** Use a table to find the sample space of tossing a coin twice.

	2nd toss	
	H	T
H (1st toss)	HH	HT
T (1st toss)	TH	HH

Sample space = {HH, HT, TH, HH}

➜ **TRY IT 5.** Use a table to find the sample space of tossing a coin and rolling a die.

List the possible outcomes. Then find the total number of possible outcomes.

6. Leo draws a letter from the alphabet of 26 letters.

7. Keisha selects a number from 2-digit square numbers.

8. Cheryl tosses a coin and selects a month of the year.

9. Mark selects an integer from 1 to 3 and a letter from the word CAT.

10. Kelly makes an outfit from two shirts (red, blue) and three skirts (tan, green, and navy).

11. Jacob makes a 2-digit number by rolling a die twice.

12. Cora makes a 2-digit number using the digits 1, 2, and 3 with repetition allowed.

13. Morgan makes a 2-digit number using the digits 1, 2, 3, and 4 without repetition.

14. Jaden randomly answers three true-or-false questions.

15. Santiago makes a 3-digit number using the digits 1, 2, and 3 without repetition.

Find each probability as a fraction. Use your answers above.

16. What is the probability that Leo draws a vowel?

17. What is the probability that Keisha selects a number greater than 90?

18. What is the probability that Cora makes an even number?

19. What is the probability that Morgan makes an even number?

20. What is the probability that Jaden answers all questions as false?

EXTRA Find the total number of possible outcomes.

21. Jack selects a day from a non-leap year. (A leap year has 366 days.)

22. Aubrey draws a card from a standard deck of 52 playing cards.

23. Jamal rolls a die and selects one day of the week.

24. Ron has a choice of ham, tuna, turkey, or roast beef and a choice of white or wheat bread to make a sandwich.

LESSON 148 Fundamental Counting Principle

☐ **COUNTING OUTCOMES OF EVENTS** ···

The **counting principle**, or **fundamental counting principle** is a method to determine the number of ways two or more events can occur in sequence. If one event can occur in p ways and a second event can occur in q ways, then the number of ways the two events can occur in sequence is $p \times q$. This rule can be extended to any number of events occurring in sequence.

➔ **EXAMPLE** Two separate events

You make a 2-digit number by rolling a die twice. How many numbers are possible?

- The tens place can be filled in 6 ways: 1 to 6.
- The ones place can be filled in 6 ways: 1 to 6.
- So, there are 6 × 6 = 36 possible numbers.

➔ **EXAMPLE** Three separate events

You make a 3-digit number by rolling a die three times, but you want an even number greater than 400. How many such numbers are possible?

- The hundreds place cannot be less than 4, so it can be filled in 3 ways: 4, 5, or 6.
- The tens place can be filled in 6 ways: 1 to 6.
- The ones place can be filled in 3 ways: 2, 4, or 6.
- So, there are 3 × 6 × 3 = 54 possible numbers.

➔ **TRY IT** Use the counting principle to solve.

1. You toss a coin five times. How many different outcomes are possible?

2. You make a 2-digit odd number by rolling a die twice. How many such numbers are possible?

3. You make a 2-digit number greater than 50 by rolling a die twice. How many such numbers are possible?

4. You make a 2-digit even number less than 40 by rolling a die twice. How many such numbers are possible?

Now let's see how to use the counting principle when events affect subsequent events.

➔ **EXAMPLE** Three events affecting each other

You make a 3-digit number by rolling a die three times, but you want a number with no digits repeated. How many such numbers are possible?

- The hundreds place can be filled in 6 ways: 1 to 6.
- The tens place can't be the same as the hundreds place, so it can be filled in 6 − 1 = 5 ways.
- The ones place can't be the same as the hundreds and the tens places, so it can be filled in 6 − 2 = 4 ways.
- So, there are 6 × 5 × 4 = 120 possible numbers.

When solving counting problems with restrictions, it is usually best to consider from the most to the least restricted events. That is why the next example starts with the ones place.

→ **EXAMPLE** Three events affecting each other

You make a 3-digit number by rolling a die three times, but you want an even number with no digits repeated. How many such numbers are possible?

- The ones place can be filled in 3 ways: 2, 4, or 6.
- The tens place can't be the same as the ones place, so it can be filled in 5 ways.
- The hundreds place can't be the same as the tens and the ones places, so it can be filled in 4 ways.
- So, there are 3 × 5 × 4 = 60 possible numbers.

→ **TRY IT** Use the counting principle to solve.

5. You make a 2-digit number by rolling a die twice, but you want a number with no digits repeated. How many such numbers are possible?

6. You make a 3-digit number by rolling a die three times, but you want a number greater than 400 with no digits repeated. How many such numbers are possible?

☐ **EXERCISE YOUR SKILLS** ···

Use the counting principle to solve. Use a calculator if necessary.

7. Kyle tosses two coins and rolls a die. How many different outcomes are possible?

8. Linsey orders a one-topping pizza from a pizzeria that offers four sizes of pizza, three types of crust, and six types of toppings. How many different pizzas can she order?

9. Jacob rolls a die, selects a day of the week, and selects a month of the year. How many different outcomes are possible?

10. Alison answers 4 multiple-choice questions. Each question has 4 choices. How many combinations of answers are possible?

11. Brian makes a 2-digit number using the digits 1 to 9. How many such numbers are possible if repetition is <u>not</u> allowed?

12. Max makes a 3-digit even number using single-digit prime numbers. How many such numbers are possible if repetition is allowed?

13. Cheryl makes a 3-digit even number using single-digit prime numbers. How many such numbers are possible if repetition is <u>not</u> allowed?

14. Harper makes a 4-digit password using the digits 1 to 9. How many different passwords can she make if repetition is allowed?

15. Mark makes a 4-letter password that starts with a vowel using the alphabet of 26 letters. How many different passwords can he make if repetition is <u>not</u> allowed?

LESSON 149 Probability of Independent Events

☐ **REFRESH YOUR SKILLS** ···

Solve. Review Lessons 146 and 148 if needed.

1. A ball is drawn randomly from a bag containing 3 red, 5 white, and 8 yellow balls. What is the probability of drawing a yellow ball?

2. How many 2-digit numbers can be formed from the digits 1 to 5 with repetition?

3. How many 2-digit even numbers can be formed from the digits 1 to 5 with repetition?

☐ **FINDING PROBABILITIES OF INDEPENDENT EVENTS** ··

Two events are **independent** if the occurrence of one event does not affect the probability of the other event. When events A and B are independent, the probability of both occurring is the product of the probabilities of each occurring: $P(A \text{ and } B) = P(A) \times P(B)$.

> Independent events
> $$P(A \text{ and } B) = P(A) \cdot P(B)$$

Suppose you toss a coin and roll a die. What is the probability of tossing heads and rolling an odd number? Tossing heads and rolling an odd number are independent because they don't affect each other. So, to find the probability of both occurring, you find the probability of each and multiply.

Remember that, as shown below, you can always find the probability of an event using the sample space also. Use whichever method you find easier! Whether you use the probability formula or the sample space, the result will be the same.

➔ **EXAMPLE** You toss a coin and roll a die. Find P(tossing heads and rolling an odd number).

Using the formula:
- $P(\text{heads}) = 1/2$
- $P(\text{odd}) = P(1, 3, \text{ or } 5) = 1/2$
- $P(\text{heads and odd})$
  $= P(\text{heads}) \times P(\text{odd}) = 1/2 \times 1/2 = 1/4$

Using the sample space:
- There are 12 possible outcomes:
  H1, H2, H3, H4, H5, H6, T1, T2, T3, T4, T5, T6
- There are 3 favorable outcomes:
  H1, H3, H5
- $P(\text{heads and odd}) = 3/12 = 1/4$

Drawing "with replacement" means putting the item drawn back into the group before drawing the next item. Draws with replacement are independent because they don't affect one another.

➔ **EXAMPLE** Two balls are drawn from a bag containing 4 red and 6 black balls, with replacement (drawing a ball, putting it back in the bag, and then drawing another). Find P(both are red).

Using the formula:
- $P(\text{1st red}) = 4/10 = 2/5$
- $P(\text{2nd red}) = 4/10 = 2/5$
- $P(\text{both red})$
  $= P(\text{1st red}) \times P(\text{2nd red}) = 2/5 \times 2/5 = 4/25$

Using the sample space:
- There are $10 \times 10 = 100$ possible outcomes.
- There are $4 \times 4 = 16$ favorable outcomes.
- $P(\text{both red}) = 16/100 = 4/25$

➔ **TRY IT** Two cards are drawn from a stack of five cards numbered 1 to 5, with replacement.

4. P(first 2, then 4)

5. P(first odd, then even)

6. P(both odd)

7. P(both greater than 4)

➔ **TRY IT** Two balls are drawn from a bag containing 2 red and 4 pink balls, with replacement.

8. P(first red, then pink)

9. P(first pink, then red)

10. P(both red)

11. P(both pink)

☐ **EXERCISE YOUR SKILLS** ··

A coin is tossed and a die is rolled. Find each probability.

12. P(heads and a 5)

13. P(tails and a multiple of 3)

14. P(heads and a prime number)

15. P(tails and a negative number)

Two balls are drawn from a bag of 2 red and 6 pink balls, with replacement. Find each probability.

16. P(first red, then pink)

17. P(first pink, then red)

18. P(both red)

19. P(both pink)

EXTRA Find each probability.

20. Two dice are rolled. What is the probability of getting two odd numbers?

21. Two dice are rolled. What is the probability of getting two prime numbers?

22. Three coins are tossed. What is the probability of landing three heads?

23. Jamal rolls a die and randomly selects one day of the week. What is the probability that he rolls an odd number and selects Monday or Tuesday?

24. A quiz consists of 4 true-false questions. If you choose answers randomly, what is the probability of getting all 4 questions correct?

LESSON 150 Probability of Dependent Events

□ **REFRESH YOUR SKILLS** ···

Solve. Review Lesson 149 if needed.

1. You toss a coin and roll a die. What is the probability of tossing heads and rolling a 5?

2. Two cards are drawn from a stack of five cards numbered 1 to 5, with replacement. What is the probability that both cards are even?

3. Two balls are drawn from a bag of 2 red and 6 pink balls, with replacement. What is the probability of drawing first a red ball and then a pink ball?

□ **FINDING PROBABILITIES OF DEPENDENT EVENTS** ···

Two events are **dependent** if the occurrence of the first event affects the probability of the second event. When events A and B are dependent, the probability of both occurring is the product of the probability of A and the probability of B after A occurs: $P(A \text{ and } B) = P(A) \times P(B \text{ after } A)$. Note that $P(B \text{ after } A)$ can also be written as $P(B|A)$.

> Dependent events
> $$P(A \text{ and } B) = P(A) \cdot P(B|A)$$

Suppose two digits are selected at random from the digits 1 through 4. If repetition of digits is not allowed, what is the probability that both digits are odd? The probability of selecting a second odd digit changes depending on whether or not the first digit is odd, meaning that the two events are dependent. So, to find the probability of both occurring, you multiply P(selecting an odd digit first) and P(selecting an odd digit second after selecting an odd digit first).

➜ **EXAMPLE** You randomly pick 2 digits from 1 to 4 without repetition. Find P(both are odd).

Using the formula:
- P(1st odd) = 2 odds / 4 digits = 1/2
- P(2nd odd | 1st odd) = 1 odd / 3 digits = 1/3
- P(both odd)
  = P(1st odd) × P(2nd odd | 1st odd)
  = 1/2 × 1/3 = 1/6

Using the sample space:
- There are 12 possible outcomes:
  12, 13, 14, 21, 23, 24, 31, 32, 34, 41, 42, 43
- There are 2 favorable outcomes:
  13, 31
- P(both odd) = 2/12 = 1/6

Drawing "without replacement" means that you draw an item and do not put it back. Draws without replacement are dependent because previous draws affect the current draw.

➜ **EXAMPLE** Two balls are drawn from a bag containing 4 red and 6 black balls, without replacement (drawing a ball, keeping it, and then drawing another). Find P(both are red).

Using the formula:
- P(1st red) = 4 red /10 balls = 2/5
- P(2nd red | 1st red) = 3 red / 9 balls = 1/3
- P(both red)
  = P(1st red) × P(2nd red | 1st red) = 2/15

Using the sample space:
- There are 10 × 9 = 90 possible outcomes:
- There are 4 × 3 = 12 favorable outcomes:
- P(both red) = 12/90 = 2/15

➡ **TRY IT** Two cards are drawn from a stack of five cards numbered 1 to 5, without replacement.

4. P(first 2, then 4)

5. P(first odd, then even)

6. P(both odd)

7. P(both greater than 4)

➡ **TRY IT** Two balls are drawn from a bag containing 2 red and 4 pink balls, without replacement.

8. P(first red, then pink)

9. P(first pink, then red)

10. P(both red)

11. P(both pink)

The probability formulas are useful, but sometimes it is simpler to use sample spaces.

➡ **EXAMPLE** A die is rolled twice. Find P(sum is 5).
Using the sample space:
- There are 6 × 6 = 36 possible outcomes.
- There are 4 favorable outcomes: 14, 23, 32, 41
- P(sum is 5) = 4/36 = 1/9

➡ **TRY IT** A die is rolled twice.

12. P(same numbers)

13. P(sum is 10)

☐ **EXERCISE YOUR SKILLS** ···

Find each probability.

14. A jar contains 3 red marbles and 3 green marbles. What is the probability of drawing two red marbles without replacing them back in the jar?

15. Two cards are drawn from a stack of cards numbered 1 to 9, without replacement. What is the probability that both cards are even?

16. Two letters are chosen at random without replacement from the word PEACH. What is the probability that they will both be vowels?

17. Three marbles are drawn from a bag of 3 red, 3 white, and 4 green marbles, without replacement. What is the probability of drawing three green marbles?

18. A die is rolled twice. What is the probability that the sum is less than 4?

19. A die is rolled twice. What is the probability that the first roll is less than the second roll?

20. Cheyenne rolls a die and spins a spinner with four equal sections numbered 1 through 4. What is the probability of getting the same number?

LESSON 151 Probability of Disjoint and Overlapping Events

☐ **REFRESH YOUR SKILLS** ···

A die is rolled twice. Find each probability. Review Lessons 149 and 150 if needed.

1. P(two odd numbers)

2. P(sum is 3)

☐ **FINDING PROBABILITIES OF DISJOINT EVENTS** ···

Two events are **disjoint**, or **mutually exclusive**, if they cannot occur at the same time. When events A and B are mutually exclusive, the probability of both occurring is 0. The probability of either occurring is simply the sum of the probabilities of each occurring: $P(A \text{ or } B) = P(A) + \mathrm{P}(B)$.

> Addition rule for disjoint events
>
> $P(A \text{ or } B) = P(A) + P(B)$

A standard deck of playing cards consists of 52 cards with 4 suits: hearts, diamonds, clubs, and spades. Each suit has 13 cards: 9 number cards (2 through 10), 3 face cards (jack, queen, and king), and an ace. Hearts and diamonds are red, while clubs and spades are black.

Suppose a card is randomly drawn from a standard deck of 52 playing cards. What is the probability that the card is a club or a red card? A card cannot be both a club and a red card, meaning that drawing a club and drawing a red card are mutually exclusive events. So, to find the probability of either occurring, you find the probability of each and add.

➔ **EXAMPLE** A card is drawn from a deck of 52 cards. Find P(club or red).

Using the formula:
- P(club) = 13/52 = 1/4
- P(red) = 26/52 = 1/2
- P(club or red)
  = P(club) + P(red) = 1/4 + 1/2 = 3/4

Using the sample space:
- There are 52 possible outcomes.
- There are 39 favorable outcomes: 13 clubs + 26 red cards
- P(club or red) = 39/52 = 3/4

➔ **TRY IT** A card is drawn from a deck of 52 cards. Find each probability.

3. P(red or spade)

4. P(heart or diamond)

5. P(ace or face)

6. P(face or number less than 5)

☐ **FINDING PROBABILITIES OF OVERLAPPING EVENTS** ···

Two events are **overlapping** if they can occur together. When events A and B are overlapping, the probability of either occurring is the sum of the probabilities of each occurring minus the probability of both occurring: $P(A \text{ or } B) = P(A) + \mathrm{P}(B) - P(A \text{ and } B)$.

> Overlapping events
>
> $P(A \text{ or } B) = P(A) + P(B) - P(A \text{ and } B)$

Suppose a card is randomly drawn from a standard deck of 52 playing cards. What is the probability that the card is a club or a number card? There are number cards that are also clubs, meaning that drawing a club and drawing a number card are overlapping events. So, when finding the probability of either occurring, be careful not to count the overlapping outcomes twice.

➔ **EXAMPLE** A card is drawn from a deck of 52 cards. Find P(club or number).

Using the formula:
- P(club) = 13/52
- P(number) = (9 × 4)/52 = 36/52
- P(club and number) = 9/52
- P(club or number)
  = 13/52 + 36/52 − 9/52 = 40/52 = 10/13

Using the sample space:
- There are 52 possible outcomes.
- There are 40 favorable outcomes: 13 clubs + 9 × 3 number cards that are hearts, diamonds, and spades
- P(club or number) = 40/52 = 10/13

➔ **TRY IT** A card is drawn from a deck of 52 cards. Find each probability.

7. P(heart or face)

8. P(red or number)

9. P(face or king)

10. P(spade or number less than 5)

☐ **EXERCISE YOUR SKILLS** ···

A die is rolled. Find each probability.

11. P(odd or prime)

12. P(odd or 2's multiple)

13. P(even or less than 4)

14. P(even or at least 4)

A card is drawn from a deck of 52 cards. Find each probability.

15. P(king or queen)

16. P(ace or club)

17. P(jack or black)

18. P(red or face)

CHALLENGE A die is rolled twice. Find each probability.

19. What is the probability that the sum is even?

20. What is the probability that the sum is a multiple of 5?

LESSON 152 Permutations and Combinations

☐ **REFRESH YOUR SKILLS** ···

Solve. Assume repetition is not allowed. Review Lessons 147 and 148 if needed.

1. How many 3-letter passwords can be formed from the letters A, B, and C?

2. List all 3-letter passwords that can be formed from the letters A, B, and C.

☐ **IDENTIFYING PERMUTATIONS AND COMBINATIONS** ···

A **permutation** is an arrangement of items in a particular order. A **combination** is an arrangement of items in which order does not matter. The difference is ordering.

➔ **EXAMPLE** Permutation

How many 2-letter passwords can be formed from the letters A, B, and C?

The password AB is not same as the password BA. Order matters, so it is a permutation problem.

➔ **EXAMPLE** Combination

How many teams of 2 players can be formed from the players A, B, and C?

The team AB is same as the team BA. Order does not matter, so it is a combination problem.

➔ **TRY IT** Identify each as a permutation or a combination. Do not solve.

3. In how many ways can a captain and a co-captain be chosen from a team of 9 players?

4. How many committees of 3 people can be formed from a group of 30 people?

☐ **COUNTING PERMUTATIONS** ···

You can use the counting principle to calculate the number of permutations.

➔ **EXAMPLE** Counting permutations

In how many ways can 3 people be seated in a row of 3 seats?

Number of permutations of 3 =

$$\begin{pmatrix} \text{1st seat} \\ \text{3 choices} \end{pmatrix} \times \begin{pmatrix} \text{2nd seat} \\ \text{2 choices} \end{pmatrix} \times \begin{pmatrix} \text{3rd seat} \\ \text{1 choices} \end{pmatrix}$$

So, there are 3 × 2 × 1 = 6 ways.

➔ **TRY IT** Solve.

5. In how many ways can you arrange the letters in the word BIRD?

6. In how many ways can you arrange 5 different books on a shelf?

➔ **EXAMPLE** Counting permutations

In how many ways can you arrange 3 of the letters in the word MOUSE?

Number of permutations of 3 out of 5 =

$$\begin{pmatrix} \text{1st letter} \\ \text{5 choices} \end{pmatrix} \times \begin{pmatrix} \text{2nd letter} \\ \text{4 choices} \end{pmatrix} \times \begin{pmatrix} \text{3rd letter} \\ \text{3 choices} \end{pmatrix}$$

So, there are 5 × 4 × 3 = 60 ways.

➔ **TRY IT** Solve.

7. In how many ways can you arrange 3 of the letters in the word MONKEY?

8. In how many ways can you arrange 2 of the letters in the word DOLPHIN?

□ COUNTING COMBINATIONS ··

To find the number of combinations, take the permutations and divide by the repeats. Why?

Think about how many teams of 3 players can be formed from the players A, B, C, and D. We know there are $4 \times 3 \times 2 = 24$ possible permutations. However, because order doesn't matter, each group below should be counted as a single combination. Each group includes 6 permutations because there are $3 \times 2 \times 1 = 6$ ways to order 3 players. So, $24/6 = 4$ teams can be formed.

Team: A, B, C	Team: A, B, D	Team: A, C, D	Team: B, C, D
ABC, ACB, BAC	ABD, ADB, BAD	ACD, ADC, CAD	BCD, BDC, CBD
BCA, CAB, CBA	BDA, DAB, DBA	CDA, DAC, DCA	CDB, DBC, DCB

➜ **EXAMPLE** Counting combinations

How many teams of 3 players can be formed from 5 players?

1. Find the number of permutations. There are $5 \times 4 \times 3 = 60$ ways to select 3 of the 5 players in order.
2. Find the number of repeats. There are $3 \times 2 \times 1 = 6$ ways to order 3 players, so 6 permutations should be counted as a single combination.
3. Divide the number of permutations by the number of repeats. So, $60/6 = 10$ teams can be formed.

➜ **TRY IT** Solve.

9. How many teams of 4 players can be formed from 9 players?

10. How many committees of 3 people can be formed from a group of 10 people?

□ EXERCISE YOUR SKILLS ··

Identify each as a permutation or a combination. Then solve.

11. In how many ways can you arrange the letters of the word WHALE?

12. How many committees of 4 people can be formed from a group of 15?

13. In how many ways can a family of 6 people line up for a picture?

14. In how many ways can you arrange 3 of the letters in the word SPIDER?

15. In how many ways can a 3-card hand be dealt from a standard deck of 52 cards?

16. In how many ways can 1st-, 2nd-, and 3rd-place prizes be awarded to 11 students?

17. In how many ways can a president, a vice-president, a secretary, and a treasurer be chosen from a club of 20 members?

18. In how many ways can you draw the names of 3 raffle winners from a basket of 25 names if every winner gets the same prize?

LESSON 153 Permutations and Combinations

☐ **REFRESH YOUR SKILLS** ··

Identify each as a permutation or a combination. Then solve. Review Lesson 152 if needed.

1. In how many ways can you arrange 3 of the letters in the word TIGER?

2. How many teams of 3 players can be formed from 5 players?

☐ **CALCULATING FACTORIALS** ···

A **factorial** is a number multiplied by every integer between itself and 1. For example, 5! is read "5 factorial" and is equal to $5 \times 4 \times 3 \times 2 \times 1 = 120$. Note that, by definition, $0! = 1$.

$$n! = n(n-1)(n-2) \dots 1$$
$$0! = 1$$

When dealing with factorials, first cancel as many factors as possible and then evaluate the rest.

➜ **EXAMPLE** Evaluate 5!/3!.

$$\frac{5!}{3!} = \frac{5 \times 4 \times 3!}{3!} = 5 \times 4 = 20$$

➜ **TRY IT** Evaluate.

3. $\dfrac{8!}{5!}$

4. $\dfrac{7!}{3! \, 4!}$

☐ **USING PERMUTATION FORMULA** ···

We know that there are $5 \cdot 4 \cdot 3$ permutations to choose 3 elements out of 5. In general, the number of permutations for n objects taken r at a time is $n(n-1)(n-2) \dots (n-r+1)$. Using the factorial, we can rewrite it as the formula shown on the right. The notation nPr represents the number of permutations for n objects taken r at a time. Here is how the formula is derived.

Permutations of r out of n

$$_nP_r = \frac{n!}{(n-r)!}$$

$$_nP_r = n(n-1)(n-2)\dots(n-r+1)$$

$$= \frac{n(n-1)(n-2)\dots(n-r+1)(n-r)(n-r-1)\dots 1}{(n-r)(n-r-1)\dots 1} = \frac{n!}{(n-r)!}$$

Note that nPr can also be written as $P(n, r)$.

➜ **EXAMPLE** Counting permutations

In how many ways can you arrange 4 of the letters in the word PANTHER?

Number of permutations of 4 out of 7 =

$$_7P_4 = \frac{7!}{(7-4)!} = \frac{7!}{3!} = 7 \times 6 \times 5 \times 4 = 840$$

So, there are 840 ways.

➜ **TRY IT** Solve.

5. In how many ways can you arrange 5 different books on a shelf?

6. In how many ways can you arrange the letters of the word FLAMINGO taking 2 letters at a time?

☐ USING COMBINATION FORMULA $\cdots\cdots\cdots\cdots\cdots\cdots\cdots\cdots\cdots\cdots\cdots\cdots\cdots\cdots\cdots$

We also know that, to get the number of combinations to choose 3 elements out of 5, we need to divide $5 \cdot 4 \cdot 3$ by $3 \cdot 2 \cdot 1$. So the formula for combinations is equal to the formula for permutations divided by $r!$. The notation nCr represents the number of combinations for n objects taken r at a time.

Note that nCr can also be written as $C(n, r)$.

> Combinations of r out of n
> $$_nC_r = \frac{n!}{(n-r)!\, r!}$$

➔ **EXAMPLE** Counting combinations

How many teams of 4 players can be formed from 7 players?

Number of combinations of 4 out of 7 =

$$_7C_4 = \frac{7!}{(7-4)!\, 4!} = \frac{7!}{3!\, 4!} = 7 \times 5 = 35$$

So, 35 teams can be formed.

➔ **TRY IT** Solve.

7. How many teams of 2 players can be formed from 8 players?

8. In how many ways can you choose 4 toppings from 10 available toppings for your pizza?

☐ EXERCISE YOUR SKILLS $\cdots\cdots\cdots\cdots\cdots\cdots\cdots\cdots\cdots\cdots\cdots\cdots\cdots\cdots\cdots\cdots\cdots\cdots\cdots$

Evaluate.

9. $_4P_2$

10. $_9P_3$

11. $_8C_3$

12. $_{10}C_7$

Solve. Use a calculator if necessary.

13. In how many ways can 5 students be chosen to represent a class of 22 students?

14. In how many ways can you arrange the letters in the word GOLDFISH?

15. How many teams of 5 players can be formed from a group of 8 boys and 7 girls?

16. How many passwords can be formed taking 4 letters at a time from the word DRAGONFLY?

17. In how many ways can you choose 6 desserts from a tray of 12 different desserts?

18. In how many ways can 3 different prizes be awarded to a group of 18 students?

19. In how many ways can a president, a vice-president, and a treasurer be elected from a class of 30 students?

20. In how many ways can you draw the names of 2 raffle winners from a basket of 40 names if both winners get the same prize?

LESSON 154 Permutations, Combinations, and Probability

☐ **REFRESH YOUR SKILLS** ···

Solve. Review Lesson 150 if needed.

1. Two cards are drawn from a stack of five cards numbered 1 to 5, without replacement. What is the probability that both cards are odd?

2. Two balls are drawn from a bag containing 2 red and 4 pink balls, without replacement. What is the probability that both balls are pink?

☐ **FINDING PROBABILITIES USING PERMUTATIONS** ···

Here is an example of using permutations to find a probability.

➜ **EXAMPLE** Probability using permutations

You randomly arrange 5 cards numbered 1 through 5. What is the probability that card 1 comes first and card 5 last?

Using the permutation formula:
- Total possible outcomes = $_5P_5$
- Favorable outcomes = permutations of 3 cards after cards 1 and 5 are set = $_3P_3$
- P(first 1 and last 5) = $_3P_3 / _5P_5$ = 3!/5! = 1/20

Using the probability formula:
- P(first 1) = 1/5
- P(last 5 | first 1) = 1/4
- P(first 1 and last 5)
  = P(first 1) × P(last 5 | first 1) = 1/20

➜ **TRY IT** Solve. Use a calculator if necessary.

3. Emma, Brian, and 4 of their friends are seated randomly in a row of 6 seats.

   a. What is the probability that Emma sits in the first seat?

   b. What is the probability that Emma sits in the first seat and Brian in the last seat?

   c. What is the probability that Emma and Brian sit at each end of the row? (*Hint*: Consider two cases separately: either Emma first and Brian last or Brian first and Emma last.)

☐ **FINDING PROBABILITIES USING COMBINATIONS** ···

Now, let's see an example of using combinations to find a probability.

➜ **EXAMPLE** Probability using combinations

You draw 2 balls simultaneously (or one after another without replacement) from a bag containing 5 red and 4 pink balls. What is the probability of drawing 2 red balls?

Using the combination formula:
- Total possible outcomes = $_9C_2$
- Favorable outcomes = combinations of choosing 2 balls from 5 red balls = $_5C_2$
- P(both red) = $_5C_2 / _9C_2$ = 10/36 = 5/18

Using the probability formula:
- P(1st red) = 5/9
- P(2nd red | 1st red) = 4/8 = 1/2
- P(both red)
  = P(1st red) × P(2nd red | 1st red) = 5/18

➔ TRY IT Solve. Use a calculator if necessary.

4. Two balls are drawn simultaneously from a bag containing 3 white and 4 black balls.

   a. What is the probability of drawing 2 white balls?

   b. What is the probability of drawing 2 black balls?

   c. What is the probability of drawing 1 white and 1 black ball?

☐ **EXERCISE YOUR SKILLS** ···

Solve. Use a calculator if necessary.

5. Emma, Brian, and 6 of their friends are seated randomly in a row of 8 seats.

   a. What is the probability that Emma sits in the first seat?

   b. What is the probability that Emma sits in the first seat and Brian in the last seat?

   c. What is the probability that Emma and Brian sit at each end of the row?

6. The letters A, E, R, W, and T are rearranged in a random order.

   a. What is the probability that an arrangement spells WATER?

   b. What is the probability that an arrangement begins with a vowel?

   c. What is the probability that an arrangement begins and ends with a vowel?

7. A club of 5 boys and 4 girls elects a president, a vice-president, and a treasurer.

   a. What is the probability that all three positions are filled by boys?

   b. What is the probability that all three positions are filled by girls?

   c. What is the probability that only the president is a girl?

8. Three balls are drawn simultaneously from a bag of 3 red, 5 pink, and 4 yellow balls.

   a. What is the probability of drawing 3 red balls?

   b. What is the probability of drawing 3 pink balls?

   c. What is the probability of drawing no yellow balls?

   d. What is the probability of drawing one ball of each color?

9. Two cards are drawn simultaneously from a deck of 52 cards.

   a. What is the probability of drawing two clubs?

   b. What is the probability of drawing no clubs?

LESSON 155 Catch Up and Review!

Catch up if you are behind. Use the review problems below to make sure you're on track.

LESSON 146 Find each probability as a percent.

1. A die is rolled. What is the theoretical probability of rolling a multiple of 2?

2. Out of 20 games, Aiden's baseball team won 11 games and tied 4 games. What is the experimental probability that the team will <u>lose</u> the next game?

LESSON 147 List the possible outcomes.

3. You toss a coin and roll a die.

4. You toss a coin three times.

LESSON 148 Find the number of possible outcomes.

5. You make a 2-digit number using the digits 1 through 5 with repetition.

6. You make a 2-digit number using the digits 1 through 5 without repetition.

7. You make a 2-digit even number using the digits 1 through 5 with repetition.

8. You make a 2-digit even number using the digits 1 through 5 without repetition.

LESSON 149 Find each probability.

9. Two cards are drawn from a stack of five cards numbered 1 to 5, with replacement. What is the probability of drawing two even numbers?

10. Two balls are drawn from a bag containing 3 yellow and 5 green balls, with replacement. What is the probability of drawing 2 yellow balls?

LESSON 150 Find each probability.

11. Two cards are drawn from a stack of five cards numbered 1 to 5, without replacement. What is the probability of drawing two even numbers?

12. Two balls are drawn from a bag containing 3 brown and 5 black balls, without replacement. What is the probability of drawing 2 brown balls?

13. A die is rolled twice. What is the probability that the sum is 4?

14. A die is rolled twice. What is the probability that the first roll is greater than the second?

LESSON 151 Find each probability.

15. A die is rolled. What is the probability of rolling an even number or a prime number?

16. A card is drawn from a deck of 52 cards. What is the probability of drawing a heart or a face card?

LESSONS 152–153 Solve.

17. In how many ways can 4 people be seated in a row of 4 seats?

18. In how many ways can you arrange 2 of the letters in the word BIRD?

19. How many teams of 3 players can be formed from 5 players?

LESSON 154 Find each probability.

20. You randomly arrange 6 cards numbered 1 through 6. What is the probability that card 1 comes first and card 6 last?

21. You draw 2 balls simultaneously from a bag containing 3 purple and 5 gray balls. What is the probability of drawing 2 purple balls?

LESSON 156 Test Preparation Tips & Self-Review

☐ **PREPARING FOR TESTS** ··

First of all, know about your test. It is important for you to understand what kind of test you will be taking. Find out the following information about your test.

o What is the test for? Why are you taking the test?

o How many questions are on the test, and how much time is allowed?

o What topics are covered on the test? How many questions are given on each topic?

o What format are the questions in (subjective or objective)?

o How will your answers be graded? Do you need to show your work?

Make a list of subtopics for each topic covered on the test. For example, suppose your final exam covers rational expressions and equations. The subtopics could include:

o Simplifying rational expressions

o Adding and subtracting rational expressions

o Multiplying and dividing rational expressions

o Solving rational equations

o Using rational equations to solve real-world problems

Make a study plan that outlines what, when, and how you are going to study. A study plan is a personal thing. There is no right or wrong way to make one. If it helps you stay organized and accomplish your goal, then it is a good plan. Here are some tips to consider.

o Place higher priority on the topics covered more in the test.

o Allocate more time on the topics and subtopics you find difficult.

o Set small and realistic goals that you can check off and feel a sense of accomplishment about when you complete them. For example, "Solve 20 rational equations and get at least 90% correct" is a better goal than "Study how to solve rational equations" because you can clearly tell whether you met the goal or not.

o Plan to make practice tests and take them in timed conditions just like the real test.

o Plan to complete all your studying and practicing a few days before the test, so that you can spend a day or two on review.

Simulate the test conditions as much as possible and take practice tests.

o Make practice tests out of your notes, study guides, and other materials, or see if you can actually find old tests or sample tests.

o Take practice tests in an environment as close to that of the real test. Take them multiple times until you feel comfortable.

Review the topics covered in the first half of the course.

1. Create a test for EP Math Algebra 1. Make 20 problems from Lessons 1 through 79. Do not just copy the existing problems. Make up your own. Include the topics you had trouble with. Write your problems neatly on a clean sheet or sheets of paper with enough space to show all work. Keep the answer key separate. Title your work as **Practice Test #1** and keep for later use.

☐ **CHALLENGE YOURSELF** ···

Answer on a separate sheet or sheets of paper, then attach to this page.

2. Pretend you are making a final exam for EP students who just finished the EP Math Algebra 1 course. How many questions will you include, and how much time will you allow? What topics will you cover and not cover? Which format of questions will you use? How would you design the exam so that you can assess how well students understand the topics?

3. Now pretend you are an EP student who just finished the EP Math Algebra 1 course. You have a final exam coming in two weeks. The information about the exam is given above. How would you prepare for your final? Make a study plan.

LESSON 157 Test Taking Tips & Self-Review

☐ **TAKING TESTS** ··

Before the test, make a test day checklist to avoid last minute fuss. The checklist can include:

o When, where, and how long is the test?

o What items can be brought to the test? What items are not allowed to be brought? For example, can you use a calculator? Can you bring a digital watch?

o What items are nice to have? For example, will you need earplugs, snacks, or water bottles? What other items can help you feel comfortable and stay focused?

Before the test, solve lots of practice problems. Here are some tips to consider.

o Make sure you know why you missed what you missed. Don't just check the answers.

o Take notes on the problems you missed multiple times or the problems you had difficulty understanding so that you can review your notes right before the test.

o Simulate the test conditions as much as possible and take practice tests. Practice pacing yourself so that you'll be able to complete the test in the allotted time.

Remember, it is also important for you to be physically ready.

o Avoid staying up late the night before the test. Get a good night's sleep.

o Eat a healthy meal and stay hydrated on the day of the test.

During the test, you can use test-taking strategies. Here are some commonly advised tips.

o As soon as the test begins, write down information that you need to remember but fear forgetting, such as formulas and equations.

o Skim over the test before you start. Answer the easy questions first. Skip difficult questions and come back to them later. If the questions are weighted differently, work on high-value ones first.

o Answer all the questions as best as you can, unless there is a penalty for wrong answers.

o Read every question closely. Read twice if you feel that a question is hard to understand.

o If you get stuck on a tough question, don't panic. Move on to another problem and come back to it later.

o When you are unsure of an answer on a multiple-choice question, eliminate nonsense answers first and go with the most logical.

o Often, your first choice is the right one. Don't keep on changing your answer unless you're sure the answer you've chosen is wrong.

o On multiple-choice questions, many consecutive answers of the same letter are unlikely.

☐ SELF-REVIEW: 2ND HALF

Review the topics covered in the second half of the course.

1. Create a test for EP Math Algebra 1. Make 20 problems from Lessons 80 through 150. Do not just copy the existing problems. Make up your own. Include the topics you had trouble with. Write your problems neatly on a clean sheet or sheets of paper with enough space to show all work. Keep the answer key separate. Title your work as **Practice Test #2** and keep for later use.

☐ CHALLENGE YOURSELF

Answer on a separate sheet or sheets of paper, then attach to this page.

2. Choose a test that you will likely take in next few years, such as PSAT, SAT, or ACT. Visit the official website of the test you have chosen and make a test day checklist.

3. Find out more about the math section of the test you have chosen above. How long is the section? How many questions are given? What topics are covered?

4. There are many test-taking strategies that are commonly recommended for students. However, not every tip is right for every student. You may prefer going through the questions in sequential order. You may like to tackle the hard ones first and get them off your mind. You may have a unique way of calming yourself down before tests. Think about what type of person you are and what strategies will work best for you.

LESSON 158 Review: Solving Linear Equations & Inequalities

Let's review solving linear equations and inequalities.

LESSONS 3–5 Solve.

1. $7x - 10 = 11$

2. $6x - 4(2x + 3) = -8$

3. $\dfrac{1}{2}x + \dfrac{5}{2} = x + \dfrac{3}{4}$

4. $\dfrac{5}{9} - \dfrac{1}{6}x = \dfrac{1}{3}x + \dfrac{2}{9}$

LESSON 6 Solve.

5. $|x - 5| = 3$

6. $|3x - 7| = 2$

7. $3 - |9x - 6| = -3$

8. $12 - 3|x - 7| = 6$

LESSON 38 Solve.

9. $4x + 7 > 35$

10. $4(x - 1) + 2 \leq 10 - 3x$

11. $\dfrac{2}{3}x + 1 \geq \dfrac{4}{3}x - \dfrac{1}{2}$

12. $\dfrac{1}{2}(2 - x) + \dfrac{3}{4} < \dfrac{1}{4}$

LESSONS 39–40 Solve.

13. $13 < 4x - 7 \leq 17$

14. $3x > 15$ or $x + 8 \geq 13$

15. $|4 - 2x| < 6$

16. $9 - |-4x| \geq 5$

17. The sum of three consecutive odd integers is 27. Find the integers.

18. Brian bought a shirt at $18.70. The price was 15% off the regular price. What was the regular price?

19. A rectangle with a width of 5.5 cm has a perimeter of 24 cm. What is the length of the rectangle?

20. Max has $1.50 in dimes and quarters. If he had 3 more dimes, then he would have twice as many dimes as quarters. How many coins of each type does he have?

21. Mark drove to visit his friend who lives 170 miles away. His average speed was 68 mph. How long did it take him to get to his friend's house?

22. Two buses leave a station at the same time and travel in opposite directions. One travels at 50 mph, and the other travels at 55 mph. How long does it take for the two buses to be 315 miles apart?

23. How much water must be added to 2 liters of a 60% saline solution to produce a 40% saline solution?

24. How much of a 10% saline solution must be added to 6 gallons of a 30% saline solution to produce a 22% saline solution?

25. Three pounds of candy costing $6 per pound is mixed with 2 pounds of candy costing $8 per pound. What is the price of the mixture per pound?

Let's review graphing and writing linear functions and inequalities.

LESSONS 16–20 Graph.

1. $y = x + 1$

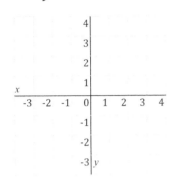

2. $y = \frac{1}{2}x - 1$

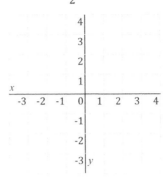

3. $x = 2$

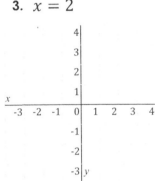

4. $2x - 3y = 6$

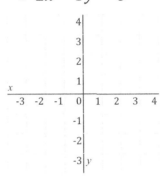

5. $y = |x|$

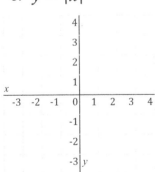

6. $y = |x - 2| - 1$

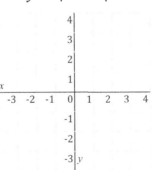

LESSON 19 Classify as parallel, perpendicular, or neither.

7. $y = 1$ and $x = 0$

8. $y = -3x + 1$ and $x + 3y = 6$

9. $x + 4y = 4$ and $4x - y = 1$

10. $y = 2x + 3$ and $4x - 2y = -3$

LESSON 41 Graph the solution set.

11. $y \leq x - 1$

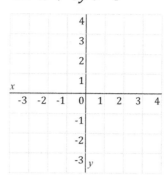

12. $x + 4y > 4$

LESSONS 22–25 Find an equation of each line in slope-intercept form and in standard form. Use only integers and the smallest possible positive integer coefficient for x.

13. slope $= -2$, through $(4, -2)$

14. through $(8, 8)$ and $(-4, -1)$

15. parallel to $y + 4x = 0$, through $(-1, 7)$

16. perpendicular to $5y + x = 4$, through $(3, 6)$

LESSONS 26–27 Solve.

17. An internet service provider charges \$38 per month plus an initial set-up fee of \$55. Write an equation representing the total cost, y, after x months of service.

18. A water tank with 350 gallons of water is being emptied at a rate of 12 gallons per minute. Write an equation representing the amount of water, y, in the tank after x minutes.

19. Anna has x five-dollar bills and y ten-dollar bills amounting to \$60. Write an equation relating x and y.

20. A 100-point test has x multiple-choice questions worth 2 points each and y short-answer questions worth 5 points each. Write an equation relating x and y.

21. A high school football game sold x general admission tickets at \$8 each and y student tickets at \$5 each. The ticket sales for the game totaled \$1,800. Write an equation relating x and y.

LESSON 160 Review: Systems of Linear Equations & Inequalities

Let's review solving systems of linear equations and inequalities.

LESSON 29 Solve by graphing.

1. $x = 1$

    $x + y = 2$

    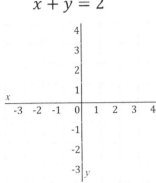

2. $x + 3y = 3$

    $4x + 3y = -6$

    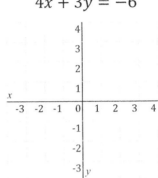

LESSONS 30–33 Solve algebraically.

3. $y = -x + 3$

    $x + 2y = 6$

4. $x + 5y = 7$

    $4x + 5y = -2$

5. $2x - 3y = 1$

    $4x - 6y = 2$

6. $x - 2y = -3$

    $x + 2y = 9$

7. $x + 4y = 5$

    $2x + 8y = 3$

8. $2x - 3y = -5$

    $3x - 2y = 5$

LESSON 42 Graph the solution set.

9. $y < -1$ and $3x - y > 1$

    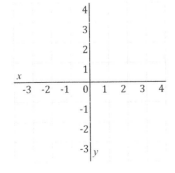

10. $y > x + 1$ and $x + 2y \leq 2$

    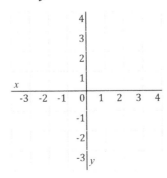

11. The sum of the digits of a two-digit number is 13. When the digits are reversed, the number is increased by 27. What is the number?

12. Movie tickets cost $9 for adults and $6 for children. A group bought 10 tickets and paid $75 in total. How many adults and how many children were in the group?

13. A cafeteria has 14 tables that can seat a total of 76 people. Some tables seat 4 people, and the others seat 8 people. How many tables seat 4 people? How many tables seat 8 people?

14. Eli took two buses to travel 360 miles. The first bus averaged 75 mph, and the second bus averaged 70 mph. The whole trip took 5 hours. How much time did Logan spend on each bus?

15. An airplane flying with the wind traveled 2,720 miles in 8 hours. The return trip took 8.5 hours flying against the wind. Find the speed of the plane in still air and the speed of the wind.

16. Two trains leave a station at the same time and travel in opposite directions. One train travels 20 mph faster than the other train. After 3 hours, they are 840 miles apart. Find the speed of each train.

17. Solution A is 45% acid. Solution B is 60% acid. How much of each should be used to produce 9 milliliters of a solution that is 50% acid?

18. Coffee A costs $10 per pound. Coffee B costs $8 per pound. How much of each should be mixed to produce 8 pounds of a coffee blend that costs $8.50 per pound?

LESSON 161 Review: Functions, Variation, and Sequences

Let's review functions, direct/inverse variation, and arithmetic/geometric sequences.

LESSONS 48–49 Find the domain and range, then identify as a function or not a function.

1.
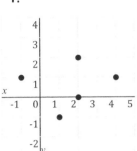

2.
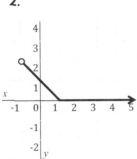

3.
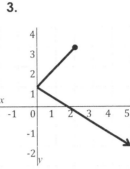

4.
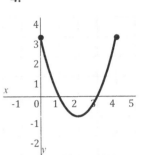

LESSON 50 Evaluate when $x = -3, 0,$ and 3. Write your answers in function notation.

5. $f(x) = |x - 2|$

6. $g(x) = x^2 - 9$

LESSONS 51–52 Classify as linear, exponential, quadratic, or none of these. If linear, write a rule.

7. $(0, 5), (1, 4), (2, 3), (3, 2), (4, 1)$

8. $(0, 2), (1, 3), (2, 6), (3, 11), (4, 18)$

9. $(0, 1), (1, 2), (2, 4), (3, 8), (4, 16)$

10. $(0, 3), (1, 5), (2, 7), (3, 9), (4, 11)$

LESSON 53 Find the average rate of change.

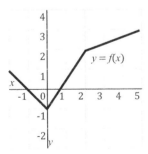

11. $0 \leq x \leq 2$

12. $-1 \leq x \leq 5$

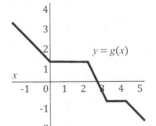

13. $1 \leq x \leq 4$

14. $-1 \leq x \leq 3$

LESSON 54 Find the inverse algebraically. Write your answers in function notation.

15. $f(x) = x + 2$

16. $g(x) = -2x + 3$

LESSONS 56–57 Write a direct or inverse variation equation, then solve.

17. Suppose y varies directly as x, and $y = 4$ when $x = -2$. Find y when $x = 3$.

18. Suppose y varies inversely as x, and $y = 6$ when $x = 2$. Find y when $x = 3$.

19. The distance sound travels varies directly with the time it travels. Sound travels 1,700 meters in 5 seconds in air. How far will it travel in 8 seconds?

20. The time it takes to empty a water tank varies inversely with the rate of pumping. If a pump can empty a tank in 16 minutes at 10 gpm (gallons per minute), how long will it take to empty the same tank at 8 gpm?

LESSONS 58–60 Identify as arithmetic or geometric, then find the explicit and recursive formulas.

21. 4, 9, 14, 19, 24, ...

22. 3, 6, 12, 24, 48, ...

23. 128, 64, 32, 16, 8, ...

24. 11, 8, 5, 2, −1, ...

LESSON 61 Solve. Round your answers to the nearest hundredth.

25. Samantha put $5,000 in her savings account with a simple interest rate of 2% per year. What will be the balance of her account at the end of the 7th year?

26. Ronald started a job that paid $48,000 a year. Each year after the first, he received a raise of $800. What was Ronald's salary in his 6th year of employment?

27. A ball is dropped from a height of 128 feet. After the ball hits the floor, it rebounds to 50% of its previous height. How high will the ball rebound after its fourth bounce?

28. As a car gets older, its resale value goes down by 20% each year. Samantha bought a new car for $20,000. What will be the value of the car after 4 years?

LESSON 162 Review: Radicals

Let's review simplifying radical expressions and solving radical equations.

LESSON 63 Evaluate.

1. $\sqrt{25}$

2. $\sqrt{0.04}$

3. $\sqrt[3]{-27}$

4. $\sqrt[4]{10,000}$

LESSONS 64–65 Simplify. Assume that all variables are positive.

5. $\sqrt{28}$

6. $\sqrt[3]{54}$

7. $\sqrt{x^3}$

8. $\sqrt[3]{64x^3y^6}$

9. $\sqrt{\dfrac{18}{49}}$

10. $\sqrt[3]{\dfrac{48}{125}}$

11. $\sqrt{\dfrac{x^3}{y^4}}$

12. $\sqrt[3]{\dfrac{x^4}{y^3z^3}}$

LESSONS 66-67 Simplify. Assume that all variables are positive.

13. $\sqrt{18} + \sqrt{32}$

14. $\sqrt{12xy} \cdot \sqrt{8y}$

15. $\dfrac{8\sqrt{15}}{\sqrt{60}}$

16. $\dfrac{\sqrt{81x^5}}{3\sqrt{3x^3}}$

LESSON 67 Rationalize the denominator.

17. $\dfrac{4}{\sqrt{2}}$

18. $\dfrac{5}{2\sqrt{5}}$

LESSON 68 Solve. Check for extraneous solutions.

19. $\sqrt{x} + 1 = 3$

20. $\sqrt{x - 6} + 7 = 5$

21. $\sqrt{5x} = \sqrt{7x - 6}$

22. $3 + 2\sqrt{x - 1} = 7$

23. $\sqrt[3]{4x} + 2 = 0$

24. $\sqrt[3]{3x + 1} = \sqrt[3]{5 - 3x}$

LESSON 69 Solve. Leave your answers in simplest radical form, if applicable.

25. The area of a square is 36 cm². What is the length of the diagonal?

26. The diagonal of a rectangle is 9 inches. The width of the rectangle is 5 inches. What is the height of the rectangle?

27. The hypotenuse of a right triangle is 15 cm, and one of its leg is 12 cm. What is the perimeter of the triangle?

28. A 14-foot ladder is leaning against a wall. The ladder reaches a height of 7 feet. How far is the bottom of the ladder from the wall?

CHALLENGE Solve. Leave your answers in simplest radical form, if applicable.

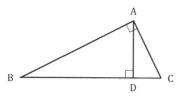

29. AD = 2 cm, DC = 1 cm, and AB:AC = 2:1. What is the perimeter of triangle ABC?

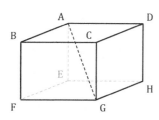

30. AB = 5 in, BC = 8 in, and BF = 6 in. What is AG?

LESSON 163 Review: Exponents

Let's review simplifying exponential expressions, scientific notation, and exponential functions.

LESSON 71 Evaluate.

1. $8^3 \cdot 4^{-5} \cdot 2^0$

2. $3^1 \cdot 6^5 \cdot 9^{-3}$

LESSONS 72–74 Simplify using positive exponents.

3. $3x^5 \cdot 4x^{-4}$

4. $x^2y^4 \cdot (3x^{-4}y^2)$

5. $(5x^3)^2$

6. $(2x^0y^{-3})^3$

7. $(3x)^{-2} \cdot (6x^2)^3$

8. $(5xy^2)^3 \cdot (5x^{-2}y^3)^{-2}$

9. $\dfrac{6x^4x^{-2}x^3}{3x^5}$

10. $\left(\dfrac{2}{x^2y^{-2}}\right)^3$

11. $\dfrac{(-4x^3)^3}{8x^8}$

12. $\dfrac{(3x^3y^2)^5}{(9x^6y^4)^2}$

LESSON 75 Simplify and write in scientific notation.

13. $(6 \times 10^2)(8 \times 10^7)$

14. $(5 \times 10^6)(6 \times 10^{-3})$

15. $\dfrac{5 \times 10^6}{2 \times 10^2}$

16. $\dfrac{1.2 \times 10^4}{4 \times 10^9}$

LESSON 76 Evaluate.

17. $4^{1/2}$ **18.** $8^{-1/3}$ **19.** $(-64)^{2/3}$ **20.** $\left(\dfrac{1}{27}\right)^{2/3}$

LESSON 77 Simplify using positive exponents.

21. $7^{1/4} \cdot 7^{3/4}$ **21.** $x^{1/3} \cdot x^{1/2}$

22. $\dfrac{8^{5/6}}{8^{1/2}}$ **24.** $\left(\dfrac{16x^{3/2}}{x^{1/6}}\right)^{1/2}$

LESSON 78 Write a function that models each situation, and then solve.

25. Melissa put $3,000 in her account that earns 4% interest compounded annually. What will be the balance of her account after 8 years?

26. During a science experiment, Jessica found that bacteria double every hour. There were 20 bacteria in the beginning. How many bacteria will be there after 7 hours?

27. As a car gets older, its resale value goes down by 10% each year. Alex bought a new car for $23,000. What will be the value of the car after 10 years?

28. The population of a town is 40,000 this year, and it is expected to decline at a rate of 5% per year. What will be the population of the town after 5 years?

29. The bear population in a national park is increasing by 15% each year. It is estimated that there about 500 bears in the park now. How many bears will be there in 10 years?

LESSON 164 Review: Polynomials and Factoring

Let's review simplifying and factoring polynomials.

LESSON 80 Add or subtract.

1. $(2x + 7) + (x - 6)$

2. $(x^2 + 3x + 1) - (2x^2 + x - 7)$

LESSONS 81–84 Multiply.

3. $-4x^2(x^2 - 2x + 1)$

4. $(x - 4)(x + 5)$

5. $(x - 3)^2$

6. $(x + 1)(x - 1)$

7. $(x + 4)(5x - 1)$

8. $(x - 4)(2x^2 + 3x - 1)$

LESSONS 85–86 Divide.

9. $(9x^4) \div (3x)$

10. $(8x^4 - 4x^2) \div (2x^2)$

11. $(x^2 + 5x + 6) \div (x + 3)$

12. $(x^2 - 15) \div (x - 5)$

LESSON 93 Factor out the GCF.

13. $x^2 + 7x$

14. $5x^3y + 5x^2y^2$

LESSON 94 Factor by grouping.

15. $x^3 - 2x^2 + x - 2$

16. $2x^3 - 3x^2 + 4x - 6$

LESSONS 95-100 Factor.

17. $x^2 - x - 6$

18. $x^2 - 4x + 4$

19. $x^2 + 9x + 14$

20. $2x^2 + 7x + 5$

21. $9x^2 - 49$

22. $6x^2 + x - 12$

LESSON 101 Factor completely.

23. $9x^3 - 6x^2 + x$

24. $2x^3 + 8x^2 - 2x - 8$

EXTRA Simplify. Write your answers in standard form.

25. $(x + 2)(x + 3)$

26. $(2x + 3)^2$

27. $(4x + 5)(4x - 5)$

28. $(3x + 1)(9x^2 - 3x + 1)$

29. $(x^2 + 2x - 24) \div (x - 4)$

30. $(2x^2 + 11x - 9) \div (2x - 3)$

EXTRA Factor completely.

31. $x^2 - 7x + 12$

32. $3x^2 + 5x - 2$

33. $6x^2 - 3x - 9$

34. $8x^2 + 12x - 20$

35. $2x^3 - 32x$

36. $x^3 - 3x^2 - 4x + 12$

LESSON 165 Review: Solving Quadratic Equations

Let's review solving quadratic equations.

LESSONS 103–104 Solve by taking square roots.

1. $(x - 7)^2 - 1 = 0$

2. $4(2x + 1)^2 - 36 = 0$

LESSON 105–106 Solve by factoring.

3. $x^2 + 6x + 8 = 0$

4. $2x^2 - 9x - 5 = 0$

LESSON 107–108 Solve by completing the square.

5. $x^2 + 2x - 4 = 0$

6. $x^2 - 4x - 8 = 0$

LESSON 109–110 Solve by the quadratic formula.

7. $x^2 + x - 3 = 0$

8. $3x^2 + 8x - 3 = 0$

LESSONS 111–112 Solve. Use any method you prefer.

9. $(2x - 1)^2 - 9 = 0$

10. $(x + 3)(x - 7) = 0$

11. $x^2 + 8x - 12 = 0$

12. $x^2 - 7x + 6 = 0$

13. $x^2 + 2x + 1 = 0$

14. $x^2 - 5x + 8 = 0$

15. $4x^2 - 8x + 3 = 0$

16. $2x^3 + 2x^2 - 12x = 0$

17. The difference between two positive integers is 4. Their product is 96. Find the integers.

18. The difference between two positive integers is 3. The sum of the larger and the square of the smaller is 33. Find the integers.

19. An isosceles right triangle has a hypotenuse of $6\sqrt{2}$ feet. Find the area of the triangle.

20. An isosceles right triangle has an area of 8 square inches. Find the perimeter of the triangle.

21. One leg of a right triangle is 7 cm longer than the shorter leg and 2 cm shorter than the hypotenuse. Find the dimensions of the triangle.

22. A rectangle has an area of 60 square inches. Its length is 7 inches longer than twice its width. Find the perimeter of the rectangle.

EXTRA Solve. Use any method you prefer.

23. $x^2 - 4x - 6 = 0$

24. $x^2 - 16 = 0$

25. $x^2 - 7x + 7 = 0$

26. $x^2 - 6x - 2 = 0$

27. $x^2 - 2x - 15 = 0$

28. $(4x + 3)^2 - 9 = 0$

29. $2x^2 + x - 2 = 0$

30. $3x^2 - 6x + 12 = 0$

LESSON 166 Review: Graphing Quadratic Functions

Let's review graphing and transforming quadratic functions.

LESSONS 116-118 Graph. Use the intercepts when possible.

1. $y = x^2 - 1$

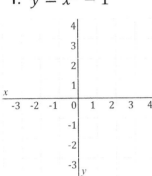

2. $y = (x - 2)^2$

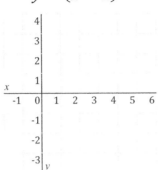

3. $y = -(x + 3)^2 + 2$

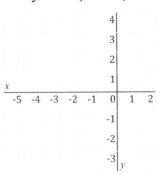

4. $y = -x(x + 2)$

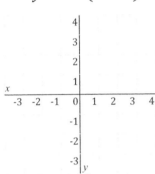

5. $y = (x - 2)(x + 2)$

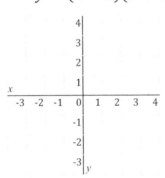

6. $y = \frac{1}{4}x(x - 4)$

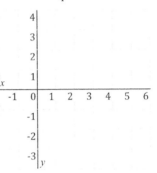

7. $y = x^2 + 4x + 3$

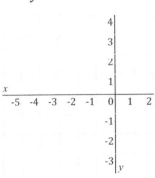

8. $y = -2x^2 + 4x$

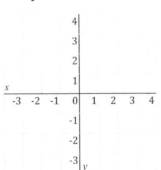

9. $y = \frac{1}{2}x^2 + 2x + 2$

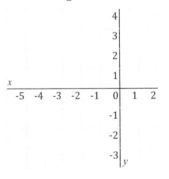

LESSONS 119–120 Find the vertex, y-intercept, and x-intercepts (if any).

10. $y = (x - 1)^2 + 3$

11. $y = 2(x + 1)(x - 3)$

12. $y = x^2 - 4x + 4$

13. $y = -x^2 + 6x - 5$

LESSON 121 Find an equation of each parabola in standard form.

14. Vertex $(3, 1)$; Point $(5, 5)$

15. Zeros at $x = 1$ and $x = 3$; Point $(4, 6)$

LESSON 122 Find an equation of each parabola obtained by transforming $y = x^2$ as described.

16. Shift left 2 units and up 3 units.

17. Scale by 2 and shift right 1 unit.

18. Flip over the x-axis and shift up 6 units.

19. Scale by 3 and flip over the x-axis.

LESSON 123 Solve.

20. A ball is thrown straight up from a height of 48 feet with an initial speed of 32 feet per second. Its height h, in feet, after t seconds is given by the function $h(t) = -16t^2 + 32t + 48$. Answer each question.

  a. When does the ball reach its maximum height?

  b. What is the maximum height reached by the ball?

  c. When will the ball hit the ground?

  d. When will the ball be at a height of 48 feet again?

21. A ball is hit from ground level with an initial speed of 64 feet per second. Its height h, in feet, after t seconds is given by $h(t) = -16t^2 + 64t$.

  a. When does the ball reach its maximum height?

  b. How high will the ball rise before it starts falling?

  c. How long will it take for the ball to hit the ground?

  d. When will the ball reach a height of 48 feet?

22. A ball is dropped from a height of 144 feet. Its height h, in feet, after t seconds is given by $h(t) = -16t^2 + 144$.

  a. When will the ball hit the ground?

  b. When will the ball reach a height of 80 feet?

LESSON 167 Review: Rational Expressions and Equations

Let's review simplifying rational expressions and solving rational equations.

LESSON 125 Simplify. State any excluded values.

1. $\dfrac{5x^4}{25x^2}$

2. $\dfrac{4x}{4x^2 - 8x}$

3. $\dfrac{x - 5}{x^2 - x - 20}$

4. $\dfrac{3x^2 + 21x - 24}{-x^3 - 7x^2 + 8x}$

LESSON 126 Multiply or divide. State any excluded values.

5. $\dfrac{x^2 + 4x + 4}{8x} \cdot \dfrac{24x}{x + 2}$

6. $\dfrac{4x^2 + 3x - 10}{x + 5} \cdot \dfrac{x + 5}{x + 2}$

7. $\dfrac{x^2 - 4}{x + 2} \div \dfrac{x - 2}{x + 1}$

8. $\dfrac{x^2 - 6x - 16}{2x^2 + 5x} \div \dfrac{x + 2}{2x + 5}$

LESSON 127 Add or subtract. State any excluded values.

9. $\dfrac{x^2}{x + 1} + \dfrac{2x + 1}{x + 1}$

10. $\dfrac{x^3}{x^4 - 81} - \dfrac{9x}{x^4 - 81}$

11. $\dfrac{1}{x} - \dfrac{1}{x + 6}$

12. $\dfrac{2x^2 - 8}{x^2 - 2x - 8} + \dfrac{4}{x - 4}$

LESSONS 128–129 Solve. Check for extraneous solutions.

13. $\dfrac{4}{x+3} = \dfrac{2}{5}$

14. $\dfrac{3x}{4} = \dfrac{x}{2} + \dfrac{1}{x}$

15. $\dfrac{4}{2x-5} + \dfrac{3}{x+2} = 0$

16. $\dfrac{x}{3} - \dfrac{1}{x} = \dfrac{x-3}{3x}$

17. $\dfrac{x}{x+4} = \dfrac{3x}{x+4} - \dfrac{x}{x-5}$

18. $\dfrac{2}{x+5} + \dfrac{1}{2x-1} = \dfrac{3}{x+5}$

LESSON 130 Solve.

19. Pipe A can fill a tank in 3 hours. Pipe B can fill the tank in 6 hours. How long will it take to fill the tank if both pipes are used?

20. Sam can mow the lawn by himself in 20 minutes. Kyle can mow the lawn in 30 minutes. How long will it take to mow the lawn if they work together?

21. Mark can assemble a computer by himself in 6 hours. If his brother Jerry helps him, it takes 2 hours. How long will it take Jerry to assemble the computer alone?

22. Kyle can clean the yard in 50 minutes. Working together, Kyle and Susie can clean the yard in just 30 minutes. How long will it take Susie alone to clean the yard?

23. Brian can complete a certain task twice as fast as Dan can. When they work together, they can complete the task in 4 hours. How long will it take each of them to complete the task alone?

LESSON 168 Review: Data Analysis

Let's review data analysis.

LESSON 138 Find the mean, median, and mode(s).

1. 3, 4, 4, 6, 9

2. 4, 5, 7, 7, 8, 8, 8, 9

LESSON 139 Find the mean, range, and standard deviation. Round to the nearest tenth.

3. 2, 5, 5, 7, 8, 9

4. 5, 6, 6, 7, 7, 8, 8, 9

LESSON 140 Find the five-number summary and interquartile range, then draw a box plot.

5. 3, 10, 5, 6, 7, 9, 8, 4, 5, 3

6. 7, 5, 7, 5, 7, 9, 6, 8, 9, 7

LESSON 142 Describe the shape of each distribution above. Which data set appears to have the greater standard deviation? What are the appropriate measures of center and variation? Explain.

7.

8.

LESSON 141 The stem-and-leaf plot shows the ages of people at a restaurant.

Stem	Leaf
2	2, 4, 6, 6
3	0, 3, 4, 6, 7, 9
4	5, 5, 6, 6, 6
5	3, 6, 7
6	1, 8

9. Find the median and range of the ages.

10. How many customers are in the restaurant?

11. What percentage of the customers are in their 30s?

12. What percentage of the customers are over 50?

LESSON 141 The histogram shows the number of movies watched over the summer by the members of a movie club.

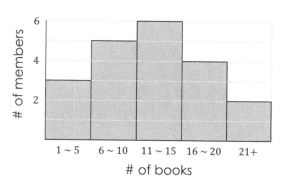

13. How many members are in the club?

14. How many members watched more than 15 movies?

15. What percentage of the club watched no more than 10 movies?

LESSON 143 Identify the type of correlation. Then draw a trend line and find its equation.

16.

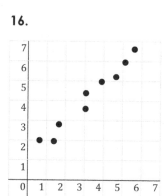

17.

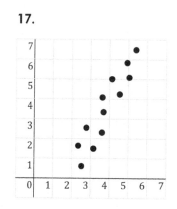

18.

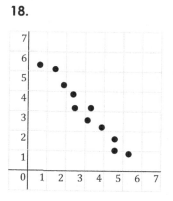

LESSON 144 Below are the results from a survey of restaurant customers. Complete the two-way frequency table, then convert your table into a two-way relative frequency table, a row-relative frequency table, and a column-relative frequency table. Round to the nearest hundredth, if necessary.

19. Two-way frequency table

	Burger	Wrap	Total
Soda	51	45	
Water			54
Total	72		

20. Two-way relative frequency table

	Burger	Wrap	Total
Soda	0.34		
Water			
Total			1.0

21. Row-relative frequency table

	Burger	Wrap	Total
Soda	0.53		1.0
Water			1.0
Total			1.0

22. Column-relative frequency table

	Burger	Wrap	Total
Soda	0.71		
Water			
Total	1.0	1.0	1.0

LESSON 169 Review: Probability

Let's review probability.

LESSON 146 A spinner with 4 equal sections labeled A, B, C, and D is spun 20 times. It landed on A six times, B nine times, and C five times.

1. What is the theoretical probability of landing on A?

2. What is the experimental probability of landing on C or D?

LESSON 148 Find the number of possible outcomes.

3. You make a 3-digit number using the digits 1 through 5 with repetition.

4. You make a 3-digit number using the digits 1 through 5 without repetition.

5. You make a 3-digit odd number using the digits 1 through 5 with repetition.

6. You make a 3-digit odd number using the digits 1 through 5 without repetition.

LESSON 149 Solve.

7. A die is rolled twice. What is the probability that the first roll is greater than 3 and the second roll is less than 3?

8. A quiz consists of 5 true-false questions. If you choose answers randomly, what is the probability of getting all 5 questions correct?

9. Two cards are drawn from a stack of ten cards numbered 1 to 10, with replacement. What is the probability of drawing two prime numbers?

10. Two balls are drawn from a bag containing 3 yellow and 6 black balls, with replacement. What is the probability of drawing 2 black balls?

LESSON 150 Solve.

11. Two cards are drawn from a stack of ten cards numbered 1 to 10, without replacement. What is the probability of drawing two prime numbers?

12. Two balls are drawn from a bag containing 3 yellow and 6 black balls, without replacement. What is the probability of drawing 2 black balls?

13. A die is rolled twice. What is the probability of rolling the same numbers?

14. A die is rolled twice. What is the probability that the sum is 8?

LESSON 151 Solve.

15. A die is rolled. What is the probability of rolling an odd number or a prime number?

16. A card is drawn from a deck of 52 cards. What is the probability of drawing a spade or a number card?

LESSONS 152–153 Solve

17. In how many ways can you arrange the letters of the word SHARK?

18. In how many ways can you arrange 3 of the letters in the word SHARK?

19. How many teams of 3 players can be formed from 5 players?

LESSON 154 Solve.

20. The letters M, A, N, G, and O are rearranged in a random order. What is the probability that an arrangement begins with a vowel?

21. Three balls are drawn simultaneously from a bag of 2 red, 4 pink, and 5 yellow balls. What is the probability of drawing 3 yellow balls?

LESSON 170 Review: Solving Linear Equations

This is a single-page worksheet. Try to complete it in 20 minutes. Afterwards, check your answers and then redo any problems you got wrong.

LESSONS 3–8 Solve. Remember that there can be no solution or infinitely many solutions.

1. $8x = -6$

2. $26 - x = 15$

3. $9x + 5 = 14$

4. $3x - 12 = 27$

5. $5x - 6 + x = 3(5 - x)$

6. $3x + 2 = 3(x + 2) - 4$

7. $x - 2(x + 3) = 5 - x$

8. $4(x + 3) - x = 2x + 5$

9. $0.5x + 4.2 = -0.3$

10. $0.03x + 0.45 = 0.02x - 0.05$

11. $\dfrac{3}{4}x + \dfrac{1}{2} = \dfrac{4}{5}$

12. $\dfrac{1}{3}x + \dfrac{1}{2} + x = -\dfrac{5}{6}$

13. $|4x| = 16$

14. $|x + 2| = 7$

15. $|4 - 3x| = 5$

16. $7 - 5|2x - 1| = -8$

LESSONS 10–11 Solve.

17. Two trains leave stations 1,000 miles apart at the same time and travel toward each other. One train travels at 140 mph while the other travels at 110 mph. How long will it take for the two trains to meet?

18. How many liters of a 20% saline solution must be added to 3 liters of a 30% saline solution to produce a 26% saline solution?

LESSON 171 Review: Solving Linear Inequalities

This is a single-page worksheet. Try to complete it in 20 minutes.

LESSON 38 Solve.

1. $-3x > 15$

2. $x + 6 < 10$

3. $7 - 8x \geq 11$

4. $5x + 8 \leq -7$

5. $x + 4(2 + x) < 3x + 6$

6. $x + 10 \geq 4x + 3(5 - 2x)$

7. $\dfrac{x}{3} < \dfrac{1}{5}$

8. $\dfrac{x}{7} + 4 > 3$

9. $\dfrac{1}{6}x - \dfrac{1}{3} \geq \dfrac{2}{3}$

10. $\dfrac{3}{8}x - \dfrac{1}{2} \geq -\dfrac{5}{4}$

LESSON 39 Solve.

11. $-2x < 6$ and $x + 6 > 8$

12. $x - 2 < 10$ and $3x - 4 \leq 2$

13. $3 - 5x \geq 9$ or $4x + 7 < 3$

14. $5x - 7 > 8$ or $7 - 6x \leq -11$

15. $0 < \dfrac{x}{3} - 1 \leq 2$

16. $\dfrac{x}{3} + 4 < 5$ or $\dfrac{1}{2} - 2x \geq \dfrac{3}{4}$

LESSON 40 Solve, then graph the solution set.

17. $|4x - 3| < 2$

18. $|5 - 2x| + 4 \geq 6$

LESSON 172 Review: Solving Systems of Linear Equations

This is a single-page worksheet. Try to complete it in 20 minutes.

LESSONS 29–33 Solve. Remember that there can be no solution or infinitely many solutions.

1. $y = 2x - 3$
   $4x + y = -9$

2. $x = 2y$
   $5x - 4y = 6$

3. $4x - 6y = 1$
   $6x - 9y = 4$

4. $2x + 7y = -8$
   $2x - 9y = -8$

5. $x + 4y = -5$
   $x + 5y = -8$

6. $3x - 4y = 2$
   $-6x + 8y = -4$

7. $4x - 2y = 2$
   $5x - 3y = -1$

8. $2x + y = -6$
   $3x + 5y = -2$

9. $2x + 3y = 1$
   $4x + 6y = 2$

10. $x - y = -8$
    $3x + 2y = 6$

11. $3x - 2y = 4$
    $5x - 3y = 8$

12. $y = 5x - 4$
    $10x - 2y = 5$

13. $7x + y = 16$
    $4x - y = 17$

14. $3x + 5y = -9$
    $2x - 3y = 13$

LESSONS 34–36 Solve.

15. Kim has 11 coins consisting of dimes and nickels. The value of the coins is $0.80. How many dimes and how many nickels does Kim have?

16. A party room has 20 tables that can seat a total of 180 people. Some tables seat 8 people, and the others seat 12 people. How many tables seat 8 people? How many tables seat 12 people?

LESSON 173 Review: Solving Radical Equations

This is a single-page worksheet. Try to complete it in 20 minutes.

LESSON 68 Solve. Check for extraneous solutions.

1. $\sqrt{x} + 2 = 3$

2. $\sqrt{x} - 3 = -1$

3. $3\sqrt{x} - 5 = 4$

4. $5\sqrt{x} + 9 = 4$

5. $\sqrt{x - 2} = 7$

6. $\sqrt{x + 4} = 5$

7. $\sqrt{5x - 1} = 8$

8. $\sqrt{6x + 7} = 5$

9. $2\sqrt{x - 4} + 5 = 3$

10. $3\sqrt{7 - x} - 6 = 3$

11. $\sqrt{x - 3} = \sqrt{2x - 7}$

12. $\sqrt{x + 4} = \sqrt{3x}$

13. $\sqrt{3x - 8} = \sqrt{7 - 2x}$

14. $\sqrt{9x + 2} = \sqrt{6x + 5}$

15. $4 - \sqrt[3]{x} = 6$

16. $5\sqrt[3]{x} - 7 = 8$

17. $\sqrt[3]{x - 7} + 8 = 7$

18. $\sqrt[3]{x + 3} = \sqrt[3]{9 - 2x}$

LESSON 69 Solve. Leave your answers in simplest radical form, if applicable.

19. A 17-foot ladder is leaning against a wall. The bottom of the ladder is 8 feet from the wall. How high up the wall does the ladder reach?

20. The formula $d = \sqrt{(x_2 - x_1)^2 + (y_2 - y_1)^2}$ gives the distance, d, between two points (x_1, y_1) and (x_2, y_2). What is the distance between the two points $(0, 1)$ and $(4, 7)$?

LESSON 174 Review: Solving Quadratic Equations

This is a single-page worksheet. Try to complete it in 20 minutes.

LESSONS 103–104 Solve by taking square roots.

1. $(x - 3)^2 - 20 = 0$

2. $3(7 + 2x)^2 - 27 = 0$

LESSON 105–106 Solve by factoring.

3. $x^2 + 8x + 15 = 0$

4. $3x^2 - 10x - 8 = 0$

LESSON 107–108 Solve by completing the square.

5. $x^2 + 2x - 1 = 0$

6. $x^2 - 6x - 3 = 0$

LESSON 109–110 Solve by the quadratic formula.

7. $x^2 - x - 1 = 0$

8. $5x^2 - 7x + 2 = 0$

LESSONS 111–112 Solve. Use any method you prefer. Remember that there can be no solution.

9. $(x - 4)^2 - 12 = 0$

10. $x^2 + 4x - 3 = 0$

11. $x^2 - 6x + 8 = 0$

12. $x^2 - 7x + 9 = 0$

13. $x^2 - 5x + 3 = 0$

14. $x^2 - 10x + 25 = 0$

15. $3x^2 + 5x + 7 = 0$

16. $4x^3 - 64x = 0$

LESSONS 113 Solve.

17. The sum of two positive integers is 16, and their product is 39. Find the integers.

18. The area of a rectangle is 70 cm². Its length is 4 cm longer than twice its width. Find the dimensions of the rectangle.

LESSON 175 Review: Solving Rational Equations

This is a single-page worksheet. Try to complete it in 20 minutes.

LESSONS 128–129 Solve. Check for extraneous solutions.

1. $\dfrac{2}{x+5} = \dfrac{1}{x+2}$

2. $\dfrac{x}{4} = \dfrac{x}{6} + \dfrac{3}{x}$

3. $\dfrac{x}{5} - \dfrac{1}{x} = \dfrac{x-4}{2x}$

4. $\dfrac{2}{x} = \dfrac{1}{2x} + \dfrac{x-3}{8x}$

5. $\dfrac{1}{3} = \dfrac{x-1}{x+2} + \dfrac{1}{3x}$

6. $\dfrac{2}{3x+2} - \dfrac{5}{x+5} = 0$

7. $\dfrac{1}{x-3} = \dfrac{x}{x^2-x-6}$

8. $\dfrac{x-2}{x-6} + \dfrac{1}{x} = \dfrac{4}{x-6}$

9. $\dfrac{2}{x} = \dfrac{1}{x+4} + \dfrac{4}{x^2+4x}$

10. $\dfrac{x-3}{x+4} = \dfrac{2}{x-2} - \dfrac{3}{x+4}$

11. $\dfrac{x}{x-3} + \dfrac{x+1}{x+3} = \dfrac{12}{x^2-9}$

12. $\dfrac{x}{x+2} = \dfrac{5}{x+4} + \dfrac{2}{x^2+6x+8}$

LESSON 130 Solve.

13. Pipe A can drain a pool in 6 hours. Pipe B can drain the pool in 3 hours. How long will it take to drain the pool when both pipes are used?

14. Elsa and Hilda can paint a fence together in 2 hours. Elsa alone can paint the fence in 5 hours. How long will it take Hilda to paint the fence alone?

15. Pipe A can fill a pool four times as fast as pipe B. When both pipes are open, they fill the pool in 4 hours. How long will it take each pipe to fill the pool alone?

LESSON 176 Study for Final Exam

1. Take **Practice Test #1** you created in Lesson 156. Grade yourself and record your score on the first page of the test. Review the questions you missed and understand why you missed them.

2. In the space provided below, make notes of the kinds of questions you get wrong repeatedly or you struggle with. Try to make your notes simple and clear so that you can review them quickly right before the final exam.

3. Attach the test to this page or keep it separately.

LESSON 177 Study for Final Exam

1. Take **Practice Test #2** you created in Lesson 157. Grade yourself and record your score on the first page of the test. Review the questions you missed and understand why you missed them.

2. In the space provided below, make notes of the kinds of questions you get wrong repeatedly or you struggle with. Try to make your notes simple and clear so that you can review them quickly right before the final exam.

3. Attach the test to this page or keep it separately.

LESSON 178 Study for Final Exam

1. Study on your own. Review lessons that caused you trouble. Solve the questions you missed and understand why you missed them.

2. In the space provided below, make notes of the kinds of questions you get wrong repeatedly or you struggle with. Try to make your notes simple and clear so that you can review them quickly right before the final exam.

LESSON 179 Study for Final Exam

1. Study on your own. Review lessons that caused you trouble. Solve the questions you missed and understand why you missed them.

2. In the space provided below, make notes of the kinds of questions you get wrong repeatedly or you struggle with. Try to make your notes simple and clear so that you can review them quickly right before the final exam.

Read the directions below carefully.

BEFORE THE TEST...

- Take 10 minutes to review your notes from Lessons 176 through 179.

- Get a calculator and blank sheets of paper for your calculations.

KEEP IN MIND...

- There are 40 questions on the test.

- Write your answers clearly in the space given. Do your work on separate paper.

- There is no time limit, but you must complete the test in ONE sitting.

- Do not use a calculator unless specifically stated that you may.

- Do NOT look at the other pages of the workbook while taking the final exam. Consider carefully cutting the pages of the final exam out of the workbook and removing the workbook from your desk.

AFTER THE TEST...

- Grade yourself and record your score on your grading sheets.

- Calculate your final grade for the course. See your grading sheets for the details.

When you are ready,

begin the test.

This page is intentionally left blank.

1. $2x - 3 = -3x + 7$

   What is the value of x that satisfies the equation above?

2. If $f(x) = 2^x$, what is $f(3) - f(0)$?

3. What is the slope of the line that passes through $(2, 4)$ and $(-3, 1)$?

4. $\sqrt{3} \cdot \sqrt{12x^2}$

   If $x > 0$, simplify the expression above.

5. $(x + 3)(x - 3) + (x - 3)^2$

   Simplify the expression above in standard form.

6. Which equation is graphed below?

   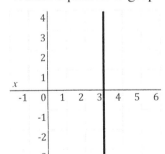

   A) $y = 3x$

   B) $x = 3y$

   C) $y = 3$

   D) $x = 3$

7. $|4x + 1| = 9$

   If a and b are the solutions to the equation above, what is the value of ab?

8. A line is perpendicular to $x + 3y = 6$ and passes through $(1, 5)$. Write an equation of the line in slope-intercept form.

9. $kx - 3y = 2$
   $5x + y = -1$

   What value of k makes the system of equations above have no solution?

10. $x^{-5}y^{-4} \cdot (2x^2y)^3$

    Simplify the expression above using positive exponents only.

11. Write an equation in vertex form for the parabola below.

    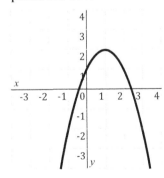

12. $|5 - 2x| \leq 11$

What is the solution set to the inequality above?

13. If $f(x) = x^2 - 8$ and $f(a) = 1$, what could be the values of a ?

14. $4x^3 + 8x^2 - x - 2$

Factor the polynomial above completely.

15. $x^2 - 2x - 2 = 0$

If a and b are the solutions to the equation above, what is the value of $a + b$?

16. What is the value of $9^{1/2} + 8^{2/3} + 81^{1/4}$?

17. Write an equation in slope-intercept form for the line below.

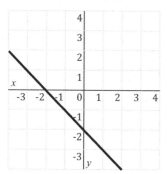

18. $2x + y = 5$
$x - 2y = 5$

What is the solution to the system of equations above? Write your answer as an ordered pair.

19. $4\sqrt{x + 1} - 2 = 6$

What is the solution to the equation above?

20. $\dfrac{x^2 - 2x + 1}{x^2 + 2x - 3}$

Simplify the expression above. Assume all denominators are nonzero.

21. The graph of $y = x^2 + 3x - 10$ has two x-intercepts. What is the distance between the x-intercepts?

22. Which equation is graphed below?

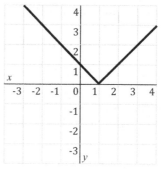

A) $y = |x - 1|$ B) $y = |x + 1|$

C) $y = |x| - 1$ D) $y = |x| + 1$

23. $\dfrac{1}{x+2} + \dfrac{2}{x-3} = \dfrac{1}{2}$

What are the solutions to the equation above?

24. The height of an object varies directly with the length of its shadow. If a tree 8 feet tall casts a shadow 10 feet long, how long will be the shadow of a tree that is 12 feet tall?

25. Owen has $1.05 in dimes and nickels. He has 3 more dimes than nickels. How many coins of each type does he have?

26. Alex can complete a certain task in 10 hours. Working together, Alex and Eli can do it in 6 hours. How long will it take Eli alone to complete the task?

27. Write an inequality in slope-intercept form for the graph below.

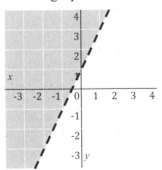

28. A water tank with 300 gallons of water is emptied using two pumps. One pump pumps water out at a rate of 11 gallons and the other at a rate of 9 gallons. Write an equation in slope-intercept form that represents the amount of water, y, in the tank after x minutes.

29. Two trains leave stations 250 miles apart at the same time and travel toward each other. One train travels at 60 mph while the other travels at 65 mph. How long will it take for the two trains to meet?

30. A restaurant has 20 tables that can seat a total of 90 people. Some tables seat 4 people and the others seat 6 people. How many tables seat 4 people? How many tables seat 6 people?

31. Which table does NOT represent a linear function?

A)

x	0	2	4	6	8
y	−7	−3	1	5	9

B)

x	−2	−1	0	1	2
y	3	4	5	6	7

C)

x	0	1	2	3	4
y	1	2	4	8	16

D)

x	−8	−4	0	4	8
y	9	7	5	3	1

32. A rectangle has a perimeter of 20 inches and an area of 24 square inches. Find the dimensions of the rectangle.

33. How many liters of a 25% saline solution must be mixed with 4 liters of a 40% saline solution to make a 30% saline solution?

34. A six-sided die is thrown three times. What is the probability of getting a prime number on all three rolls?

You may use a calculator for questions 35–40. Round your answers to the nearest whole number, if necessary.

35. 5, 12, 19, 26, 33, ...

What is the 15th term of the sequence above?

36. $h(t) = -16t^2 + 48t + 64$

A ball is thrown vertically upwards from the top of a building of height 64 feet with an initial speed of 48 feet per second. Its height h, in meters, after t seconds is given by the function above. How long will the ball be in the air before it hits the ground?

37. The hypotenuse of a right triangle is 17 cm, and one of its legs is 8 cm. What is the perimeter of the triangle?

38. During a science experiment, Lisa found that bacteria double every 20 minutes. There were 10 bacteria in the beginning. How many bacteria will be there after 3 hours?

39. A survey asked a group of teens and adults whether they prefer online shopping or in-store shopping. The table below shows the results of the survey. What percentage of the teens prefer online shopping?

	Online	In-store	Total
Teens	64	13	77
Adults	53	35	88
Total	117	48	165

40. Brian randomly arranged six textbooks on his shelf. What is the probability that math comes first? Write your answer as a fraction in simplest form.

STOP

This is the end of the test.
Review your answers before grading.

Appendices

EP Math Algebra 1 Grading Sheet 1

Record up to 5 points for completing each lesson.

Algebra Basics

Lesson	Score	Notes
1	/ 5	
2	/ 5	

Solving Linear Equations

Lesson	Score	Notes
3	/ 5	
4	/ 5	
5	/ 5	
6	/ 5	
7	/ 5	
8	/ 5	
9	/ 5	
10	/ 5	
11	/ 5	
12	/ 5	

Graphing Lines

Lesson	Score	Notes
14	/ 5	
15	/ 5	
16	/ 5	
17	/ 5	
18	/ 5	
19	/ 5	
20	/ 5	

Finding Equations of Lines

Lesson	Score	Notes
22	/ 5	
23	/ 5	
24	/ 5	
25	/ 5	
26	/ 5	
27	/ 5	

Systems of Linear Equations

Lesson	Score	Notes
29	/ 5	
30	/ 5	
31	/ 5	
32	/ 5	
33	/ 5	
34	/ 5	
35	/ 5	
36	/ 5	

Linear Inequalities

Lesson	Score	Notes
38	/ 5	
39	/ 5	
40	/ 5	
41	/ 5	
42	/ 5	

Quarterly Review

Lesson	Score	Notes
44	/ 5	
45	/ 5	

First Quarter Total: /200

EP Math Algebra 1 Grading Sheet 2

Record up to 5 points for completing each lesson.

PSAT Practice

Lesson	Score	Notes
46	/ 5	
47	/ 5	

Functions

Lesson	Score	Notes
48	/ 5	
49	/ 5	
50	/ 5	
51	/ 5	
52	/ 5	
53	/ 5	
54	/ 5	

Variation and Sequences

56	/ 5	
57	/ 5	
58	/ 5	
59	/ 5	
60	/ 5	
61	/ 5	

Radicals

63	/ 5	
64	/ 5	
65	/ 5	
66	/ 5	
67	/ 5	

Radicals

Lesson	Score	Notes
68	/ 5	
69	/ 5	

Exponents

71	/ 5	
72	/ 5	
73	/ 5	
74	/ 5	
75	/ 5	
76	/ 5	
77	/ 5	
78	/ 5	

Polynomials

80	/ 5	
81	/ 5	
82	/ 5	
83	/ 5	
84	/ 5	
85	/ 5	
86	/ 5	

Quarterly Review

88	/ 5	
89	/ 5	
90	/ 5	

Second Quarter Total: /200

EP Math Algebra 1 Grading Sheet 3

Record up to 5 points for completing each lesson.

PSAT Practice

Lesson	Score	Notes
91	/ 5	
92	/ 5	

Factoring Polynomials

Lesson	Score	Notes
93	/ 5	
94	/ 5	
95	/ 5	
96	/ 5	
97	/ 5	
98	/ 5	
99	/ 5	
100	/ 5	
101	/ 5	

Solving Quadratic Equations

Lesson	Score	Notes
103	/ 5	
104	/ 5	
105	/ 5	
106	/ 5	
107	/ 5	
108	/ 5	
109	/ 5	
110	/ 5	
111	/ 5	
112	/ 5	
113	/ 5	

Graphing Parabolas

Lesson	Score	Notes
115	/ 5	
116	/ 5	
117	/ 5	
118	/ 5	
119	/ 5	
120	/ 5	
121	/ 5	
122	/ 5	
123	/ 5	

Rational Expressions and Equations

Lesson	Score	Notes
125	/ 5	
126	/ 5	
127	/ 5	
128	/ 5	
129	/ 5	
130	/ 5	

Quarterly Review

Lesson	Score	Notes
132	/ 5	
133	/ 5	
134	/ 5	
135	/ 5	

Third Quarter Total: /205

EP Math Algebra 1 Grading Sheet 4

Record up to 5 points for completing each lesson. Record your final exam score.

PSAT Practice

Lesson	Score	Notes
136	/ 5	
137	/ 5	

Data Analysis

Lesson	Score	Notes
138	/ 5	
139	/ 5	
140	/ 5	
141	/ 5	
142	/ 5	
143	/ 5	
144	/ 5	

Probability

Lesson	Score	Notes
146	/ 5	
147	/ 5	
148	/ 5	
149	/ 5	
150	/ 5	
151	/ 5	
152	/ 5	
153	/ 5	
154	/ 5	

Review: All Topics in Algebra 1

Lesson	Score	Notes
158	/ 5	
159	/ 5	
160	/ 5	
161	/ 5	
162	/ 5	
163	/ 5	
164	/ 5	
165	/ 5	
166	/ 5	
167	/ 5	
168	/ 5	
169	/ 5	

Review: Solving All Types of Equations

Lesson	Score	Notes
170	/ 5	
171	/ 5	
172	/ 5	
173	/ 5	
174	/ 5	
175	/ 5	

Final Exam

180	/ 40	

Fourth Quarter Total: | /220 |

Write down your total score from each quarter.

First Quarter	Second Quarter	Third Quarter	Fourth Quarter

Total Possible: 200   Total Possible: 200   Total Possible: 205   Total Possible: 220

Add up your scores above, then determine your grade using the table below.

Course Total	Grade
742 and above	A
660 to less than 742	B
577 to less than 660	C
495 to less than 577	D
Below 495	F

Course Total	**Course Grade**

Total Possible: 825

Congratulations!

You completed the course!

LESSON 46 PSAT Practice   Date: Score:

1. Ⓐ Ⓑ Ⓒ Ⓓ   6. Ⓐ Ⓑ Ⓒ Ⓓ   11. Ⓐ Ⓑ Ⓒ Ⓓ   16. Ⓐ Ⓑ Ⓒ Ⓓ

2. Ⓐ Ⓑ Ⓒ Ⓓ   7. Ⓐ Ⓑ Ⓒ Ⓓ   12. Ⓐ Ⓑ Ⓒ Ⓓ   17. Ⓐ Ⓑ Ⓒ Ⓓ

3. Ⓐ Ⓑ Ⓒ Ⓓ   8. Ⓐ Ⓑ Ⓒ Ⓓ   13. Ⓐ Ⓑ Ⓒ Ⓓ

4. Ⓐ Ⓑ Ⓒ Ⓓ   9. Ⓐ Ⓑ Ⓒ Ⓓ   14. Ⓐ Ⓑ Ⓒ Ⓓ

5. Ⓐ Ⓑ Ⓒ Ⓓ   10. Ⓐ Ⓑ Ⓒ Ⓓ   15. Ⓐ Ⓑ Ⓒ Ⓓ

Cut Here

LESSON 47 PSAT Practice   Date: Score:

1. Ⓐ Ⓑ Ⓒ Ⓓ   6. Ⓐ Ⓑ Ⓒ Ⓓ   11. Ⓐ Ⓑ Ⓒ Ⓓ   16. Ⓐ Ⓑ Ⓒ Ⓓ

2. Ⓐ Ⓑ Ⓒ Ⓓ   7. Ⓐ Ⓑ Ⓒ Ⓓ   12. Ⓐ Ⓑ Ⓒ Ⓓ   17. Ⓐ Ⓑ Ⓒ Ⓓ

3. Ⓐ Ⓑ Ⓒ Ⓓ   8. Ⓐ Ⓑ Ⓒ Ⓓ   13. Ⓐ Ⓑ Ⓒ Ⓓ

4. Ⓐ Ⓑ Ⓒ Ⓓ   9. Ⓐ Ⓑ Ⓒ Ⓓ   14. Ⓐ Ⓑ Ⓒ Ⓓ

5. Ⓐ Ⓑ Ⓒ Ⓓ   10. Ⓐ Ⓑ Ⓒ Ⓓ   15. Ⓐ Ⓑ Ⓒ Ⓓ

Cut Here

LESSON 91 PSAT Practice   Date: Score:

1. Ⓐ Ⓑ Ⓒ Ⓓ   6. Ⓐ Ⓑ Ⓒ Ⓓ   11. Ⓐ Ⓑ Ⓒ Ⓓ   16. Ⓐ Ⓑ Ⓒ Ⓓ

2. Ⓐ Ⓑ Ⓒ Ⓓ   7. Ⓐ Ⓑ Ⓒ Ⓓ   12. Ⓐ Ⓑ Ⓒ Ⓓ   17. Ⓐ Ⓑ Ⓒ Ⓓ

3. Ⓐ Ⓑ Ⓒ Ⓓ   8. Ⓐ Ⓑ Ⓒ Ⓓ   13. Ⓐ Ⓑ Ⓒ Ⓓ

4. Ⓐ Ⓑ Ⓒ Ⓓ   9. Ⓐ Ⓑ Ⓒ Ⓓ   14. Ⓐ Ⓑ Ⓒ Ⓓ

5. Ⓐ Ⓑ Ⓒ Ⓓ   10. Ⓐ Ⓑ Ⓒ Ⓓ   15. Ⓐ Ⓑ Ⓒ Ⓓ

Cut Here

LESSON 92 PSAT Practice

Date: Score:

1. Ⓐ Ⓑ Ⓒ Ⓓ   6. Ⓐ Ⓑ Ⓒ Ⓓ   11. Ⓐ Ⓑ Ⓒ Ⓓ   16. Ⓐ Ⓑ Ⓒ Ⓓ

2. Ⓐ Ⓑ Ⓒ Ⓓ   7. Ⓐ Ⓑ Ⓒ Ⓓ   12. Ⓐ Ⓑ Ⓒ Ⓓ   17. Ⓐ Ⓑ Ⓒ Ⓓ

3. Ⓐ Ⓑ Ⓒ Ⓓ   8. Ⓐ Ⓑ Ⓒ Ⓓ   13. Ⓐ Ⓑ Ⓒ Ⓓ

4. Ⓐ Ⓑ Ⓒ Ⓓ   9. Ⓐ Ⓑ Ⓒ Ⓓ   14. Ⓐ Ⓑ Ⓒ Ⓓ

5. Ⓐ Ⓑ Ⓒ Ⓓ   10. Ⓐ Ⓑ Ⓒ Ⓓ   15. Ⓐ Ⓑ Ⓒ Ⓓ

LESSON 136 PSAT Practice

Date: Score:

1. Ⓐ Ⓑ Ⓒ Ⓓ   6. Ⓐ Ⓑ Ⓒ Ⓓ   11. Ⓐ Ⓑ Ⓒ Ⓓ   16. Ⓐ Ⓑ Ⓒ Ⓓ

2. Ⓐ Ⓑ Ⓒ Ⓓ   7. Ⓐ Ⓑ Ⓒ Ⓓ   12. Ⓐ Ⓑ Ⓒ Ⓓ   17. Ⓐ Ⓑ Ⓒ Ⓓ

3. Ⓐ Ⓑ Ⓒ Ⓓ   8. Ⓐ Ⓑ Ⓒ Ⓓ   13. Ⓐ Ⓑ Ⓒ Ⓓ

4. Ⓐ Ⓑ Ⓒ Ⓓ   9. Ⓐ Ⓑ Ⓒ Ⓓ   14. Ⓐ Ⓑ Ⓒ Ⓓ

5. Ⓐ Ⓑ Ⓒ Ⓓ   10. Ⓐ Ⓑ Ⓒ Ⓓ   15. Ⓐ Ⓑ Ⓒ Ⓓ

LESSON 137 PSAT Practice

Date: Score:

1. Ⓐ Ⓑ Ⓒ Ⓓ   6. Ⓐ Ⓑ Ⓒ Ⓓ   11. Ⓐ Ⓑ Ⓒ Ⓓ   16. Ⓐ Ⓑ Ⓒ Ⓓ

2. Ⓐ Ⓑ Ⓒ Ⓓ   7. Ⓐ Ⓑ Ⓒ Ⓓ   12. Ⓐ Ⓑ Ⓒ Ⓓ   17. Ⓐ Ⓑ Ⓒ Ⓓ

3. Ⓐ Ⓑ Ⓒ Ⓓ   8. Ⓐ Ⓑ Ⓒ Ⓓ   13. Ⓐ Ⓑ Ⓒ Ⓓ

4. Ⓐ Ⓑ Ⓒ Ⓓ   9. Ⓐ Ⓑ Ⓒ Ⓓ   14. Ⓐ Ⓑ Ⓒ Ⓓ

5. Ⓐ Ⓑ Ⓒ Ⓓ   10. Ⓐ Ⓑ Ⓒ Ⓓ   15. Ⓐ Ⓑ Ⓒ Ⓓ

Made in the USA
Columbia, SC
24 August 2024